Freemasonry
The Esoteric Tradition

Freemasonry
The Esoteric Tradition

Fabio Venzi

Lewis Masonic

To my dear Friend and Brother
Spencer Douglas David Compton
7th Marquess of Northampton
with whom I have shared many of the topics addressed in this volume

First published 2016

ISBN 978 0 85318 534 5

Published by Lewis Masonic

an imprint of Ian Allan Publishing Ltd, Addlestone, Surrey KT15 2SF.
Printed in Malta.

Visit the Lewis Masonic website at www.lewismasonic.co.uk

Picture Credits
Every effort has been made to identify and correctly attribute photographic credits. Should any error have occurred this is entirely unintentional.

Front cover: 'The mysteries that are shown are only to a Mason known' by Tringham (1755).
The Library and Museum of Freemasonry, London

Back cover: A symbolic illustration from a French manuscript book c1760 called *Précis des huit premiers grades, ornés de discours er d'histoires allégoriques relatifs au respectable Ordre de la Franc-Maçonnerie*.

CONTENTS

INTRODUCTION

Everybody enjoys the freedom he deserves, which is measured by the stature and dignity of his person.
Julius Evola
Men among the ruins

René Guénon viewed Freemasonry, irrespective of its degenerations and deviations, as the sole heir throughout the western world of an ancient symbolism based on *Tradition*. Although his frequently violent and radical criticism of modern-day Freemasonry is widely acknowledged, the French thinker maintained that, despite its marked initiatic and esoteric decline, Freemasonry had succeeded in perpetuating and preserving, albeit unconsciously, the principles of *Tradition,* and would, if circumstances allowed, be in a position to 'revive' and once again transmit the authentic 'traditional' doctrine through use of its symbols and rituals.

Guénon, in conjunction with other scholars and historians who put forward or supported similar theories, were of the opinion that the origins of Freemasonry dated back to ancient times, attributing its birth to the medieval cathedral builders. They maintained that, over time, Freemasonry had slowly, but relentlessly, changed, overlooking the significance of its symbology and distancing itself from its initial aims and purposes, ultimately assuming its current, and definitive, form through the creation, in 1717, of the Grand Lodge of London.

More recent historiographic studies concur that this theory was not based on reliable documentation. On the contrary, documents available today lead us to reasonably maintain that the birth of Freemasonry, as practiced and interpreted in contemporary society, originated in considerably more recent times than those indicated by Guénon, taking on its current semblance in the second half of the 1600s, in the context of the London Masons Company.[1]

Thus, Freemasonry was established *ex novo* in England in the mid-seventeenth century, although the origins and nature of the movement were immediately subjected to widespread speculation and theories. This form of Freemasonry was initially characterised by a meagre and elementary, almost non-existent, esoteric component, as an analysis of the first rituals adopted by the Lodges present during this period of development readily demonstrates. Speculatively, Freemasonry may have been deemed prevalently an associative phenomenon, the rituals of which were subsequently subjected to variation, ultimately resulting in an increasingly complex and 'esoteric' structure and nature.

These constant, and significant, transformations led to the creation of a ritual, achieved through the hard work and efforts of the Lodge of Reconciliation. Between 1813 and 1816, the Lodge conceived a unique form of ritual that ratified the union between the two English Grand Lodges, the Moderns and Ancients (this division had taken place in 1751 with the creation of the Grand Lodge of the Ancients): thus, the United Grand Lodge of England was born.

Stability and Emulation are the two forms of ritual still in use today that best resemble the original, and undoubtedly most complex, ritual ever to be conceived by Anglo-Saxon Freemasonry. The ritual established a perfect and fully complete initiatic pathway of an esoteric nature, with true significance being achieved only through a careful *exegesis*; in my opinion, this represents the highest peak reached by English Freemasonry.

Paradoxically, it was from that time of greatest splendour that a departure from the exquisitely esoteric interpretation of Freemasonry began, to be progressively replaced by a moralist and charitable interpretation (in addition to, particularly in Europe and South America, the perception of a political and anticlerical movement). The ritual is purported to no longer disclose any 'hidden' elements, there is nothing to 'reveal', indeed, the ritual appears to have made everything clearer; the individual, the Freemason, is merely the principled person par excellence, whose sole aim is to do good and set a good example. Over time, the increasingly rare individuals who behold something of a deeper nature in the Masonic ritual are considered as somewhat 'singular', or 'fantasisers'; they are charitably tolerated as long as they do not overstep the mark with their fantastical interpretations. However, as will be expounded later in this volume, tolerance is finite and may even, in a few cases, lead to the expulsion from the Order of individuals who persevere in using the term 'esotericism' (Welcome back Inquisition! This time however within the confines of Freemasonry).

This volume is devoted to those members of society who maintain that Freemasonry should be interpreted, experienced and lived as an authentic Initiatic School, as was doubtless intended by the creators of its complex ritual forms, brimming with symbols, allegories and hidden meanings. However, as stated previously, this initiatic and esoteric connotation, still evident in the rituals, has been progressively obliterated, and Freemasonry has evolved into something in profound contrast with the intentions of those who skilfully and patiently conceived the complex symbolism.

However, on observing Freemasonry today from an esoteric and initiatic viewpoint, it is evident how far removed the current day Masonic Obediences are from the established characteristics of an authentic School of Wisdom, which it is frequently purported to be. Nonetheless, the initiatic potential of Freemasonry is still conspicuous, and conceivably primed for 'activation'; although, to achieve this aim, several fundamental transformations would need to take place both internally, and, more importantly, among the higher ranks.

This volume is based on inspiration gained from a series of personal experiences I have enjoyed as Grand Master of the Regular Grand Lodge of Italy, Obedience established in 1993, and the sole in Italy to be officially recognised by the United Grand Lodge of England. In two *European Grand Masters* Meetings, the first held in London in 2007, and the second in Geneva in 2013, the two Pro Grand Masters of the United Grand Lodge of England, Lord Northampton and Peter Lowndes, essentially emphasised, at a distance of six years, the same concept: as an Institution Freemasonry plays no direct role in society. In particular, Lord Northampton went on to specify how the United Grand Lodge of England:

> Firmly believe that it is not Freemasonry but the individual who can have a positive influence on society. We see Freemasonry as an intensely personal journey of self-discovery, knowledge and personal development. We hope that the individual, during his journey, will absorb the principles and tenets of Freemasonry, so that they become a part of his nature. In that way he will make a contribution for the good of society. If the individual, imbued with the principles of Freemasonry, does not work for the good of society we should then question whether Freemasonry has fulfilled its purpose.[2]

In truth, this important message, delivered with the specific aim of dispelling all clouds and shadows, which, not only in Italy, have frequently surrounded Freemasonry, and contributed towards providing a distorted, at times even disturbing, view of the same, was not, on both occasions, shared unanimously. Indeed, several of the Grand Masters present manifested, albeit not openly (the risk of losing the much sought after recognition by the English advocated the need for caution …) uncertainty and impatience towards the stance adopted by the United Grand Lodge of England, continuing to maintain that the social, political, and economic role played by Freemasonry should be given due acknowledgement.

Taking for granted that I heartily agree with the stance adopted by the United Grand Lodge of England, it should be emphasised how in these two meetings, the message, although clearly delivered, was not subjected to any degree of discussion or debate. In addition to the two meetings mentioned above, similarly no comment was passed or further analysis undertaken on the initial affirmation of 'Freemasonry plays no role in Society' during meetings held in either 2009 or 2011. Although, in the light of the issues that have since arisen throughout numerous aristocratic European Masonic Obediences (i.e. the revoking or suspending of recognition by the United Grand Lodge of England to the Grand Orient of Italy in 1993 and, more recently, to the Gran Loge Nationale Francaise, following use of a combination of Freemasonry and the profane world), this uttering should have constituted a fundamental focus for debate. Perhaps today the concept of 'regularity' is no longer viewed as strictly as it once was (but why then should this become something about which *the orthodox* Freemasons would boast to the derogatorily defined *spurious* members?), and a strangely unsettling 'ecumenism' is thus stirring on the horizon.

Conversely, on striving to adhere to the basic principles of Masonic regularity, an answer should be provided to the key question posed by the working hypothesis: If Freemasonry does not occupy a specific role in society, what does it represent for members of the fraternity, and what appeal does it hold for those who wish to become members? Moreover, most of all, what is a Freemason in the modern world? Does his presence in contemporary society make sense, or should he merely be considered an anachronistic reminder of a time long past? Or, worse still, should Freemasonry be left to operate undisturbed, in the same way as the most *profane* of Associations, within the confines of political, economic and social dynamics?

Veritably, although the position of the United Grand Lodge of England has been made undeniably clear, there is a prevailing concern amongst many Masonic Obediences that their size, and consequently their standing, may increase merely from a numerical point of view, thus envisaging a potentially important role or 'strategic' position (or rather, a position of 'power') in society. Freemasonry is seen as being in a position to influence political, economic, social, and even religious issues, whilst, on the contrary, no thought is spared as to what Freemasonry is in a position to do for the individual; the *single* individual, to help him decipher his condition, the 'human condition', as Malraux would put it, and embark on a journey with introspective analysis as a mandatory starting point. This theme will be amply addressed in the present volume, albeit from a different perspective, as the main focus will not be the associative phenomenon of Freemasonry, but rather, to use the words of Ernst Junger[3], the 'form' or 'figure' of the Freemason himself.

From a metahistorical point of view, the figure of the Freemason will be portrayed as a sort of 'ideal type', beneath which lies a recognisable archetype that is presented cyclically under different semblances or figures, such as the Freemason, the archetype of an 'Initiate'.

From the Epoptes of the Eleusinian Mysteries, to the Hermetic of the first centuries B.C.; from the Magician and the Neoplatonist of the Renaissance to the Rosicrucian; from the Alchemist to the Freemason, the same human type, an individual featuring a series of common characteristics and, in particular, a similar 'vision of the world', is manifested cyclically in specific historic moments.

The Schools of Wisdom[4], the singularity of which related largely to communications carried out by 'esoteric', and therefore 'symbolic' means, were established; although the schools were not set up in opposition to the official Religions and Cults, at a time of severe social crisis and unrest, when man was distracted by a sense of pessimism and dissatisfaction with the traditional forms of life and thought, they clearly set themselves apart. The doctrines imparted by these Schools reintroduced the ancient archetype of the *Wise Old Man*, the Initiate. The Initiatic or Philosophical Schools thus cyclically came to light in an attempt to aggregate individuals fired by a deep desire for knowledge based on the principles of hermetic thought, the ultimate purpose of which is the union of the *Individual* with the *Universal*. The term 'Initiate' is applied to an individual featuring a mandatory and essential qualification, i.e. a predisposition to embark on a pathway of gnostic development that culminates in an authentic transmutation, which may even be detached from the strictly ritual connotation of initiation.

The end of the Initiatic Schools, with their binding thread of the secret and mysteries, is marked by a return to awareness of the divine nature of an individual (or, as Jung would say, the rediscovery of Self and the achievement of an integrated personality). Indeed, although the premises and doctrines of these Schools appear to diverge somewhat, in line with the differences encountered in the historic contexts in which they take place, their symbology and principal aims evolve into a form and tension unwaveringly focused on the *Transcendent*, in an attempt to obtain a reprieve, a return to an entity lost over time.

This arduous journey is obviously not suited to all, and can be achieved only by minds free from superstructures and opinions, uncorrupted, and above all, unconditioned minds. The ideal type of Initiate requires no ideological support to enable him to manifest his innate freedom and originality and is concomitantly, thanks to this singular feature, qualified to survive in and endure even the most oppressive historic context. This particular type of human elaborates arguments at a deeper and higher level, having achieved total inner freedom.

To this regard, the equivalent of the Jungian 'Wood' in which the *Waldgang* (the Rebel) has sought refuge, comes to represent, in the specific case of the Freemason, the Masonic Lodge or Temple; a tangible site, but also a metaphor used to indicate a virgin territory in which to retreat from a civilisation scarred by nihilism, a hermitage in which to hide from the obligations of the hordes. For a Freemason therefore, the Lodge represents first and foremost an inner dimension, although of course possessing spatial proportions, a concrete place for the Initiate to continue his retrograde fight against the rampant decay.

In my opinion, the Initiate, and its most recent historic representation, the Freemason, specifically embodies a spiritual aristocracy; the higher the degree of standardisation, the greater the spiritual merit and force of the few who succeed in extricating themselves. The Freemason therefore is the true aristocrat, he lives in emancipation, and he adheres to the doctrine of the Tao 'act without acting'. He is, in the words of Evola in *Ride the Tiger,* the differentiated man, who is affected neither by the ruins nor by modernity, he is not corroded by nihilism, on the contrary, affirming his 'complete, replete and absolute freedom from everything, even detachment from himself: he is indeed sovereign unto himself'.

Thus, the Initiate is representative of a human figure cyclically presented under different guises, all bearing essentially similar symbolic characteristics. As the Hermetic who carries out his work in the search for an absolute purity, and the Alchemist focuses on his ability to achieve, from an imperfect and impure matter, a perfect substance capable of transmitting this perfection to other substances; so the Freemason represents a roughly hewn stone that will need to be smoothed by means of an concerted inner effort.[5] It should however, be underlined that both the alchemical procedures and the undertaking of the Masonic and hermetic pathway are performed in the presence of the transcendent. The hermetic, alchemical and Masonic initiatic journeys will never be achieved as the result of a theoretical or experimental knowledge, but, on the contrary, represent the outcome of an endeavour, an *opus*, in which the spirit is returned to the matter, animating and ennobling the same.

Ultimately, the main aim of the Schools of Wisdom, both Initiatic and Philosophical, elitist schools of thought and spiritual communities, was to achieve the 'transmutation' of an individual who, by embarking on an initiatic journey would succeed in ontologically altering his status. The archetype of an Initiate is repeatedly and cyclically brought to light to free, in men who avert the need, the most elementary forces imprisoned within the depths of the psyche, forces that represent the 'source of life' of humans, thus enabling the initiate to gain awareness of his inner essence, his Self.

In the last chapter of the book, I will illustrate how Nature is a crucial reference point for an Initiate, Nature intended as a place in which the *elementary* is unfailingly present. Accordingly, the ideal type of Initiate features a close, almost holistic, relationship with Nature, which draws characteristically directly from the elementary forces.

It should be highlighted that the forms or figures assumed by the archetype of the Initiate, albeit invested in this interpretation with metahistorical connotations, in view of their singular atemporal nature, are firmly incorporated into their own time. Consequently, although present in a specific social context, these figures will inevitably represent mythical figures, in no way indicative of social class or standing, and thus, although apparently located in time, are in a certain sense unconnected to the latter, irrespective of the realisation that they have evidently been generated as a result of historic events.

Throughout the volume therefore, we shall embark on a journey into modern-day society in the search for this ideal type, the Initiate, to reveal the figure or form potentially assumed in the current historic context; this journey will be undertaken in the firm belief that we may identify this figure in the person of the Freemason.

In a speech delivered on 13 June 2012, the Grand Master of the Grand Lodge of New South Wales and the Australian Capital Territory, a 'regular' Masonic Obedience recognised by the United Grand Lodge of England, categorically 'forbade' use of the term 'esoteric' or its derivatives, stating that use of the term may give rise to being misconstrued and cause 'detriment' to the Order. Subsequently however, the Grand Master specified that, to ensure the acquisition of correct Masonic knowledge, any studies or discussion were to be conducted through an understanding of the secrets and mysteries of the Craft, and the expositions described as merely 'speculative', and by no means 'esoteric'. Issues relating to alchemy, profane mysticism (?), rosicrucianism and occultism, virtually all phenomena that had 'contaminated' Masonic thinking and symbols over the centuries and led to the creation of the Order, were likewise prohibited.[6] Members failing to comply with this edict would have been expelled from the Order.

The above edict would seem to imply the presence of a degree of confusion, or perhaps we should term it ignorance, within the confines of Freemasonry, stemming indeed from the crucial terminology adopted as means of expression by the Freemasons.

In the first chapter I shall analyse the term 'esotericism', commenting on the significance of this term in the contemporary world, and highlighting how, particularly in academia, the term is associated with Freemasonry. Although studies focusing on esotericism have abounded in recent decades, even underlying the establishment of University chairs, I will clarify how, in the conclusions of the *esoterologist* (a scholar of esotericism), the rational approach and analysis applied will unfailingly divulge a marked and inevitable disorganisation, outcome of the constant strains produced through the stubborn attempts to pigeonhole esoteric, and frequently pseudo-esoteric phenomena in rigid, logical, consequential categories. Fired by external taxonomic concerns, historians of esotericism would like to artificially separate what, in truth, are concomitant or closely linked phenomena or processes.

With regard to Freemasonry, an analysis of the differences between the first, fundamental, Three Degrees and the High Degrees, will highlight the vulgar errors of evaluation made by academic scholars who tend to assess the phenomenon from a 'quantitative' rather than a 'qualitative' point of view. The expectations of esoterologists relating to the regimentation of aspects that belong to the innermost layers of an individual will prevent them from ever achieving a true knowledge of the initiatic phenomena, which, accordingly, will continue to be seen as a mere historic expression within the confines of different socio-cultural contexts. As the 'vision of the world' of the Initiate is essentially symbolic, with the symbol constituting the means and form used in the perception and representation of reality, to enable an interpretation and distinction between the authentic Schools of Wisdom and pseudo-initiatic contexts (in the case of Freemasonry, this is of particular importance due to the abundance of spurious or irregular Obediences), the symbology and complex rituals adopted should be carefully analysed. This, however, is undertaken extremely rarely.

The main defect characterising academic studies focusing on esotericism is that they tend to overlook almost completely the human component of the phenomenon, i.e. the 'ideal type' identified in the Initiate and forms or figures through which it is historically manifested. In the absence of a constant human point of reference the esoteric contexts analysed by the authors will appear to be unrelated, determined essentially by exquisitely profane mechanisms (social, political or other), rather than inspired by inner needs. The historicist vision is therefore reiterated, with each manifestation and phenomenon, including the initiatic phenomena, being assessed on the basis of its historic and progressive nature, as the outcome of a precise logic of necessary development. Naturally, this takes place along a linear time trend, although, on the contrary, to aid understanding of the true nature of Initiatic Schools, a circular view of the time implicated in the 'Cosmic Cycles' or 'Eternal Recurrence' should be employed.

A deeper understanding of the sense and spiritual function of the Schools of Wisdom, avoiding a peremptory classification based merely on the specific time in history in which they are collocated, will contribute towards clarifying the role played by a specific human type in binding agent and characterising the phenomenon. This human type may indeed be presented within a historic context, but will not be entirely determined by the same, or created *ex novo*, but merely recalled. Thus, an ideal type unrelated to its specific context is once again manifested; it *is* and opts to manifest itself independently, whenever the situation may so dictate.

In the second chapter I shall analyse one of the most widely used, and possibly abused, terms relating to esoteric phenomena: the term 'Tradition'. We shall once again be faced with the contrast between the academic vision entailing a historicisation of Tradition and the metaphysical vision held by the so-called Perennialists, according to whom Tradition, essentially a synonym of esotericism, is a sort of common metaphysical language that has succumbed to the languages of the individual traditional doctrines. In the Traditional School, esotericism is seen as no more than a theoretical concept, rather than a reference to a historically identifiable religious tradition; to fail to attribute specific traditions to the term 'esotericism' would, in the opinion of those favouring this view, facilitate a better comprehension of its metaphysical and metahistorical nature, an indispensable aspect of every Tradition. According to this interpretation, the individual Traditions should be viewed as mere esoteric vehicles containing metaphysical truths, rather than the Truth itself.

Subsequently, I will introduce a representation of Tradition according to the interpretation of the German philosopher Karl Jaspers, a Tradition that, in Jaspers' view, constituted a *Perennial Philosophy* in the true sense of the word. The chapter will continue by expounding the Jungian theory of archetypes, and its possible association with the idea of Tradition, to conclude with the theory of 'Morphic Fields' by the biologist Rupert Sheldrake, which suggests a view, seen as somewhat risky by some, of a scientific form of Tradition.

In the work of Carl Gustav Jung, the *Myth* is depicted as an independent form of cognitive thought and organisation of the world, expression of the true mystery of man, the Myth manifests, by means of its images and symbols, the obscure and fragile parts of the human existence, thus providing the individual with the possibility of gaining experience. As the complete course of knowledge acquired and experienced by man since his creation is present in Myth in a symbolic and coded form, its archetypes will allow us to grasp, through the Jungian doctrine, the meaning of Tradition. In discussing Jung's theory, we shall observe how, among the archetypes exposed in the dynamics of the process of identification, i.e. in the search for an integrated personality and psychic totality, as intended by the Wise Old Man, the Initiate is the archetype that emerges from the collective unconscious into the conscience of the individual contemplated herein. Indeed, the individual is he who has already been acquainted with his *Shadow* and his *Soul*, and now, facing the Wise Old Man, is ready to undertake, in the Initiatic School, the final part of his journey, the recognition of his inner Self.

In support of this belief, I will attempt to underline how, in his theory, Jung described the integration of the unconscious as a process that, in addition to healing psychic conditions, assumes the connotations of an authentic gnostic and initiatic pathway. Using the archetype of the Initiate, I shall attempt to delineate the *weltanshauung* of our ideal type, of his vision of the world, or, in the words of Jung, his attitude. This implies the vision of the world held by an individual who is already advanced in the process of consciential evolution and has chosen to embark on the last, and most arduous, part of his journey together with other similar individuals. He has decided to place himself beyond the confines of the common collective conscience to interpret the world in a diverse manner, as the result of his predisposition, or rather, his innate qualification.

I therefore intend to apply an adapted version of the Jungian concept of identification to the dynamics of the Initiatic Schools; the process of identification, intended as an evolutionary process of the psyche towards totality, thus represents, in this parallelism, the aim of the Schools of Wisdom and their adepts. During the course of identification, we encounter the process of education and characterisation of individuals, in particular the development of a psychological individual distinct from the general population, from the collective psychology, and thus a process of differentiation aimed at developing individual personality. In the same way, in the Initiatic Schools, a process of identification targeting the accomplishment of becoming oneself is clearly present and is expressed initially through a differentiation of the individual personality from the collective personality achieved mainly by means of Initiation. Subsequently, the purpose of the true journey of wisdom will be to elicit a further evolution of the individual conscience.

In the Eleusinian ritual, the purpose of initiation to the Mysteries was to produce an authentic 'ontological change', namely, a psychic modification of the pre-existing status by means of an *operative-realisational* rather than quiescent and quietist approach similar to that present in Hermeticism, Alchemy, and, particularly, in the Masonic rituals in which the personal experience of the Freemason, the so-called 'secret', represents a supremely *inner* experience, which, for this very reason, cannot be communicated, a secret that is revealed only through spiritual development and consequent transformation of the individual personality. The 'vision' provoked in the Epoptes or in the hermetic Adept of the *Ogdoad and the Ennead*, in the same way as the suggestion produced in the Freemason during the 'initiatic death', draws the candidates – as occurs in the Jungian process of identification – towards an *awareness* of the existence of a deeper inner Self, which is differentiated from the conscious I.

In the light of the premises made previously in this Introduction, and in reference to the study of Alchemy undertaken by Jung, we may assume that in the realm of Masonic symbology and dynamic rituals, the adept, in the same way as the alchemist, has *unknowingly* developed an authentic identification process aimed at connecting his conscious (I), depicted by the 'Raw Stone', with knowledge of the central nucleus of his psyche (Self), or the 'Smooth Stone'. I have used the term *unknowingly* because, as stated previously, from the time of its creation Freemasonry has frequently opted to attribute a largely, if not indeed exclusively, sanctimonious significance to its rituals and symbology, although I am persuaded that in the depths of his soul, or rather in his psyche, the 'Initiate' to the 'Mysteries' of Freemasonry will realise that the craved 'hewing' of the Stone, merely represents the symbol of an entity that can only be reached in the deepest recesses of the psyche.

The volume will conclude by analysing one of the dynamics that best highlights the distress perceived by modern, contemporary man, the 'Loss of the Centre'.

As I will demonstrate, this 'Loss of the Centre' is largely underpinned by the degeneration and loss of control over so-called progress, together with the most perfect representation of the latter, *Technique*, a decadence and corruption portrayed in the indiscriminate and devastating attack carried out on Nature in the name of economic overgrowth and of an uncontrollable scientific prometheism. Modernity has thus been transformed during the period of *nihilism*, and the Earth has been devastated by the will to power of Technique.

In this age of absolute and inevitable entropy brimming with negative and destructive significance, it will be in the passive nihilism that the Initiate will be required to recognise the true enemy to overcome. Accordingly, for the Initiate, the recovery of his 'Centre' assumes the preeminent relevance of restoring *rapture* to the world and to men, a rapture swept away by a rampant nihilism.

Nihilism, as mentioned previously, a phenomenon that characterises modern-day society, is the process within which, affirms Nietzsche in his *Will to Power,* 'the supreme values deteriorate', thus implying that it is indeed this depreciation and disappearance of spiritual values that the figure of the Freemason, the last of the Initiates, will be expected to recover and defend. Heidegger emphasises how the essence of nihilism, the main source of which lies within contemporary progress and Technique, 'is in the forgetfulness of being' or rather, in nihilism the forgetfulness of being is accomplished, being located in a realm of *Nothingness*. In rediscovering his Centre, the Freemason undertakes to locate the being lost within the entropic dynamics of contemporary nihilism.

I shall analyse the symbols of the Centre, seeking the origins of the same in ancient alchemical manuscripts, and furthering examination up until the time of the doctrines put forward by Jung. Emphasis will be placed on how the process of loss of the centre, first commenced with a progressive detachment of man from Nature, resulting in the consequent impoverishment of the latter, and thus depicting the dynamics of nihilism in all their destructiveness.

The abrupt change in the concepts of 'Time' and 'Space', and the negative consequences produced by these changes on the lives and psyche of modern, contemporary man, resulting in an increased sensation of discomfort, estrangement and acceleration of the process, will complete the analysis; all undertaken in line with a panoramic view of *secularisation*, the latest consequence of the degenerative process that has led modern-day man towards loss of the 'Centre'.

The hypothetical possibility of overcoming this regression should originate from a recovery of the Transcendent, and a return to the search for an inner awareness in which the Initiate, the Freemason, the solitary spiritual researcher, will play a key role.

What conclusions can be drawn therefore? Undeniably that, in the light of the above, political and social activism does not necessarily constitute the only way of providing tangible contributions aimed at yielding a much sought-after better world. On the contrary, we run the risk of not achieving anything at all if a mere material effort is used to elicit an external change without first implementing an inner transformation.

Indeed, the true action rises from the accomplishment of a new vision, a new awareness than has grown within, but which will be forever be impressed on the external field, thereby determining the potentially rapid and abrupt evolution of the same.

CHAPTER ONE
ESOTERICISM, INTERPRETATIONS AND FABRICATIONS

Lines, circles, figures: there's everything in there. If only someone could read that!
Georg Buchner
Woyzeck

1
Esotericism and its meanings

Definitions of the term 'esotericism'
'The question of how to distinguish the 'authentic' Schools of Wisdom, with their 'real' access to the 'transcendent forces' from the mere pseudo-organisations, has long been a subject of lively debate amongst the followers of esotericism.'
With these words the scholar of esotericism and traditional thinking Hans Thomas Hakl introduces the work by Julius Evola *The Mask and the face of contemporary spiritualism*; a study aimed at warning those who feel the need to embark on an authentic initiatic journey, of the perils constituted by all institutions that are in no way linked to the authentic *Tradition*. In Evola's book the term 'spiritualism' is used essentially as a synonym for esotericism; indeed, the phenomena constituting the focus of Evola's studies are routinely grouped by modern historians under the umbrella of esoteric phenomena.

Several decades after the publication of Evola's work, and despite the escalation and increased visibility of studies on esotericism, particularly amongst academics, the errors of judgement and consequent confusion between the *authentic* and *pseudo* Initiatic Schools have, regrettably, remained largely unchanged.

One, and possibly the most important, explanation lies in the fact that scholars of esoteric phenomena invariably address the issue using the typical approach of an *esoterologist*, an aseptic and unmovable specialist' in the field, thus, as external observers. However, to succeed in grasping the true essence of esotericism it is essential to approach the phenomenon as a 'follower', or rather, as an *esotericist.*

In the absence of an esotericistic approach, or indeed without becoming an esotericist, academic scholars will never be in a position to perceive the actual differences between the authentic Initiatic Schools with their specific aim of searching for the inner Self, the 'divine' essence of an individual, achieved by means of an authentic transformation (or 'realisation'), and those organisations that, confusingly, appear to advocate the same aims.

As mentioned previously, the analysis of genuine or seemingly genuine esoteric phenomena is frequently carried out by the esoterologist in a cold, sterile and logical manner, based on the presence of 'constants' that allow them to classify the phenomenon into well-defined and acknowledged categories, in a vain attempt to bridle something which, by its very nature is elusive, changeable, impossible to define in a logical or rational manner. Esotericism, a tangibly appreciable metaphysical concept, a list of historically-identifiable religious and lay traditions, particularly represents a dimension, a vision of the world, accessible and understandable only to those who have effectively adhered to and striven to achieve the same. Those individuals who strive towards esotericism are the adepts of the authentic Schools of Wisdom, their common *weltanschauung* is of an esoteric nature, they constitute the ideal type I have defined as an Initiate.

Therefore, if we wish to identify the existence of an ideal type in modern-day society, or rather, the figure in which the latter is cyclically manifested, it is mandatory to start by establishing the correct meaning of the term 'esotericism', and to subsequently discern the potential existence of authentic Schools of Wisdom, or Initiatic Orders, in the context of which the ideal type has been newly manifested, reactualised.

It may seem feasible to maintain that in the confused melting pot of esotericism, one should encounter similar figures, but Evola warns the reader and, in his previously mentioned book, makes a net distinction between 'pure' and 'spurious' esoteric doctrines, even making an interesting reference to Freemasonry[7]:

> Rekindled by each aggravation of the crisis in the western world, a considerable number of these tendencies remain – spiritism alone accounted for millions. Esoteric doctrines of all types are imported; the greater the degree of strangeness and mystery, the more fascinating they prove to be. Indeed, every sort of concoction will find a place in the container of 'spiritualism' – forms of Yoga, a series of spurious mysticisms, 'occultism' relegated to the edges of Masonic lodges, neo-Rosicrucianism, naturalistic and primitivistic regressions based on pantheism, neo-gnosticism, together with astrological, parapsychological, and medianic digressions and similar issues – to say nothing of all that is pure mysticism.[8]

It is clear therefore, that Evola relegates the phenomenon of occultism to the edges; although it would be more appropriate to say 'beyond the confines' of traditional Freemasonry, presenting the occultist digressions as a distorted representation of the latter, rather than as an authentic manifestation (the approach of Freemasonry to occultism, or even to Satanism or Luciferism is an error that is frequently committed even by renowned scholars and modern-day academics).

To deposit such widely diverse experiences and institutions in the same container is particularly detrimental to the authentic Initiatic Schools which, compared to other phenomena bearing frequent negative connotations in the social imaginary (spiritism and occultism for all), with at times hasty and misleading associations, are thus interpreted in an erroneous and depreciatory manner. In his texts, Evola emphasises this risk repeatedly, reiterating the same even in his autobiography, *The path of Cinnabar* in which, on referring to his attempts at distinguishing between the authentic Initiatic Schools and the pseudo-organisations apparently featuring the same aim, he underlines the difficulty of raising awareness of these differences in the academic world: 'the spokesmen of profane culture had no conception of the crucial distinctions in rank'.[9] The term 'esotericism' was coined relatively recently (it was first used by Jacques Matter in his *Historie critique du gnosticisme*, published in 1828), and for many years was seen as a synonym of a secret, occult manifestation, in the most negative sense of the word. A similar occurrence has been observed for the phenomena of Gnosticism and Hermeticism which, although in the past the focus of authoritative studies, subsequently came to be viewed with suspicion or, worse still, total indifference. However, following the Second World War, religious historians set out to investigate the various contexts of the previously scorned Western esoteric traditions, and, fortunately, in recent decades the study of esotericism has found its rightful place in academia. Without doubt, the actual turning point coincided with the publication of the writings of the Renaissance historian Frances A. Yates, in particular her work *Giordano Bruno and the Hermetic Tradition* (1964), in which Ms Yates carried out a thorough revision of the historiography verging on an overt 'revolutionisation', no longer representing the Nolan philosopher as a martyr of scientific progress, but rather as a full-blown hermetic magician. The effects of this volume, together with others by the same author (*The Rosicrucian Enlightenment, The Art of Memory, The Occult Philosophy in the Elizabethan Age,* and *Astrea*) have succeeded in securing the inclusion of studies on the hermetic traditions of the Renaissance into the realms of academic research. However, despite the progress made, the term 'esotericism', contrary to Hermeticism, is frequently still subject to misinterpretations or denigration. As rightly emphasised by an expert in the field, the Dutch historian Wouter Hanegraaff, this may suggest that although Hermeticism and esotericism both form part of the same field of investigation, the possibility of the latter acquiring a vestige of credibility in academia will only come about if the scholars concerned apply 'politically correct' or socially acceptable terms, with the aim of avoiding conflict with their colleagues: the term 'Hermetic' is acceptable, whilst 'occult' and 'esoteric' are not![10] To solve this issue Hanegraaff proposes that the so-called 'Yates paradigm', according to which the Hermetic tradition constituted a significant factor in the development of scientific progress, be overlooked. On the contrary, he maintains that the studies of Hermeticism and similar phenomena, including esotericism, do not need to be legitimised, frequently achieved through a sheer act of force, by means of hypothetical scientific or social progress deriving from the original Hermetic or esoteric doctrines. Indeed, the Dutch historian opined that tradition did not need to be seen as progressive in order to be worthy of scientific acclaim. I fully agree with Hanegraaff in this regard.

Subsequently, Hanegraaff criticised the presentation of 'Hermetic tradition' as a unitarian and self-sufficient phenomenon, placing his confidence in an innovative approach to the study of traditional phenomena, a new method emphasising an increased complexity rather than an artificial sense of uniformity. Studies focusing on Western esoteric currents (including post-Renaissance developments, some of which were not strictly of a Hermetic nature) would consequently be called upon to free themselves from the notion of esotericism seen as a counter-tradition and from the obsession with justifying esotericism in terms of a modernistic narration of secular progress.[11]

In the wake of Ms Yates, numerous scholars from a series of disciplines have contributed towards furthering the knowledge of and reappraisal of the western esoteric corpus. Among these, I should like to mention Gershom Scholem, who provided an important contribution to the study of the Jewish Kabbalah, François Secret, who studied the Christian Kabbalah, Alexandre Koyré for his studies on German mysticism and theosophy, Charles Puech for Gnosticism and Manicheism, Mircea Eliade and Carl Gustav Jung for Alchemy. This renewed enthusiasm heralded the birth of a discipline independent from all other disciplines focusing on the study of esotericism as an historic, social and religious phenomenon with its own singular identity.

In 1964, François Secret was appointed to the Chair of 'History of Christian Esotericism' at the *Ecole Pratique des Hautes Etudes* (EPHE) in Paris. Secret was succeeded in 1979 by Antoine Faivre, under the directorship of whom the chair changed name, taking on the title of 'History of esoteric and mystical currents in modern and contemporary Europe'. In 2002, following the arrival of Jean-Pierre Brach at EPHE, the term 'mystical' was removed, and esotericism became the sole subject matter of the discipline. The fecundity of this scientific investigation was confirmed by the creation of numerous chairs in other nations. In 1980, the Hermetic Academy was established in the USA, a study group investigating the esoteric traditions linked to the American Academy of Religion, in the context of which, in 1986, first the Esotericism and Perennialism Group'(from 1993 onwards Theosophy and Theosophical Thought Seminar), and more recently the Western Esotericism Group were set up. In 1999, Amsterdam University witnessed the creation of a specific department (directed by Wouter J. Hanegraaff) devoted to the history of modern Western esoteric currents under the title of 'History of Hermetic Philosophy and Related Currents'. In 2005, the European Society for the Study of Western Esotericism was set up and lastly, in 2006 at the University of Exeter in the United Kingdom, the Centre for the Study of Esotericism, directed by Prof Nicholas Goodrick-Clarke was established.

These institutional initiatives were supported by specialist journals of considerable interest, including *ARIES*, published in four languages, founded in 1985 by Faivre and Edighoffer, published by the Brille University press, the name of which was subsequently changed in 2001 to *Aries: Journal for the Study of Western Esotericism*, and, in the United States, the *Theosophical History* founded by Leslie Price in 1985 and directed since 1990 by James A. Santucci.

An Attempt at Classification

Following this brief overview of the origins of a new discipline, our research continues with particular focus on the meaning and content of the term 'esotericism' from a specifically academic point of view.

The classification put forward by the Frenchman Pierre A. Riffard, professor of pedagogy and philosophy, and renowned expert in the field, is one of the most widely accepted, presenting the esoteric phenomena according to *ideal types*:

Ecstatic Esotericism. This induces brief, intense, heavy states of consciousness in which *exaltation* is the predominant factor; in this type of esotericism, possession and medianity play a key role, the initiate is no longer himself, he succumbs to mania, dragging the others with him. To this regard, Riffard cites the well-known tragedy of Euripides, *the Bacchae*, which illustrates the practices of the faithful who worship Dionysius (or Bacchus) who, at the height of exaltation, which coincided with the ecstasy, ripped apart and devoured raw the sacred animal to take possession of the deity himself.

Metaphysical Esotericism. In this form, esotericism is mediated by a tool, presenting not as a spiritual but as a material, or rather, materialised esotericism. This type of esotericism, which may also assume doctrinarian, philosophical, speculative, and theoretical forms, is based substantially on knowledge; consequently, the initiatic pathway coincides with gnosis. For the anthroposophist Rudolf Steiner, Riffard represents the ideal type of metaphysical esotericist, whilst in Hinduism, the French historian perceives the presence of the Vedanta.

Operative Esotericism. This type is not essentially practical, but operates in the context of practices that are not conditional to Initiation, but are rather conditions accepted by the Initiate. According to this definition esotericism is denoted by efforts, activity, its aim is to achieve completion of the world, and thus man needs to perfect himself, the Principle needs to be conquered. The works elicited by means of this process are esotericism in their own right: works of art, the martial arts, social institutions, physical practices, and craftsmanship.

Symbolic Esotericism. Essentially recalling the imaginary world, which is neither entirely spiritual nor wholly material, but a connection between the two. This ideal type is based on two main trends: the first of a *pantheistic*, and the second a *pancosmic* nature. The former seeks the divine in nature, surprises the prodigies, reveals the archangels, and sacralises events: the typical figure is Paracelsus. The latter seeks for nature in the divine, invests God with cosmic attributes (GAOTU), and justifies its spiritual nature using data from nature: for Riffard, the characteristic figure of this type of esotericism is the German philosopher and mystic, Jakob Bohme.[12]

In the analysis of another renowned academic, Professor Antoine Faivre, considered one of the leading authorities in the study of esotericism, it is clear how the French historian adopted an exclusively historic arrangement, radically different from the perennialist interpretation represented in the twentieth century not only by Guénon (who favoured a Traditionalist, and particularly initiatic perspective), but also by Massignon, Jung, Corbin and Eliade (who all remained within a scientific and academic context).

To Faivre, goes the undeniable credit of having provided esotericism with its rightful academic dignity; in particular, in the volume *Western Esotericism and the Science of Religion,* he clarified how he intended to view esotericism as a distinct and independent field of study within the context of Religious studies:

> Since the present volume intends to contribute to the recognition of 'western esotericism' as a specific field of research within the science of religions, one focus of interest concerns the meaning(s) of various terms which belong to the vocabulary common in this domain.[13]

As mentioned previously, Faivre intended to illustrate the esoteric phenomena mainly from an historic and social point of view, revealing in each single phenomenon the presence of a process of emancipation from the esoteric doctrines, compared to the increasingly exoteric official religion. At variance with Riffard, Faivre historically confined his analysis to commence at the start of the sixteenth century, thus from the Christian Theosophy or Natural Philosophy advocated at that time, in order that all subsequent forms of esotericism would be so defined merely in consideration of their vicinity or distance from the characteristics that this first Theosophy possessed, and which Faivre termed 'The Golden Age' of Western esotericism.

Faivre maintained that one should only refer to esotericism in the presence of *six fundamental characteristics*, or components, varyingly distributed throughout the historic context in which the phenomenon is manifested:

Correspondences. Both symbolic and actual correspondences are present between all parts of the visible and invisible Universe, recalling the ancient notion of the *microcosm* and the *macrocosm*. Essentially, two types of correspondence can be distinguished, those existing between visible and invisible nature, for example between the seven metals and the seven planets, between the planets and parts of the human body or character (or society), thus forming the basis for astrology; secondly, those observed between the natural world and the invisible regions of the celestial and supercelestial worlds.

Living Nature. The cosmos is seen as complex, plural, hierarchical phenomenon – as observed previously in discussing the issue of correspondence. Accordingly, Nature occupies a strategic position. Stratified, rich in potential revelations of all types, it should be interpreted and referred to as a book.

Imagination and mediation. The two concepts are interlinked, complementary. The notion of correspondence conveys a form of imagination prone to identifying and adopting mediations of all kinds, including rituals, symbolic images, mandalas, and intermediary spirits.

The experience of Transmutation. Faivre underlines the fundamental importance of the initiatic element, which allows us to distinguish between an esoteric phenomenon and a spirituality confined to a speculative expression. It is indeed 'Initiation' that facilitates a 'metamorphosis' produced by the 'second birth' that occurs as a result of 'Initiation'. Faivre explains how the aim is not to separate knowledge (gnosis) from inner experience, or intellectual activity from active imagination.

The practice of concordance. This concept is not reserved solely to western esotericism as a whole, but rather marks the start of the modern Era (in line with the *Philosophia Perennis*) to emerge at the end of the past century under a changed and more forceful guise. A trend is displayed that underlines the need to establish a common denominator between two or more, or even between all different traditions, in the hope of achieving enlightenment, a higher gnosis.

Transmission. Esoteric teachings can, and should, be transmitted by the Master to his disciple according to a formerly channelled direction, a previously forged pathway. Two specific notions are associated with this occurrence: a) the validity of the knowledge transmitted through filiation, the regularity or authenticity of which is undeniable (association with a tradition viewed as an organic set the integrity of which should be left intact); b) Initiation, generally undertaken between Master and disciple (self-initiation cannot be performed arbitrarily, an initiator or guru is required).[14]

In his studies, Faivre, in line with a design previously applied by Yates in the case of Hermeticism, likewise proposed a paradigm of *enchantment-disenchantment* with the world in which the above-listed singularities of esotericism would be fully defined. According to this interpretation, esotericism essentially represents a *response* to the disenchantment produced by the Cartesian philosophy and Newtonian and positivist science, a metaphysical vision based on the correspondences inspired by the Plotinian ideas of sympathy within the Universe. This is contrary to the pervasive mechanistic vision which suggested the presence of subtle entities that join the *spirit* to the *matter,* access to which may be gained through the *vis imaginativa*, together with the possibility of achieving, for those seeking the same, a transmutation leading man to his original Divine status.

Personally, I maintain that this list of presumed indicative components of esotericism proposed by Faivre and Riffard, is somewhat artificial, and, at times, rather bizarre. If we were to adhere blindly to this list in choosing whether or not to view esotericism as a doctrine, we would indeed need to exclude the ideas of the French esotericist René Guénon right from the very start, particularly, as we will learn hereafter, in view of his renowned categorical exclusion of *Living Nature*.

I envisage therefore, that all attempts to historify, catalogue, place or, paradoxically, rationalise esotericism in order to make the same better understandable are destined to fail miserably.

This is clearly highlighted when Faivre, attempting to apply his design to Freemasonry, states that: 'Moreover, only some aspects of specific institutions, such as Freemasonry can be construed as belonging to esotericism (some forms of Freemasonry are devoid of these aspects.)'[15] In referring to the statement uttered by Faivre, it would be more precise to say that some Masonic Obediences may possess some, all or none of the peculiarities highlighted, but the essence of Freemasonry, the *authentic* Freemasonry, interpreted as the Form or Aspect of Tradition, will inevitably continue to be an esoteric movement. Furthermore, to aid an intimate comprehension of Freemasonry (and to better understand all other authentic Initiatic Schools), an analysis will need to be undertaken that takes into account the 'human type' constituting the same, i.e. the reference ideal type or figure to which it refers. It will clearly be impossible to identify this ideal type by adhering blindly to the above categories proposed by Riffard[16] and Faivre.

In a rational representation of esotericism, an anatomy that explains, catalogues and subdivides the issue into categories, one inevitably loses sight of the Myth, the major motivation underlying all esoteric phenomena, which is, and will continue to be, a crucial 'initiatic' phenomenon. Thus, a Tradition is transformed into a mere historic event, revealing the degeneration and loss of sacred vision of the world that, in the words of Max Weber, has produced a disenchantment in modern man. Indeed, to classify esotericism would be to rip out its soul.

To enable an in-depth comprehension of esotericism, the latter would thus need to be accomplished, experienced, lived, and only subsequently could an individual attempt to represent the latter, whilst continuing however to be far removed from its true *essence*.

The analysis performed by Faivre, Riffard and other scholars, as the product of a typically historicist vision, proposes an interpretation and evaluation of the esoteric phenomenon solely in the light of the time and the historic context in which it occurs, disregarding, either wholly or in part, the *universal* models. Historicism, focusing on unique and unrepeatable historic events, cannot contemplate the possibility of unique and repeatable human figures, therefore, instead of seeking Man, focus is placed solely on individual historic events, frequently of scarce interest, in the belief that by studying the latter, one may penetrate the essence of the phenomenon.

To return to other scholarly analyses, the Dutch historian Wouter Hanegraaff, in the same way as Faivre, limited his assessment of esotericism to the Western world, although correctly emphasizing how the same term 'Western Esotericism' is a mere academic construct coined on the basis of the constants detected by scholars in the context of similar phenomena:

> In short, 'Western esotericism' is a modern scholarly construct, not an autonomous tradition that already existed out there and merely needed to be discovered by historians. This does not mean, however, that there is nothing 'real' about the field. On the contrary, the category of 'Western esotericism' emerged because intellectuals and historians became attentive to structural similarities that actually did exist between the ideas and world-views of a wide variety of thinkers and movements.[17]

The Dutch historian Gilles Quispel, lecturer in the History of Christianity at the University of Utrecht, used Gnosis as a term of reference in his studies of Western Esotericism, even suggesting a sort of affinity, and indeed almost interchangeability, between the two terms. On the matter of religious experience, Quispel learnt considerably from the teachings of Carl Gustav Jung, and was thus in a position to distinguish and interpret the complicated gnostic myths. His work *Gnosi Als Weltreligion* was published as the outcome of a series of conferences held at the Jung Institute in Zurich, with the specific aim of illustrating to Jung and his entourage the new findings of Nag Hammadi. His admiration for the Swiss psychoanalyst was unblushing, with Quispel once declaring that Jung 'has done more for the interpretation of religion than any other living person'.[18]

In the interpretation put forward by Quispel, *Gnosis* assumes the connotations of a constant in the history of religions, a constant that, although universal, is manifested under specific historic guises. Essentially, according to Quispel, Gnosis represents the intuitive knowledge of the true nature of man, of God and of the world, conveyed by mythical images and, therefore, a spontaneously emerging possibility open to men of all eras.

The approach adopted by Quispel clearly differs from that of the academic vulgate; in referring to Gnosis as a universal constant, a possibility of spiritual development afforded to men, Quispel more closely approaches the true essence of esotericism. Esotericism is seen no longer as a mere historic phenomenon, but rather, from a trans-historic point of view, as a phenomenon within which the diverse esoteric manifestations are contaminated, follow in succession, *converge*, from a blatantly metaphysical perspective, represented by an individual who 'may emerge spontaneously in all eras', in whom to identify the ideal type mentioned in this work.

The Accomplishment of Esotericism

The definitions and classifications of esotericism as deduced from its historic manifestations, are, as mentioned previously, represented with a clear intrinsic weakness due to the fact that, in line with this approach, the fundamental element that facilitates the existence of the esoteric phenomenon, or rather he who accomplishes and practices esotericism, the Initiate, is ignored. Indeed, academic scholars tend to focus exclusively on the historic-social context in which the phenomenon is presented. If however, on the contrary, we attempt to approach esotericism in a different manner, acknowledging the centrality of the figure of he who actually embarks on the initiatic pathway, the *opus*, and analysing the psychological and consciential requirements thereof, the object of our investigations would start to seem less confused and arduous.

By approaching the range of historic manifestations of esotericism from a different viewpoint, and examining the human figures that gave rise to the birth and diffusion of the Schools of Wisdom, and the reasons underlying their choice to embark on unprecedented, alternative pathways frequently scorned by the social and cultural contexts in which they were manifested, (in the same way as Freemasonry today), we would indeed ascertain how these figures are representative, with a view to the personality and vision of the world, of a series of interesting constants constituting an actual ideal type, an ideal type which, over time, is represented with largely similar characteristics.

This ideal type or figure, this 'differentiated' man, to use the words of Evola, is he who aspires to a transmutation of his conscience, his soul, an acceleration of his evolutionary pathway, thanks to his singular predisposition, or rather the total unconditioning of his mind, freedom from all types of ideological, religious or social superstructures.

As mentioned previously, use of the term 'figure' is inspired by the German writer and thinker Ernst Junger, who used this term to define 'a superior entity that confers a sense to the phenomena.'[19] By applying this definition the German intellectual averted a need to identify an average term to establish a new system of knowledge, and finds the same by syncretistically representing the possibility of a union between the essence and the existence, thus, a sort of immanent transcendence comprising an idealtypical figure. According to Junger, this figure is governed by its own laws, its own designs, and thus replaces a linear conception, whilst at the same time remaining static in the typical world of an historic approach, a dynamic, or rather cyclical, temporal representation, which, in the sheer cyclicity of its apparition, conceals its true transhistoric, or metaphysical, meaning.

It should be emphasised how in the figures through which the phenomenon is manifested and reactualises the ideal type I refer to here, i.e. the Initiate, I have opted not to highlight specific rules of conduct, but rather depict these figures as metahistoric constants of a subsequent archetype. This archetype or ideal type is historicised in the notion of a form or figure based on well-defined individuals who diverge from their peers in view of their singular vision of the world, their original *Weltshauung*. In my opinion, to recognise these characteristics, identify the origin of the inner motivation to seek a pathway of gnosis, the need for a transmutation, constitutes an inescapable condition in achieving the knowledge and understanding of the nature of esotericism.

The previously cited French historian Riffard seems to grasp the difficulty involved in providing an academic interpretation of esotericism, emphasising the latter in the previously mentioned differentiation between an esotericist and an esoterologist: 'Let us therefore address once more the main issue faced by he who practices esotericism (esotericist), and the fundamental question focused on by he who studies esotericism (esoterologist): are we legitimised to express (to create, examine, present) secret doctrines and initiatic practices, to loosen the subtleties of 'traditional symbols' and the authenticity of 'spiritual experiences'? When claiming to speak of esotericism, it should first be mentioned that esotericism refuse to be communicated, debased, to speak of itself, to become the topic of conversation.'[20] We should therefore ask ourselves if there is any point to writing books about *Esotericism*? If we do not feel we are legitimised to speak of, and to express the contents and the purposes of the Traditional doctrines, what must we do if we wish to approach esotericism? Riffard, an academic, thus addressed the central issue:

> This is the main difficulty for an esoterologist: can one be the latter without being an esotericist?...One would need to be 'capable of' but not 'qualified to' practice esotericism, in other words, you would need to be initiated in order to comprehend initiation, whilst it is indeed possible to be an epistemologist without being a scholar, a professor of literature without being a writer, an art critic without being a creator, an ethnologist without being 'primitive'. This implies that esoterology is impossible, that esotericism is unknown, and is not studied. This leads us to a quandary: one is either an esoterologist, uninitiated, and for this very reason presents oneself by admitting to knowing little or nothing about the matter at hand, or one is an esotericist and obeys the arcane discipline by not revealing the same, for fear of debasing what may have been revealed.[21]

Thus, Riffard held the opinion that an esoterologist (he himself) is incapable of understanding esotericism, knowing little or nothing about the topic, but may indeed perceive the need to write a 1500-page book on the subject.

To remain in the world of academia, I should like to mention a series of interesting studies undertaken by Prof Nicholas Goodrick-Clarke, Director of the *Centre for the Study of Esotericism* established in 2006 at the University of Exeter. In his studies,

Goodrick-Clarke, one of the most widely acknowledged experts in the field of esotericism, on referring to the Western esoteric tradition, collocates its roots within a singular approach to religion stemming from the Gnosticism, Hermeticism and Neoplatonism of the Hellenic era in the first centuries AD. Goodrick-Clarke opines that subsequently, from the Renaissance to modern times, esoteric thought has assumed a series of forms, identifying a semblance even in the context of the dynamics of Jungian analytical psychology:

> In the Renaissance, the rediscovery of ancient texts led to the scholarly revival of magic, alchemy, and Kabbalah. Following the Reformation, this spiritual current gave rise to theosophy, Rosicrucianism, and Freemasonry, and the modern occult revival extended from nineteenth-century spiritualism, H. P. Blavatsky's Theosophy, and ceremonial magical orders to twentieth-century esotericists such as Rudolph Steiner, Alice A. Bailey, and George Ivanovitch Gurdjieff, and the analytical psychology of Carl Gustav Jung.[22]

In my opinion, the hypothesis put forward by Goodrick-Clarke is of particular interest, as he also viewed esotericism as an authentic vision of the world, a *weltanshauung* that produced an important influence on the philosophical, scientific and religious changes throughout the Western world, an esoteric behaviour springing from a mental attitude based on a spirituality aspiring to a knowledge of the absolute which was not enmeshed in purely historic and social reconstructions:

> My own perspective is that definitions of 'the esoteric' in terms of discourse, social constructions, and legitimacy lack a hermeneutic interpretation of spirit and spirituality as an independent ontological reality. By seeking to define the esoteric in terms of human behaviour and culture, it becomes a reflected cultural category rather than a philosophical or spiritual insight, which remains the essential component of any claims to real or absolute knowledge.[23]

In the world of academia, among those who have approached the esoteric phenomenon from an authentically initiatic point of view, undoubtedly one of the most interesting characters is the North American historian, Arthur Versluis.

Professor Arthur Versluis, Chair of the Department of Religious Studies and Professor at the College of Arts & Letters of Michigan State University, in order to achieve a correct understanding of the authentic esoteric experience and thus succeed in identifying with the latter, adopts a method he terms 'sympathetic-empirical', Versluis writes:

> It is essential for scholars to engage at minimum in a process of imaginative participation ... Yet I will go further, I am suggesting that in order to fully understand what we are studying, there is a point in this field at which the

practitioner's expertise takes on more importance than purely academic knowledge.[24]

Therefore, according to Versluis, an esoterologist should practice the doctrine, whilst the esotericist should transform himself into an individual whose experience has originated from his embarking on the pathway, with all that this entails, including an initial desire to seek spiritual rebirth.

In referring to Western Esotericism, Versluis aimed to highlight the characteristics of a hidden inner or spiritual knowledge, transmitted throughout the historic currents in Western Europe, and subsequently passed on to North America and other extra-European contexts. According to this simple definition, esoteric knowledge can be traced throughout the course of Western history from ancient times to the present in a series of different forms, ranging from the Mysteries of Ancient Greece and Rome, to the gnostic groups, and the observers of hermeticism and alchemy, and even up to the modern-day esoteric or new religious movements.

Versluis openly criticises the approach adopted by Faivre who, in his opinion, whilst bearing in mind the cosmological aspect of Western Esotericism (the correspondences and the living nature) fails to grasp the undeniably central element in Gnosis. Versluis further maintains that it is typical of esotericism to affirm the possession of Gnosis. The US historian is of the view that to select Gnosis as a common denominator for esoteric phenomena would afford the advantage of providing studies with a characteristic that is sufficiently broad to include the entire range of esoteric traditions, but likewise sufficiently limited to exclude figures and movements featuring exoteric connotations, and to distinguish on the one hand between traditional knowledge, i.e. knowledge obtained through largely rational means, and an authentic Gnosis on the other. Alchemists sought direct spiritual knowledge in nature, with the aim of transforming specific substances; astrologists sought direct spiritual knowledge in the cosmos and exploited the same to analyse events; magicians sought direct spiritual knowledge to be used in changing the course of events; theosophists sought direct spiritual knowledge to accomplish their angelical nature. Versluis concluded that in all these cases the aspiring candidates sought direct spiritual knowledge of the hidden nature of the cosmos and of self: they sought Gnosis.[25]

Versluis was thus of the opinion that esotericism refers to the series of traditions that have emerged in the context of the numerous approaches to Gnosis, resulting in the view that 'Western gnostic' is a synonym for 'Western esoteric' traditions, i.e. esoteric traditions which, although differing significantly as to their form and nature, share a series of common denominators:

Gnosis or gnostic insight, i.e. knowledge of hidden or invisible realms or aspects of existence (including both cosmological and metaphysical gnosis)

Esoterism, meaning that this hidden knowledge is either explicitly restricted to a relatively small group of people, or implicitly self-restricted by virtue of its complexity or subtlety.

In his studies, Versluis identified a 'Cosmological gnosis', or rather a 'Knowledge or direct perception of the hidden esoteric aspects of the cosmos' from a 'Metaphysical gnosis' intended as a 'spiritual intuition focused on a complete transcendence'. The former remains today a form of knowledge in which the corresponding forms of subject-object dualism are still observed in the field of alchemy, astrology and magic. The latter is a non-dualist spiritual pathway similar to the *negative pathway* referred to by Meister Eckart, or the *Ungrund* of Jacob Böhme; it was revealed originally in the *Corpus Hermeticum* in the guise of a divine Mind or *Nous*, and is likewise acknowledged in the Indian philosophy in the form of the *Advaita Vedanta*.

Versluis also criticised the methodological approach adopted by Hanegraaff who, Versluis maintained, made a sharp division between a 'Religionist' (essentialist and conspicuous) and an 'Empirical' perspective, although he likewise opined that the recourse to an empirical rather than a prominent approach indicated an arrogant dismissal of the volumes of alchemy, magic or theosophy, viewing these as unimportant or misleading.

However, Versluis particularly abhorred the use of rationalism in approaching the esoteric phenomena, specifically when referring to mysticism and magic, upholding that:

> In magic and mysticism we see areas of study that by their very nature are not entirely reducible to objects of rationalist discourse and manipulation, but instead border on and open into dimensions of life that remain partially veiled to us unless we enter into them for ourselves. Esotericism, in other words, borders on consciousness studies, and its experiential centre results in its inherent and definitive syncretism (mingling disparate religious beliefs) or syncrasis (mingling practices). From antiquity to the present, esoteric practitioners have consistently mingled together disparate beliefs, traditions and practices in order to create new esoteric syntheses. As the study of esotericism continues, it will have to develop more sophisticated phenomenological ways of approaching and understanding what is esoteric.[26]

In an interesting essay, 'Religion of Light', Versluis investigates the topic of light, one of the most pervasive themes in the field of religions and esotericism but which, inexplicably in Versluis' opinion, the majority of scholars have failed to study in greater detail. The explanation provided by the US historian is that the academic community, defined by its exponents as an exquisitely secular environment, knowingly rejected topics that might have challenged its method. However, Versluis further stated how, on observing the topics of light and illumination in a religious context, we realise that the contemporary academic boundaries seem to be decidedly artificial, constructs to be used in the shaping of particular areas of knowledge that contribute to the existing social order. However, Versluis maintains that the symbolism of light, is unrestricted by these disciplinary boundaries, and how a debate focusing on the religion of light would inevitably entail the need for a debate on the philosophy and literature of light, light in art and architecture, light in culture and light perhaps, in science and neuroscience. It would be to discuss the sublime, the very nature of which is transcendent, invisible, but which concomitantly renders things visible, or rather, stimulates discussion into those aspects of extreme commonness, which are simultaneously of such importance that their significance surpasses our ability to describe it.

Versluis thus questions himself as to the existence of any element capable of inhibiting or limiting a religion/ philosophy of light. How can such a prominent issue present not only in the religious texts, but also in everyday life, pass unobserved to such a degree? Perhaps, responds Versluis, the mere thought of the implications associated with light may induce us into an area that questions some of our most deeply held, and at times unconscious, beliefs relating to our true nature and that of our world. Versluis is indeed of the opinion that the latter may account for the extirpation of *Mani* and his religion. For Judaism and Christianity, particularly those variants that clung firmly to anthropomorphic conceptions of deity, Manicheism was seen as a profound threat, and was detested and opposed in Asia by many Buddhists and Taoists. Where the Jewish and Christians deemed the religion too oriental, the Asians saw in it an excessive similarity with monotheism, and an unreasonable association with anthropomorphism. Nonetheless, the religion established by Mani was undeniably a religion of light; it is moreover of considerable interest that this religion, in the same way as its founder, was so thoroughly eliminated that still today we possess only fragments, shards of what it must have been in the past. Perhaps then, as now, a religion of light represented, and continues to represent today, a threat to the *status quo*.

Versluis hypothesised that the theme of light was too abstract, too ethereal, for those endowed with a religious inclination in modernity; the emotional pitch of veneration and fevers of conversion, the call to a personal relationship with a personal God hold far greater appeal. Nevertheless, the historian continues, the more one delves into the religion of light, the more profound the subject is reveals to be, retaining a strong hold on the popular imagination: it is indeed a commonplace belief that death entails a movement *towards the light*. This theme is pervasive in New Age thought, and is present in every sort of popular religious movement. Indeed, Versluis holds the view that it is there for a good reason. There is something about this theme that goes beyond any particular religious or philosophical tradition, that is in a certain sense built into human consciousness, often in ways that we find hard to recognise or understand. Accordingly, Versluis affirms that his approach to the ‘Religions of Light’ is not to explore a particular religious tradition, but rather to identify those forms of religious, or sacred, expression and understanding that recur throughout the numerous religious and philosophical traditions:

> Although I use the term 'religion of light', I don't identify that term with any particular religious tradition, nor does it denote something separate from existing or historical religions. Rather, as we explore this theme, we find glimpses of it here and there. Even Manichaeism, sometimes known as 'the religion of light', represents only a small part of what we are exploring here… we will investigate, not every reference in religious literature to light, that would be an encyclopedic task indeed, but rather what we might term the keys to the mysteries. Those keys, I have come to believe, are to be found primarily in the tradition known to us as 'Platonism', though it also could be termed 'Pythagoreanism', or even more broadly, the Hellenic illuminative mysteries. Whatever one terms it, one finds it hinted at not only in the works of Plato and Speusippus, as well as Plotinus, Porphyry, Iamblichus, the Emperor Julian, Proclus and Damascius, but also in the body of Hermetic texts known as the Corpus Hermeticum, and in the remaining fragments of the Gnostics, notably Valentinus and Basilides. It is possible that, behind these many tantalising hints, behind the stone monuments of great antiquity, behind the traditions of the sacred fire and the hearth, behind the prophets of light, there is something else, aspects of which we begin to see, but which is not yet recognised for what it is? Is it possible that, as we begin to explore the metaphysics and the traces of a religion of, we are glimpsing not only what existed in the past, but also what might exist in the future? After all, to speak of a metaphysics of light is to begin to consider non-dualism and all its implications, as well as how one begins to move from a subject-object dualism toward transcendental (non-dual) gnosis, from outer toward inner science. Here of course we are embarking on an exploration that might result in the discovery – scandal of scandals – that there is an empirical basis for inner science too. It is possible that the Platonists offer us something that we might not be interested in accepting, but that is no less valid if it is refused. What is offered, of course, is a metaphysical reference point, a way of understanding in the West what is understood in the East, too, in the traditions of Vedanta and of Buddhism. Ascent toward non-dual gnosis might look very similar even from different cultural-religious vantage points, after all.[27]

Light, concludes Versluis, is a central theme in all Asian religions, and likewise present in indigenous traditions; for this reason therefore, to explore the theme would imply a need to address not only the subject of light in religion, but also, more fundamentally, the experience and significance of being human.

To this regard, I should here underline the constant, fundamental presence of light in Masonic rituals, a symbology acquired through the important contaminations elicited by Neoplatonic thought on the Masonic doctrines, a symbology that has resulted in the inclusion of Masonic thought and methods among those defined by Versluis as Religions of Light.

To conclude, of the scholars who proposed an 'operative' approach to esotericism, I would like to highlight the British philosopher and researcher John Holman, expert of Western esotericism, and one of the leading experts of hermetic psychology, member of the Association for the Study of Esotericism, the Association for Transpersonal Psychology, and the Scientific and Medical Network. In his *The return of the Perennial Philosophy*, Holman reached the conclusion that if we are to understand esotericism in its authentic guise, this will only be possible in the role of Initiate, indeed, only in this way will we be able to fully grasp and fathom the essence of the phenomenon.[28]

Goodrick-Clarck, Holman and Versluis are among the representatives of a diverse approach to esoteric phenomena that is finally on the verge of being manifested throughout academia, traditionally impermeable to change to its acquired paradigms, a new means of approaching the true nature of esotericism.

However, it is particularly amongst the leading Western thinkers, located beyond the confines of bureaucracy and academic rules that, as I will describe in greater detail in the next chapter, we detect the most inspired representations of esotericism, including the widely renowned philosopher and mystic Frithjof Schuon, whose definition constitutes a veritable model. Indeed, his representation of esotericism is devoid of classifications or constants; through this definition he proposes to reach the very *essence* of the esoteric experience:

> We should begin by agreeing on the meaning of the word 'esoterism': According to common understanding the term 'esoterism' designates doctrines and methods that are more or less secret, because they are regarded as transcending the limited capacities of average men. It should however be explained why this view is possible, indeed necessary, and how it is suited to all planes of human existence...Without doubt all esoterism appears to be steeped in heresy when compared to its corresponding exoterism, which indeed is no disgrace if it is intrinsically orthodox, and thus corresponds to the truth itself and to the traditional symbolism on which it depends; it is however true that the most genuine form of esoterism may eventually deviate from this context and be related to extraneous symbols, although it may never be syncretistic in the same form or substance. What concerns us here is not so much the historic esoterisms — such as Pythagorism, Shivaist Vedanta, Zen — but esoterism as such, which we would willingly call sophia perennis and which in itself is independent of particular forms, since it is their essence... Only esoterism, in referring to the total truth, is capable of justifying the jagged edges and restoring the lost truth; can provide answers that are neither fragmentary nor compromised in advance by a denominational bias. Just as

> rationalism can remove faith, so esoterism can restore it. Esoterism, by its interpretations, its revelations and its interiorizing and essentializing operations, tends to realise pure and direct objectivity; this is the reason for its existence. Objectivity takes account of both immanence and transcendence; it is both extinction and reintegration. It is not other than the Truth, in which subject and object coincide, and in which the essential takes precedence over the accidental — or in which the principle takes precedence over its manifestation — either by extinguishing it, or by reintegrating it, depending on the various aspects of relativity itself.
>
> The esoterist sees things, not as they appear according to a certain perspective, but as they are: he takes account of what is essential and consequently invariable under the veil of different religious formulations, while necessarily taking his own starting point in a given formulation... Everything which, in metaphysics or in spirituality, is universally true, becomes 'esoteric' in so far as it does not agree, or does not seem to agree, with a given formalistic system or 'esoterism.[29]

Esotericism and the Catholic Church

What stance has been adopted, both in the past and at the current time, by the Catholic Church with regard to esotericism? An interesting analysis of this issue is provided by the Jewish historian of Greek origin, Guy G. Stroumsa, Professor Emeritus of Comparative Religion at the Hebrew University of Jerusalem. In his interesting book *Hidden Wisdom, Esoteric Traditions and the Roots of Christian Mysticism*, Stroumsa highlights how the Christian doctrines initially included an important presence of esoteric elements which, as testified particularly by the opposition to Gnosticism, were subsequently expelled:

> The most developed anti-esoteric argument in Patristic literature can perhaps be found in a sermon of Augustine. The analysis of its argument shows the complexity of the reasons which brought to the disappearance of esoteric traditions from Christian thought in late Antiquity. An obvious and simple explanation for this disappearance lies in the transformation brought by the Peace of the Church; when Christianity was no more religio illicita, the need to hide was gone. But this explains the end of cultic secrecy, not that of doctrinal esotericism. A more convincing answer lies with the fight of the Church Fathers against Gnosticism. Various Gnostic groups seem to have accepted and developed, sometimes in baroque fashion, early Jewish-Christian esoteric traditions. The appropriation of these traditions by the Gnostics made them suspect in the eyes of 'orthodox' Christian intellectuals. In their merciless fight against the Gnostics, the Church Fathers felt the need to reject these esoteric traditions, which had accompanied Christianity since its beginning, but which had become an embarrassing burden. Victory over

> Gnosticism thus meant the eradication of esotericism from Christian doctrine.[30]

Thus, once all esoteric elements have been removed from its midst, the Christian doctrines, and in particular the Catholic Church, became concerned that esotericism might cause harm from the outside to its faithful; to publicise these dangers, several so-called experts in the field diffused a series of writings. I have selected two in particular and will quote a series of explanatory sentences.

The first book I will examine, entitled *L'Esoterismo* is written by an expert (as he defines himself) on the topic, the priest don Curzio Nitoglia, who introduces his theory:

> Esotericism (or exoterism) is a doctrine in which the teachings are open to all, it is a public concern, conversely to esotericism which is confined to a small group of initiates or the adept. In the majority of cases, the latter are misfits or unbalanced persons who strive to compensate their own limits through recourse to a mythical 'super-man', i.e. an initiate who is persuaded he is a 'God', if not something more, or a...poor megalomaniac...Religion is free for all, whilst esoterism is accessible only to the few, and naturally these few will maintain they are the true master and initiate. He truly believes he is 'someone', whilst the others have not risen to the same heights.[31]

Therefore, in Nitoglia's opinion, the esotericists should indeed be classified as psychiatric patients; being essentially'unbalanced' or 'misfits'. Likewise, with regard to the purposes of esotericism the priest seems to have very clear ideas:

> The false mystic gnostic-esotericist who strives at all costs to become 'deified' or towards self-deification by means of gnosis or knowledge aimed at salvation, is prouder and more foolish than the attempts made by Lucifer, who merely wanted to resemble God, whilst Gnostics strive to achieve equality with God, or even to surpass him. This, regrettably, is a path that leads not to union with God, but rather to complete, absolute and eternal separation from Him, in the eternal fires of hell…[32], adding that 'Esotericism scorns the Catholic dogma of salvation or eternal damnation, asserting how these have been invented by Man to keep the people in awe of authority. Esotericism does not strive to save souls, but rather strives towards deification. A deep, obscure and dark illusion that leads to a final impenitence, to a sin committed against the Holy Spirit which can never be forgiven, as man does not want to seek forgiveness.[33]

Thus, destined to eternal damnation, the esotericist can only resign himself, although, Nitoglia finally concludes by reassuring the reader who is likely worried by the decidedly aggressive tones:

> My intention in writing about esotericism is not merely to raise a controversy. I want to warn those who are attracted by mystery, the occult, secrecy which catch our eye and raise our at times morbid curiosity, they are at risk of embarking on the road to final impenitence – the true goal of esotericism... Esotericism, gnosis or initiation are thus pure Satanism, a desire to be deified, but whilst Lucifer was an Angel, and therefore highly intelligent, and did not attempt to achieve a total resemblance with God, the esotericists strive to achieve a total resemblance, or even surpass the superiority of God... In its insane pretence towards self-divinisation, esotericism is a contradiction of terms that leads man into a doctrinal error, towards moral depravation and, on persisting until the end of the mythological fable, into sin against the Holy Spirit and eternal damnation...He truly believes he is 'someone', whilst the others have not risen to the heights as he has.[34]

Father Paolo M. Siano, a member of the Order of the Franciscan Friars of the Immaculate, and the recent Congregation of Pontificial Rights was even more specific. Father Siano is a well-known scholar in the Catholic world, taking part in programmes aired by the IEC (Italian Episcopal Conference), *TV2000*, during one of which (denoted by the explicative title 'Vade Retro!!' focusing on the topic of the renowned problem of Masonic Rosaries) was introduced by the speaker as a leading expert on the subject of esotericism and Freemasonry. Father Siano, in his book *Freemasonry between Mysticism, Rituals and Symbolism*, expressed the conviction that the Masonic spirit, present throughout the world of Freemasonry, was not confined merely to the principles of solidarity and philanthropy, nor even to relativism, but, in his opinion, included three additional important elements: 1) a subjectivist, relativist and anti-dogma humanism; 2) an intrinsically magical rituality; 3) an esotericism that focuses on the deification of the Initiate (the great temptation of the infernal Serpent!). But particularly, opines the Franciscan scholar: 'by means of the theory of the union-coincidence-harmony-equilibrium of Opposites, Masonic esotericism is open to 'veneration', or 'cult', or 'sympathy' towards those entities that we Catholics call indistinctly with the following names: Lucifer, Devil, Satan, Serpent of Genesis'.[35]

It is clear how the opinions expressed by Father Siano on esotericism are in line with those conveyed previously by Father Curzio Nitoglia; indeed, Siano is even more explicit and maintains he can detect the satanic component of esotericism within the Masonic doctrines: 'I personally believe that in Freemasonry there is an explicitly luciferian cult. I believe that the Masonic cult of the Great Architect of the Universe is, objectively and intrinsically, a gnostic, esoteric and luciferian cult. Although the Devil is never named in the rites of the 'High Lodges', this is of no account; what counts is the 'inner' or 'esoteric' understanding of the more deeply 'Initiated' Masons...'[36]

I fail to grasp what Father Siano meant by the 'High Lodges', or to identify who the 'more deeply Initiated' Masons might be and where they carry out their esoteric activities. Father Siano continues by stating that 'an accurate search and examination of Masonic documents has proven that Freemasonry (and the Freemasonries) is intrinsically provided with a 'quid' that conveys it a natural ease in currying favour and interest in magical esotericism and Lucifer'. In the Chapter 'Introduction to the Study of Masonic Luciferism', become even more enterprising and includes Masonic esotericism among the types of Satanism.

In addition to rationalist and occultist Satanism, in the view of Father Siano, there is a form of gnostic-manicheistic luciferism or Satanism which should be ascribed to Masonic Satanism, a Satanism, 'according to which the Devil (or rather Lucifer) is not evil (in line with the judgement reported in the Bible or held by the Catholic Church), but which is actually a principle (personal or impersonal) – luminous, good and necessary to the sacred and divine, signifying that he is truly the bearer of knowledge and light (Lucifer)'.[37] Father Siano subsequently proposes a further distinction between ritual Satanism, cultural or philosophical Satanism, and initiatic-esoteric Satanism in which, 'in exercising the magic-esoteric rituals, the adepts or Initiates (all or part of the latter, a majority or minority) 'activate' their 'attraction' or full-blown inner veneration (from which the term 'esoteric' stems) towards Lucifer – Satan, although failing to expressly name him in their rites'.[38]

This is almost laughable, if it were not for the fact that these documents are in the public domain and anyone purchasing them is free to conceive a disturbing, but above all false, idea of esotericism and Freemasonry.

2
Esotericism and Freemasonry

Esotericism in the first Three Degrees. The errors of the 'esoterologists'

How should Freemasonry be collocated in the context of this study of esotericism? In the previous chapter, we have demonstrated that to assess *Esotericism* on a par with any other social phenomenon would not help to solve the issue, as emphasised by Riffard himself:

> But how can we acknowledge the existence of several forms of esotericism within the context of one esotericism alone? The problem is raised by esotericism itself on encountering a form of esotericism that differs from its own. To recognise a plurality of esotericisms may prove more embarrassing than acknowledging the existence of a series of philosophies, as philosophy purports to represent a search for the truth, whilst esotericism is presented as being in possession of a secret. How therefore can we study esotericisms as if they were one alone?[39]

To overcome this problem, the solution proposed herein was to step outside the exquisitely phenomenological field of esoteric forms and to liaise with he who practices esotericism, to reveal the constant aspired to by Riffard in the ideal type identified in the person of the Initiate.

With regard to the relationship between esotericism and Freemasonry, I should start by saying that, in my opinion, to define the Masonic initiatic pathway as ‘esoteric’ would be purely pleonastic, although this axiom is far too frequently at the centre of debate. It is even more serious that this occurs not only in the myriad of frequently confused pamphlets circulating on Freemasonry, but also in important studies of esotericism, in which a presumed *absence* of esoteric content is highlighted particularly for the first Three Degrees of Freemasonry.

Accordingly, the above-mentioned Faivre and Riffard, as already mentioned, two of the most widely renowned representatives of studies focusing on Western esotericism, on referring to Masonic esotericism, in my opinion, seriously misjudge the issue. Indeed, the works of the two Frenchmen display a clear and inexplicable underestimation of the esoteric component of the first Three Degrees of English Freemasonry, commonly known as the Degrees of Blue Lodge or ‘Symbolic’ Freemasonry. The two French scholars maintain that in the Masonic doctrines and rituals (and generally speaking, to refer to ‘rituals’ may be misleading, due to the hundreds of rituals contemplated) the esoteric components are present only in the subsequent Degrees, the so-called ‘High Degrees’. I completely disagree with this view, which is wholly unsustainable from both an historic and an initiatic point of view, which I shall now demonstrate.

Let us commence with the Frenchman Pierre Riffard, who wrote:

> The esotericism of the XVIII century largely coincides with a mystic form of Freemasonry...from an esoteric point of view, the crucial date is not the year 1717, although that same year the Grand Lodge of London was formed, the break occurred in 1736. This gave rise to the occult form of esoteric Freemasonry. The Knight of Ramsay cites ‘the necessary qualities’ to become a member of the ‘highly noble and illustrious Order of Masons’...The order claimed to date back to the Knights Templar. Thus, Freemasonry was viewed as a ‘Universal Dictionary of liberal Arts and useful Sciences’ which however did not include theology and politics. From this date onwards, a period of splendid developments followed. The great names of Freemasonry are: A. Court de Gobelin, L.C. de Saint Martin, J.-B. Willermoz, N.A. Kirchberg, Joseph de Maistre, F. Tienman; the most important organisms are the Strict Templar Observance (S.T.O., 1753), the *Order* of *Knight*-Masons Elect Priests of the Universe (1738), the Hermetic Rite (1770), the *Holy Order of Knights* Beneficient of the *Holy* City (H.O.K.B.H.C, 1778). The enlightened Freemasonry of the XVIII century is a global form of esoterism. Through the creation of those known as the high degrees, which were conferred subsequent to those commonly used in ancient Freemasonry (apprentice, fellow craft, master mason), the thinkers were in possession of the ritual tool to be applied

in a detailed speculation into the symbols used in Solomon's Temple and in construction.[40]

Essentially, along the same lines as Riffard, Antoine Faivre in his Esotericism writes: 'As we have had occasion to observe, it is particularly the high degrees in Freemasonry in which esoteric tendencies are expressed'[41], further adding that: 'Naturally, the high degree Rites are those suffused with esoteric content. For this reason, the English Freemasonry is virtually devoid of such aspects,[42] concepts that were likewise supported in other writings published by the French author:

> Undoubtedly, it (Freemasonry) is not by its very nature 'esoteric' in the sense implied by this term herein. Although for the first three degrees (blue) that form the basis, there is a link to symbolic and initiatic aspects, this is not sufficient to define esotericism. We have however seen that in the high degrees of certain Masonic systems there exists a level of esotericism, together with an esotericism-like nature of Masonic literature.[43]

To this regard, another renowned scholar of esotericism, Jean-Paul Corsetti, is in partial agreement with the previous theories and, in his *History of Esotericism and the Occult Sciences* wrote: 'The English Freemasonry is scarcely esoteric, only becoming so from the Third Degree of Master Mason, which was included in 1730 and was not known to Anderson.'[44]

It is now mandatory to ask ourselves, where does this mistaken perception of English Freemasonry derive from? Which authors, and in particular, which rituals, have the scholars addressed in forming their opinions? The issue is not easy to solve, and is particularly inexplicable in view of the fact that both Faivre and Riffard in their writings refer to major esotericists such as René Guénon and Oswald Wirth who however, as I shall reveal subsequently, with regard to this same issue, have expressed views in open contrast to those of Riffard and Faivre.

The opinion conveyed by the renowned French esotericist Guénon on the High degrees could not be clearer:

> Masonic initiation comprises three successive phases, and there can thus be only three grades, representing these three phases; from this it would seem to follow that the system of high grades are completely useless, at least in theory, since in their entirety the rituals of the three symbolic grades describe the complete cycle of initiation. However, since Masonic initiation is in fact symbolic, it produces Masons who are only symbols of true Masons, simply outlining for them the course of the steps they must take in order to arrive at real initiation. It is this goal that, at least originally, was the aim of the various systems of high grades, which seem to have been instituted precisely in order to realise in practice the Great Work that symbolic Masonry teaches in theory.

> It must be recognided, however, that very few of these systems actually achieve their proposed goal; in most cases, one meets with points of incoherence, lacunae, and superfluities, and the initiatic value of certain rituals appears quite meagre, especially when compared to that of the symbolic grades. These failings are all the more conspicuous the greater number of degrees the system contains; and if such is already the case with the Scottish Rites of 25 and 33 degrees, what of those Rites having 90, 97 or even 120 degrees? This multiplicity of degrees is all the more useless in that one is obliged to confer them successively.[45]

However, the Swiss Oswald Wirth states the clearest view, and one I personally share. In addition to possessing a highly 'esoteric' view of Freemasonry, with regard to the differences between the first Three Degrees and the High Degrees, Wirth wrote:

> The goal of Masonic initiation is to enlighten men that they might be taught to work usefully, in full conformity with the very purpose of their existence. Now in order to enlighten men, it is first necessary to rid them of all that might keep them from seeing the Light. They are therefore submitted to certain purifications intended to eliminate heterogeneous residues, themselves the causes of the opacity of the layers that serve as so many protective shells for the spiritual kernel of man. As soon as they are made clear, their complete transparency allows the rays of outward Light to penetrate to the conscious centre of the initiate. Then his entire being is progressively saturated by Light until he is enlightened in the highest sense of the word; he is thereafter known also as an adept, himself transformed into a radiant focus of Light. Masonic initiation is thus made up of three distinct phases, consecrated successively to the discovery, assimilation, and propagation of Light. These phases are represented by the three grades of Apprentice, Fellow, and Master, corresponding to the triple mission of the Masons, which consists first in searching for, then possessing, and finally being able to spread the Light.
>
> The number of these grades is absolute: there can be only three, no more, no less. The invention of various systems known as high grades rests solely on an equivocation, by which the initiatic grades, strictly limited in number to three, are confused with the degrees of initiation, the multitude of which is necessarily indefinite. The initiatic grades correspond to the triple program pursued through Masonic initiation. They carry in their esotericism a solution to the three questions of the Sphinx's riddle: Where do we come from? What are we? Where are we going? And they thereby correspond to all that can interest men. They are immutable in their fundamental character, and in their trinity, they form a complete whole, to which nothing can either be added or taken away: Apprenticeship and Fellowship are the two pillars supporting Mastery. As to the degrees of initiation, they allow the initiate to penetrate

> more or less deeply into the esotericism of each grade. From this there results an indefinite number of different ways of entering into possession of the three grades of Apprentice, Fellow, and Master.[46]

Indeed, Guénon and Wirth relentlessly moved the focus of the issue, an initiatic ritual cannot be interpreted from a 'quantitative' point of view (the more Degrees there are, the higher the content of esotericism), but obviously, from a qualitative aspect, an operation which, to reach conclusion, dictates the need for a thorough exegesis of the text, or rather of the Ritual. It is almost unbelievable that such competent scholars had failed to take into account the opinions of two of the most renowned experts in the field who were indeed cited in their works, but almost certainly not understood.

It could be argued that it was indeed often the Anglo Saxon Freemasons themselves who, in a certain sense, undermined the Masonic doctrines, reducing the latter to a prevailingly moralistic interpretation, as indeed had been emphasised previously by the Italian esotericist and Freemason Arturo Reghini, who referred to the excess of moralism in Freemasonry as follows:

> In the Anglo Saxon countries, in line with the prevalently moralistic trend adopted to date by Protestantism, better suited to being known as moralism, the exquisitely moral nature of the Masonic initiation, being the demise of vice and the birth of Masonic initiation, is underlined...To take pride in this moralistic interpretation of the Masonic allegory invariably implies to sacrifice, misunderstand, or at the very least contort the esoteric, universal, non-sectarian character of the Order; it is unbelievable how much pleasure is taken in dressing Freemasonry in white dress for its First Communion and wallowing in morals up to one's knees...The ancient Masonic tradition and the inspiration of rituals used in pagan ceremonies denote how the prevailing sense of the Masonic allegory is of a metaphysical nature, yielded by a true spiritual palingenesis.[47]

It is undeniable how Anglo-Saxon countries have a tendency to interpret the Masonic ritual in a typically moralistic manner, although it would be over-simplified and misleading to generalise. Indeed, numerous English scholars have represented the esoteric nature of Freemasonry, among which the Englishman Walter Leslie Wilmshurst is undoubtedly one of the key players.

Walter Leslie Wilmshurst was born in Chichester in 1867 and died in London in 1929. He worked as a solicitor in Huddersfield and was initiated into the Huddersfield Lodge no.290 of the United Grand Lodge of England. Wilmshurst subsequently became a member of the Lodge of Harmony no.275 and the Lodge of Living Stone; he was appointed Provincial Grand Registrar in 1913 and held the position of Past Provincial Senior Warden in 1926 and Past Assistant Grand Director of Ceremony in 1929.

Wilmshurst was a true *esotericist*, and several of his articles were published on *The Occult Review*, a monthly journal that from 1905 to 1951 published interesting articles by a series of renowned esotericists and occultists of the time, among which Franz Hartmann, Arthur Edward Waite, Meredith Starr, and Aleister Crowley. He wrote, among other things, a considerable introduction to the volume 'Early Magnetism' by the English author Mary Ann South who wrote of hermeticism and alchemy.

Wilmshurst's most renowned article 'The Meaning of Masonry', published in 1922, is one of the highest expressions of an esoteric vision of Freemasonry, and the pages proposed here are a living example of an almost mystical view which, at the same time, underline the perilous internal degeneration that was taking place. With regard to initiation, Wilmshurst, as cited below, affirms that this event is frequently seen as a mere formality, with membership in the Order in no way influencing the 'reawakening' of initiates who view it almost as a sort of social club. Conversely, Initiation should be interpreted as a new beginning, a break with the old methods and order of life and admission into a new, profound, supernatural order of self-discovery and knowledge, it implies leaving the common scopes of the outside world behind – these are merely shadows and scarce imitations of the underlying eternal Reality that is hidden within each of us. Initiation, in the interpretation provided by Wilmshurst, thus represents a reawakening of the hidden faculties of the soul, leading to Light and Awareness:

> Their admission is quite a lottery; their initiation too often remains but a formality, not an actual awakening into an order and quality of life previously unexperienced; their membership, unless such an awakening eventually ensues from the careful study and faithful practice of the Order's teaching, has little, if any, greater influence upon them than would ensue from their joining a purely social club. For 'Initiation' – for which there are so many candidates little conscious of what is implied in that for which they ask – what does it really mean and intend? It means a new beginning (initium); a breakaway from an old method and order of life and the entrance upon a new one of larger self-knowledge, deepened understanding and intensified virtue. It means a transit from merely natural state and standards of life towards a regenerate and supernatural state and standard. It means a turning away from the pursuit of the popular ideals of the outer world, in the convinction that those ideals are but shadows, images and temporal substitutions for the eternal Reality that underlies them, to the keen and undivertible quest of that Reality itself and the recovery of those genuine secrets of our being which lie buried and hidden at 'the centre' or innermost part of our souls. It means the awakening of those hitherto dormant higher faculties of the soul which endue their possessor with 'light' in the form of new enhanced consciousness and enlarged perceptive faculty.[48]

Wilmshurst, adopting a vaguely Jungian representation, emphasised how the main purpose of Freemasonry was the acquisition of knowledge of Self, knowledge that is not acquired by passing from one Degree to the next, or through a sense of knowledge in general which, on the contrary, should be overlooked on the difficult and unique pathway that alone is capable of guaranteeing the achievement of the true aim:

> And Masonry was designed to teach self-knowledge. But self-knowledge involves a knowledge much deeper, vaster and more difficult than is popularity conceived. It is not to be acquired by formal passage through three or four degrees in as many months; it is a knowledge impossible of full achievement until knowledge of every other kind has been laid aside and a difficult path of life long and strenuously pursued that alone fits and leads its followers to its attainment.[49]

The Author highlights the existence of a higher, more secret path of life compared to that usually undertaken, underlining how sooner or later, as the outside world fails to meet our innermost needs, we shall turn to ourselves and knock on the door of the inner world. This is the pathway that Freemasonry promises to illuminate, indicating the qualifications required and conditions necessary to proceed:

> The fact that there exists a higher and more secret path of life than that which we normally tread, and that when the outer world and its pursuit and rewards lose their attractiveness for us and prove insufficient to our deeper needs, as sooner or later they will, we are compelled to turn back upon ourselves, to seek and knock at the door of a world within; and it is upon this inner world, and the path to and through it, that Masonry promises light, charts the way, and indicates the qualifications and conditions of progress. This is the sole aim and intention of Masonry.[50]

Wilmshurst underlines how this, the sole aim and intention of Freemasonry, should never be forsaken or overlooked in favour of other moralistic forms of expression. Wilmshurst continues by stating that Freemasonry, which for too many people and for too long a period failed to be deemed as such, has had its energy diverted along previously foreign social and philanthropic channels: 'But because, for long and for many, Masonry has meant less than this, it has not as yet fulfilled its original purpose of being the efficient initiating instrument it was designed to be; its energies have been diverted from its true instructional purpose into social and philanthropic channels, excellent in their way, but foreign to and accretions upon the primal main intention.'[51]

The definition of Freemasonry as an 'initiatic instrument' leaves us in no doubt as to the esoteric vision of Wilmshurst, although it is however in the mystical connotations he attributed particularly to the Hiramic allegory that, in my opinion, he reaches the peak of his analytical capabilities. On mentioning the 'death of the body' referred to in the legend, Wilmshurst underlines how this should be interpreted as the symbolic sign of *rebirth* or *regeneration*, particularly in view of the fact that through *self-discipline* and inner development, the candidate overcomes his shortcomings and attains an immortal 'incorruptible body':

> Although distinct reference to the death of the body is made, yet such death is obviously intended to be merely symbolical of another kind of death, since the candidate is eventually restored to his former worldly circumstances and material comforts, and his early Masonic career is not represented as coming to a close at this stage. All that has happened in the third degree is that he has symbolically passed through a great and striking change: a re-birth, or re-generation of his whole nature. He has been 'sown a corruptible body'; and in virtue of the self-discipline and self-development he has undergone, there has been raised in him 'an incorruptible body', and death has been swallowed up in the victory he has attained over himself.[52]

This concept is once again emphasised towards the end of the essay when the author affirms that solely the Initiatic process should be aimed at stimulating and reawakening in candidates a sense of *direct* cognition, irrefutable demonstration of facts and truths he was previously unaware or only notionally informed of; to bring him into direct conscious contact with the realities underlying the surface-images of things, so that, instead of holding merely beliefs or opinions about himself, the Universe and God, he is directly and convincingly confronted with the Truth; and finally moves him to become the Good and Truth revealed to him by identifying with the same:

> The purpose of Initiation may be defined as follows: it is to stimulate and awaken the candidate to direct cognition and irrefutable demonstration of facts and truths of his own being about which previously he has been either wholly ignorant or only notionally informed; it is to bring him into direct conscious contact with the Realities underlying the surface-images of things, so that, instead of holding merely beliefs or opinions about himself, the Universe and God, he is directly and convincingly confronted with Truth itself; and finally it is to move him to become the Good and the Truth revealed to him by identifying with it.[53]

As mentioned, the excerpts cited from Wilmshurst clearly recall the Jungian theories of the process of individuation, theories I will expound on later in the volume.

In referring to the esoteric nature of the symbolic Three Degrees, Wilmshurst highlights how the latter enclose all forms of esotericism without any additional notions or superfetations. In passing from one Grade to the next Grade the candidate is led from an old to an entirely new quality of life; through discipline, he is transformed from a natural being into a perfect, *regenerated* man. To achieve this transmutation and metamorphosis the candidate is taught to purify and develop his mental nature, to finally, surrendering his old life, rise from the dead as a Master, a Perfect Man with vaster consciousness and faculties, an effective instrument in the hands of the Great Architect in his plan to rebuild the Temple of fallen Humanity, capable of initiating and advancing other men to take part in the same great work:

> To sum up the import of the teaching of the three degrees, it is clear, therefore, that from grade to grade the candidate is being led from an old to an entirely new quality of life. He begins his Masonic career as the natural man; he ends it by becoming through its discipline, a regenerated perfected man. To attain this transmutation, this metamorphosis of himself, he is taught first to purify and subdue his sensual nature; then to purify and develop his mental nature; and finally, by utter surrender of his old life and losing his soul to save it, he rises from the dead a Master, a just man made perfect, with larger consciousness and faculties, an efficient instrument for use by the Great Architect in His plan for re-building the Temple of fallen humanity, and capable of initiating and advancing other men to a participation in the same great work.[54]

However, we then wonder why two key scholars such as Faivre and Riffard would have made such a blatant mistake, assigning a lesser esoteric connotation to the first *Three Degrees* of Freemasonry to that conveyed to the Higher Degrees, and maintaining how the English Freemasonry was essentially devoid of esoteric content? There are two reasons for this in my opinion. The first is an *underestimation* of the issue, with Freemasonry frequently being dealt with in a rather smug manner, using common stereotypes irrespective of whether or not these are based on fact or correspond to the actual situation. A careful examination of the Anglo Saxon Masonic rituals would undoubtedly have helped the authors to avoid taking up such an unforgiving stance. However, this is where another issue arises: the *interpretation* of rituals. Faivre and Riffard were the first to dichotomise and divide the esoterologists from the esotericists, the former notably study esotericism and associated rituals, whilst the latter practice the same. However, as already mentioned, on addressing a ritual, the historic approach undertaken by an esoterologist is quite different from the exegetic approach of the esotericist, the sole method capable of revealing the hidden content of the ritual. The esotericist alone is capable of carrying out the exegetic tasks required to achieve an esoteric interpretation of any type of ritual, not only Masonic rituals. Indeed, even on reading a ritual, the esoterologist, the scholar of esotericism, may fail to grasp its true significance, its esoteric and initiatic content; regrettably, there is no solution to this problem.

The esoterologist, with his historic approach, does not contemplate the presence of Myth in his method, and moreover, does not identify in the various esoteric phenomena the presence of the ideal type, the Initiate, the nature of which and need for an intimate and profound search into his inner self, the result of his vision of the world, is at the basis of an authentically esoteric phenomenon, the need that witnesses his birth and stimulates the initiate to pursue this as his aim.

In this authentically initiatic representation, man is interpreted not with a view to what he is, or seems to be, but rather with a view to what he could *become*, and therefore from the point of view of his possible evolution. Indeed, the possibility of achieving an actual change and extending of the human conscience represents the aim of the authentic Wisdom Schools, and the presence of the ideal type, the Initiate, is an essential starting point. The Initiate, in this case represented by the figure of the Freemason, finds his answers within himself, not externally, indeed, the Master does not intend to undertake a revolution, but rather to *transform* society by instilling an awakening of the individual, in the intimate realms of his conscience. In a world lacking direction, the Initiate, the Freemason, is entrusted with the sacred mission of saving himself, and no form of ideology can elicit this metamorphosis in him. All actions should be undertaken in the Lodge, a territory of the spirit.

In relation to the second motivation, it should be underlined how numerous scholars of Freemasonry with their frequently abstruse theories have proved considerably misleading and complicated a correct comprehension of the same. Regrettably, many of these scholars, of whom I will mention a few, form part of academia. The Dutch historian Wouter Hanegraaff, previously cited several times, provides a somewhat superficial account of Freemasonry, presenting it as a sort of role play, in which particularly those hailing from the lower social classes are given the opportunity to become 'for fun, important and respected persons:

> It is certainly true that Freemasons are supposed to make 'progress' through their initiations, but there can be no doubt that many of them simply take pleasure in the 'serious play' of dressing up in ceremonial costume and performing their well-defined roles in what amounts to a kind of elaborate ritual theatre. The pleasure may be further enchanted by the opportunity of a temporary escape from normal society and its constraints: an individual may well make social (apart from spiritual) progress within the organisation of Freemasonry and become an important end generally respected person in the lodge, even if in general society he has a low-status job and lives a mostly boring life.[55]

This corresponds to a false and over-simplified representation of Freemasonry, I would even go as far as calling it offensive, but is above all a misleading portrayal, as it does not provide the possibility, to those who would so wish, to truly comprehend the singularities of the phenomenon. Freemasonry, in spite of the critical aspects repeatedly highlighted in this book, still today represents, at least in the intentions of those, numerous, who practice it, an authentic Initiatic school featuring a wealth of esoteric notions and manifestations. Also, most importantly, throughout the Anglo Saxon world.[56]

Amongst the theories portraying a view of Freemasonry, which was far removed from reality, I should like to mention the views held by the American historian Margaret Jacob, who has, regrettably, written several books on the topic. Ms Jacob states:

> 'The constitutional and legislative environment was what attracted men on the Continent to the first lodges. Within their confines, Brothers adjudicated new forms of personal power and they could imagine themselves involved in governance as well as opposition'[57]; 'Masonic discourse, in whatever Western European language, although permitting the expression of local interests and circumstances, did so within the framework of a rhetoric that was British in origin as well as invariably civic, hence political, and most frequently progressive and reformist'[58];'The central element of Masonic discourse was its intention of acting on a political level'[59]; 'It is the contention of this book that the Masonic experience in every Western European context – from Edinburgh to Berlin, from the 1730s to the 1780s – was resolutely civil, and hence political.[60]

Similar utterances convey a completely distorted and unrealistic view of Freemasonry. These are indeed theories purporting that the origins of Freemasonry are based on political undertakings, and the mere possibility that Freemasonry may *also* represent an Initiatic School does not even cross the mind of the North-American author. It is clear that throughout all the sentences quoted there is no reference to rituals, to their esoteric or initiatic content, nothing at all. Ms. Jacob views Freemasonry as nothing more than a purely associationist-political movement, an association with exclusively profane aims:

> Certain characteristics of Masonic associations differ not at all from the many other private societies that sprang up throughout Europe in the course of the eighteenth century. Members, proposed and chosen by other members, paid dues, attended meetings, voted and discussed, gave loyalty, and sought conviviality, if not self-improvement, from their association.[61]

These theories, devoid of any firm basis, have unfortunately influenced several scholars who, taking them in good faith, have frequently gleaned elements and cues for the purpose of elaborating further hypotheses, naturally invalidated from the start. One of the better known of these relates to an alleged illuminist origin of Freemasonry.[62]

Esotericism and the Schools of Wisdom

The Schools of Wisdom have long constituted the living expression of a particular human type, a 'figure', in turn the image and expression of an archetype, historically presented in different guises and under different names, whilst unfailingly possessing a similar vision of the world and an unavoidable and singular relationship with the transcendent, with the sacred.

The Schools of Wisdom in turn constituted a 'form' of Tradition, although, it should be pointed out, to be the bearer of a Tradition does not imply the blind reproduction of ideas and thoughts, the re-evoking of symbols, or the carrying out of complex ritual ceremonies by means of which the spiritual current was manifested throughout its past incarnations. On the contrary, the task of the custodians of Tradition was to succeed in incarnating the latter into the new forms in which today it aspires to be manifested, or in other words, updating the same to the new historic context, acting through the figure, by means of which the archetype of the Initiate will once again see the light, will be reawakened.

Thus, esotericism represents the dimension in which the Schools of Wisdom should be rightly collocated, as the vision of the world of the figure representing the same is of an esoteric nature. It should be underlined that the esoteric horizon, particularly due to its multiform and polyhedric nature, shall never display those traits of unity and homogeneity that may be attributed to religious phenomena and, consequently, in order to detect some degree of common denominator to share the range of expressions of esotericism (in this case the Schools of Wisdom referred to herein, forms of Tradition from which the creation and consolidation Freemasonry gleaned inspiration), the only possible way is to apply as a paradigm the individual who practices esotericism, the Adept, the Initiate, or rather the ideal type cyclically represented throughout the seasons, particularly at the present time, an era in which man, as emphasised by Bulgakov:

> Has become too free, too devastated by his empty freedom, too exhausted by this lengthy period of crisis. Thus, man has begun to feel a yearning for organicity, synthesis, a religious centre, a mystery.[63]

It is therefore crucial that, when the times are ripe and this archetype begins to re-emerge from the collective unconscious of particular individuals, they are in a position to recognise correctly the authentic Schools of Wisdom to which to adhere, and avoid misjudgements, underlining the need for an appropriate differentiation and insight. In his *Ride the Tiger*, Evola warned of the scarce likelihood of achieving an authentic Initiation in the contemporary world. Despite the fact that the democratic vision of the world has succeeded in persuading modern man of the possibility of those who so desire accomplishing a self-initiation:

> One must assume a priori that it is not even a hypothetical possibility in an

> epoch like the present, in an environment like the one we live in and also given the general inner formation of individuals. Anyone who sees things differently either does not understand the matter, or else is deceiving himself and others. What has to be negated most decisively is the transposition to this field of the individualistic and democratic view of the 'self-made man,' that is, the idea that anyone who wants can become an 'initiate,' and that he can also become one on his own, through his own strength alone, by resorting to various kinds of exercises and practices. This is an illusion, the truth being that through his own strength alone, the human individual cannot go beyond human individuality, and that any positive result in this field is conditioned by the presence and action of a genuine power of a different, non-individual order.[64]

In the doctrines adopted by the Schools of Wisdom, Tradition, of which the term 'esotericism' is no more than a synonym, permits man to escape from the vicious circle of his profane existence and retrace the way that will once again lead him to his origins. Of course, a similar pathway cannot be either contingent or transient, contrary to ideologies, philosophies, religions, and political regimes, and thus the singularities of the Initiatic Schools, which, even from a spatio-temporal viewpoint, have long been collocated on the edges of the profane world. Indeed, if the notion of modernity is based on an idea of linear time, then the Initiatic Schools propose an opposing notion of cyclical time or duration, as these extend beyond time, particularly as their principles belong to a metaphysical, and therefore atemporal, dimension.

Consequently, the opposition between the modern world and the traditional world, between modern man and traditional man, is not merely an historic issue, but, to use the words of Evola, is *ideal*, *morphological* and, particularly, *metaphysical*. Consequently, if the contrast between the 'historical world' and 'world of Tradition' is a juxtaposition between the action displayed 'in' history and a 'meta-historical' action, the Initiatic Schools should not have to operate in history unless this is on an exclusively *indirect* basis. The action 'in history' indeed constitutes the distinctive sign of the modern world based, as mentioned previously, on a concept of linear time, or rather on the succession that separates and distinguishes events, a concept in which ideas of development, of theological redemption, emancipation and progress are collocated. On the contrary, the indirect meta-historical action represents the distinctive sign of the Initiatic Schools, and is based on a concept of the *eternal*: the action is; it is unfailingly ongoing but is expressed in terms of space rather than time.

3
Theosophism, a pseudo-esotericism

I shall now analyse a phenomenon that is emblematic of what could be defined as the Twentieth century transformation, or rather, the degeneration, of the *sacred*, the Theosophical Society.

Long before the religious historians, the modern-day psychologists and sociologists, several 'traditionalist' thinkers, *in primis* René Guénon and Julius Evola, realised as early as the 1920s that in the secularised societies, the sacred would not have disappeared altogether, but would have been deformed by its new users and moulded to fit with the numerous disorders of modern-day society, not certainly in open contrast to the latter, but almost becoming a parody of the same, even more dangerous than materialism itself.

Others, such as the German philosopher Oswald Splengler, coined the negative term of 'second religiosity', a phenomenon inevitably associated with the end of a cycle of civilisation, which does not represent a return to a sacred vision of life, but rather confirms the decomposition of the civilisation and its inability to achieve a true 'enchantment'. No longer therefore a return to the world of Tradition, but, on the contrary, as highlighted by Guénon, dangerous 'cracks in the Great Wall', the ultimate defence against the uncontrollable obscure forces.

Evola reminds us how the risk of pseudo-initiatic schools is that they may irreparably confuse, or rather overturn the idea of Initiation and the figure of the Initiate from whom the latter stems. In Evola's opinion, this confusion is largely advocated by the academic world that tends to liken the authentic Initatic Schools, the sole to possess the requisites required to transmit Initiation, with movements featuring improbable esoteric and initiatic connotations. Evola wrote:

> It is not easy, today, to give an exact idea of what is meant by Initiation and to define the figure of the 'Initiate'. The main difficulty lies in the necessity of referring to a vision of the world and man, and to structures, which belong essentially to traditional civilisations, distant from the present one, not only from the modern mentality and culture, but also, to a large extent, from the religion which has come to predominate in the West. In addition, there is the disgraceful circumstance that, if, today, one still hears of Initiation, outside of the empty ritualistic remains of modern Freemasonry and such amateurish literary exercises as, for example, the well-known book The Great Initiates, by E. Schuré, it is on the sidelines of the various theosophical, anthroposophical, or generally occult sects. The discredit, which has rightly become attached to these frivolous 'neo-spiritualistic' forms, which are sometimes outright hoaxes, could not but create a prejudice, which impedes the understanding of what Initiation really is.
>
> This state of affairs has provided those who claim to represent 'modern critical thought' and contemporary 'culture' with a pretext to assimilate the world of Initiation to that of the 'magicians', 'clairvoyants', and so on, of the lower classes, and to disregard the fact that, historically, Initiation was an integral and frequently essential part of the great traditions and civilisations of the past to which, in other regards, respect and gratitude are paid.[65]

For Evola therefore, the pseudo-esoteric organisations differ from the authentic Schools of Wisdom and Initiatic Schools in the fact that their very integration and ultimate aim are not focused on an Initiation and true esotericism. When authentic, Initiation constitutes the sole division, or rather litmus paper, capable of distinguishing between the authentic and the false, allowing the individual who wishes to approach a genuine initiatic experience to proceed without mistake; this entails two possibilities, the first if to ontologically modify one's personality, by means of a correct Initiation, higher, to ascend towards a state of superior being, or, on the contrary, to descend with one's personality towards a state of inferiority:

> Etymologically, 'to initiate' means to provide a new commencement. In this respect, one could also speak of a 'rebirth'; but then it would be necessary to give this term a strictly ontological signification. As a matter of fact, the fundamental premise of Initiation is that the human condition, with the limits which define the common individuality, can be surpassed. It is a change of state, a passage from a way of being to another way of being, in the most objective sense. This is why in some testimonies Initiation is described almost as a physical fact, to underline its real, ontological character. The opposition between 'Superman' and 'Initiate' can be helpful to explain the concept of Initiation. The term 'Superman' refers to the extreme and problematic strengthening of the species 'Man'. However, in principle, the Initiate no longer belongs to this species at all. If one has in mind High Initiation, it can be said that the 'Superman' belongs to a Promethean plane (Man remains as he is but seeks, illegitimately, to gain a superior dignity and power), while the Initiate in the proper sense belongs to an Olympian plane (he has acquired an innate, distinct, and justified dignity). The theory according to which the being possesses multiple states, of which the human is only one, is therefore the premise of the concept of Initiation. These states must however be considered as not only superior, but also inferior to the one characteristic of the common and normal human personality. Thus we can conceive of a double possibility of opening of this personality, upwards and downwards; consequently, an 'ascending' overcoming (true to the strict etymological sense of the word 'to transcend', i.e., 'to go beyond by rising') must be well distinguished from a 'descending' overcoming.[66]

Theosophy or Theosophism?

With regard to the Theosophical Society, founded by Helena Petrovna Blavatsky, a Russian medium who emigrated to England, its first, fierce critic was the Frenchman René Guénon who, in a renowned book on the subject entitled *Theosophism,* proposed a marked distinction between the late medieval authentic Theosophy and the new reality created by Ms Blavatsky. Guénon wrote: 'The doctrines, indeed all modern, supported by the Theosophical Society are completely different in almost all aspects from those legitimately contemplated under the name of Theosophy, that could be mixed up for reasons of deceit or ignorance.' Guénon was of the opinion that the true Theosophy, the most renowned representatives of which included Jacob Böhme, Gichtel, Swedenborg, Louis-Claude de Saint-Martin, and Eckartshausen, was in possession of, contrary to the improbable syncretism of the wide variety of oriental theories relating to Theosophism, a common basis founded on the Christian doctrines. Theosophy however depicted as its main aim that of going beyond the devotional practices of religion, and leading he who practiced the same into the world of *esoteric gnosis*, a true knowledge of the divine.

In *Theosophism*, Guénon highlighted the role played by a series or pseudo-initiatic organisations in the establishment of the movement set up by Blavatsky, denouncing from the start the shortcomings and the syncretistic nature of the former. In the course of his analysis, Guénon moreover emphasised the connivances between the theosophist contexts and political undertakings linked to British imperialism and the British protestant missionary movement. Guénon's analysis, carried out on a series of documents, led to the conclusion that Theosophism should not be seen in any way as an authentic spiritual institution, and even less as a phenomenon displaying esoteric features and singularities. To briefly summarise, and in complete agreement with Guénon, I opine that the 'Theosophy' supported by Ms Blavatsky was established essentially as a syncretistic revival of religious and oriental esoteric motivations combined with other Western ideals, all amalgamated by medianic visions of doubtful origin, not to forget the association, manifest or otherwise, with Spiritism. For the above reasons, Theosophism and its means of expression should be ascribed to the history of 'pseudo-religions' rather than to the field of esotericism.

Julius Evola was likewise a fervent adversary of the Theosophical Society. The traditionalist Roman thinker, who in 1932 completed his work *The Mask and Face of Contemporary Spiritualism*, following in the wake of Guénon, warned readers to avoid confusing the ancient and traditional Theosophy with the Theosophy proposed by the Theosophical Society and, for the same reason, defined the organisation created by Ms Blavatsky as 'Theosophism' rather than 'Theosophy'. Evola, similar to Guénon, underlines how the latter goes beyond a mere fideistic religious standpoint a, as the authentic Theosophist is not concerned solely with believing in a specific theology, but also maintains the possibility of an effective *experience* and knowledge of divine order; on the contrary, Theosophism is essentially presented as heteroclite and syncretistic complex of a series of different doctrinal elements, lacking any form of thorough critical examination, and combined with data deriving from personal visions and experiences intended to convey a higher truth.[67] Accordingly, it should be defined, disparagingly, as 'Theosophism' which, concludes Evola: 'instead of leading, as trye theosophy would, beyond 'beliefs', it tended frequently to replace a given belief or religion with another, even indeed adding a dreadful and acritical philosophy resulting in resonance on the notions of the modern science'...

Theosophism, to the silence and practice, to the post latore scientia referred to also by the Western hermeticists, has preferred the unbridled digressions focused on invisible planes and bodies, on 'planetary patrols', on plots, evolutions and involutions of all types, on visions of the fate of the worlds, of masters, races, sub-races, cosmic eras and so on, leaving aside the dressing of humanitarianism, optimism and progressivism.'[68]

As mentioned previously, Evola warned against the risks that organisations such as the Theosophical Society were capable of producing, including an increased possibility of *unknowingly* making contact with essentially negative forces or entities 'forces that are not above, but rather below man as a personality'. For this reason the neo-spiritualist phenomena, among which Evola collocated *Theosophism*, might 'be of a regressive nature and the 'spiritual' component may prove to be 'infranatural' rather than 'supernatural'; this, inevitably concretely and existentially, notwithstanding the doctrinal and intellectual confusion and deviations encountered.'[69]

In the view of the Roman traditionalist, it is particularly the approach Nature, or rather the relationship between *man and Nature* intended in its non-dualist and clearly metaphysical representation, that the greatest differences between an authentic spiritual doctrine and modern pseudo-spiritualism can be detected:

> To gain an idea of the influences one is dealing with when these openings are manifested, being directed upwards and not downwards and implying a descending rather than ascending move, it may be appropriate to mention what is meant n a broad and complete sense by 'nature'. When speaking of 'nature' today, we generally refer to the physical world, perceived through the physical senses of all awakened persons and measured by an exact science. In reality, this is only one aspect of nature, an image that has formed in relation to the human personality, and which at a certain stage of its historical development, was ascribed as an experience associated to nature, and not to other possible stages and forms of existence. Man perceives nature in these forms defined by the physical reality as he has become detached from nature itself, he has been released and disbanded and now averts the same as something extraneous, as a 'non-Self'. Nature itself is not a mere apparition in space: it can be seized whence this sense of extraneousness wanes, diminishing in correlation to the state of awakening of the conscience and replaces states in which the objective and the subjective, the 'inside' and the 'outside' become blurred. From here the first domains of an 'invisible' and 'psychic' world commence which, to be decreed thus, do not cease to be 'nature', indeed, they are eminently 'nature', and not at all 'supernaturalness'. By means of objective scientific investigation into matter and energy, man moves in a sort of magic circle he has created. He steps beyond this circle and reaches nature, only he who steps backwards from the formed personal conscience towards the subconscience along the way will

> encounter obscure organic sensations, with the emergence of freely manifested psychic complexes and automatisms – i.e. free of cerebral control – which will subsequently develop and descend to the depths of the physical subconscience.[70]

Evola therefore supports the existence of an occult area beyond the ordinary conscience, to all effects real and not imaginary, which should not be confused with the spiritual or the supernatural, but should be termed 'infranatural', an area that is opened *passively*, in mystic and ecstatic forms and that demotes he who practices the same from a higher to a lower degree. Conversely, the spiritual is encountered, in Evola's opinion, solely in the presence of a 'clear, active and distinct' conscience; indeed, this conscience alone will allow the individual to ascend on the ladder of spirituality.

In fact, as a youth, Evola came into contact with the theosophical world, and thanks to his version of the *Tao Te Ching,* in 1924, he met Decio Calvari, who presided over an independent theosophical circle in Rome, and who introduced him to Tantrism. In *Ultra*, the journal of the Theosophical League edited by Calvari, Evola developed several of his philosophical theories, particularly his notion of solipsistic autarchy that incited man to 'act as God' in material undertakings, although to a lesser degree in detachment or with regard to the interiorised philosophic view:

> If therefore by religious solution one does not imply the abandoning of all positions, the bankruptcy of coherence and certainty in the name of the cold stoicism of faith, then it should be related to a mystic, or rather magical, process in which God is but a mere ghost if not generated within ourselves, not by means of words, concepts, fantasies or noble sentiments, but rather by means of an outright concrete undertaking, in which the empiric existence is truly transfigured and resolved in divinity.[71]

Obviously, the subjective intuition was not alone capable of achieving such an undertaking and therefore Evola saw Occultism as a means of obtaining the desired result. Indeed, Occultism was moreover represented in the severe discipline he conveys in performing the techniques of Theosophy and Anthroposophy that were so criticised by Guénon, and that were meant to contribute towards the creation of the 'absolute individual'. Accordingly, Philosophy and Occultism are viewed as the sole possible means of achieving a magical idealism, and consequently a concretisation of the absolute individual:

> Thus the construction of immortality; the establishment of self-consciousness, the merging of reality with the dead areas represented by sleep, the time before birth and the time following death of the body; the consuming of a need for space and time through a spiritual vision developing up to the creation of a

> cosmic consciousness – these are the main points on which occultism and theosophy focus their attention, their studies, their disciplines, and which, in the same way as the steps on the 'road to persuasion', resemble the latter to magical idealism, both featuring a common destination constituted by the establishing of a concrete Self in an absolute existence, in a living, current eternity – *interminabilis vitae tota simul et perfecta possessio* – one truth in the name of the Stirnerian Unique One and of the pure Aristotelian Act.[72]

Subsequently however, Theosophy did not escape his criticism; formulated organically at a later date and inspired by the previously mentioned book by Guénon, as well as by a subsequent volume published by the French traditionalist, *The Spiritist Fallacy,* a work in which Guénon clearly indicates the risks associated with Spiritism, particularly when the later purports to being scientific and scientifically proven. In *The Spritist Fallacy*, Guénon adopts the term 'Neo-spiritualism', a term also used subsequently by Evola, with whom the French esotericist largely designed the 'pseudo-religious' conceptions that initially diffused throughout the United States, and subsequently in Europe towards the mid-nineteenth century. These phenomena were viewed by Guénon fundamentally as misdirected attempts at creating a religious imprint, experiences founded more on a modern faith in science than on an intimately experienced spirituality. However, as we will see subsequently, Guénon opines how the authentic expression of a genuine spirituality is detected solely in the presence of a pure metaphysics, a metaphysics that Guénon will achieve largely from the study of oriental religions.

To conclude, I would like to mention briefly the association between another traditionalist thinker, Ananda Coomaraswamy, and the International Theosophical Society, which, at the time I refer to, had passed under the presidency of Annie Besant. Coomaraswamy, at the time situated in Ceylon where he was director of Mineralogical Research, also presided over the Ceylon Social Reform Society, an organisation created to reawaken the conscience of the Ceylonese in an attempt to maintain and privilege the national traditions over the European customs, an attempt to reawaken people's pride in their origins. In 1907, he invited to give a talk Annie Besant, the President of the International Theosphical Society, an organisation that, as mentioned previously, operated in line with the British colonial interests, and advocated a systematically distorted activity of the Hindu tradition.[73] Subsequently however, the initial interest and attraction displayed by Coomaraswamy in Theosophy declined drastically and in a negative manner, as attested by letters exchanged between Coomaraswamy and A. More, in which the art historian claims that: 'Theosophy is largely a distorted perennial philosophy'[74], a view that is fundamentally in line with that supported by Guénon and Evola.

CHAPTER TWO
TRADITION

My heart has become capable of every form: it is a pasture for gazelles and a convent for Christian monks, and a temple for idols and the pilgrim's Kaa'b, and the tables of the Torah and the book of the Quran. I follow the religion of Love: whatever way Love's camels take, that is my religion and my faith.
Ibn 'Arabi

1
Definitions of Tradition

The meaning of Tradition
The word 'Tradition' is observed recurrently in writings focusing on esoteric topics, although at times assuming significantly different, and often contrasting, meanings depending on the author by whom it is used. As previously undertaken for the term 'esotericism', the concept of Tradition will be analysed both from an academic perspective, that of the esoterologist, and a strictly initiatic point of view, that of the esoterist, placing particular emphasis on the so-called Perennialist current.

According to French historian Antoine Faivre, the term 'Tradition' possesses two complementary meanings:

> On the one hand, it represents the means (books, institutions, chains of masters) through which norms of beliefs and practices are transmitted; in this case it can be used as a synonym of 'transmission'. On the other hand, the term represents the same norms, or the authorised sources on which these norms are based.[75]

In another paper entitled *L'ésotérisme*, Faivre provides a historical *excursus* aimed at demonstrating that Tradition is no more than a reintroduction, albeit with different terms depending on the context and historical period, of the same *Sophia Perennis* which subsequently gave form to all religions and sacred expressions. To this regard, Faivre remarks that:

> During the Renaissance, the *prisca theologia* of the Middle Ages underwent a transformation. It became *philosophia occulta* and *philosophia perennis*, terms that were not interchangeable, but that were applied to a nebula endowed with

> relative autonomy in the mental universe of the epoch, and detached from theology properly speaking. It already constitutes, give or take a few nuances, what some starting from the beginning of the nineteenth century would call 'Tradition'.[76]

Faivre starts his analysis with the renowned doctrine of Renaissance philosopher Marsilio Ficino, according to whom Zoroaster, Hermes Trismegistus, Orpheus, Pythagoras, Plato and the Sybils were viewed as the exponents of an uninterrupted chain sustained by a single source of Truth, which later gave rise to all other sources. Consequently, only by investigating the common denominators of all historical expressions of the *Sophia Perennis* will it be possible to identify this unique source.

The term *Philosophia Perennis* most likely derives from an engaging text dated 1540 by the Italian philologist and philosopher Agostino Steuco, entitled *De perenni philosophia*. Steuco, an avid interpreter of biblical texts, attempted to highlight the 'conformities' (*conformationes*) between pagan traditions and the Jewish-Christian Revelation, based on the assumption that the only true Truth had originally been imparted without any particular connotations, a sort of common metaphysical language which only later acquired different attributes according to the context in which it was used. After a period of obscuration, (no clear references to the *Sophia Perennis* were found in the German Theosophy of the 1500s and 1600s, and in Rosicrucianism), the term appeared again more than a century later, having been transformed into Primitive Tradition in an essay from 1784, entitled *Le Monde Primitif*, by Antoine Courte de Gébelin, whose ambition was to represent the traditions of all civilisations known at the time, hinting at the existence of a shared primitive tradition. Another Frenchman, Fabre d'Olivet, would later introduce an idea of 'Primordial Tradition', which better resembled the idea of Tradition subsequently proposed by the Perennialist current.

Among those who approached Tradition in the sense of Philosophia Perennis, British writer and essayist Aldous Huxley is particularly worthy of mention. Huxley was not only a successful science fiction novelist, but also took a great interest in philosophical mysticism. In 1944, he wrote *The Perennial Philosophy,* an anthology in which he studied the metaphysical principles and peculiarities of the traditional thought, promoting the creation of an *ideal society*, clearly based on the diffusion and general acceptance of one of the forms with which the Perennial Philosophy historically and doctrinally presented itself. It should be underlined that Huxley referred to the distinction between the Perennial Philosophy in itself, interpreted as the 'Principles' deriving from Divinity, and the 'metaphysical schemes' which tried to define it, albeit in an approximate manner. Divine Reality, he wrote, cannot be directly and immediately apprehended: 'except by those who have chosen to fulfil certain conditions'. Its Principles are scattered across the different historical expressions, from the traditions of the primitive populations to the more sophisticated theological doctrines, but in substance:

> It is the metaphysic that recognises a divine Reality substantial to the world of things and lives and minds; the psychology that finds in the soul something similar to, or even identical with, divine Reality; the ethic that places man's final end in the knowledge of the immanent and transcendent Ground of all being. Rudiments of the Perennial Philosophy may be found among the traditionary lore of primitive peoples in every region of the world, and in its fully developed forms it has a place in every one of the higher religions. A version of the Highest Common Factor in all preceding and subsequent theologies was first committed to writing more than twenty-five centuries ago.[77]

According to Huxley, Perennial Philosophy should therefore be considered as the only divine Reality substantial to the manifold world of things and lives and minds. However, the nature of this one Reality is such that it cannot be directly apprehended except by those who have chosen to fulfil certain conditions, making themselves 'loving, pure in heart, and poor in spirit'. In every age, there have been some men and women who chose to fulfil the conditions upon which alone such immediate knowledge can be had. Of these, few have left accounts of the reality they were thus enabled to apprehend and have tried to relate, in one comprehensive system of thought, the given facts of this experience with the given facts of their other experiences. To such first-hand exponents of the Perennial Philosophy those who knew them have generally given the name of saint, prophet, sage or enlightened one.[78] In this book, they will be referred to simply as Initiates.

2
The Perennialists

Origins of the word

As discussed previously, the term 'Perennialism' and the name by which its followers were known, the Perennialists, were attributed by the academic community to this current and its exponents who, it should be underlined, never referred to themselves using this name. I will hereby provide a brief, and of course inexhaustive, overview of its main exponents in an attempt to identify the main distinctive traits of this current

In his book *The Only Tradition* (1997), American scholar William Quinn analyses the perennialist thought and, in particular, the ideals of those he regards as the two founders of the current, René Guénon and Ananda Coomaraswamy. To avoid any misunderstandings, the author makes a clear distinction between the authors who contributed to the divulgation of the Perennial Philosophy, the scholars who disseminated its principles and significance without explicitly mentioning the term, and those who simply discussed it, such as historians and, above all, philosophers:

> First, there are those who can be called perennial philosophers because of their promulgation of the philosophia perennis (though none actually calls himself, to my knowledge, a 'perennial philosopher'). These individuals who promulgate the philosophia perennis per se (like Guénon, Coomaraswamy, Wilbur Urban, and others) must be distinguished from (a) those who promulgate the same or similar principles without using the specific term philosophia perennis (e.g., Carl Jung, J. J. Poortman, Huston Smith) and from (b) those who do not promulgate but merely write about or discuss the principle as having existed or existing – for example, modern philosophers and/or academic historians of philosophy (the two are different but not exclusive) like Franz Sawicki, Charles B. Smitt, and James Collins.[79]

Quinn highlights how Perennialists identified philosophers as their major antagonists, and held them responsible for the secularisation of their thought and the separation of Tradition from its founding element, the *sacred*, which is the antithesis of the *secular*. For these reasons, Perennialists believed that modern philosophy, with a secular essence even in its metaphysical version, will never be able to understand the deepest meanings of Philosophia Perennis and will always be inclined to analyse it exclusively from a secular perspective.

In the same way as esotericism, the approach adopted by academic historians highlights their inability to understand Tradition from any perspective other than a 'rational' and 'historicist' one. Dutch scholar Wouter Hanegraaff, for instance, went as far as saying that inclusion of the perennialist thought in the study of esotericism was undertaken in error. According to Hanegraaff, the scholars of this current used the term' esotericism' mainly from a metaphysical perspective in referring to an assumed unity of all religious traditions, thus essentially reducing the perennialist thought to a comparative study of religions. In Hanegraaff's opinion, the limit of perennialist thinkers was that, to them, esotericism simply represented a 'theoretical concept' rather than a reference to a historically manifest religious tradition:

> It voluntarily distances itself from the academy world...The common assumption that perennialism is applicable to the study of esotericism is largely based on a misunderstanding. In perennialist usage, 'esoterism' is a metaphysical concept referring to a supposed 'transcendent unity' of all great religious tradition. Perennialism is, in other words, an approach to the comparative study of religions. In the context of that pursuit, 'esoterism' is a theoretical concept which refers to the transcendent unity of exoteric religions, rather than to any historical religion or religious tradition in particular. Perennealist authors have never intended 'esoterism' to be a general etic label applicable to specific historically manifest traditions. And when historical traditions are presented as exoteric vehicles for esoteric truth, one notices a marked preference for such religions as Hinduism or Islam. Historical currents

> which are regarded by almost everybody else as typical examples of western esoteric traditions (such as hermetic alchemy, or Christian theosophy) enjoy no special prominence in the perennialist perspective. It must be concluded that 'esoterism' in a perennialist sense is not intended to be, and should not be misunderstood as, a proposal for construing an 'esoteric tradition' in any accepted historical sense of that word. Instead it is a proposal for interpreting not esotericism but the phenomenon of religion as such.[80]

These words reveal how the Dutch scholar struggled to comprehend, or accept, that the fact that *no* specific historically manifest traditions were attributed to esotericism was the natural consequence of its fundamental *characteristic*, i.e. its being a metaphysical and meta-historical phenomenon, an indispensable condition for any authentic Tradition. For this reason, Traditions originate from Perennialists, and from their predecessors who embraced the concept of Philosophia Perennis, and are considered as simple vehicles of metaphysical truths, not the Truths themselves. We are aware, however, that the 'metaphysical' is not among the subjects accepted by historians; the solution to the problem, therefore, seems to be nigh on impossible to find as, in the words of Guénon, metaphysics can only be studied metaphysically.

In the above-mentioned paper, Hanegraaff also maintains that the perennialist thought never displayed an interest in Hermetic alchemy; the latter claim, however, is completely unfounded, as demonstrated by Julius Evola's papers on Hermetic Tradition or those by Swiss-German scholar Titus Burckardt on Alchemy, among others.

Although for the Perennialists esoterism is synonymous with Philosophia Perennis, with Guénon referring to it as 'Primordial Tradition', it should be noted that even within the same perennialist current Tradition has been described according to multiple variations of the concept. For instance, the Swiss thinker Frithjof Schuon, regarded the *Advaita Vedanta* (undifferentiated) philosophy, as conveyed by its greatest exponent, Shankara, as its most perfect expression:

> In those who accept esoterism or philosophia perennis, which is all the same, although emotionally sharing a given religious climate, the temptation is great to confuse the sublime with the esoteric and to believe that everything that they venerate pertains ipso facto to esoterism, starting with theology and sanctity. To escape all confusion of this kind, it is important to have a precise, not a vague, idea of what is in question; we shall choose as point of reference the example of the impersonalistic and unitive personalistic non-dualism of Shankara and shall contrast it with the personalistic and separative monism of Ramanuja. On the one hand, the perspective of the latter is substantially similar to the Semitic monotheisms, and on the other hand, the perspective of Shankara is one of the most adequate expressions possible of philosophia perennis or sapiential esoterism.[81]

All differences aside, what unites the thinkers of this current is the solid certainty of the existence of an ensemble of undifferentiated metaphysical principles which will give rise to a common vision of the world based on a rejection of modernity; the latter elements will represent the starting point of our overview of the greatest exponents of the perennialist current.

The founder, René Guénon

René Guénon is unanimously considered as the founder of the perennialist current; his writings constantly depicted the Perennial Philosophy (which he refers to as 'Primordial Tradition') as the highest knowledge accessible to intellectual intuition, a Tradition predating the single religious traditions. According to Guénon, this primordial Wisdom did not arise within a specific culture; its metaphysical principles, indeed, convey the Truth by means of symbols and myths, which are common to all major religions but did not specifically originate from any of these. To this regard Guénon, in an issue dated 1925 of the Catholic magazine *Regnabit*, stated that:

> When one finds such agreement everywhere, is this not more than a simple indication of a Primordial Tradition? After all, a little unprejudiced research suffices to reveal the marks of this essential doctrinal unity, the consciousness of which has at times been obscured among men.[82]

Only individuals carrying out extensive research and gnosis will be capable of fully comprehending the true meaning hidden behind these symbols, starting from the teachings of their own religious tradition. Indeed, according to Guénon, traditional exoteric forms represented the solid foundations of an esoteric path.

Similarly to the other Perennialists, Guénon also viewed the term 'Tradition' as being synonymous with esotericism, the doctrine of the superior states of being. Whilst distancing himself from the Catholic tradition he initially sought reference models in Hinduism (*Vedanta*) and subsequently in Islam (Ibn 'Arabi).

The French thinker maintained that the absolute principles on which Tradition is based have been, and will continue to be, passed down from man to man by means of the Traditions, provided that this transmission is carried out uninterruptedly within a regular Initiatic School, including Freemasonry and Compagnonnage. With regard to the concept of regularity, Jean-Pierre Laurant, one of Guénon's most prominent biographers, asserted the following:

> The search for proof of the existence of an eternal and universal primordial Tradition dominated his entire written production. This Tradition had shaped human destiny and had stayed alive in the Orient: India had preserved and transmitted the essence of the original metaphysical message...All his written texts were specific dissertations on that one certainty, whose presentation in literary form became necessary after the interruption in the Western world of

> 'normal' transmission, i.e. the oral communication between master and student within the relevant religious institutions for every tradition, such as Sufi confraternities in the Muslim world or medieval Christian esoteric societies, or even operative initiatic societies, such as Compagnonnage and Freemasonry. Only those who have received the original spiritual deposit without interruption can consider themselves traditional and regular.[83]

Guénon was often notoriously argumentative and renowned for disregarding or belittling Western esoteric traditions and underrating the exponents of classical Theosophy and, to an even greater extent, those of the Hermetic alchemical tradition. More importantly, Guénon failed to show any interest whatsoever in Nature and the manifest world which, in his opinion, 'has even less reality than our shadow projected on a wall', marking a sharp separation from the other exponents of modern and contemporary Western esoteric currents. In the words of Guénon:

> No one in the world has ever shown less inclination than the Easterners to follow the cult of nature, as it was followed in Greco-Roman times, since for them nature has always meant the world of appearances; appearances no doubt possess a reality of their own, but it is only transitory and impermanent, contingent and not universal. Therefore, to men who are metaphysicians by temperament, 'naturalism', in the many guises it is capable of assuming, only appears as an aberration, or even as a positive intellectual monstrosity.[84]

As stated previously, Guénon replaced the term 'Philosophia Perennis', too close to the Renaissance spirit which he rejected, with Primordial Tradition or, simply, metaphysics. His traditionalism, as well as that of the majority of his followers, was essentially based upon three postulates, which French historian Antoine Faivre exhaustively summarised as follows:

> 1) There exists a primordial Tradition of non-human origin – man did not invent it but rather received it – which has been obscured by a succession of historical vicissitudes (the idea of a progressive obscurement of truths). The different metaphysical traditions of humanity represent the remains of the original Tradition. This primordial Tradition does not appear to be based on a single revealed scripture. Its origin cannot be accurately identified, based on scientific historiography.
> 2) Western modernity (culture, civilisation, and modern science) is essentially incompatible with Tradition; humanity, in fact, had never found itself as detached from Tradition as it is now.
> 3) Tradition may be found again, at least partially, through the search for the common denominators between the different traditions (religious and/or metaphysical). This quest, which is of a qualitative nature, implies certain

> choices, value judgments and a form of ascesis that is both intellectual and spiritual. It also implies an 'Initiation' through specific channels whose authenticity – the initiatic regularity – makes them increasingly rare and necessary, whilst humanity finds itself involved in a process of cyclical obscuration.[85]

Guénon first expressed his view on Tradition in his book *Introduction to the Study of Hindu Doctrines* (1921), in which the French thinker explicitly articulates his thoughts in the chapter 'What is meant by Tradition?':

> A civilisation is the product and expression of a certain mental outlook common to a more or less widespread group of men, making it possible to treat each particular case separately as regards the exact determination of its constituent elements. However that may be, it remains nonetheless true, as far as the East is concerned, that the identification of tradition with the entire civilisation is fundamentally justifiable: every Eastern civilisation, taken as a whole, may be seen to be essentially traditional, which appears immediately evident from the explanations provided in the previous chapter. As for Western civilisation, we have shown that it is on the contrary devoid of any traditional character, with the exception of the religious element, which alone has retained it. Social institutions, to be considered traditional, must be effectively attached in their principle to a doctrine that is itself traditional, whether it be metaphysical or religious or of any other conceivable kind. In other words, those institutions are traditional that find their ultimate justification in their more or less direct, but always intentional and conscious, dependence upon a doctrine which, as regards its fundamental nature, is in every case of an intellectual order; but this intellectuality may be found either in a pure state, in cases where one is dealing with an entirely metaphysical doctrine, or else it may be found mingled with other heterogeneous elements, as in the case of the religious or other special modes which a traditional doctrine is capable of assuming. In Islam tradition exists under two distinct aspects, one of which is religious – it is upon this aspect that the general body of social institutions is dependent – while the other, which is purely Eastern, is wholly metaphysical. In a certain measure something of the same sort existed in medieval Europe in the case of the Scholastic doctrine, in which Arab influences moreover made themselves felt to an appreciable extent, although metaphysics was never sufficiently clearly distinguished from theology…In India we are in the presence of a tradition that is purely metaphysical in its essence; to it are attached as so many dependent extensions, the diverse applications to which it gives rise, whether in certain secondary branches of the doctrine itself, such as that relating to cosmology, or in the social order.[86]

Whereas in the East, India represented the most accomplished expression of a Tradition, in the West, Tradition – in Guénon's opinion – had been definitively eclipsed in the Middle Ages, with a progressive and inexorable distancing from metaphysics taking place from the Renaissance onwards. This criticism of the West highlights how Guénon and the Perennialists were not really concerned with the unity of religions or Traditions, but rather with their degree of conformity with a primordial Tradition dating back to a mystical past. It should be remembered that in the English perennialist literature use of the term 'esoterism' tends to prevail to define this hidden aspect and this quest, as opposed to esotericism, which is used to identify the ensemble of Western esoteric currents.

Guénon discussed Tradition in several other essays, examining at the same time other fundamental elements of his doctrine, such as the idea that the most suitable Tradition for a person is that belonging to the social and cultural context in which he was born and in which he places himself, and, most importantly, the idea that the most complete traditional form is one in which the *exoteric*, i.e. the religious aspect, and the *esoteric*, i.e. the initiatic aspect, are present *simultaneously* in order to enable all individuals of the traditional community, depending on their predispositions, to adhere to it:

> We can say that every particular traditional form is an adaptation of the primordial Tradition, which they all more or less directly derived from, in certain special conditions of time and space; what varies from one form to the other, therefore, is not the essence of the doctrine, which is above all these contingencies, but only the external aspects which surround it and through which it expresses itself. As a result of this, on the one hand, all these forms are inevitably equal to each other in terms of foundation, and on the other hand, human beings find it advantageous to connect, wherever possible, to the Tradition belonging to the environment in which they live, which is usually the one that best suits their individual nature...Distinction between exoteric and esoteric. We can identify the former with the religious domain and the latter with the initiatic domain; in the case of the latter, this assimilation is correct in all instances; as far as the former is concerned, as long as it does not acquires the purely religious form which characterises certain traditional forms, these are the only ones we will be dealing with at the present time. Having said that, this is the question that we should now consider: when a traditional form is complete, both from an exoteric and an esoteric viewpoint, it is clearly possible for everybody to adhere to it simultaneously, whether they intend to limit themselves to the religious perspective or also follow the initiatic path, as both domains will be open to them. After all, it should be clearly understood that, in a similar case, the initiatic order always receives its support and backing from the religious order, upon which it imposes itself without contrasting it in any way; as a consequence, it is never possible to set aside the rules belonging

> to the religious order, especially as far as rituals are concerned, as the latter bear the greatest importance from this point of view and are able to effectively establish a connection between the two orders...In order to have some sort of efficacy, the same initiatic practices necessarily presuppose a connection to an organisation from the same order; formulas such as that of the dhikr or the wird, or mantras from the Hindu tradition, may be repeated indefinitely without the slightest result, if they were not received via a regular transmission, as they would not be 'revived' by any spiritual influence.[87]

Guénon ended his analysis by briefly touching upon the extensively discussed issue of regular transmission, a topic that Guénon failed to fully elaborate, essentially limiting himself to saying that the transmission of traditional doctrines needed to be performed *without interruption,* and emphasising the fact that the initiatic Order should receive fundamental support from the religious Order, an interpretation that, as will be commented on subsequently, was not shared by Evola.

In *Introduction to the Study of Hindu Doctrines*, Guénon examines the other fundamental concept of his thought: the metaphysics, which was to represent the cornerstone of his later studies. The use Guénon makes of the term 'metaphysics' highlights his evident anti-historicism and anti-scientism, as evidenced in his definition of the word:

> Literally 'beyond physics', taking the word 'physics' as 'knowledge of nature' in the widest sense...Metaphysics is essentially the knowledge of the Universal, or the knowledge of principles belonging to the universal order, which moreover alone can validly lay claim to the name of principles...No opposition or conflict of any sort between metaphysics and the sciences is conceivable, precisely because their respective domains are so widely separated; and exactly the same thing applies to the relationship between metaphysics and religion...The domain of every science is always dependent upon experimentation in one or other of its various modalities, whereas the domain of metaphysics is essentially constituted by that which cannot be investigated externally: being 'beyond physics' we are also, by that very fact, beyond experiment...This implies a formal condemnation of any attempt at applying the 'historical method' to the metaphysical order; the metaphysical point of view is itself radically opposed to the historical point of view, or what passes for such, and this opposition will be seen to amount not only to a question of method, but also, what is far more important, to a real question of principle, since the metaphysical point of view, in its essential immutability, is the very negation of the notions of evolution and progress. One might say in fact that metaphysics can only be studied metaphysically...Knowledge belonging to the universal order of necessity lies beyond all the distinctions that condition the knowledge of individual things, of which that between

> subject and object is a general and basic type; this also goes to show that the object of metaphysics is no wise comparable with the particular object of any other kind of knowledge whatsoever, and indeed it can only be referred to as an object purely by analogy, because, in order to speak of it at all, one is forced to attach to it some denomination or other...Metaphysical truths can only be conceived by the use of a faculty that does not belong to the individual order, and that, by reason of the immediate character of its operation, may be called 'intuitive', but only on the strict condition that it is not regarded as having anything in common with the faculty which certain contemporary philosophers call intuition, a purely instinctive and vital faculty...The distinction between metaphysical and scientific knowledge: the first is derived from the pure intellect, which has the Universal for its domain; the second is derived from reason, which has the general for its domain...Science could be indefinitely extended without ever joining metaphysics, from which it will always remain as completely separate as ever, because metaphysics alone embraces the knowledge of the Universal.[88]

This harsh criticism of science was not shared by certain thinkers, followers of Guénon, including the French writer and thinker Raymond Abellio, the pseudonym of Georges Soulès (1907–1986). Abellio criticised Guénon's view, as he firmly believed it was possible to be simultaneously an esotericist and modern, that the adherence to a Tradition does not automatically preclude the possibility of adopting a scientific approach to a series of issues.

Initially a specialist technician with strong political interests, Soulès later left politics to devote himself to esotericism, which he was drawn to thanks to the influence of Pierre de Combas, an expert in initiatic issues, whom he met in 1943. Regarded as one of the most prominent French writers of prose, from 1946 until his death he published his works, novels, autobiographical texts and theoretical essays under the pseudonym Raymond Abellio. Thanks to this variety of different genres he developed an all-encompassing system for the interpretation of the world and its history, supported by elements deriving from various esoteric traditions, which he had been introduced to by Pierre de Combas, and by the Husserlian phenomenology, which had first aroused his interest in 1950. In 1965 he published *The Absolute Structure,* considered the key to his philosophical system; the structure in question is partly inspired by the arithmological tradition and partly by the Kabbalistic practice of gematria, the I Ching, Tarot Cards, Astrology and, as previously stated, by Edmund Husserl's philosophical phenomenology. The absolute quality attributed to this Structure is justified by Abellio's conviction that the same structure could be applied within a doctrine of universal interdependence, or universal correspondences, throughout the field of reality, including history. Essentially, Abellio made an attempt to represent the invisible history or metahistory of civilisation by means of a transdisciplinary vision involving psychology, politics, physics and biology, with the aim of achieving a full comprehension of the transcendent Self of humanity.

As previously mentioned, Guénon was at times deeply argumentative, and not even psychoanalysis was spared his criticism, although in this instance he expressed his judgement in a more generalised and superficial manner. More specifically, Guénon believed that the theories put forward by Jung only appeared to be spiritualistic, whereas in reality their only achievement was to lead to the 'diffuse psychism of the most inferior regions of the subtle world'.[89]

In his book *The Crisis of the Modern World*, Guénon analyses the current cycle experienced by humanity and explains that the original Tradition of the Western world is of a Hyperborean nature, the remnants of which were transported throughout various regions; here they mingled with already existing traditions to result in the creation of other doctrines, including the Celtic doctrine, as the product of this fusion.[90] Guénon, however, expressed serious doubts as to the possibility, entertained by some but which he deemed remote, of a reconnection with these Nordic doctrines. He believed that it these doctrines could no longer be detected in their pure state and sufficiently vital to serve as a basis for other doctrines. Guénon's book was published in 1927, and a few years later the Nazi regime provided him with the answer he so desperately sought; Jung's work 'Wotan', published in 1936, explained through the theory of archetypes what Guénon, due to his reluctance to psychoanalysis, would have failed to grasp through his metaphysical doctrines. In this paper, published in the journal *Neue Schweizer Rundschau*, and subsequently transformed into the first chapter of the book *Essays on Contemporary Events*, Jung explained that the archetype of *Wotan* (Odin), god of war and death, had always been present in the collective unconscious of Germans, a population of warriors since the epoch of Germanic barbarians, and that, like all archetypes, could have been brought back to light by the German population to promote the rebirth of the Norse and German mythology. Those doctrines were present in their pure state, featuring a vitality that was revealed to be both powerful and destructive in the collective unconscious of the German population.

To return to the notion of metaphysics, Guénon identified *intellectual intuition*, yet another concept, which forms the foundation of his thought, as the main gateway to knowledge:

> When describing the essential features of metaphysics, we said that it constitutes an intuitive, or in other words, immediate knowledge, as opposed to the discursive and mediate knowledge that belongs to the rational order. Intellectual intuition is even more immediate than sensory intuition, for it is beyond the distinction between subject and object which the latter allows to subsist; it is at once the means of knowledge and the knowledge itself, and in it subject and object are identified...The immediate consequence of this is that knowing and being are fundamentally but one and the same thing; they are,

> so to speak, two inseparable aspects of a single reality, being no longer even really distinguishable in that sphere where all is 'without duality'...Cartesian dualism which consists in artificially opposing knowing and being, an opposition that is the negation of all true metaphysics.[91]

Guénon repeatedly elaborated on the concept of metaphysics, particularly in his book *The Multiple States of Being* (1932), in which metaphysics is once again represented as the knowledge of that which exists beyond nature but, at the same time, as an opportunity of awareness of what gnosis allows us to approach intuitively, in a dynamic perspective in which the unity of principles is manifested 'through an infinity of degrees', in the passage from potency to act, expressions which reveal the influence of Arab mystic, Ibn Arabi.

Guénon's later writings directed intense criticism towards the contemporary Western civilisation, guilty of having transformed itself into an 'anti-traditional' civilisation through a process of decline which began after the Middle Ages. This decline could only be interrupted thanks to a reconstruction of the traditional spirit, based on the sole form which, in Guénon's opinion, still preserved revivable elements of the lost Tradition:

> In the present state of the world then we have on the one hand all the civilisations that have remained faithful to the traditional standpoint – namely the civilisations of the East – and on the other a veritably anti-traditional civilisation, namely that of the modern West...In certain periods, of which the nearest to us is the medieval, the Western mentality was much more akin, in its more important features, to what is still the Eastern mentality than to what it has itself become in modern times...We think that if a Western tradition could be rebuilt it would be bound to take on a religious form in the strictest sense of this word, and that this form could only be Christian; for on the one hand the other possible forms have been too long foreign to the Western mentality, and on the other it is only in Christianity – and we can say still more definitely in Catholicism – that such remnants of a traditional spirit as still exist in the West are to be found...The fact that somebody calls himself a 'traditionalist' does not prove that he knows, even vaguely, what tradition is in the true sense of the word. For our part, we refuse absolutely to give this name to anything that is of a purely human order...The real traditional outlook is always and everywhere essentially the same, whatever outward form it may take; the various forms that are specially suited to different mental conditions and different circumstances of time and place are merely expressions of one and the same truth. But this fundamental unity beneath apparent multiplicity can be grasped only by those who are able to take up a point of view that is truly intellectual.[92]

Whilst discussing the manner in which the West would have been in a position to return to a traditional form, Guénon proposed a sort of an East-West syncretism; having stated that the restoration of a traditional form in the West should be based on Christianity and, specifically, Catholicism, he also added that:

> A Western elite can by definition only be established by Western initiative, and therein lies the whole difficulty. This initiative could come in one of two ways: either the West would have to find in itself the means of bringing it about through a direct return to its own tradition, a return that would be a sort of spontaneous reawakening of latent possibilities; or certain Western elements would have to bring about this restoration with the help afforded by a knowledge of the Eastern doctrines; this however could not for them be quite direct, since they would have to remain Westerners, but it might be obtained by a sort of second-hand influence working through intermediaries such as those of whom we have just spoken.[93]

Guénon firmly believed that the return to an integral Tradition in the West was prevented by an anti-traditional action aimed at radically altering the general mentality and, at the same time, destroying all Western traditional institutions; an action which, according to the French thinker, would have been triggered by the Renaissance Humanism, identified as the precursor of the future Rationalism, which expected to be able to attribute all things to purely human elements, thereby completely excluding anything that was classified as super-individual and metaphysical. To this regard, Guénon underlined the main terminology differences between *traditionalist* and *traditional*:

> The people just referred to are such as can properly be described as 'traditionalists', meaning people who only have a sort of tendency or aspiration towards tradition without really knowing anything at all about it; this is the measure of the distance dividing the 'traditionalist' spirit from the truly traditional spirit, for the latter implies a real knowledge, and indeed in a sense it is the same as that knowledge. In short, the 'traditionalist' is and can be no more than a mere 'seeker', and that is why he is always in danger of going astray, not being in possession of the principles which alone could provide him with infallible guidance...All misuses of the word 'tradition' can serve this same purpose in one way or another, beginning with the most popular of all, whereby it is made synonymous with 'custom' or 'usage', thus bringing about a confusion of tradition with things that are on the lower human level and are completely lacking in profound significance. But there are other and more subtle deformations, all the more dangerous because of their subtlety; but all have as a common characteristic that of bringing the idea of tradition down to a purely human level, whereas on the contrary there is nothing and can be

> nothing truly traditional that does not contain some element of a superhuman order. This indeed is the essential point, containing as it were the very definition of tradition and all that appertains to it; this is also therefore the very point which must on no account be allowed to emerge if the modern mentality is to be maintained in its state of delusion.[94]

According to Guénon, in addition to the Catholic Church, Freemasonry, the last of the large Initiatic Societies to have survived the destruction of the *Kali-Yuga*, could have encouraged the Western civilisation to escape the grip of the reigning materialism and nihilism, although Freemasonry itself, in Guénon's opinion, had undergone a certain degree of decline and degeneration from a spiritual point of view. A sort of revivification of traditional symbols, knowledge and doctrines could have indeed been activated, although only under favourable circumstances, despite a detachment from operative Tradition. It was Guénon's belief, in fact, that these doctrines had been transmitted without interruption, albeit *unknowingly*, by the Freemasons, who had long forgotten their initiatic significance.

In conclusion, Guénon's esotericism, synonym of Tradition, essentially represents an ensemble of metaphysical principles rather than specific historical realities; principles which have clearly been present in and transmitted by the Traditions, a body of metaphysical knowledge included within the generic term 'esotericism'. It is precisely through esotericism, understood as an ensemble of metaphysical principles, that the perennialist current managed to achieve a diffusion and reawakening of conscience in the different levels of reality that are associated with it, followed by the individuation of a way of life allowing to identify and sense the presence of the sacred in everyday life.

Ananda Coomaraswamy

Ananda Coomaraswamy is considered, alongside René Guénon and Frithjof Schuon, one of the three most prominent exponents of Perennialism, or, as they preferred to call it, the Traditionalist School. Coomaraswamy, unlike Guénon and Schuon, was an academic and made academia his reference target; for this reason, as underlined by Giovanna Monastra in an interesting essay on the Ceylonese art historian, Coomaraswamy, 'represents the perfect example of how one can profitably operate in the modern world by means of the instruments available in our time to transmit a cultural message which clashes with the values of Modernity. Coomaraswamy demonstrates that the thought of the great metaphysical traditions can be expressed through the Western academic culture, without needing to be trivialised or sterilised, and therefore deprived of its 'unsettling' wisdom value.'[95] In the light of the critical observations directed towards the academic culture with regard to Esotericism and Tradition, it is precisely thanks to this distinctive feature that Coomaraswamy is viewed as one of the most original and enlightened art historians of the twentieth century and, at the same time, one of the greatest exponents of the traditional thought.

Coomaraswamy therefore developed his academic exegesis by means of the instruments and methods pertaining to philology, archaeology, history of art, ethnology, folklore and history of religions, approaching spiritual documents (myths, symbols, figures, rituals and theological systems), similarly to the other perennialist Henry Corbin, both as a scholar and a philosopher.[96]

Despite the posthumous publication of several of Coomaraswamy's essays on Hinduism and the Perennial Philosophy in the quarterly journal *Studies in Comparative Religion*, alongside, amongst others, papers by Schuon and Guénon, Coomaraswamy differentiated himself from the other authors of the Traditional School due to his absolute lack of interest in the 'divulgation' of his thought:

> It isn't my primary function to write 'readable' books or articles: this is just where my function differs from Guénon's. All my willing writing is addressed to the professors and specialists, those who have undermined our sense of values in recent times, but whose vaunted 'scholarship' is really so superficial. I feel that rectification must being at the reputed 'top', and only so will find its way into schools and textbooks and encyclopaedias.[97]

As far as his position within the perennialist current is concerned, William Quinn described him more as a 'complementor' of the Tradition than a *continuator* like Guénon and Schuon, who were referred to as 'continuators' because, unlike Coomaraswamy, they had undergone an actual initiation to the Tariqa Islamic esotericism. To this regard, Quinn asserted that:

> Guénon and Schuon were successive 'continuators' of the Tradition, while Coomaraswamy was a 'complementor'. This position, which can be described as the initiatic analysis of the Traditional perspective, primarily involves a strong Sufi or orthodox Islamic influence, insofar as Guénon and Schuon were both regularly initiated into Sufi tariqas or spiritual fraternities as were a number of other later Traditional writers, whereas Coomaraswamy was a Hindu and by comparison with the former was neither a specialist in Arabic nor Islamic metaphysics.[98]

As perceptively underlined by another renowned traditionalist scholar, British orientalist Martin Lings, a student of Frithjof Schuon, whereas Coomaraswamy's approach may be referred to using the term 'truth', Guénon's may be summarised by means of the word 'orthodoxy'; Guénon's writings, in fact, are unfailingly characterised by a thinly veiled attempt to create a minority qualified to undertake an efficient spiritual action. If Coomaraswamy's works are written with the same intentions, and indeed, they most certainly are, the reader is undoubtedly less aware of it. The immediate impression given by Coomaraswamy's writings is that of an enormous fresco of metaphysical and cosmological truth aimed at the development, expansion and enlightenment of intelligence beyond its limits, and its preparation for the spiritual work, which represents the methodological complement of doctrine – a complement that tends to be implicit with Coomaraswamy, and explicit with Guénon.[99]

As previously mentioned, although Coomaraswamy's idea of Tradition and universal concepts is well integrated with that of his master Guénon, the form of his works differed greatly from that of the French thinker. Coomaraswamy's studies highlight a thorough integration, or *fusion*, of *religion* and *sacred culture*, a combination that distinguishes an authentically Traditional society from the others; it is only in this kind of society, in fact, that all activities, be they of a priestly or of any other nature, are carried out and interpreted in an entirely initiatic manner. Guénon did not fully reject this viewpoint but clearly specified that the traditionality of a given culture is to be found in the *orthodox* elements of the great religions and esoteric initiatic associations, both in premodern and modern societies, and constantly promotes the opportunity to restore the lost Tradition through a regular initiation in certain realities that have survived within the Christian, Buddhist, Hindu and Islamic traditions.

According to Coomaraswamy, similar to the other Perennialists, the terms Tradition and Philosophia Perennis were virtually interchangeable, with the only difference being linked exclusively to their application: whereas the use of the term *Tradition* is more frequently associated with a culture, Philosophia Perennis is used by Coomaraswamy to describe the ensemble of all metaphysical principles that do not refer to any specific culture or tradition, or on the contrary refer to all of them.

William Quinn, once again, highlights how Coomaraswamy and Guénon essentially make use of the same *Hermeneutics* by means of intellectual intuition, albeit from two different perspectives, an *anagogical* one in Coomaraswamy's case and a strictly *esoteric* one in Guénon's:

> Coomaraswamy's anagogic exegesis and Guénon esoteric exegesis, by the application of one's 'intellectual intuition' to the particular principle in question, result in the same hermeneutic; that in which the tradition, the philosophia perennis, is brought to light. In the execution of this method, it was Coomaraswamy's style always and everywhere to compare, to cross reference, to establish consistency, while it was Guenon's style to seek the principal heart of the matter and expound upon its metaphysical qualities and significance.[100]

Despite their diverse doctrines, numerous themes are common to both Guénon and Coomaraswamy – one of the most renowned being the presence of a *principle of hierarchy* in the Universe, symbolised by an axial element, or vertical axis, which, like the rungs on a ladder, would allow the selected few able to perform an exegesis of the traditional Principles in sacred texts to reach the *vertex* of the ladder, the Truth.

This concept naturally resulted in both of them being accused of elitism by the exponents of the culture of political correctness.

In 1906, Coomaraswamy started his project of divulgation of Indian art in the West. He returned to London from Ceylon armed with a vast collection of photographs of artefacts and, seeing as he was aware he would not have been able to rely on the collaboration of museum curators or other exponents of the cultural establishment of the time, he tried to make their existence known to the largest possible number of contemporary artists. To this regard, in 1908 he wrote:

> The main difficulty so far seems to have been that Indian art has been studied so far only by archaeologists. It is not archaeologists but artists who are the best qualified to judge of the significance of works of art considered as art.

In 1909, he became acquainted with Jacob Epstein and Eric Gill, two of the most influential modernist artists in the city and among the first to include elements of Indian aesthetics in their works (their pieces represent the result of what is viewed as the first British Modernism).

Coomaraswamy possessed a strong aesthetic perceptiveness and, despite having been formed by the Hindu tradition, boasted an extensive knowledge of the Western tradition, and a considerable experience of and interest in Greek metaphysics, particularly Plotinus. Indeed, although one of his greatest merits had undoubtedly been that of facilitating a better understanding of Indian art, which subsequently determined an increase of its value in the West, when performing his exegeses Coomaraswamy also made use of extra-Indian parallelisms, using the comparativist method typical of perennialists. His writings featured constant references, aside from the above-mentioned Plotinus, to Plato, Clement of Alexandria, Augustine, Thomas Aquinas, Shankara, Meister Eckhart and other Asian and Western mystics. For this reason, and precisely in relation to the principles of the Perennial Philosophy, he loved being referred to as a 'Metaphysician'.

His perennialist approach ultimately led him to attempt to build a bridge between the East and the West; his metaphysical writings, in particular, highlight his constant attempts to reveal interesting connections and parallelisms between certain elements of the two cultures, such as the Vedanta doctrine and Platonism. His written works likewise reveal an attempt to re-establish the original Buddhist doctrine, a tradition which Guénon constantly overlooked and regarded negatively, reducing it to a revolt of the Kshatriya caste against the British authority.

Coomaraswamy's interest in Indian art became a lifelong passion, and his Hermeneutic method progressively evolved and went through several different phases. What we can refer to as the second stage registered an increasing familiarity with certain issues of the history of religions, and particularly with the symbolism of Chtonic fertility represented by the *Magna Mater*, cosmogony, water rituals and mythology; however, it is only around 1932, in the third stage of his intellectual journey, that he developed a systematic interest in the various expressions of the Philosophia Perennis, a primordial and universal tradition whose presence was detected in every authentic civilisation.

Due to a lack of specific writings on Tradition, his view on the Philosophia Perennis needs to be elicited from his art essays, which American scholar Roger Lipsey gathered and included in a three-volume collection published by Princeton University Press.[101]

In the last chapter of Volume 3, 'Tradition: An Introduction to the Later Writings', Lipsey collected a significant number of quotes from his different papers, to summarise the meaning of what Coomaraswamy intended as 'Tradition':

> Coomaraswamy never fabricated anything like an abstract of all traditional expressions of a given idea, which he believed could only lead to a mechanical and lifeless monstrosity...a sort of religious Esperanto. Rather he progressed by a comparative method, collating the formulae of one tradition with another, which kept in view the likelihood that all religions have a common source.'[102]

Lipsey's words highlight how Coomaraswamy, similarly to all other Perennialists, never intended to dialectically *prove* the reliability of every single doctrine, but rather aimed at demonstrating their coherence and, consequently, their clarity and comprehensibility:

> All are speaking what is essentially one and the same spiritual language, employing different words, but expressing the same ideas, and very often by means of identical idioms. Otherwise stated: there is a universally intelligible language – not only verbal but also visual – of the fundamental ideas on which the different civilisations have been founded.'[103]

Coomaraswamy's typically traditionalist vision of the world became perfectly evident in the Ceylonese historian's dichotomy between *Religion of Time* and *Religion of Eternity*, the latter interpreted as a *Sophia Perennis* allowing individuals to discover their own divine 'Self':

> The life or lives of man may be regarded as constituting a curve, an arc of time-experience subtended by the duration of the individual Will to Life. The outward movement on this curve – Evolution, the Path of Pursuit, the Pravritti Marga – is characterised by self-assertion; the inward movement – Involution, the Path of Return, the Nivritti Marga – is characterised by increasing Self-realisation. The religion of men on the outward path is the Religion of Time; the religion of those who return is the Religion of Eternity. If we consider life as one whole, certainly Self-realisation must be regarded as its essential

> purpose from the beginning; all our forgetting is but that we may remember the more vividly.[104]

Those who, on the contrary, opt for the outward path, largely undertaken in the West where ethics acts as the referee amongst competitors, will not see a long road ahead of them:

> The acquisition of wealth (artha) and the enjoyment of sense-pleasure (kama), subject to such law (dharma) as may protect the weak against the strong, are the legitimate preoccupations of those on the outward path. This is the stage attained by modern Western society, of which the norm is competition regulated by ethical restraint. Beyond this stage no society can progress unless it is subjected to the creative will of those who have passed beyond the stage of most extreme egoism, whether we call them 'heroes', 'guardians', Brahmans, Samurai, or simply 'men of genius.[105]

As illustrated previously, Coomaraswamy often made use of parallelisms between Vedanta and Platonism, although his analysis frequently afforded original comparisons between the Western thought and Christian theology, as in the following passage on the concept of reincarnation and the fascinating contrast between the age of the *soul* and the age of the *body*:

> The doctrine of reincarnation corresponds to a fact which everyone must have remarked; the varying age of the souls of men, irrespective of the age of the body counted in years. 'A man is not elder because his head is grey.' (Dhammapada, 260). Sometimes we see an old head on young shoulders. Some men remain irresponsible, self-assertive, uncontrolled, unapt to their last day; others from their youth are serious, self-controlled, talented, and friendly…An essential factor is to be recognised in the dogma of the rhythmic character of the world-process, determined by the great antithesis of Subject and Object, Self and not-Self, Will and Matter, Unity and Diversity, Love and Hate, and all other 'Pairs'. The interplay of these opposites constitutes the whole of sensational and registrateable existence, the Eternal Becoming (samsara), which is characterised by birth and death, evolution and involution, descent and ascent. Every individual life – mineral, vegetable, animal, human, or personal god – has a beginning and an end, and this creation and destruction, appearance and disappearance, are of the essence of the world-process and equally originate in the past, the present, the future. According to this view, then, every individual ego, or separate expression of the general Will to Life, must be regarded as having reached a certain stage of its own cycle. It is further considered that the turning point of this curve is reached in man, and hence the immeasurable value which Hindus (and Buddhists) attach to birth in human

> form. Before the turning point is reached – to use the language of Christian theology – the natural man prevails; after it is passed, regenerate man.[106]

According to the perennialist thought, individuals will occupy a different position on an hypothetical scale of values based not on their anagraphical age but rather on their *spiritual* one:

> According to their position on the great curve, that is to say, according to their spiritual age, we can recognise three prominent types of men. There is first the mob, of those who are preoccupied with the thought of I and Mine, whose objective is self-assertion, but are restrained on the one hand by fear of retaliation and of legal or after-death punishment, and on the other by the beginnings of love of family and love of country. These, in the main, are the 'Devourers' of Blake, the 'Slaves' of Nietzsche. Next there is a smaller, but still large number of thoughtful and good men whose behaviour is largely determined by a sense of duty, but whose inner life is still the field of conflict between the old Adam and the new man. Men of this type are actuated on the one hand by the love of power and fame, and ambition more or less noble, and on the other by the disinterested love of mankind. But all these, who have but begun to taste of freedom, must still be guided by rules. Finally, there is the much smaller number of great men – heroes, saviours, saints, and avatars – who have definitely passed the period of greatest stress and have attained peace, or at least have attained to occasional and unmistakeable vision of life as a whole. These are the 'Prolific' of Blake, the 'Masters' of Nietzsche, the true Brahmans in their own right, and partake of the nature of the Superman and the Bodhisattva. Their activity is determined by their love and wisdom, and not by rules. In the world, but not of it, they are the flower of humanity, our leaders and teachers.[107]

Coomaraswamy's view of the ritual in his art writings essentially coincided with the interpretation provided by Guénon. Similarly to the latter, Coomaraswamy also believed that, whilst the ritual is essential in the initial phase of the cognitive path, it inevitably becomes superfluous once the peak of the same path is reached, the one in which intuitive knowledge is used:

> The ritual, like that of the old Vedic Sacrifice, is an interior procedure, of which the outward forms are only a support, indispensable for those who – being still on their way – have not yet reached its end, but that can be dispensed with by those who have already found the end, and who, though they may be still in the world, are not of it. In the meantime, there can be no greater danger or hindrance than that of the premature iconoclasm of those who still confuse their own existence with their own being, and have not yet 'known the Self';

> these are the vast majority, and for them the temple and all its figurations are signposts on their way.[108]

Coomaraswamy, in the same way as Guénon, albeit not with the same vigour and argumentative streak displayed by the Frenchman, sharply criticised modernity; his negative judgement is particularly evident in the following comparison between medieval art and the already degenerate modern art:

> Our traditional art is thus 'ideal' in the philosophical sense of the word; as Guénon expresses it with bitter clarity, 'in the whole of medieval art, and otherwise than as in modern art, we meet with the embodiment of an idea, and never with the idealisation of a fact'. Traditional art is never 'idealistic' in the modern and sentimental sense, according to which we conceive 'ideals' or 'heart's desires' after which we could wish to reshape the world. For the medieval philosopher, the world could not have been better or more beautifully made than it is, for him the perfection of artistic judgement and height of aesthetic pleasure was touched when 'God saw everything that he had made, and behold, it was very good.[109]

Coomaraswamy particularly stigmatised the fact that modern art became incapable even of understanding the very *essence* of the materials used; after quoting Thomas Aquinas, according to whom 'Art is the imitation of Nature in her manner of operation'.[110] Coomaraswamy added, in the wake of the theological scholar, that:

> Nature's manner is to imitate the form of humanity in a nature of flesh. The form of humanity does not only exist in this way, but also – for the Middle Ages and the East, if not for us – in a nature of light, transformally. This means that to make our statue right we must have understood both human nature and the nature of stone, or wood, or whatever our material: only so can we imitate the form of a man in the nature of stone or wood.[111]

A deep knowledge of Nature and the materials it provides for use in the creation of art is an essential element for Coomaraswamy, representing a drastic difference of opinion with Guénon.

According to Coomaraswamy, in creating their art pieces human artists should essentially behave like God, the only difference being that man finds his materials ready and simply needs to impose new 'forms' on them, whereas God also creates his own materials:

> Art imitates Nature in her manner of operation. In other words, as every traditional treatise on metaphysics or theology continually asserts, the human artificer works like the Divine Artificer, with only this important distinction,

> that the human artificer has to make use of already existing materials, and to impose new forms on these materials, while the Divine Artificer provides his own material out of the infinitely 'possible', which is not yet, and is therefore called 'nothing', whence the expression ex nihilo fit.[112]

For the above reasons Coomaraswamy believed that, in Traditional civilisations, art should be placed not among the purely physical useful and pleasurable activities, but rather in a metaphysical domain, where it is possible to encounter, and represent, the 'form' of humanity:

> To have seen in his artefacts nothing but the things themselves, and in the myth a mere anecdote would have been a mortal sin, for this would have been the same as to see in oneself nothing but the 'reasoning and mortal animal', to recognise only 'this man', and never the 'form of humanity'. It is just insofar as we do now see only the things as they are in themselves, and only ourselves as we are in ourselves, that we have killed the metaphysical man and shut ourselves up in the dismal cave of functional and economic determinism. Do you begin to see now what I meant by saying that works of art consistent with the Philosophia Perennis cannot be divided into the categories of the utilitarian and the spiritual, but pertain to both worlds, functional and significant, physical and metaphysical?[113]

How is such a process of metaphysical *perception* activated in an artist? First of all, by means of meditation techniques aimed at distancing him from profane concerns so as to enable him, as it is particularly evident in the specific case of the icon, to *intuit* the form of the Divinity as described in the sacred scripture. In the above process the knower and the known merge into each other and are no longer distinguishable. Coomaraswamy skilfully described the origin of masterpieces as follows:

> The formal element in art represents a purely mental activity, *citta-sañña*. From this point of view, it will appear natural enough that India should have developed a highly specialised technique of vision. The maker of an icon, having by various means proper to the practice of Yoga eliminated the distracting influences of fugitive emotions and creature images, self-willing and self-thinking, proceeds to visualise the form of the devata, angel or aspect of God, described in a given canonical prescription. The mind 'pro-duces' or 'draws' this form to itself, as though from a great distance. Ultimately, that is, from Heaven, where the types of art exist in formal operation; immediately, from 'the immanent space in the heart', the common focus of seer and seen, at which place the only possible experience of reality takes place...The whole process, up to the point of manufacture, belongs to the established order of

> personal devotions, in which worship is paid to an image mentally conceived; in any case, the principle involved is that true knowledge of an object is not obtained by merely empirical observation or reflex registration, but only when the knower and known, seer and seen, meet in an act transcending distinction. To worship any Angel in truth one must become the Angel: 'Whoever worships a divinity as other than the self, thinking 'He is the one, and I another', knows not'.[114]

In Coomaraswamy's opinion, this union between the seer and the seen, achieved thanks to an intuitive process, is absolutely necessary and essential for the creation of an authentic work of art. It is evident that this dynamic does not determine a contrast between the intelligible and the sensitive; reality, in fact, comes about as a result of knowledge and is not independent of the act of thought:

> It should be realised that from the Indian (metaphysical) and Scholastic point of view, subjective and objective are not irreconcilable categories, one of which must be regarded as real to the exclusion of the other. Reality (satya) subsists there where the intelligible and sensible meet in the common unity of being, and cannot be thought of as existing in itself outside and apart from, but rather as, knowledge or vision, that is, only in act. All this is also implied in the Scholastic definition of truth *adae quatio rei et intellectus*, Aristotle's identity of the soul with what it knows, or according to St Thomas, 'knowledge comes about in so far as the object known is within the knower', in radical contradiction to the conception of knowledge and being as independent acts.'[115]

The typically perennialist approach of the Ceylonese historian is underlined, in the above passage, in the juxtaposition of different systems of thought and traditions, specifically the Indian metaphysical and Aristotelian Scholastic perspectives, eventually leading (something that did not happen in Guénon's approach) to an interesting parallelism with the modern scientific paradigms: 'Thus Indian types representing sentences or powers are analogous to those of Scholastic theology and the energies of science.'[116]

The nature of a sacred work of art is, therefore, depicted by Coomaraswamy as an ideal product, and regarded as the result of a process, which excludes the purely *visual* ability of an artist. To this regard, Coomaraswamy explains that the differences between Oriental and Christian (medieval) art are to be observed in the employment, by the former, of the *imaginative* ability rather than the more limited *visual* one, resulting in the creation of a work of art starting from the very idea of Divine whose presence is indispensable for humanity:

> The Indian or Far Eastern icon, carved or painted, is neither a memory image nor an idealisation, but a visual symbolism, ideal in the mathematical sense.

> The 'anthropomorphic' icon is of the same kind as a yantra, that is, a geometrical representation of a deity, or a mantra, that is, an auditory representation of a deity. The peculiarity of the icon depends immediately upon these conditions, and could not be otherwise stated, even were we unaware that in actual practice it is the mantra and not the eye's intrinsic faculty that originates the image...There is no feeling of texture or flesh, but only of stone, metal, or pigment, the object being an image in one or other of these materials, and not a deceptive replica of any objective cause of sensation...In Western art the picture is generally conceived as seen in a frame or through a window, and so brought toward the spectator; but the Oriental image really exists only in our own mind and heart and is thence projected or reflected onto space. The Western presentation is designed as if seen from a fixed point of view, and must be optically plausible; Chinese landscape is typically represented as seen from more than one point of view, or in any case from a conventional, not a 'real', point of view, and here it is not plausibility but intelligibility that is essential...Where European art naturally depicts a moment of time, an arrested action or an effect of light, Oriental art represents a continuous condition. In traditional European terms, we should express this by saying that modern European art endeavours to represent things as they are in themselves, Asiatic and Christian art to represent things more nearly as they are in God, or nearer to their source.[117]

In conclusion, to illustrate what happens at the end of the intuitive, or imaginative, approach, at the time of the union between the seer and the object of his contemplation, i.e. the creation of a work of art, Coomaraswamy uses the Indian term *Sadrsya*, meaning 'similarity', clearly interpreted not as facsimile but rather as *likeness*:

> It is in fact obvious that the likeness between anything and any representation of it cannot be a likeness of nature, but must be analogical or exemplary, or both of these. What the representation imitates is the idea or species of the thing, by which it is known intellectually, rather than the substance of the thing as it is perceived by the senses.[118]

A particularly interesting reference highlighted in Coomaraswamy's studies of various symbolisms relates to the symbolism of 'Ornaments'. Ornaments are amongst the most significant symbols of Masonic rituals; despite being subject to a *moralising* interpretation, which contributed to the loss of their profoundly initiatic aspects, Coomaraswamy's analysis may contribute to the recovery of their original meaning, the meaning intended according to a traditional, i.e. esoteric, context.[119] In a fascinating etymological and philological analysis of the term, Coomaraswamy highlights how, depending on the context in which it is used, the word lends itself to different meanings and potential misunderstandings:

> The words 'decoration' and 'ornament', whether with reference to the embellishment of persons or of things, can be considered simultaneously in Latin and in English. Ornare is primarily to 'fit out, furnish, provide with necessaries' (Harper) and only secondarily 'embellishment', etc. Ornamentum is primarily 'apparatus, accoutrement, equipment, trappings' and secondarily 'embellishment, jewel, trinket', etc., as well as rhetorical ornament (Sanskrit alamkara).[120]

Unfortunately, in modern and contemporary society, the term 'Ornament' has undergone a progressive decline, as remarked by Coomaraswamy, and now no longer represents a necessary element in a work of art, or in a sacred object, but simply a sort of insignificant accessory:

> We know that in traditional philosophy the work of art is a reminder; the summons of its beauty is to a thesis, as to something to be understood, rather than merely enjoyed. Unwilling as we may be to accept such a proposition today, in a world increasingly emptied of meaning, it is even harder for us to believe that 'ornament' and 'decoration' are, properly speaking, integral factors of the beauty of the work of art, certainly not a significant part of it, but rather necessary to its efficacy.[121]

Coomaraswamy then moves on to a suggestive description of the original meaning of the word 'ornament' or 'decoration', an *action* aimed at the completion of the object or, more importantly, of the personality of the individual who possessed it:

> Let us consider now the history of various words that have been used to express the notion of an ornamentation or decoration, and which in modern usage for the most part import an aesthetic value added to things of which the said 'decoration' is not an essential or necessary part. It will be found that most of these words originally implied a completion or fulfilment of the artefact or other object in question; that to 'decorate' an object or person originally meant to endow the object or person with its or his 'necessary accidents', with a view to proper operation; and that the aesthetic senses of the words are secondary to their practical connotation. Whatever was originally necessary to the completion of anything, and thus proper to it, naturally giving pleasure to the user; until still later what had once been essential to the nature of the object came to be regarded as an 'ornament' that could be added to it or omitted at will; until, in other words, the art by which the thing itself had been made whole began to mean only a sort of millinery or upholstery that covered over a body that had not been made by 'art' but rather by 'labour'... Without going into further detail, it can easily be seen what was once the meaning of an 'adornment', viz, the furnishing of anything essential to the validity of

whatever is 'adorned', or enhances its effect, empowering it. For example: 'The mind is adorned (alamkriyate) by learning, folly by vice, elephants by mast, rivers by water, night by the moon, resolution by composure, kingship by leading.[122]

It ensues that, through the use of Ornaments, the ornamented individual (or space) acquires specific characteristics, which are representative of his rank or of the sacredness of a place:

Whatever is unornamented is said to be 'naked'. God, 'taken naked of all ornament' is 'unconditioned' or 'unqualified' (nirguna): one, but inconceivable. Ornamented, He is endowed with qualities (saguna), which are manifold in their relations and intelligible. And however insignificant this qualification and this adaptation to finite effects may be when contrasted with His unity and infinity, the latter would be incomplete without them. In the same way, a person or thing apart from its appropriate ornaments ('in the subject or externally adapted to it') is valid as an idea, but not as species. Ornament is related to its subject as individual nature to essence: to abstract is to denature. Ornament is adjectival; and in the absence of any adjective, nothing referred to by any noun could have an individual existence, however it might be in principle. If, on the other hand, the subject is inappropriately or over-ornamented, so far from completing it, this restricts its efficiency, and therefore its beauty, since the extent to which it is in act is the extent of its existence and the measure of its perfection as such-and-such a specified subject. Appropriate ornament is, then, essential to utility and beauty: in saying this, however, it must be remembered that ornament may be 'in the subject' itself, or if not, must be something added to the subject in order that it may fulfil a given function.[123]

To return to the parallelism with Freemasonry, a Lodge would be 'naked' without its Ornaments, as it would be deprived of the elements which make it complete from a sacred and initiatic viewpoint; for this reason, the *act* of decorating a Lodge should be understood as an *action* intended to provide it with its full potential. Indeed, without its Ornaments (Mosaic Pavement, Blazing Star and Indented Border), without its *cosmological* value, the Lodge would, simply, be unable to exist.

Coomaraswamy's considerations on another founding element of the perennialist doctrine, the concept *of metaphysics*, for the most part correspond to those previously encountered when discussing Guénon:

The metaphysical doctrine simply contrasts time as a continuum with the eternity that is not in time and so cannot properly be called everlasting, but coincides with the real present or now of which temporal experience is impossible. Here confusion only arises because for any consciousness

> functioning in terms of time and space, 'now' succeeds 'now' without interruption, and there seems to be an endless series of nows, collectively adding up to 'time'...In any case, any division of the continuity of time into a series of immobile instants would be just as artificial as a division of a line into a series of points: one might as well think of time as a thing created by the jerky motion of the hands of a clock.[124]

In the same way as Guénon, Coomaraswamy also adopted a metaphysical approach in which the concepts of Space and Time inevitably became relative, the notion of a linear interpretation of Time being replaced by a cyclical representation, and Time interpreted as an 'Eternal Return'.

To return to his theories of art, Coomaraswamy depicted himself as the guardian of a traditional philosophy of art, i.e. the doctrine handed down to us in the exemplified forms of works from the Middle Ages and the East, in all his writings. In the framework of this traditional interpretation, a purely *aesthetic*, i.e. *disinterested*, contemplation of the work of art would be unconceivable and contradictory. According to Coomaraswamy, the aim of a work of art should be to transmit a significance to the observer, who should then acknowledge and elaborate the same; indeed, to achieve a full comprehension of the art of a population and a civilisation, it is essential to understand the *spirit* which moves and compenetrates this civilisation by empathising with it:

> We do not have the special modern and aesthetic or sentimental concept of art in mind, but that Platonic and once universally human point of view on which 'art' is the principle of manufacture and nothing but the science of the making of any things whatever for man's good use, physical and metaphysical.[125]

Coomaraswamy was also extremely argumentative towards some of the concepts that underlie the basis of the typical Western self-righteousness, such as the widely used, and abused, term 'tolerance':

> We are, in proposing to teach about other peoples, faced with the problem of tolerance. The word is not a pretty one: to tolerate is to put up with, endure, or suffer the existence of what are or appear to be other ways of thinking than our own...Tolerance is a merely negative virtue, demanding no sacrifice of spiritual pride and involving no abrogation of our sense of superiority; it can be commended only in so far as it means that we shall refrain from hating or persecuting others who differ or seem to differ from ourselves in habit or belief. Tolerance still allows us to pity those who differ from ourselves, and are consequently to be pitied! Tolerance, carried further, implies indifference, and becomes intolerable. Our proposal is not that we should tolerate heresies, but rather come to some agreement about the truth. Our proposition is that the

> proper objective of an education in comparative religion should be to enable the pupil to discuss with other believers the validity of particular doctrines, leaving the problem of the truth or falsity, superiority or inferiority, of whole bodies of doctrine in abeyance.[126]

As we have seen, one of the concepts frequently used by Coomaraswamy to describe the creation of a work of art, also appears to be a recurring theme in the various doctrines of the perennialist thought: i.e. intellectual intuition. Only through intellectual intuition, or imagination, will art be able to reveal to us the side of reality that we are not usually allowed to perceive and that only the artist can offer us access to through his *intuition*:

> A real art is one of symbolic and significant representation; a representation of things that cannot be seen except by the intellect. In this sense art is the antithesis of what we mean by visual education, for this has in view to tell us what things that we do not see, but might see, look like.[127]

Unfortunately, as remarked by Coomaraswamy, this intuitive ability no longer characterises the modern artist; despite the fact that the latter presents his art as being derived from, or inspired by, 'primitive' art, the affinities are, in fact, purely superficial. Modern art, therefore, reveals itself to be no more than a mere mannerism with nothing to do with the 'metaphysical' approach of the primitive artist. In Coomaraswamy's opinion, the main culprit in this degeneration is the introduction of a word which somewhat changed the approach to works of art, namely *aesthetics*:

> We shall have to begin by discarding the term *aesthetic* altogether, for these arts were not produced for the delectation of the senses. The Greek original of this modern word means nothing but sensation or reaction to external stimuli; the sensibility implied by the word aìsthesis is present in plants, animals, and man; it is what the biologist calls 'irritability'. These sensations, which are the passions or emotions of the psychologist, are the driving forces of instinct... Aesthetic experience is of the skin you love to touch, or the fruit you love to taste. 'Disinterested aesthetic contemplation' is a contradiction in terms and a pure non-sense.[128]

On the contrary, Coomaraswamy believed that art should not represent a merely physical but also an intellectual virtue, and that the concept of beauty should necessarily be associated with that of knowledge and ethics; the function of a work of art, in fact, should not simply limit itself to the attraction it produces in the observer but rather communicate with him.

To conclude his argument, Coomaraswamy discusses the main objective of a work of art, and of those who create it within a traditional civilisation:

> There can be no doubt about the purpose of art in a traditional society: when it has been decided that such and such a thing should be made, it is *by art* that it can be properly made. 'There can be no good use without art'; that is, no good use if things are not properly made. The artist is producing a utility, something to be used. Mere pleasure is not a use from this point of view... Our 'aesthetic' appreciation, essentially sentimental because it is just what the word aesthetic means, a kind of feeling rather than an understanding, has little or nothing to do with their raison d'être. It is luxurious to make mantelpiece ornaments of the artefacts of what we term uncivilised or superstitious peoples, whose culture we think of as much inferior to our own, and which our touch has destroyed...Manufacture, the practise of an art, is thus not only the production of utilities but in the highest possible sense the education of men. It can never be, unless for the sentimentalist who lives for pleasure, an 'art for art's sake', that is to say a production of 'fine' or 'useless' objects.[129]

We shall now briefly take a step back to the essay by Monastra mentioned at the beginning of the present paragraph, particularly with regard to Arturo Schwarz's opinion as quoted in the Preface to the Italian edition of Coomaraswamy's *Introduction to Indian Art*. According to Schwarz, Coomaraswamy's esoteric teachings have their roots in the collective unconscious of man, a statement that did not meet with Monastra's approval:

> This is as false as it gets, clearly the result of an approximate and general interpretation. Coomaraswamy, on the contrary, had explicitly explained that the dimension of the 'superconscience', from which esoteric knowledge derives, 'cannot in any way be associated to the subconscious of modern psychology', whose 'inferior' status he, and Guénon, acknowledged. It is no coincidence, in fact that he also criticised C. G. Jung's psychological reductionism.'[130]

To this regard, I shall now provide some clarifications: as we will see in the next chapter, Jungian doctrines are regarded as being almost heretical in the field of modern psychology, his rift with Freud and the underlying motive being a well-known fact in the field. Moreover, although the notion of metaphysical vision cannot in any way be referred to Jung, his concept of 'collective unconscious' (latent traces from an individual's ancestral past, a psychic residue of man's evolutionary process) has nothing to do with the concept of personal subconscious, a notion which, at any rate, was dismissed after the birth of the psychoanalytical theories due to its vagueness and ambiguousness. It should moreover be borne in mind that the Jungian theory of Active Imagination, an intuition for images, is precisely the instrument by means of which the artist is provided with the opportunity to conceive a work of art in the manner and with the dynamics expressed by Coomaraswamy himself. To this regard, the above-mentioned Monastra subsequently pointed out that 'art, always impersonal, should portray archetypes, never copy objects, thus becoming the copy of a copy; in other works, it should embody ideas, not idealise facts'[131]; at this point we wonder, which instruments should an artist use to access these *archetypes*? Jung's Active Imagination, as we will observe in the next chapter, is exactly one of these instruments.

Frithjof Schuon

Another great exponent of the perennialist current, who we will present in this brief and, due to the limited space available, incomplete overview, is the Swiss philosopher and mystic Frithjof Schuon. Schuon was, perhaps, the individual who, more than all other Perennialists, devoted himself to trying to prove the existence of timeless metaphysical Truths which transcended the establishment of the various religions; these metaphysical principles were by him referred to as *Religio Perennis*, which was discussed in countless writings, and subsequently translated into numerous languages. When speaking about one of these writings, *The Transcendent Unity of Religions*, Nobel Prize winner T. S. Eliot observed: 'I have met with no more impressive work in the comparative study of Oriental and Occidental religion.'

According to Schuon, the 'transcendent unity of religions' should not be sought in terms of faith or ideas, but rather in terms of metaphysical symbols; it is indeed precisely through a metaphysical homogeneity and concurrence that traditions pertaining to Buddhism, Christianity, Islam, etc., come together and merge into a single trans-religious mind. For this reason, the sources from which the Religio Perennis originated would not only include sacred Scriptures but also writings by the great spiritual masters. To this regard, Schuon wrote:

> The term philosophia perennis, which has been current since the time of the Renaissance and of which neo-scholasticism made much use, signifies the science of the primordial and universal ontological principles; a science as unchanging as these principles, primordial due to its universality and infallibility. Perhaps it would be better to speak of a sophia perennis, since it is not a question of artificial mental constructions, generating from ignorance, doubt and conjectures, even from the excitement for novelty and originality, as is too often the case in philosophy, or we could use the term religio perennis to refer to the operative side, the mystic or initiatic aspect, of this knowledge. In order not to forget this aspect, and to point out that universal and primordial knowledge requires a full commitment from man, we chose the title 'Religio Perennis' for the book; this also served to demonstrate that the quintessential element of every religion is to be found in this metaphysical religion, which one has to know if he desires to be aware of the simultaneously human and divine mystery represented by the religious phenomenon.[132]

Said metaphysics mainly expresses itself by means of symbols: 'Symbolism is the primordial language, that of sophia perennis.'[133]

As mentioned previously, Schuon recurrently discussed in his writings the meaning of the term 'Religio Perennis', and is perhaps the perennialist thinker who elaborated it more clearly than the others:

> If it were necessary or useful to prove the Absolute, the objective and transpersonal character of the human, Intellect would be a sufficient testimony, for this Intellect is the indisputable sign of a purely spiritual first Cause, a Unity infinitely central but containing all things, an Essence at once immanent and transcendent. It has been said more than once that total Truth is inscribed in an eternal script in the very substance of our spirit. What the different Revelations do is to 'crystallise' and 'actualise', in different degrees according to the case, a nucleus of certitudes that not only abides forever in the divine Omniscience, but also sleeps by refraction in the 'naturally supernatural' kernel of the individual, as well as that of each ethnic or historical collectivity of the human species as a whole.[134]

Schuon's reference to the existence of a 'naturally supernatural kernel' in the ethnic or historical collectivity of the human species, of a 'nucleus of certitudes' with references to this Religio Perennis, that is, to Tradition, is particularly interesting as it strongly resembles Jung's concept of the collective unconscious and biologist Rupert Sheldrake's 'morphogenetic fields', which will be discuss in the following chapters. The symbolic representation of Religio Perennis, the symbology of the 'Centre', which we will discuss extensively in one of the next chapters, is illustrated by Schuon in his book *Light on the Ancient Worlds*, as follows: 'Truth can expand and differentiate indefinitely, but it is also contained in a 'geometrical point'; grasping this point is everything, whatever the symbol – or symbolism – that in fact brings about intellection.'[135] The above reference is particularly significant in terms of the (esoteric and metaphysical) interpretation provided by Freemasonry, which we will examine in this book. It is an acknowledged fact that one of the most important symbols in Masonic rituality is, indeed, represented by the 'Point within a Circle': if the Point within a Circle represents the, single, Truth, the 'Parts of the Circumference equidistant to the Centre' are nothing other than its single historical representations. For this reason, to refer to Freemasonry as 'Deist', 'Theist', or, even worse, 'Relativist' is tantamount to not appreciating the metaphysical essence of Truth as interpreted by the Masonic doctrine, a Truth which is symbolically represented, it should once again be underlined, by a Point, or Centre, (the Sophia Perennis) within a Circle, whose every part (the single Religions) is equidistant from the Centre. The concept is elaborated by Schuon as follows:

> Truth is one, and it would be vain to refuse to look for it except in one

> particular place, for the Intellect contains in its substance all that is true, and truth cannot but be manifested wherever the Intellect is deployed in the atmosphere of a Revelation. Space can be represented by a circle as well as by a cross, a spiral, a star, or a square; and just as it is impossible for there to be only one figure to represent the nature of space or extension, so it is also impossible for there to be only one doctrine giving an account of the Absolute and of the relations between the contingent and the Absolute.[136]

As mentioned previously, Schuon regards the Vedanta philosophy as the purest form of esotericism; his acceptance of this doctrine, and of the caste system as a natural consequence of the same, reveals, as previously observed also with Guénon and Coomaraswamy, Schuon's elitist interpretation of Tradition:

> The pure and direct nature of the Vedanta metaphysics would be unimaginable without the caste system; transcendent intellectuality in India enjoys total freedom, whereas the same intellectuality in other traditions is obliged to adapt to more or less enigmatic or even 'tortuous' esoteric expressions, and often also to certain sentimental constraints; this is the price for the simplification of the social context. In Semitic religions, esoterism supports exoterism, and viceversa; the absence of castes forcedly leads to a certain mental uniformity which causes no fewer inconveniences, from a purely metaphysical perspective, than those caused by the caste system in terms of imponderable human factors; exoterism often lapses into esoterism, whence a pendular movement between these two levels... Wherever there exists a characterised esoterism, esoterism cannot help but walk on exoteric 'stilts', even though it represents the essence of truth, which surpasses forms and incidentally breaks them.[137]

Schuon's exclusivist vision could not be clearer, the 'mass' is excluded from the search for Truth, the latter being is the exclusive prerogative of an elected few:

> It should not be forgotten that the collectivity represents a principle of condensation and complication: it often provides facts with an absolute value and it is this tendency that is considered a priori by religious dogmatism. If esoterism can instill some of its mysteries and its graces in the mass, the mass will reward it – in so far as esoterism gives itself to the mass – with its 'condensing' and, at the same time, 'dispersing' tendencies, whence a doctrinal simplification and a longing for outward activities which are the antipodes of intellection and contemplation.[138]

As mentioned, one of the recurring themes of the perennialist current is the use of the term 'metaphysical' in connection with anything regarding Tradition, which gave rise to a sharp contrast, as already witnessed with Guénon, between metaphysics and philosophy. In the preface to *The Transcendent Unity of Religions*, Schuon informs us that:

> This book is founded on a doctrine that is metaphysical in the most precise meaning of the word and cannot by any means be described as philosophical. Such a distinction may appear unwarrantable to those who are accustomed to regard metaphysic as a branch of philosophy, but the practice of linking the two together in this manner, although it can be traced back to Aristotle and the Scholastic writers who followed him, merely shows that all philosophy suffers from certain limitations that exclude a completely adequate appreciation of metaphysics. In reality, the transcendent character of metaphysic makes it independent of any purely human mode of thought. In order to define clearly the difference between the two modes in question, it may be said that philosophy proceeds from reason (which is a purely individual faculty), whereas metaphysic proceeds exclusively from the Intellect. The latter faculty has been defined Meister Eckhart – who fully understood the import of his words – as follows: 'There is something in the soul that is uncreated and uncreatable; if the whole soul were this it would be uncreated and uncreatable; and this is the Intellect.[139]

A similar - yet even more concise and symbolically representative - definition can also be found in Islamic esotericism: 'The Sufi (that is to say man identified with the Intellect) is uncreated.'

Because of its super-individual nature, intellectual knowledge, which derives from pure Intelligence, is thus projected beyond the individual; it exceeds his ratiocinating intelligence, and likewise goes beyond his idea of faith in the general sense of the word. Indeed, whereas religion is based on the Revelation, an indirect and passive dynamic emanating from God and subsequently transmitted to man through his Word, intellectual intuition allows for a *direct* and *active* participation of man in the discovery of the Divine. Through intellectual intuition, an individual can therefore, obtain an identity between the knower and the known, as he is no longer differentiated from his Divine Principle.

Schuon's notion of Tradition, implicit in the transcendent unity of religions, implies that this unity is based on a purely metaphysical vision of the nucleus that these religions are influenced from, because:

> The unity of the different religions is not only unrealizable on the external level, that of the forms themselves, but ought not to be realised at that level, even were this possible, for in that case the revealed forms would be deprived of their sufficient reason. The very fact that they are revealed shows that they are willed by the Divine Word. If the expression 'transcendent unity' is used,

> it means that the unity of the religious forms must be realised in a purely inward and spiritual way and without prejudice to any particular form.[140]

In 1932, Schuon travelled to Algeria and met the renowned Shaykh Ahmad al-Alawi, who initiated him into his *tariqa*, a Sufi confraternity. It is doubtful whether he later actually became a *moqadden* or even a Sheik (Master), as it appears that al-Alawi himself had only authorised him to transmit elementary teachings of Islam and not to personally initiate other disciples, which Schuon most likely did regardless. These are presumably the reasons that caused, from 1947, a rift in his relationship with Guénon. Whereas the French thinker continued to abide by sapiential instructions, Schuon did not limit himself to initiate (already violating his Master's teachings) new disciples, but he also expected to indoctrinate them with his own personal, somewhat syncretistic vision, insomuch as he was accused of blasphemy by Sheik Nuh-Keller, a successor of Al-Alawi's. Schuon certainly also relished the opportunity to teach his doctrines to Christian believers, whilst his vision of Islam was characterised by a remarkable tolerance towards its rituals and obligations, such as fasting during the month of Ramadan. The syncretism of his doctrine became particularly evident especially during the meditation exercises, in which Islamic rituals were alternated with Taoist and Christian elements. According to Guénon, this would have only contributed to compromising the purity of the Islamic doctrine.

Guénon first took a stance on the matter in the essay 'The Necessity of Traditional Exoterism' (published by *Edizioni Studi Tradizionali* in October-November 1947). In this paper, the author displayed his outright aversion to the possibility of syncretism between different Traditions, and to the idea of experimenting with an esotericism that bears no connections to the current exoteric traditional form. Guénon, indeed, believed that the release of esotericism from its original religious form, which would have subsequently implied its birth in a profane environment, could potentially transform it, or let it degenerate, into occultism. According to the French thinker, true esotericism is inextricably linked to its corresponding exoterism, with which it constitutes the true traditional form. In said traditional form, esotericism represents the inner aspect (core) which can only be accessed through the external aspect (or shell).

Many years later, Schuon clearly expressed his contrasting opinion on the matter in an essay entitled 'The Limitations of Exoterism', included in *The Transcendent Unity of Religions*, an excerpt of which is quoted below. The paper highlights how Schuon's and Guénon's views had drifted further apart over the years:

> One must not confuse the function of the exoteric viewpoint as such with the function of exoterism as a spiritual means: the viewpoint in question is incompatible, in one and the same consciousness, with esoteric knowledge, for the latter dissolves this viewpoint as a preliminary to reabsorbing it into the centre from which it came; but the exoteric means do not for that reason

> cease to be utilisable, and will, in fact, be used in two ways: on the one hand, by intellectual transposition into the esoteric order – in which case they will act as supports of intellectual 'actualisation'; and on the other hand, by their regulating action on the individual portion of the being... The exoteric claim to the exclusive possession of a unique truth, or of Truth without epithet, is therefore an error purely and simply; in reality, every expressed truth necessarily assume a form, that of its expression, and it is metaphysically impossible that any form should possess a unique value to the exclusion of other forms...The foregoing can be summed up in the following formula: pure and absolute Truth can only be found beyond all its possible expressions; these expressions, as such, cannot claim the attributes of this Truth; their relative remoteness from it is expressed by their differentiation and multiplicity, by which they are strictly limited.[141]

Several years later, in his book *Esoterism as Principle and as Way,* Schuon returned to the topic to underline those, which, according to him, were the limits of exoterism:

> Exoteric salvation consists in establishing an individual human subject, or the incorruptible soul of the divine Object, so to speak; esoteric salvation for its part is the reintegration in divine Subjectivity of the intellectual human subject; this second mode of salvation – the deliverance (moksha) of the Vedantists – implies the first mode, for man as such can never become God. Certainly, the immutable substance of man, which coincides with the Supreme Self, is liberated from the accident of the ego; but it does not destroy it, any more than the reality of God does not prevent the existence of the world...We could say, simplifying a little, that exoterism puts the form – the credo – above the essence – Universal Truth – and accepts the latter only as a function of the former; the form, through its divine origin, is here the criterion of the essence. Esoterism, on the contrary, puts the essence above the form and only accepts the latter as a function of the former; for esoterism, and in accordance with the real hierarchy of values, the essence is the criterion of the form; the one and universal Truth is the criterion of the various religious forms of the Truth... For exoterism, appearances have little importance, unless it be that Revelation and Tradition concern themselves with them to a certain degree; for pure esoterism, on the contrary, appearances have all the importance that results from their nature on the one hand, and from the nature of man on the other.[142]

The definitive break between Guénon and Schuon became apparent after the publication by Schuon of an article entitled 'Christic Mysteries', in which he maintained that all Christian sacraments (particularly Baptism and Confirmation) had preserved an initiatic value, proposing a parallelism between the Lesser and Greater Mysteries, and therefore attributing all Christians the role of Initiates, who were not however fully aware of their status due to a lack of appropriate teachings. Guénon's opinion on the matter differed greatly, as he believed that the esoteric element had already been completely lost in Christianity, or alternatively it was so well hidden that it had become virtually inaccessible; only the exoteric element remained, and, accordingly, it would have been inaccurate to discuss the existence of a Christian esotericism.

Compared to the other founder of the perennialist current, Coomaraswamy, it can be observed that the two thinkers displayed both conformity and divergence of opinion on a number of topics, particularly with regard to the interpretation of works of art. Conformity can undoubtedly be witnessed with regard to the *atemporal* condition of works of art, a conformity which manifests itself in Schuon's criticism of the modern world and contemporary mentality, which was dealt with in the typical perennialist style:

> The mentality of today seeks in fact to reduce everything to categories connected with time: a work of art, a thought, a truth have no value in themselves and independently of any historical classification, but their value is always related to the time in which they are rightly or wrongly placed; everything is considered as the expression of a 'period' and not as having a timeless and intrinsic value; and this is entirely in conformity with modern relativism, and with a psychologist or biologist that destroys essential values.[143]

Schuon's viewpoint differs from Coomaraswamy's on the subject of *aesthetics*, which was scorned upon by the Ceylonese historian:

> As a general rule form takes precedence over aesthetic expression, since the normative character of form, hence its regularity of substance and proportions, constitutes the prime condition of aesthetic value; for wherever harmony or balance are lacking in the form itself, beauty of expression no longer appears as a decisive factor on the level of sensible beauty, for this level is by definition that of formal perfection or truth in form.[144]

As illustrated previously, Schuon was also highly critical of modern and contemporary society, which he held responsible for the diffusion of disenchantment in the world. The main reason for this existential tragedy which overwhelms the contemporary man is a disconnection from and a forgetting of his divine nature; because of this he desacralised his existence and lost sight of the ultimate Principles of his being:

> Independently of doctrinal atheism and of cultural peculiarities, modern man moves in the world as if Existence were nothing, or as if he had invented it; in his eyes it is a commonplace thing like the dust beneath his feet – more

> especially as he has no consciousness of the Principle at once transcendent and immanent – and he makes use of it with assurance and inadvertence in a life that has been de-consecrated into meaninglessness.[145]

Julius Evola.

Julius Evola's interpretation of the meaning of the word Tradition strongly resembles, albeit with significant differences, the vision held by the founder of Perennialism, René Guénon.

Similarly to Guénon, Evola, in his writings, consistently reiterated the metaphysical connotation of Tradition, based on principles featuring a 'superior legitimacy', and therefore incontestable. These principles are meta-historical due to the fact that, despite being manifested in a specific social context, their deepest essence will never be fully revealed by the latter:

> Tradition, in its essence, is something simultaneously meta-historical and dynamic: it is an overall ordering force, in the service of principles that have the chrism of a superior legitimacy (we may even call them 'principles from above'). This force acts through the generations, in continuity of spirit and inspiration, through institutions, laws, and social orders that may even display a remarkable variety and diversity...Even where these principles are objectified in a historical reality, they are not at all conditioned by it; they always point to a higher, meta-historical plane, which is their natural domain and where there is no change. The ideas that I call 'traditional' must be thought of along the same lines.[146]

Whereas for Guénon, Tradition represented essentially an ensemble of metaphysical principles rather than a form destined to operate in history, Evola, though identifying with the transcendent unity of the various Traditions, considered Tradition as an immanent form of every historical cycle, which transmits spiritual values destined to influence the evolution of the human cycle, and which is represented by the *élites* of the communities in which it is detected.

According to Evola, Tradition thus constituted a 'force from above' which was manifested by bestowing spiritual and super-individual values on human assemblies, the *transmission* of an invisible and formative energy revealed in the course of a constructive and educational *action*. It is precisely this concrete action, which allowed it to confer a superior significance and legitimacy to the social forms by which it was adopted.

In addition to the metaphysical aspect, Evola also highlighted a second, significant, esoteric and doctrinal aspect of Tradition; in this instance, clear reference was made to the 'transcendent unity of the various Traditions', Traditions which, by virtue of the existence of a unique *Sophia Perennis,* could be of a religious, sapiential or mystical nature.

It was Evola's belief that, historically, Tradition had existed in two forms, a primordial Hyperborean or Nordic-Western Tradition, which included the entire group of Indo-European traditional civilisations, and a Tradition that involved the culture of the Far East.[147] The transmission of traditional doctrines, in Evola's opinion, had been undertaken and was feasible solely through the authentic Sapiential Schools, as it is only through the latter that an actual initiation can be achieved. For this reason, realities not based on the authentic principles of Tradition were seen by Evola as neo-spiritualist *pseudo-organisations*; as mentioned in the previous chapter, the most renowned among the latter, the Theosophical Society, was the object of harsh criticism by Evola and Guénon.

In the same way as Guénon, Evola was also critical of psychoanalytical thought, accused of focussing on the unconscious (both in the individual, Freudian form and the collective, Jungian one), thus neglecting or underestimating the potential of the conscious personality, but, above all, guilty of approaching the unconscious without adequately *structuring* one's own I first, thus running the risk of providing access into the individual conscience to latent and lurking 'demonic' forces. Moreover, Evola deemed unacceptable the Psychoanalytical notion of extending theories developed by means of experiments on the mentally ill to psychiatrically healthy individuals.

As regards Jung's theories, Evola furthermore underlined that the Swiss scholar used oniric visions brought to light by the collective unconscious as means to analyse symbols and myths which belong to the world of the superconscious, as depicted in the old sapiential writings, and to compare the 'individuation process', created to achieve the recovery of psychically unstable people, with the 'initiation process', which implies a total transformation of the being compared to the common man.

It should, however, be clarified that Jung's individuation process was not conceived by Jung exclusively for use with the mentally ill and that, above all, as we will see in the next chapter, Jung's studies were not based merely on psychiatric disorders but also on the visions (Active Imagination) and dreams of perfectly healthy people. It should also be borne to mind, with regard to the accusation of a poor *structuration* of the I, that Jung seemingly preferred the method of Active Imagination to that of dreams, as in the latter case, during the transcendent function, the conscious Ego is asleep and is therefore not able to interact (whence Evola's criticism) in an equal manner with the unconscious. Based on the Jungian theory, the transcendent function is capable of operating at full capacity only when in the presence of sufficient tension between the two opposites; for this reason, the Ego, the I, has to be fully awake and capable of standing its ground when interacting with the images of the unconscious. The image generated by the unconscious, in fact, necessarily has to interact with the Ego by creating the tension necessary for the execution of the transcendent function. The accusation of a poor structuration of the I in Jung's theories is therefore refuted by the method of Active Imagination in which the Ego is not subjugated but fully awake and functional, as it interprets and experiences the contents generated by the unconscious. The I, therefore, is not a *passive* element which suffers the consequences of a process, but rather an active player which elaborates the experience produced by the imagination, gaining benefits that will result in a superior structuration.

Amongst all his works on Tradition, in *Revolt against the Modern World*, published in 1934, Evola offered circumstantial criticism to the modern Western society by drawing inspiration from Guénon's *The Crisis of the Modern World*; the latter and other works by the French traditionalist will guide and direct Evola thus allowing him to form his own personal notion of Tradition. In *Revolt Against the Modern World*, Evola highlighted how the idea of a differentiation between a superior state of *being*, placed in a metaphysical context, and an inferior state of *becoming*, located in a purely physical context, was progressively lost over time, previously representing an essential concept, or rather vision of the world, for man living in a traditional society, but nowadays forgotten and absent from the individual lifestyle in the current materialistic society. In the light of the above, Evola constantly strived to underline the evident contrast between a transcendent, supersensitive, invisible, essentially initiatic reality to which the man from Traditional civilisations belonged, and the immanent, sensitive, tangible, substantially profane society into which the modern individual had sunk.

Similarly to Guénon, in *The Crisis of the Modern World*, Evola attempted to highlight how the authentic *Tradition* had previously represented, both in the East and the West, a central and essential principle around which the religious, political, social and cultural hierarchies present in these traditional societies revolved; in a civilisation thus structured, the principles on which Tradition was based granted man the possibility of spiritual transformation, moving from the inferior to the superior level.

In the first part of *Revolt against the Modern World* entitled *The World of Tradition*, the author carried out a comparative analysis of different civilisations, different myths and human institutions, in an attempt to demonstrate which are the universal categories and elements making up Tradition, such as regality, priesthood, the law, the empire, the masculine principle of spirit, chivalry, the caste system, and initiation.

In the second part of the book, entitled *Genesis and Face of the Modern World*, Evola illustrated how the latter was mainly characterised by a loss of transcendence, anthropomorphisation and by the secularisation of religion and politics, including the deriving phenomena of decadence, including: the inversion of the traditional order with the revival of castes, the extreme yet complementary equalisation of collectivism and individualism, the technological-economic-industrial colonisation of the planet carried out in equal measure by Bolshevism and Americanism, but likewise a decline of the principle of aristocratic sovereignty, determining a shift of power from spiritual aristocracy to the amorphous masses created by consumerist materialism. These processes of decadence were placed by Evola within a framework of historical metaphysics which he shaped on the foundations of the traditional doctrine of the four ages: the golden, silver, bronze and iron ages, based on the Greco-Roman tradition, or Satya-Yuga, Treta-Yuga, Dvapara-Yuga and Kali-Yuga, based on the Indian doctrine. According to Evola, evidently influenced by Guénon, man is currently living in the 'dark age' (Kali-Yuga), an age in which antitraditional forces have gained the upper hand and are leading the West towards decline and destruction.[148]

Contrary to Spengler, who deterministically believed this dynamic to be unstoppable and cyclical, Evola regarded this decadence as the result of a development process historically started by man himself. A rediscovery of Tradition appeared to be the only solution to interrupt this process. Whereas, in theory, this would still be possible today, seeing how Tradition continued to exist irrespective of revolutions and historical turmoil, guarded by spiritual élites who have constantly revived and reawakened it after periods of obscuration, the intervention of the selected few aimed at achieving recovery of the traditional spirit and principles is quite simply no longer possible, thus, the sole viable alternative is to wait in anticipation of a more appropriate time. The only feasible option is to 'ride the tiger', to allow the selected few to maintain the centre and be on hand to come into play when circumstances allow. In the words of Evola:

> Tradition begins wherever it is possible to rise above these notions by achieving a superindividual and nonhuman perspective; thus, I will have a minimal concern for debating and 'demonstrating'. The truths that may reveal the world of Tradition are not those that can be 'learned' or 'discussed'; either they are or they are not...Let me repeat that in every ancient persuasion, traditional truths have always been regarded as nonhuman. Any consideration from a nonhuman perspective, which is 'objective' in a transcendent sense, is a traditional consideration that should be made to correspond to the traditional world...Those who begin from a particular traditional civilisation and are able to integrate it by freeing it from its historical and contingent species, and thus bring back the generative principles to the metaphysical plane where they exist in a pure state, so to speak – they cannot help but recognise these same principles behind the different expressions of other equally traditional civilisations...Thus what I call 'traditional method' is usually characterised by a double principle: ontologically and objectively by the principle of correspondence, which ensures an essential and functional correlation between analogous elements, presenting them as simple homologous forms of the appearance of a central and unitary meaning; and epistemologically and subjectively by the generalised use of the principle of induction, which is here understood as a discursive approximation of a spiritual intuition, in which what is realised is the integration and the unification of the diverse elements encountered in the same one meaning and in the same one principle.[149]

Once again, in *Revolt against the Modern World,* Evola elaborated on the concept of regality, one of the themes which best distinguished him from Guénon. The earliest forms of Tradition, in Evola's opinion, were not characterised by a separation between temporal power and spiritual authority; indeed, the latter originally provided the foundations and legitimated the former. Although the two powers, temporal and sacerdotal, were later synthetised in the figure of the consecrated king, Evola believed, unlike Guénon, that regality would unfailingly have gained supremacy over priesthood. The Middle Ages, during the Holy Roman Empire, witnessed the final act of the dispute between the universality of the Church and the notion of incarnated regality, which bestowed the title of *caput ecclesiae* upon the Emperor, thus providing the latter with the opportunity to replace and perform the tasks of the sacerdotal caste. The Emperor, therefore, came to simultaneously represent the chief of the kingdom and of the Church, claiming to have been invested by God, rather than by the Pope, with the right to govern humanity, with God being the only entity he recognised as being above him. Despite his role in the consecration of the Emperor, the head of the sacerdotal hierarchy was, therefore, reduced to simple mediator and found himself unable to revoke, even by means of excommunication, a supernatural force which had already been disseminated and had already entered into operation:

> Every traditional civilisation is characterised by the presence of beings who, by virtue of their innate or acquired superiority over the human condition, embody within the temporal order the living and efficacious presence of a power that comes from above. One of these types of beings is the pontifex, according to the inner meaning of the word and according to the original value of the function that he exercised. Pontifex means 'builder of bridges', or of 'paths' (pons, in ancient times, also meant 'path') connecting the natural and the supernatural dimensions. Moreover, the pontifex was traditionally identified with the king (rex)...The most important foundation of the authority and of the right of kings and chiefs, and the reason they were obeyed, feared and venerated, was essentially their transcendent and nonhuman quality. This quality was not artificial, but a powerful reality to be feared...The root of every temporal power was spiritual authority, which was almost a 'divine nature disguised in human form'. According to an Indo-European view, the ruler is not a 'mere mortal', but rather 'a great deity standing the form of a man'. The kings of Alba and of Rome were supposed to be the incarnations of Zeus; the Assyrian kings, of Baal; the Persian shahs, of the god of light; the Nordic-Germanic princes were believed to derive from the race of Tiuz, of Odin, and of the Aesir. Beyond the variety of mythical and sacred expressions, the recurrent view of kingship is expressed in terms of an 'immanent transcendence' that is present and active in the world. The king – who was believed to be a sacred being and not a man – by virtue of his 'being', was already the centre and the apex of the community. In him was also the

> supernatural strength that made his ritual actions efficacious. In these actions people could recognise the earthly counterpart of supernatural 'ruling', as well as the supernatural support of life in the world of Tradition.[150]

The early 1930s played a crucial role in Evola's formation: indeed, he progressively abandoned his philosophical theories on 'magic idealism' and 'solipsism' to turn his attention to the traditional approach, proposing the restoration of the thought and action of Tradition as the foundation for a new anthropology, gnoseology and, above all, a new action. In several passages of his autobiography *The Path of Cinnabar*, published in 1963, Evola underlined how thanks to the assimilation of the traditional approach, he was able to focus, centre his thought and, more importantly, his own personality. From the perennialist doctrine, and particularly from Guénon, Evola assimilated the principle of a primordial metaphysical Tradition and that of a cyclical decline culminating in the current 'age of darkness' (Kali-Yuga in the Hindu doctrine); within this new mental framework, however, the Roman traditionalist developed his own peculiar doctrine which, as we will see, often failed to coincide with that of Guénon.

One of the themes around which the views of the two traditionalist thinkers diverged significantly, was represented by Christianity as contemplated by the Traditionalist perspective. It is an acknowledged fact that Guénon regarded Christianity as an originally initiatic traditional form, which abandoned the esoteric aspect by virtue of an intentional sacrifice imposed by the providential need to obtain the salvation of a civilisation – that of the late Roman Empire – otherwise destined to perdition due to the extreme degeneration that the Greco-Roman tradition was experiencing, at least among the masses. From Evola's perspective, on the other hand, primitive Christianity represented a tragic doctrine of salvation, addressed to the masses of disinherited and those without tradition, for which it 'affirmed and indicated the alternative of an eternal salvation or eternal perdition to be decided once and for all on this earth'. The latter would have been 'a way to arouse, in certain nature, an extreme tension, which, a type associated to the myth of Jesus as 'Redemptor', could also give its fruits: if not in this life, at least at the point of death or in the post-mortem, that these indirect means acting on the human emotivity could succeed in modifying the basal force of the human being in their depth.' Essentially, whereas for Guénon Christianity was a religion within the Kali-Yuga, which gave up its original elitist approach to save the masses, for Evola, primitive Christianity was a religion of the Kali-Yuga, capable of saving the deprived masses without the intervention of an initiatic *élite*.

For this reason, Evola distanced himself from Christianity and turned his attention to Oriental spirituality, as highlighted in his work *Pagan Imperialism*, dated 1928, in which the author proposed a daring and radical 'pagan restoration':

> Pagan restoration should represent the foundation of a society based on values of hierarchy, organisation from the top, aristocracy, domination and wisdom…

> It should be emphasised that it is necessary to create élites that are so by nature but not by name, in which superiority is not based on power and charge, but power and charge are based on superiority; as far as this superiority is concerned, it should be stressed that the latter should never be reduced, for us, to factors of 'culture', practical prudence, administrative ability and the likes, but it should base itself on a qualitative, substantial and actual differentiation of life. This differentiation should be confirmed and defined according to specific relations of distance in a system which should not be identical, but certainly analogous, to that of the Oriental castes.[151]

In later works such as *Ride the Tiger*, published in 1961, Evola once again addressed the same theories on Tradition previously expressed in *Revolt against the Modern World*, an ongoing contrast between the historical world and the world of Tradition. This antithesis highlighted the difference between action in history and meta-historical action, the former representing for Evola the distinctive mark of the modern world based on the concept of time, having progress as its main objective, whereas the latter, in which 'time' is replaced with the eternal, represents the distinctive mark of Tradition. The old relation with the Myth reappeared in the latter, having taken on a supertemporal and no longer human connotation.

In *Ride the Tiger*, Evola underlines how historical time has imposed itself over the eternal time of Tradition in a clearly degenerative dynamic. Hope however remains: indeed, the world of Tradition has not been completely clouded; it continues to exist, and resist, thanks to a few differentiated, incorruptible individuals, the sole in a position to identify a strategy to overcome this crisis and once again find the Centre.[152]

In his work, *The Bow and the Club* (1968), in an essay entitled 'The Concept of Initiation', Evola addresses the notion of 'high initiation' from a theoretical point of view. He was firmly convinced that a *true* initiation was the indicator of authenticity of a Sapiential School; in this essay, he set out to outline the differences between 'Traditional' initiation – i.e. a radically and ontologically different way of being for man – and pseudo-initiations, such as those practiced by theosophists, anthroposophists and other Neo Spiritualist organisations. The paper had been based on an article entitled *Uber das Initiatische*, first published in 1965 on the German journal *Antaios*, officially (although not actually) edited by Mircea Eliade and Ernst Junger. In the second edition of *The Bow and the Club*, Evola added a further essay on the so-called *initiatic centre*, highlighting how authentic initiation is generally imparted by well concealed and not easily accessible centres, which have become increasingly rare and are nowadays almost impossible to access.

It should be underlined how Evola and Guénon featured radical differences in their consideration of the so-called regular initiation. According to Guénon and his students, regular initiation could only be achieved if the disciple lived, in an exoteric sense, within the framework of one of the great religions of the world, therefore following its commandments; in the French thinker's opinion, an esoteric education alone was, therefore, not sufficient. Evola's opinion on the matter was significantly less strict, as he believed that it was also possible to achieve self-initiation, without affiliation to a specific group or religious community. The divergences between the two ways of thinking were thoroughly analysed by Evola himself in an essay from the 2nd Volume of *Introduction to Magic*, entitled 'On the Limitations of 'Esoteric regularity':

> The view held by Guénon is briefly as follows. Initiation consists in a surpassing of the human condition and in the realisation of improved conditions of self; this is of course impossible to achieve by individual means alone. This could indeed have occurred in the beginning, in the presence of a human race that largely differed from the modern-day model; today however intervention from external sources is required, the transmission on a 'spiritual influence' into the initiate. This transmission is achieved through the performing of rituals and by association to a regular initiatic organisation. These are the baseline conditions, which if not met, in Guénon's opinion, imply the impossibility of a true initiation, allowing merely an empty parody of the latter (a 'pseudo-initiation'). The 'regularity' of an organisation consists in its being associated, either directly or through other centres, to a Sole Supreme Being; moreover, it implies the presence of an uninterrupted chain of transmission assuring continuity in time through living representatives, whilst continuing to recede to reach the 'primordial tradition'. To ensure the actual undertaking of the transmission of spiritual influences affecting initiatic development, it would suffice for rites contemplated to be carried out by individuals regularly appointed for the purpose; whether or not the latter would include the performing of rites, and whether the person concerned believes in their efficacy would be of no effect. Consequently, 'an association with improved conditions of self-established through the transmission of spiritual influences is not necessarily implicit on the reaching of a true state by means of awareness'; particularly, Guénon 'rejects any possibility of an 'ideal' association – as he calls it –with a tradition, by this implying all associations not achieved by means of the above-described rituals or following contact with live, present representatives authorised to convey the tradition. Lastly, a 'spontaneous' initiation is likewise to be excluded.[153]

According to Evola, therefore, the possibility of receiving any kind of initiation from 'degraded' organisations was to be excluded categorically, because 'the continuity of 'spiritual influences' is at its most illusory if worthy and conscious representatives in a given chain no longer exist and transmission has almost become mechanical.[154]

Evola's words reveal his perplexity over a potential initiatic transmission carried out by individuals who are completely unaware of the profound significance of the rituals they use, and his reluctance to accept that initiation can only be achieved through designated organisations, a sort of 'bureaucratisation' of the initiatic path, is equally evident. For this reason, Evola considered it necessary to:

> Place a limit to the insistence of several traditionalist elements as to the inevitability of a 'regular', almost bureaucratic association with organisations for individuals seeking to surpass their limited existence. The fact is that this association may be mandatory for many people, but for an even larger number is not sufficient, thus leading to the legitimate question as to whether all this is truly necessary.[155]

Yet another difference between the two thinkers related to the interpretation and role of contemporary Freemasonry. In 1972, in an article published on the Journal *La Destra*, Evola enunciated the reasons for their disagreement:

> A point of divergence between Guénon's views and mine concerned Freemasonry. *I* acknowledged that original forms of Freemasonry (such as the so-called operative Freemasonry) may have had an initiatic, almost spiritual character. But after, due to its increasing politicization, as in speculative Freemasonry, starting with the establishment of the Grand Lodge of London (1717), Freemasonry assumed a significantly different form and historically carried out an antitraditional action (like one of the societés de pensée it already had to prepare for the French Revolution)...Guénon, on the other hand, recognised in Freemasonry the character of a regular initiatic organisation, perhaps the only one in the West. Although he acknowledged its current degenerescence, because of his formalist viewpoint, he also believed that it had maintained said character.[156]

But, as mentioned previously, Evola's views on Freemasonry were not negatively preconceived, and his criticism was mainly addressed to its modern form (in complete agreement with the Fascist Regime), which, in his opinion, was far removed from its traditional origins. To this regard, in *Pagan Imperialism* Evola explained that:

> The esoteric and initiatic sciences are based on yet another identical tradition (although not specifying whether oriental or western) the origins of which, we must repeat, are lost in the origins of history. By means of hermetism, and a symbolism that is part evangelical (pertaining to 'edification') and part Roman (Collegia Fabrorum), a particular form of the esoteric tradition – leaving out numerous other distinctive forms – was adopted by Freemasonry for the purpose of hermetic, spiritual, in no way extra-political endowment, at least up until the time of the French Revolution. It is indeed quite laughable that the Fascists deemed it necessary to fight against a similar Masonic order, and that biased rumours spread following the puerile behaviour of Bodrero have

> produced such an effect. But once Freemasonry took on the semblance of a political association infected – which came as no surprise! – by social-Christian and Jacobean ideologies, its initiatic element gradually started to wane. As indeed this was the movement so openly opposed by Fascism, it is undeniable that to associate with Freemasonry all that is occult science in order to alarm the Fascists and take advantage of the same, is no more than a trick, which we denounce and admonish.[157]

Furthermore, whereas Guénon had hurled abuse at the English Freemasonry since its inception, Evola identified Masonic degeneration mainly in its continental version, and particularly in the French chapter, which had been subjected to Jacobin political influences and the principles of the French Revolution (which are still today evident in the rituals of the *Grand Orient de France*).

An accomplished example of Tradition in the West was represented, for Evola, by the archaic and imperial Roman World, the approach of which to the divine represented, for the Italian thinker, the highest expression throughout the Nordic-Western world. The idea that Roman Tradition may constitute the true, legitimate tradition of the ancient world was suggested to Evola by the studies and writings of Arturo Reghini, with whom, following an initial friendship, an irreparable rift formed; these are the words with which Evola retraced his troubled relationship with Arturo Reghini:

> Around this time, I met a number of different people. One of these was Arturo Reghini, a curious and most interesting character. A few years older than myself, Reghini was a trueborn Florentine who had once been close to the Lacerba group. Reghini was apparently responsible for Papini's frivolous attempt (described in his autobiographical book) to retire in a secluded place to 'become a god' by means of a condensed two-week initiation course. When I first met Reghini, he had reached the thirty-third degree of Scottish Rite Freemasonry, and had written an impressive volume on the sacred key words employed in the first degree of the sect, on which subject he appeared to possess an uncommon knowledge. A mathematician and philologist, as well as a highly critical mind, Reghini was devoted to the study of initiation with a seriousness and objectiveness unknown to 'occultists' and Theosophists (which were ever the victims of the man's caustic sarcasm). It is thanks to my encounter with Reghini (and, soon after, with Guénon, who Reghini first mentioned to me) that I decidedly broke with what 'occultist' or Theosophical tendencies I still possessed, and came to acknowledge the complete separateness and transcendence of initiatory wisdom... Reghini was fond of the idea of a Western esoteric tradition (which might also be termed an 'Italic' tradition, given Reghini's often problematic references to Pythagorean doctrine). Consequently, Reghini had sought to revive Masonic rites and

> symbols. Reghini also praised 'pagan' Roman culture, which he refused to interpret merely as a political and juridical reality set in a framework of cults and superstitious practices, as was common at the time. Rather, Reghini emphasised the sacred, if not initiatory character of many aspects of Roman culture, and on this basis argued in favour of Roman wisdom and of the Roman view of life and holiness – something he explicitly contrasted with Christianity. Given Reghini's approach, it is clear that his opposition to Christianity was of a very different kind from that of Nietzsche. Reghini argued that Christianity was an exotic belief founded on a dubious spirituality that appealed to the irrational, sub-intellectual and sentimental side of man...What was new in Reghini was his reference to the sacred wisdom and Mystery doctrines that could be accessed by means of a more profound study of Classical Antiquity. Reghini's analysis also contained a strong tendency towards the 'idealisation' of Roman culture, since Roman culture could not have yielded to Christianity, had it not already been undermined by the presence of cults, ideas and tendencies of an equally un-Roman and Asian nature.[158]

Reghini published his article entitled 'Pagan Imperialism', prior to his conflicts with Evola, in *Salamandra* journal in January 1914. As recalled by Roberto Sestito, Reghini had not intended 'Pagan Imperialism' to merely represent the fatigues of an élite preparing for a war of national redemption, but also a means of promoting a true political movement based on the Roman, Dantesque, Campanellian and Pythagorean concepts of the spiritual unity of Italians. The latter movement started to take shape around and within the only secular and Ghibelline 'State party' capable of appreciating it at the time. Its failure was partly due to preconceptions and partly to internal rivalry amongst the Italians.[159] The publication in 1928 of Evola's essay, bearing the same title as Reghini's but significantly different contents, eventually triggered controversies between the two. It is likely, however, that the conflicts between Evola and Reghini dated back to an earlier time; one of the many disagreements between the two thinkers concerned Pythagoreanism, a fundamental element in the doctrine of the Tuscan thinker but an object of open hostility for Evola, which is evident in his introduction to Bachofen's *The Mothers and Olympian Virility* (1949). The Swiss historian observed in Southern Italy the predominance of lunar cults and culture, an idea that was later used by Evola in his criticism to the initiatic Mystery order, which represented the foundation of Hellenic and Pythagorean Esotericism. To this regard Evola maintained that:

> The fact that with Pythagoreanism the maternal principle regained its supremacy and the importance it previously had with the Mysteries is revealed by multiple elements, the most significant of which is the superior position that Pythagoreanism itself attributed to women...an essentially physical and sensitive philosophy, which did invite to the contemplation of supreme divinity

> but all the while preserving a lunar element, without solar clarity – these premises, indeed, prove the congeniality of Pythagoreanism with the feminine nature...After all, just like the moon which is sometimes considered as an extinguished sun, Pythagoreanism can be seen as representing a veiled and undefined profanation of an old Arian (Atlantic-Western) tradition which had spread around the Mediterranean basin, rather than the sublimation of the inferior Tellurism of aboriginal populations.

Several years later in 1959, in an introductory essay to *The Golden Verses of Pythagoras*, he was just as critical, highlighting, incidentally, an interesting parallelism between the Pythagorean and the Masonic symbologies and ritualities:

> The system reproduces the essential structure of every regular initiatic organisation. Pythagorean 'esoterists' used specific signs – ways of greeting and symbols (their most important symbol seemed to be the pentagram) – to recognise each other in Pythagorean centres other than their own and similar organisations. This is a well known characteristic of secret societies, which has preserved itself until modern times (ending its echo with Freemasonry).[160]

As far as his position and his expectations towards the Fascist experience in Italy are concerned, Evola imagined that Fascism itself would have made it possible to return to a traditional representation; in the journal *La Torre*, indeed, Evola declared that he wanted to 'signal to the foreign world the point up to which strict imperial and traditional thought has a chance of survival in Fascist Italy', a thought devoid of any political purpose and which simply reflected his will to defend an idea. It was Evola's belief that Fascism should have risen against civil Europe, reaffirming the Mediterranean tradition and creating an *élite* through which it could once again have experienced the old initiatic and operative wisdom, the only means of achieving the reestablishment of invisible chiefs and a Centre. Fascism should have established the principle of true restoration, which for Evola, was represented by the *Imperium* with a transcendent foundation. This anti-Europe would also have been anti-Christian, particularly as Evola regarded Christianity as venom to the greatness of the Roman Empire and the ultimate cause of decline of the West. It should be underlined that the Christianity Evola refers to does not merely entail survival of the Christian religion, but comprises all degenerative processes featured throughout the modern world, from the Reformation to the French Revolution, anarchism, Bolshevism and the typical modern European society. Christianity represented the great fall of the Roman-Pagan culture, in the same way as the Reformation for the Nordic-Germanic civilisation following the Ghibelline Empire.

Evola contrasted the above with the Mediterranean tradition of Mysteries, which, according to the Roman traditionalist, was transmitted until the present day by means of an uninterrupted and secret chain: 'Anti-Europe means Anti-Christianity. And anti-Christianity consists in the Mediterranean classical, and pagan tradition that is our own.'

In Evola's view, resurgence of this Tradition would have determined the fate of the entire West; for this reason he addressed Mussolini in attempt to restore the pagan tradition within a pagan Empire, pinpointing the identification of the Western Tradition with Christian and Catholic practices as the most vulgar and nefarious mistake. The divergence with Guénon was particularly evident in this instance.

Evola's thesis and traditionalist programme of 1928, essentially likened Rome with paganism, upholding that imperial restoration would be a concept devoid of all significance in the lack of pagan restoration. As mentioned previously, Evola's idea of Tradition was influenced by Guénon, but supported in a way that contradicted Guénon, who believed that the legitimate Western tradition was the Christian and Catholic tradition. Evola denied this concept, affirming how 'Christianity is beyond tradition', not due to a lack of traditional elements, but to the profane pollution of their sources.

Despite having initially found inspiration in Guénon, the two later developed views which were at times in sharp contrast; in the introduction to Guénon's *The Crisis of the Modern World*, Evola himself highlighted their divergence of opinion, as specified in the passage below, which thoroughly describes the respective positions of the two thinkers:

> Guénon's point of view involves the valorisation of a tradition – albeit an august one – not for its reserved and particularistic nature, but for any aspects that may recall the metaphysical contents which, perhaps in other forms, with a higher or lower degree of completeness, can also be observed in any other tradition worthy of the name. It is an esoteric and non-empirical traditionalism...Guénon explicitly claims the primacy of 'knowledge', 'contemplation' and 'pure intellectuality' over action. Can this be accepted without reservations? We believe this is possible only as long as the action that is considered inferior and to be subordinated is the deconsecrated and materialised action, what we would call unrest or fever rather than real action due to its being devoid of any light, any true sense, any principle: in other words, action as it has more or less been conceived by the modern West...The two symbols of contemplation and action have always been related, the former to the priestly, the latter to the warrior. When this has been said we must go back to a teaching that Guénon himself refers to on more than one occasion, i.e., that the two powers merged in an apex that was both royal and sacerdotal. It is only later that the two dignities separated and not infrequently were even in strife...Now, the mindset which characterised Guénon as an individual prevented him from recognising in these terms the consequences of a doctrine

which he himself approved. Whence the non-irreproachability of the theory he defended on the unconditional primacy of intellectuality and contemplation, and the rejection of the possibility that even the world of action (in the traditional, not the modern, sense of the word) may have the potential for reintegration…It is strange that in his many references to traditional civilisations, Guénon practically ignores Japan. This is the result of his personal idiosyncrasy in which the Brahmanical-pure knowledge interpretation predominates with regard to everything traditional. But it is Japan that until yesterday offered us a most interesting example of a civilisation which in externals had been modernised for purposes of defence and offense, nevertheless preserving in its inner essence a millennial tradition; this tradition, which was in some ways akin to that of the Holy Roman Empire, was, however, based mainly on the symbols of action, the warrior caste and regality rather than on the priestly element, with the concept of Order, like a warrior aristocracy integrated with sacred, and, in some cases, initiatic (Zen as well as Shintoism) elements, playing an essential role – in the Samurai caste, which represented the backbone of that tradition…Guénon replaced the East-West antithesis with that between traditional world and modern world. The forms of the traditional world did not diverge significantly in the East and the West, but were equally the direct opposite of modern civilisation. Guénon believes that, due to a series of circumstances, the East still preserves said forms, which have disappeared in the West; this originated his idea that a contact with the East, where the traditional spirit is still alive, would help the West not to lose touch with its itself but rather find itself again and try to revive a traditional form. We would now have to wonder where exactly in the East tradition is actually still alive: China no longer comes within the picture, India nationalistic and Europising trends are steadily gaining ground, the Arab countries are in confusion.[161]

One final, significant difference of opinion between the two great thinkers is represented by alchemy. As mentioned in the previous paragraph, Guénon considerably underrated the alchemical thought by referring to it simply as *cosmology*. Evola, on the contrary, especially in his book *The Hermetic Tradition* from 1931, took the alchemical doctrine extremely seriously and devoted himself to the exegesis of its symbolism from a strictly initiatic perspective, taking the opportunity to reintroduce, in the dynamics of the *opus*, the differences between the two main traditional lines, the regal one, active and virile, opposed to the sacerdotal or ascetic-contemplative line. It is precisely within the framework of alchemical Hermetism that Evola detected the practical, operative instance, the primacy of 'art', and therefore of *action*, 'experimentalism' extended to the spirit. The most common designation of said discipline was already significant: *Ars Regia*, that is, regal art, a special formulation of the initiatic way, characterised by an affirmative orientation that was also 'regal' in a figurative sense, more than contemplative or simply intellectual or sapiential.

3
Karl Jaspers and the 'Philosophia' Perennis

German philosopher Karl Jaspers frequently made use of the term 'Philosophia Perennis' in his writings, with an interpretation that differed, however, from that adhered to by the Perennialist thinkers. Indeed, Jaspers approached the Philosophia Perennis by identifying in it those Principles that are undoubtedly transcendent, but also historically present and historically accessible to those who capable of approaching them through the philosophical faith. The line adopted by Jaspers, implied an interpretation of the world based on the transcendence, or rather, the overcoming of the objectivity of sciences, through a differentiation of the scientific statement, which proposed a representation of the world whose validity could be measured and verified through the intellect, from the philosophical one which originated from the clarification of existence and from metaphysics as a result of transcendence understood as ulteriority:

> Philosophically, transcendence can always be understood historically, and comes to be present only historically. This means, however, that its objective appearance cannot become valid and true for all men. For the revealed faith of religion, on the other hand, transcendence is contained in a historical, unique form that is objective for all, exclusively valid, and the condition of salvation for everyone.[162]

Philosophia Perennis, in its Jasperian interpretation, essentially aimed at providing the individual with a 'world orientation', through his own thought, and at reaching the *origins*, i.e. *Transcendence*, through philosophy: 'it will be possible to listen to the great philosophers and draw from their spring through them'.[163]

As mentioned previously, Jaspers' interpretation of the concept of Philosophia Perennis differed from that expressed by the Perennialists, and particularly René Guénon. The dissonance with Guénon, who, as we know, consistently avoided use of the term 'Philosophia Perennis' in his writings, is particularly evident with regard to man's relationship with Nature. According to Guénon, metaphysics, i.e. the only dimension within which the true Principles of reality can be found, was 'what is beyond nature', which is the reason for its exclusion from his doctrine. Jaspers, on the contrary, regarded the relationship between man and Nature as a fundamental element for the achievement of the Immanent-Transcendence, which represented the objective of his philosophising and the foundation of his idea of Philosophia Perennis:

> That which does not allow us to base ourselves exclusively on non-sensitive Transcendence, unless we find ourselves on the edge of a sudden conversion, is not only the fragility of our finitude, but also our love for the world, as a creature of God.[164]

The act of transcendence, in Jaspers' view, equalled the overcoming of the objective and existence itself, it meant going beyond the clarification of existence, beyond thought, beyond everything that could be accessed by thought; it meant reaching the transcendent, the One, the origin, the being[165]. For this reason, Philosophia Perennis represented for Jaspers a gnostic path towards the origin, the Transcendence, a path which went through the three phases of the philosophical world orientation, in which the knowable is first learned and then rejected, followed by the clarification of existence (by waking up from simply being in the world, the activity of our own realisation will be activated), to finally reach metaphysics (the evocation of being).

In his book *Philosophy of Existence*, Jaspers discussed the unavoidable connection between an individual and a common tradition, which represented a 'single world historicity', concepts that we will later observe in Jung's theories of the 'collective unconscious' and biologist Rupert Sheldrake's 'morphogenetic fields':

> What is granted to everyone as his historicity, his recollection, his One, what stands before him at the boundary, is indeed inseparably linked with a common tradition. This tradition becomes more profound, alive and concentrated the more it incorporates into its own recollection a historicity broadened to include the plurality and incessant dynamism of all human possibilities and actualities' whilst nevertheless preserving an individual character: 'because the irreplaceable historicity of the individual should not cause the immediacy and autonomy if its transcendent origin to be obliterated by being subsumed under the generality of a single-word.[166]

It is precisely through his own individuality, the result of his freedom, that man will be able to modernise the principles of the Philosophia Perennis, which have rested in a common tradition, and have therefore been inherited, nevertheless possess a sort of dynamism that determines their constant evolution and transformation.

In his introduction to Jaspers' work, *Philosophical Faith and Revelation*, Umberto Galimberti underlined how Jaspers ,'virtually exiled himself from his time in order to search the philosophia perennis, which forms the basis of every time'.[167] His main publication, *Philosophy*, in particular, reveals the progressive detachment of his philosophy from 'scientific objectivity' and the focus on the being, which, in its entirety, transcends the partial expressions of time. Man, thus assumes the role of philosophical subject and is faced with a choice between two possibilities: he can deal exclusively with the entities that are before him by objectifying them with scientific categories which allow him to dominate the totality of the manifest world, or he can take care of the being, which, whilst hidden in its totality, faintly manifests itself through the same entities, which should no longer be seen as an object of investigation, but as ciphers that refer to the being that encompasses them all (Umgreifende).[168] Jaspers, therefore, evidently reintroduced a symbolic interpretation of the world, in which entities were symbolically brought closer, and the 'cipher', the Symbol, became once again the cognitive tool for the comprehension of the deepest Truths.

This superiority of the Symbol, the cipher, on discursive reason, was a recurring theme throughout Jaspers' works; symbolism, indeed, represented the only means through which it was possible to draw from and teach the Philosophia Perennis in a manner that even philosophy would not have been capable of achieving. It was mainly through symbolism, therefore, that Jaspers managed to reintroduce and recover the transcendent dimension, a symbolism which, having been previously rejected and neglected by the modern spirit, was revealed to be perfectly adequate for the expression of the Truths which belonged to the order of pure intellectuality. Human nature, due to its not purely intellectual essence, requires a sensitive basis from which to soar into the highest spheres, and symbolism represents the perfect instrument to satisfy man's intellectual requirements. Whereas language continues to be an analytical and discursive tool of human reason, symbolism, on the other hand, is an essentially synthetic and, consequently, intuitive mechanism. These properties make it better suited than language to provide support for the recovery of the transcendent dimension, as the symbol possesses an ontological reality that goes far beyond all forms of mental construction.

Whereas Guénon's 'metaphysics' was based on a clear distinction between *Immanence* and *Transcendence*, the determination of which was achieved through logical categories deriving from the first principles that were believed to be identical in all men, Jaspers, on the contrary, believed that Transcendence should be searched for *in* the world, for it is:

> The being that never becomes world, but which equally speaks in the world through the being. There can exist no Transcendence until the world, by showing that it does not subsist for itself and that it does not contain the foundation of its own being, redirects to what is beyond. If the world represents totality, then Transcendence does not exist. But if Transcendence does exist, then the reality of the world should bear the signs that can lead to it.[169]

It was Jaspers' belief, therefore, that the encounter between existence and Transcendence took place 'in the world', as reality was placed in the temporality of being in the world, and an investigation of the world remained the sole gateway to our knowledge. It is for this reason that realisation in the world represents the sole means of achieving an existential realisation, and giving up the world would, therefore, entail renouncing the opportunity of self-discovery.[170]

Jaspers' Transcendence is an announcement of the ulteriority that is manifested in the borderline situations experienced by existence, explaining why, in the view of the German philosophers, a philosophy which fails to address the transcendent dimension is inevitably destined to collapse. Jaspers' philosophical and religious faith, the Philosophia Perennis and the Religio Perennis, albeit originating from an unavoidable tension towards the dimension of *Transcendence* obtained through the cipher, the Symbol, i.e. the instruments that indicate the pathway to the Truth, nevertheless follow two radically different paths:

> The philosophical faith does not attribute the value of a universally valid truth to the cipher believed, because it perceives that this character belongs to the apodictic knowledge of conscience, which presides over the scientific organisation of the world, rather than to existence which, by obeying an unconditional need, surpasses the world to land in a Transcendence in which worldly categories inevitably flounder. Certain of not gaining access to a universally valid truth, religious faith does not excommunicate, it does not declare dissenters as heretics, nor does it light stakes or possess sacred books that are held preferable due to their content of absolute truth; the philosophical faith is aware that it is on its way to the truth and is not willing to trade the uncertain way with the definitive destination; it is for this reason that it fails to recognise any authority outside the cipher in which it believes, based on the indications it provides rather than to its imposition on temporal realisations; philosophical faith acknowledges the authority of the cipher as lying in Transcendence (and thus denies the world), and does not contemplate its involvement as a world authority.[171]

In particular, Jaspers' works focused on the analysis of modern Nihilism provided the background for an in-depth examination of the essentiality of reinstatement of the transcendent dimension, and a return of philosophy to the fundamental issue of being: 'in view of the Western catastrophe, philosophy should once again renew awareness of its own independence, in the discovery of its relation with the original source of human'.[172]

As previously mentioned, Philosophia Perennis, in its Jasperian interpretation, is detached from all institutions, it is not based on sacred texts or authorities, but rather lies in the interiority of each individual, being accessible only through a return to *Transcendence*; it places itself within Tradition, which Jaspers maintains is constituted by the entire body of human knowledge hoarded over the centuries, of which it represents the indispensable source:

> It only exists in individual consideration, it lacks the objective protection of an institution, it is what it remains after everything is broken, and it means nothing for those who wish to interpret it as an aid in the world; its presence

> however is reached from time to time when we return to ourselves, drawing inspiration from tradition…there will be no possibility to catch up in time with the philosophia perennis, unfailingly present in the very notion of philosophy and the general project of philosophical truth, as its three-thousand-year-old history which fulfils itself in a single present…Even the highest tradition remains hung in time and fails to offer definitive support or a real community, it does not result in a collection of sacred texts and it does not entail any unquestionably valid writings. A definitive truth does not exist, but the tradition which encompasses the entire history of philosophy, from China to the West, represents the inexhaustible spring that still flows incessantly as we return to its source, which remains present in anticipation of being reactualised.[173]

Jaspers continues by concluding that:

> The philosophical truth is the *philosophia perennis* which no individual possesses, around which all philosophers rotate, with its omnipresence as a truly authentic thought…in the view of philosophy, religious incarnations deceptively hide divinity, yielding a false impression of vicinity and approach…this is the difference between philosophy and religion, which will subsequently determine the difference between divinity and God, conceived Transcendence and living God; what belongs to philosophy will not be contemplated in the Bible.[174]

Jaspers focused on highlighting how the essence of man was not merely to *exist*, but rather to *exist* where 'possible existence' was manifested, thus obliging mankind to choose whether or not to transcend his existence. Whereas an animal, unlike man, is faced with the sole option of *existing*, and cannot thus transcend beyond this condition, man, on the contrary, to recall Pico della Mirandola's famous *Oration*, can choose what to become, whether to remain in the world of pure animality or climb towards divine Transcendence. For Jaspers the principle of philosophising comprised a leap from the totality of Immanence to Transcendence, marking the passage from that which is experienced in time and is known timelessly (and thus remains a mere appearance) to the true eternal being (which is not temporally cognisable although manifested in the context of our temporal existence). It is the leap from our actual encompassing[175], pertaining to existence, consciousness, and spirit, to the encompassing that we *could* be, or authentically are as an existence. Indeed, a leap from the world of encompassing as we know it, to the encompassing constituted by the act of being. This leap is decisive for my freedom. For freedom only exists with and by Transcendence.[176]

It is evident that, unlike Evola and Guénon, Jaspers' theories did not feature a contrast between 'historical world' and 'world of Tradition', which is little more than a contrast between action *in* history and meta-historical action. Evola was particularly critical of existentialism as he believed that in the human type that existentialism proposed, in which Transcendence had awakened, the individual still remained uncentreed with regard to it; on the contrary, the man that Evola aimed at outlining is an individual centred on himself, who senses the dimension of Transcendence within himself and secures himself to it. Now, without delving deeper into the dialectic controversy between Evola and the Existentialist thought, it should simply be noted that, whereas Evola's opinions with regard to Heidegger and Sartre are distinct and categorical, his disagreement with Jaspers' doctrine turned out to be more problematic.

Evola, indeed, considered Jaspers as 'perhaps the only one among the existentialists to make a few superficial references to "metaphysics"'[177], which, according to Evola, Jaspers tended to confuse with mysticism. Evola's criticism of Jaspers' thought, referred in particular to the writings in which the German philosopher displayed a tendency to exalt the so-called 'rational illumination', the 'liberty and independence of the philosophical', but especially to the texts which emphasised Jaspers' intolerance of 'any form of spiritual and secular authority', and of any claim of obedience for men believed to be 'God's microphones'.[178] With regard to Jaspers' exaltation of rational illumination, it should be remarked that Evola himself later wrote that:

> Jaspers speaks of the 'unconditioned demand' through which is manifested the Being, the eternal, or whatever one likes to call the other dimension of being. It is a command to act in a way that has no motive or justification in objective, rational, or naturalistic terms. One might almost think it was the detached, 'pure action' that I have described,[179] maintaining that the so-called 'unconditioned demand' to which Jaspers makes references to is inevitably destined to fall into the orbit of religious or social morality, a Transcendence to be understood 'as a species of paralyzing and anguishing 'stone guest'. By projecting it outside oneself, one's relationship to transcendence if off centre, exterior, and dependent. This is so much like the relationship in religious consciousness'.[180]

Even as far as the concept of 'all-embracing' (das *Umgreifende*) is concerned, which Evola saw as a 'distant reflection of ideas typical of traditional teaching', the Roman traditionalist could not deny that Jaspers displayed a rejection of the dual conscience whereby the object is always objectified and set against the I as subject, making it impossible for it to acknowledge the deep root of the real being, which is antecedent to duality. Evola thus admitted that Jaspers' doctrine, through the 'dissolution of the I' and the 'fall into the all-embracing', offered the opportunity for one to overcome the object-subject antithesis, and achieve the experience of unity, that is, the 'All-embracing'.

Evola acknowledged that according to Kierkegaard, considered the spiritual father of the Existentialists, the very existence of man revealed the presence of Transcendence, and that his concept of *Existenz*, which Evola shared, represented both the physical presence of the I in the world and the metaphysical presence of the Being (of Transcendence) of the I.

To conclude, Evola recognised in 'a certain Existentialism', Jaspers' doctrine, a positive Antitheism, that is, the existential overcoming of the concept of God-as-person, an object of faith and doubt:

> Since the centre of the I is also mysteriously the centre of Being, 'God' (transcendence) is a certainty, not as a subject of faith or dogma, but as *presence* in existence and freedom. The saying of Jaspers: 'God is a certainty for me inasmuch as I exist authentically', relates in a certain way to the state already indicated, in which calling Being into question would amount to calling oneself into question.[181]

Lastly, the following passage from *Philosophy of Existence* demonstrates how the Jasperian interpretation of Transcendence is inextricably linked to the concept of *origin*, and highlights how the views of the two thinkers were actually closer than Evola himself realised:

> But although as finite temporal existence we remain veiled, and must uneasily make do with do from moment to moment with preliminaries, yet there is within us a hidden depth that we can feel in exalted moments, something that permeates all modes of the encompassing and that becomes certain for us precisely through them. Schelling said that we are 'privy to creation' – as if in our ground we had been present at the origin of all things and then had lost this awareness in the confines of our world. In philosophising, we are engaged in awakening the memory through which we will return to our ground.

4
Carl Gustav Jung, The Archetypes as 'Sophia Perennis'

Jung, the last esoterist?

Trying to establish whether Swiss psychoanalyst Carl Gustav Jung should be included among the interpreters of Tradition or whether he should simply be remembered as one of the most original theorists in the field of psychoanalysis, represents a long-standing debate among scholars.

One of the most salient features of Jung's studies has undoubtedly always been represented by his attempt to provide a psychological explanation to the processes of *transformation of personality*, which form the foundation of religious, gnostic and alchemical practices. It should, however, be clear from the start that Jung's theories will fall outside of the field of pure metaphysics typical of Perennialist authors; Jung himself, indeed, repeatedly stated that it had been his intention to limit his studies to everything relating to the psychic 'experience', thus apparently rejecting metaphysics.

We now find ourselves wondering whether Jung was actually able to maintain the two domains, the physical and the metaphysical, the immanent and the transcendent, so strictly separated.

According to Spanish philosopher and theologian Raimon Panikkar, the dichotomic separation of the sphere of the immanent from that of the transcendent is an action that will never be mirrored in reality and, consequently, in the search for Truth.

Immanence and *Transcendence* should therefore be considered as twin and inseparable arches; neither would be able to support itself without the other, as divine Immanence is based on divine Transcendence and *vice versa*.[182]

Jung himself, in his autobiography, announced the existence in his theories of an openness towards the spirit and the transcendent; according to Jung, indeed, the Self is represented by an individual's essentiality, which defines him in the *hic et nunc* whilst simultaneously opening up towards a transcendent reality.[183] Starting from his basic theory, that is, that the religious factor par excellence, the principle of correspondence with the divine, the archetype of the *imago dei* which is the indispensable condition of all religious forms, is to be found in the depths of the human psyche, Jung recognised the discovery of one's own Self as: 'the most immediate experience of the Divine which it is psychologically possible to imagine.'[184]

In order to formulate and subsequently describe his theories, which strove towards the achievement of psychological self-knowledge, Jung constantly drew inspiration from gnostic models. Jung himself referred to this doctrine as an 'inner sun', an inner light within the human psyche through which man can gain access to the *Numinosum*, to a personal spiritual 'trans-reality':

> We cannot suppose that this aspect of the unconscious or of the hinterland of man's mind is something totally new. Probably it has always been there, in every culture. Each culture gave birth to its destructive opposite, but no culture or civilisation before our own was ever forced to take these psychic undercurrents in deadly earnest. Psychic life always found expression in a metaphysical system of some sort.[185]

Jung's approach to the transcendent dimension occurred, in particular, through his method of Active Imagination, which, as underlined by psychoanalysis scholar Robert Mercurio, had not been conceived, as some had speculated, as a sort of spiritual exercise, but rather as a specific psychological instrument, allowing its users to touch the religious possibilities in the depths of the human soul and to nurture their relationship with this mystery:

> Jung reminds us that our task towards this deep mystery, towards God, is no longer to invoke him, as servants or needy children, but rather to actively participate in the resolution of the conflicts within the unconscious and to facilitate the incarnation of Divinity in our humanity.[186]

Certain scholars in the academic world have made reference to the existence of a Jungian esotericism, particularly Prof Nicholas Goodrick-Clarke who highlighted how Jung, thanks to his studies, which embraced the fields of Gnosticism, Alchemy and often focused on Paracelsus' theories, had created a true esoteric theory in which the 'individuation process' was nothing other than the discovery, or rather the *rediscovery*, of our divine side, which Jung referred to as Self:

> The work and influence of the Swiss psychologist Carl Gustav Jung has been an important factor in the development of an inner variety of esotericism through the twentieth century...He advanced the theory that the stage of individual development (ontogeny) recapitulated the stage of the development of the human race (phylogeny). This led Jung to postulate a 'phylogeny of the soul' whereby the early religions and mythologies of mankind would correspond to the lower, unconscious strata of the mind. By 1909, Jung conceived of the idea of mining the unconscious by first investigating Greco-Roman mystery cults, later focusing on the Gnostics. By the end of the First World War, Jung had conceived a theory of universal symbols produced by the collective unconscious, which he defined as archetypes. This theory, continually developed between 1920 and 1940, drew Jung into new formulations of esoteric imagination. Jung suggested that dreams prefigured the evolution of the soul. Another Key idea was 'active imagination', a notion Jung took from Herber Silberer (1882-1923), a Swiss Freudian analyst interested in alchemy, which involved the transmutation of the unconscious archetypes by their integration into a unified archetype of the Self. By the 1930s, these ideas, essentially esoteric, had led Jung from Gnostic mythology to alchemical texts as sources of the archetypes, and he published studies of Paracelsus and psychological interpretations of alchemy...Although Jung's earliest inspiration lay with older German psychologists such Karl Eschenmayer, Justin Kerner, and Carl Gustav Carus, all representative of Romantic Naturphilosophie, his work has had a powerful influenced on New Age religion in its sacralisation of the Self as the divine counterpart within the human being.[187]

Jung's theories undoubtedly instructed and inspired numerous twentieth-century thinkers, but as far as traditionalist thinkers are concerned, despite Jungian scholar Sonu Shamdasani remarking that 'many proponents of the Perennial Philosophy, Hermeticism, Gnosticism, Alchemy and Magic were quick to claim Jung as one of their own and use his name to lend credibility and legitimacy to their ideas,'[188] we are aware that Jung was indeed heavily criticised by some, particularly Evola, Guénon and Burckhardt.

Jung's scholars and critics used a series of labels to identify him over the years, one of the most original definitions of which originated from a well-known work by Richard Noll, *The Aryan Christ*. The text is based on the theory that the establishment of a Psychological Club in 1916, determined the birth of a Jungian cult, based on Jung's charisma and ultimately aimed at his Self-deification as an Aryan 'Christ'. Noll defined the Psychological Club as the government body of a spiritual *élite* made up of patients and analysts sharing an equal relationship, and based his theory on a document, a brief transcript of a speech delivered by Jung on the day of the inauguration of the Club, a text which outlines a model of psychological transformation for the individual by drawing analogies with the life of Christ, Goethe's *Faust* and Wagner's *Parsifal*, ending with the definition of an 'ideal' analytical community and suggestions for the organisation of the Club.

One of the biggest critics of Noll's theory was the above-mentioned Shamdasani, who highlighted how the text on which Noll based his theory, is basically one single, untitled document consisting of five typed pages of foolscap with handwritten corrections in two different scripts. Moreover, according to Shamdasani, Noll's essay exponentially amplified the significance of this talk, seen as an attempt to redeem the world, and portraying Jung's analysis techniques as a 'rite of initiation' through which patients were transformed into 'apostles'.[189] Shamdasani remarked that it was somewhat curious, given the significance attributed to the text as the inaugural address to a new world order of a spiritual elite, that only one copy had surfaced so far, in Boston. Shamdasani mainly challenged Noll's thesis by referring to writings by Jung, in which the Swiss scholar himself heavily criticised the psychological dynamics, which formed the basis of the establishment of cults. In fact, according to Jung, cults arose through identification on the part of the cult leader with the archetype of the *prophet,* and on the part of the follower with the archetype of the *disciple*, stemming from a failure to come to terms adequately with the collective unconscious. Following on from this, Jung considered his theories and methods, contrary to the theories put forward by Noll, as the first line of defence *against* cult-mindedness.[190]

Without delving deeper into Shamdasani's criticism of Noll's text, I would like to underline how the reducing of the contents of Noll's essay to the theory of the creation of an Aryan cult was a reductive and simplistic move on Shamdasani's part. Noll's text, indeed, offered an interesting analysis of one of Jung's earlier works, *Transformations and Symbols of the Libido* (1912), which, as highlighted by Noll, contributed to the establishment of psychoanalysis not only as a science but as a true solution to *revive* culture and the individual, and which, above all, underlined Jung's increasing interest in Volkisch Arianism and, to an even greater extent, in the 'solar cult', which was reproposed in many later works:

> *In Wandlungen und Symbole der Libido* Jung cannot help but rely on the ideas of the volkisch movement, as around 1910 the most intelligent and accepted blend of the scholarly literature on comparative philology, comparative mythology, and evolutionary biology in German could be found in the various literatures of this movement on the differences between Aryan peoples and Semitic peoples. Volkisch ideas permeate scholarly publications from the eminent Muller and Haeckel on down to the esoteric books and pamphlets of Theosophists and other occultists, and many were used (and some cited) by Jung in Wandlungen. This is, perhaps, most apparent in the relentless syncretism of solar mythology and psychoanalysis that begins in the last section of part 1 – *The Song of the Moth* – and continues throughout the enormous part 2, thus making the second part of Wandlungen as bulky and unintelligible as the second part of Faust. It is especially in these sections that Jung's text becomes a liturgy of sun worship and volkisch Aryanism.[191]

The symbolism of sun which Jung referred to, is that of the mystery cult of Mithras, a survival of the Mazdaist (Zoroastrian) dualistic religion of Ancient Persia (600 B.C.), which was imported into the Roman culture in the Late Antiquity (100-400 A.D.), 'the all-male cult (primarily Roman soldiers and merchants) was based on a masonic lodge-type model of grades of initiations'.[192]

To this regard, it is interesting to observe how, in the same period, the Mithraic cult also piqued the interest, and was recurrently discussed in the studies of another previously examined traditionalist, Julius Evola.

Shamdasani also refuted the theory that Jung had made use of Christian metaphors to conceal his Pagan nature, using his research on Alchemy as a façade to convince others that his religious vision remained of a Christian and monotheistic nature, even though Noll's analysis of the matter appeared coherent and well documented.

The theme of the relationship with and conception of God in Jung has always been object of a controversial debate. Noll's analysis of the matter, however, is clear, as he firmly believed that Jung had distanced himself from Christianity to direct his attention to an antecedent Pagan religion:

> The experience of God within was always a key promise of Jung and his method of psychotherapy, and it is indeed a central part of Jung's repudiation of traditional Christianity that offered a God that was distant, transcendent, and absolute. Having a god within could lead to the experience of becoming one with God, or merging with this God-force in some way. It is clear from his many statements in Wandlungen that Jung felt that the central experience of transformation in the ancient mystery cults of the Hellenistic world involved just such a process or experience of self-deification.[193]

Noll's hypotheses are of particular interest in the light of Jung's later studies on

Gnosticism and the Mystery Cults, which provided support to his theories on the unconscious:

> The natural Urreligion of the prehistoric Aryans was Jung's idea of the true source of all the Hellenic mystery cults (e.g. the Great Mother, Isis, Osiris, Dionysus), but this was especially true of Mithraism. Mithraism was a direct survival of the Urreligion from the primordial homeland or Urheimat of the ancient Aryans, the Indo-Iranian region. In Jung's view, based on the scholarship of his day, the ancient Greco-Roman mystery cults were all based on the experience of rebirth for their initiates through special secret rites of initiation that focused on the transformative experience of becoming one with god. In the Mithraic cult, therefore, this would mean becoming one with an ancient Aryan god. The Aryan peoples – unlike the Semites – held onto their natural religion longer than any other group and were thus closer to the Urreligion of the sun and sky of all original humans.[194]

In other words, they were closer to the authentic and original Tradition.

Jung's conclusions based on the above hypotheses appeared obvious: in the individual psyche there are strata that comprise the sediment of two thousand years of Christianity, and the internalisation of bourgeois-Christian civilisation is a 'mask' that covers the true Aryan god within, a natural god, a sun god, perhaps even Mithras himself. This was highlighted, according to Jung, both by the universality of the symbolism of the sun in materials derived from the unconscious, and by the practice of the solar cult, which still existed in certain primitive societies throughout the world, expressions of prephylogenetic memories of our innate history. This gave rise to an interpretation of the Jungian method as an opportunity to get in touch with the pre-Christian ancestral stratum of the unconscious mind, the ancestral pagan images of which can be transformed into an immediate and direct experience.

Noll also dealt with the connections between Jung and National Socialism, yet another extensively discussed and debated theme, stating that:

> The similarity between Jungian psychology and National Socialism is that both movements promoted Weltanschauungs based on (1) the traditional Germanic symbolism of volkisch mysticism and (2) 'Nietzscheanism' in the elist and psedutoliberational sense astutely identified by Tonnies. They both, in their unique ways, offered what Stern calls 'the promise of miracle, mystery and authority' to those of predominantly Aryan heredity.[195]

The references to the ancient Germanic symbolism are particularly evident in the above-quoted essay from 1936, 'Wotan', according to which Germans turned to their collective unconscious to 'reactivate' those Myths of which, according to Jung, they had never freed themselves.

In the light of the above premises, it is possible to detect in the Jungian doctrine certain dynamics and themes which could constitute yet another representation or aspect of Tradition. References to Traditions, indeed, make continuous appearances in his writings, depending on the themes discussed by the Swiss scholar; when discussing human figures, for instance, Jung maintained that all character manifested in our dreams or in a process of Active Imagination, albeit linked to personal past experiences, contain a far more ancient and deeper psychic stratum, 'the two million-year-old man', i.e. 'the ancient but not forgotten wisdom that we preserve within ourselves', a sort of archetypal substratum of primordial wisdom[196].

In support of this theory, I shall attempt to highlight how, in the Jungian theory, the integration of the unconscious is manifested as a process, which, in addition to the treatment of psychic disorders, is associated with a further fundamental objective: the generation of a true growth of consciousness. The Jungian process of individuation will, therefore, acquire the characteristics of a true gnostic and initiatic pathway, granting the individual access to a 'primordial wisdom'.

I shall proceed to examine some of these elements.

Collective unconscious and archetype as psychic expressions of Tradition

Jung's *collective unconscious* has been defined as the storehouse of latent memory traces inherited from the ancestral past of mankind, the psychic residues of human evolution, which have gathered following the repeated experiences of countless generations.

Therefore, what is learnt through personal experience is inevitably subjected to the influence of the collective unconscious, which, since the beginning of life, produces a direct action on individual behaviour, as explained by Jung, on the occasion of a Conference held in 1936, specifically on this subject:

> The collective unconscious is a part of the psyche which can be negatively distinguished from personal unconscious by the fact that it does not, like the latter, owe its existence to personal experience and consequently is not a personal acquisition. While the personal unconscious is made up essentially of contents which have at one time been conscious but which have disappeared from consciousness through having been forgotten or repressed, the contents of the collective unconscious have never been in consciousness, and therefore have never been individually acquired but owe their existence exclusively to heredity. Whereas the personal unconscious consists for the most part of complexes, the content of the collective unconscious is made up essentially of archetypes.[197]

The Archetype

The archetype, another key term in the Jungian doctrine, has been defined by Jung essentially as a universal form of thought provided with emotional content. This form of thought creates images or visions, which correspond, in the normal state of wakefulness, to certain aspects of conscious life. The archetype, contained within the collective unconscious, is therefore essentially inherited, as in a certain way it represents the product of the experiences of the world lived by the human race, experiences that are for the most part similar to those lived by every individual:

> The concept of the archetype, which is an indispensable correlate of the idea of the collective unconscious, indicates the existence of definite forms in the psyche which seem to be present always and everywhere. Mythological research calls them 'motifs'; in the psychology of primitives they correspond to Lévy-Bruhl's concept of 'représentations collectives', and in the field of comparative religion they have been defined by Hubert and Mauss as 'categories of the imagination'. Adolf Bastian long ago called them 'elementary' or 'primordial thoughts'. From these references, it should be clear enough that my idea of the archetype – literally a pre-existent form – does not stand alone, but is something that is recognised and named in other fields of knowledge. My view along my studies, then, is as follows: in addition to our immediate consciousness, which is of a thoroughly personal nature and which we believe to be the only empirical psyche (even if we tack on the personal unconscious as an appendix), there exists a second psychic system of a collective, universal, and impersonal nature which is identical in all individuals. This collective unconscious does not develop individually, but is inherited. It consists of pre-existent forms, the archetypes, which can only become conscious secondarily and which give definite form to certain psychic contents...The concept of collective unconscious is neither speculative nor philosophical but an empirical matter. The question is simply this: are there or are there not unconscious, universal forms of this kind? If they exist, then there is a region of the psyche which one can call the collective unconscious.'[198]

Several scholars compared the Jungian archetypes to Plato's ideas, although it is an acknowledged fact that by his ideas the Greek philosopher aimed essentially at representing the pure content of thought, whereas, in Jung's theory, the archetype is, in substance, synonymous with Myth.

In order to comprehend fully the concept of archetype it is essential to understand the distinction that Jung applied between the true archetype and the archetypal image, the representation, idea or phantasy. Archetypes, in fact, in the words of Jung, are unobservable structures; only when they are stimulated through internal and external necessities (internal compensatory processes or external stimuli), do they produce archetypal images, archetypal fantasies, thoughts or intuitions, which can be defined as archetypal as they are also detectable in other civilisations or populations. Individuals, therefore, would essentially inherit the archetypal structures, not the images through which they are brought to light in the conscious part of the individual.

What is inherited is the disposition and the archetypal structures, which will produce mythological or non-mythological, identical or corresponding images.

One of the greatest scholars of the Jungian thought, Marie-Louise von Franz, Jung's student and collaborator, summarised the thought of the Swiss scholar as follows:

> When an inborn archetypal structure passes into the manifest form of an archetypal fantasy or image, the psyche makes use of impressions from the external surroundings for its means of expression; therefore, the individual images are not entirely identical but only similar in structure. For example, an African child, when an image of something overwhelmingly terrifying needs to take shape in him, will perhaps fantasise about a crocodile or a lion, and a European child in the same situation will imagine a truck that is barrelling toward him. Only the structure of something overpoweringly threatening will be the same in this case. The image is of course enriched by impressions from the external world. The archetypal disposition shows itself most clearly in man in the fact, to which Jung therefore referred the most often, that all of his religious systems and myths and mythological customs and folk talks, with all their individual differences, show structural similarity...Most interesting are the conceptions of space-time, for they all derive from the archetypal image of the omnipresence of a deity or the omnipresence of the divine pneuma. This was already implicitly formulated by Plato, then explicitly by Plotinus: 'God is an intelligible sphere whose centre is everywhere and whose periphery is nowhere'. Here we also already have the modern conception of the omnipresent point.[199]

We will return to the fundamental symbology of the Centre in the final chapter of this book.

As mentioned previously, Jung illustrated the concept of collective unconscious from an empirical, i.e. demonstrable, perspective. He later explained *how* and *where* it was possible to locate the components of the collective unconscious, that is, the archetypes, identifying dreams and the Active Imagination as two means through which the archetypes can be accessed:

> We must now turn to the question of how the existence of archetypes can be proved. Since archetypes are supposed to produce certain psychic forms, we must discuss how and where one can get hold of the material demonstrating these forms. The main source, then, is dreams, which have the advantage of being involuntary, spontaneous products of the unconscious psyche and are therefore pure products of nature not falsified by any conscious purpose... Another source for the material we need is to be found in 'active imagination'. By this I mean a sequence of fantasies produced by deliberate concentration.'[200]

We will later discuss how, to an even greater extent, the method of Active Imagination, interpreted by Jung as the product of deliberate concentration, permitted the individual to proceed along a true gnostic pathway, the 'process of individuation'. According to Jung this method represented the most powerful and reliable means of gaining access to the archetypal material, to the Myth, or if one wishes, to Tradition.

The Myth as expression of Tradition

Before delving deeper into Jung's theories on the process of individuation and Active Imagination, the concept of Myth in relation to the theory of archetypes should be examined.

Jung believed that the origin of archetypes could not be explained if not by interpreting said archetypes as storehouses of the experiences repeated by humanity. One of the most frequent and, at the same time striking experiences was represented, in Jung's view, by the daily and visible motion of the sun. As long as we deal with the physical process that we are all familiar with, we cannot discover anything about it in our unconscious, but, within the same unconscious, we can frequently observe it disguised as Myth in the representation of the *solar hero* and all its variations. As specified by Jung, the Myth obviously represents the solar archetype, not the physical process through which it manifests itself, and the same can be applied to the lunar phases. The archetype thus presents itself as a sort of disposition to reproduce constantly the same or analogous mythical representations, by impressing in the unconscious exclusively the fantastical, subjective representations created by the physical process. It could therefore be assumed that archetypes are the impressions of subjective reactions to repeated experiences.[201] As an analogy to the Jungian conception of archetypes, it is particularly interesting to read the definition of Myth provided by Mircea Eliade in his *History of Religions*:

> Any myth, of any nature, enounces an event that occurred *illo tempore*, and sets an exemplary precedent for all the actions and 'situations' that replicate the even as from them. Any ritual, or any meaningful action performed by man is the repetition of a mythical archetype…The consequence of repetition is the abolition of profane time and the projection of man into a magic-religious time that has nothing to do with duration in the strict sense of the word, but which is the 'eternal present' of mythical time.[202]

The Myth, as a fundamental component of the archetype, was thus considered by Jung as a primary and exemplary category, which had existed prior to the history of man but was nevertheless imprinted in the unfathomable depths of the human mind, destined to surface in the conscience of few individuals, to take form and substance in the mind of the conscious man. It should now be underlined how in the processes of *becoming aware* and *awareness*, élites were necessarily the ones taking advantage of their inclination to a relation with the Myth. To quote Eliade:

> In archaic societies recitation of the mythological traditions remains the prerogative of a few individuals. In some societies the reciters are recruited among the shamans and medicine men or among members of the secret societies...accordingly the role played by creative minds must have been greater than one is led to believe...briefly, when privileged religious experiences are conveyed by means of a scenario of overwhelming imagination, they are capable of imposing specific models or sources of inspiration onto the entire community.[203]

In our search for Tradition among the complex Jungian theories, the concept of Myth therefore acquires a fundamental significance; it is, indeed, the Myth, or rather 'the mythological materials', within the vast field of archetypes, that represents what may be defined as an expression of Tradition, a pre-existing, inherited Tradition, only accessible to a selected few, or rather, to those who, through *Intellectual Intuition* (in the Perennialist vision) or Active Imagination (in the Jungian doctrine), which can both be interpreted as *access methods*, can approach and discover it. Tradition, in this representation, becomes a common unconscious form, bearer of the universal Principles present in the archetypes, which will contribute to the development of the human consciousness. To quote Marie-Louise Von Franz:

> Bound up with the archetypes is the presence of something like *knowledge* in the form of symbolic images. This is a kind of luminosity or partial consciousness on the part of archetypes, a knowledge that is conscious only in the archetypal realm, but not conscious for the ego; it is something that makes a sudden appearance in ego consciousness.[204]

Archetypes thus conceal, hidden and veiled in the form of symbolic images, a *form of knowledge*, a sort of comprehensive collection of all universal wisdom, which the ancient populations had already identified with the mythical *Akasha*:

> A huge library containing in symbolic form all the knowledge of the universe. After all, this realm beyond space and time, and the mythical and mysterious 'Akasha', which has been handed down in Oriental traditions, are exactly the same thing. In order to access the laws of the universe in its proper light, it is essential for the psyche to connect with this 'cosmic web'. Its duty is to inform the mind which, confronted with the concrete reality, will subsequently develop the scientific law by using the required mathematical apparatus.[205]

It should further be underlined that whenever Jung described the Myth, the latter was never represented as a more or less pathological aspect of psychic life, which would entail a decrease in the autonomy of the Myth; on the contrary, Jung demonstrated how the Myth, in the countless variations in which it can manifest itself within the different societies, is nothing other than the concrete – different and variable from time to time but essentially uniform - expression of an atemporal structure of every individual's unconscious. Jung's objective was, therefore, to demonstrate how in the purely formal nature of the unconscious one can find the *universal matrices* of the mythological themes, which, due to their frequency and diffusion, should rightly be referred to as universal:

> The collective unconscious appears to consist of mythological motifs or primordial images, for which reasons the myths of all nations are its real exponents. In fact, the whole of mythology could be taken as a sort of projection of the collective unconscious.'

In conclusion, whereas for the Freudian school the Myth had its roots in a complex of man's personal unconscious, Jung identified the Myth's atemporal origin in a formal structure of the collective unconscious.

Archetypes, i.e. forms of representation that are older and more general than humanity, would thus possess a life of their own, an independent life similar to the existence of partial souls, as readily recognisable in the philosophical or gnostic systems based on the perception of the unconscious as a source of knowledge. The images of angels and archangels, thrones and dominations that can be observed, for instance, in St Paul's writings, Gnostic archons, Dionysius the Areopagite's celestial hierarchy all surface precisely thanks to this, sometimes uncontrollable, archetypal autonomy. This determined Jung's suggestion that religious symbols have some kind of independent psychic reality that they are, so to speak, already swimming around in the depths of the unconscious mind.[206]

Among the archetypes that have been represented by Jung, the archetype of Self invariably occupied a central place in the theories of the Swiss psychoanalyst; indeed, according to Jung, the Self, as Centre, should be considered as the *spiritus rector* of daily life. Moreover, it was Jung's belief that the experience of the Self was almost impossible to distinguish practically from the experience of 'what has always been referred to as God'. For this reason, the experience of the Self, according to the Swiss analyst, would be, from the perspective of the ego an *experience* of the Divine that presents it with problems and issues it would just as soon avoid.[207]

The starting point for this theory was represented by Jung's belief that men are religious, or rather *spiritual*, by nature, whereas the human mentality is nowadays directed towards a disenchanted perspective, a loss of the Myth, which is destined to inevitably lead to displays of neurosis. The concept of divinity was thus considered by Jung as an irrational and insuppressible psychological function, which, however, has nothing to do with God's existence: 'The self is a God-image, or at least cannot be distinguished from one. Of this the early Christian spirit was not ignorant, otherwise Clement of Alexandria could never have said that he who knows himself knows God.'[208] But how can one know God by knowing himself? After analysing the theories of the gnostic doctrine and those of the Indian philosophy, as well as Meister Eckhart's writings, Jung concluded that:

> These utterances on the nature of the Deity express transformations of the God-image which run parallel with changes in human consciousness, though one would be at a loss to say which is the cause of the other. The God-image is not something invented, it is an experience that comes upon man spontaneously – as anyone can see for himself unless he is blinded to the truth by theories and prejudices. The unconscious God-image can therefore alter the state of consciousness, just as the latter can modify the God-image once it has become conscious.[209]

The doctrines imparted by the Sapiential Schools, from the Pythagorean school and the Eleusinian Mysteries to the Gnostic and Hermetic communities, and the Alchemist and Neoplatonic societies, contributed to a modification of the God-image, and their disciples were thus able, by imagining God, to reach 'psychic wholeness': 'The symbolism of psychic wholeness coincides with the God-image.'[210]

Due to the impossibility to provide tangible proof, the question of God's existence continued to constitute an unsolvable problem for Jung; indeed, in the light of the conscious and unconscious, archetypal presence of a being with unlimited power, the ability to produce such proof became superfluous for the Swiss scholar. Some ask themselves whether Jung believed in God; the answer is that in his scientific works he never specifically discussed God, but limited himself to using the term 'God-image in the human soul':

> I have been accused of 'deifying the soul'. Not I but God himself has deified it! I did not attribute a religious function to the soul, I merely produced the facts which prove that the soul is *naturaliter religiosa*, i.e., possesses a religious function. I did not invent or insinuate this function, it produces itself of its own accord without being prompted thereto by any opinions or suggestions of mine. Accordingly, when I say as a psychologist that God is an archetype, I mean by that the 'type' in the psyche. The word 'type, as we know, derived from 'blow' or 'imprint'; thus an archetype presupposes an imprinter...We simply do not know the ultimate derivation of the archetype any more than we know the origin of the psyche. The competence of psychology as an empirical science only goes so far as to establish, on the basis of comparative research, whether for instance the imprint found in the psyche can or cannot reasonably be termed a 'God-image' Nothing positive or negative has thereby been asserted about the possible existence of God, any more than the archetype of the 'hero' posits the actual existence of a hero...The archetypes of the unconscious can be shown empirically to be the equivalents of religious dogmas.[211]

The existence of the Divine archetype in all human civilisations was observed by numerous anthropologists and scholars of religion; Mircea Eliade, in particular, highlighted in several essays how a series of civilisations represented the myth of the Eternal Return, in which the act of creation (still regarded as an atemporal phenomenon) witnessed the origin of the archetypal images of all human things and actions. The subsequent earthly imitations represented a constant and unstoppable decadence, leading man to the renovation of the archetypal images through the narration of creation myths and the repetition of rituals, in an attempt to restore their original purity.[212]

It should also be borne to mind, in order to avoid misunderstandings, that Jung did not consider the Myth as an archetype, but rather as the *product* of its action. And as this action comprises conscious and unconscious contents, superficial or deep materials within the human mind, which is ever changing in its historical evolution, it produces infinite and infinitely different images. Just as the individual Traditions do not account for Tradition itself, but merely act as a vehicle, in the same way the archetypal image does not constitute the archetype, but merely the result of its incessant action. These universal matrices, the archetypes, will thus represent the precious material from which 'predisposed' man will draw his own Myths; this collective and unconscious legacy of ancestral memories will lead to development stages in man, which can be regarded as a representation of Tradition.

The individuation process

Before moving on to examine the dynamics of Active Imagination as an access tool to archetypes, it is imperative to analyse the individuation process, the most efficient method of which, according to Jung, was represented by Active Imagination itself.

As mentioned previously, Jung's theories were not aimed exclusively at the creation of solutions for the recovery of individuals affected by psychic disorders, but rather intended to propose a true *weltanschauung*, an interpretation of the world, or even better, an instrument allowing man to *adapt* his soul to life and seize its potential in terms of individual expression and specificity. This pathway was termed 'individuation'.

Jung defined the individuation process as a rather complex and challenging pathway made up of diverse, at times extremely painful stages, which could simplistically be interpreted as a detachment, or rather, a *differentiation* from the external values, which Jung referred to as 'collective values', causing the individual to open up to more authentic and essential values, identified as 'individual values'. In this way therefore, the individual, who up until that moment had been influenced by and adapted to common beliefs, and had thus been divided between the two, seizes the opportunity of transformation into a unique being in possession of an inner coherence, his own Centre. Jungian scholar Mario Trevi, thoroughly described this dynamic in his introduction to the Italian translation of Jung's *Two Essays on Analytical Psychology*:

> One of the greatest risks for the individual is to identify himself with his own Persona, that is, the ensemble of behaviours deriving from the collective conscious psyche: the collapse of the Ego in the collective represented by the cultural regulations of a given society is seen by Jung as a psychological disaster comparable to the collapse of the Ego in the archaic structures of the unconscious. In both cases the individual loses sight of the unique and irreducible meaning of his own existence, he loses himself in the impersonal, opts for the anonymous and parts with the effort of individuality. In this sense the dynamic of the Ego is configured by Jung as a dual possibility of identification: on the one hand, the social role, the Persona, urges the Ego to wear itself out among canonical behaviours, collective approaches, preconceptions and impersonal standards; on the other hand, the unconscious, with its archetypal structures, offers the Ego the opportunity to regress to archaic, childish models of behaviour, as devoid of authentic individual responsibility as those offered by the Persona. Both scenarios represent an attempt to avoid the identification with an aspect of the collective, an attempt to replace the identification with a particular dynamic relation between the Ego and the forms of the collective, so that the values of a historical society are not passively endured or ignored, but rather lived with critical responsibility; and so that the archaic forms that preside over the life of the unconscious are not endured or ignored either, but inwardly accepted as the poles of a creative dialectics...Only when the Ego overcomes the barrier of the identification with the social role, with the mask imposed to him by the authentic interpersonal relation, that is, the Persona, can the disidentification from the elements of the unconscious begin.[213]

The individuation process thus implied a psychic process, unique and inimitable for every individual, comprising an approach of the Ego to the Self, made possible through an increasing integration and unification of the complexes that form one's personality. According to Jung, the only possible solution to withdraw from the trammels of the conscious and unconscious collectivity was represented by individuation:

> Individuation means becoming a single, homogeneous being, and, in so far as 'individuality' embraces our innermost, last, and incomparable uniqueness, also implies becoming one's own self. We could, therefore, translate individuation as 'coming to selfhood' or 'self-realisation'.[214]

This process is enabled by an attribution of meaning and an interpretation of the symbols, deriving both from the external and the inner world, manifested to the individual during the evolution of his existence.

From an esoteric or initiatic point of view, the individuation process could be interpreted as a sort of spiritual journey towards an increased self-awareness, a journey in which the reaching of the final destination is the result of a continuous collaboration between Consciousness and Unconscious, the Ego and the Self. The search for a cooperation between the conscious and the unconscious sides represents for the individual a true initiatic path, the objective of which is represented by the realisation of an *integral* or *total* personality, the integration of Ego into Self, or, if Self is seen as coinciding with the divine, *deification*. During the course of his journey the individual encounters and collides with certain archetypal organisations of his own personality; indeed, only by facing these will he be in a position to increase and expand his own consciousness; these archetypes are represented by the *Shadow*, the *Animus* or *Anima*, the *Wise Old Man* and, the final stage, Self.

The Shadow, the Animus and the Anima

The first archetypal depiction encountered along the inner pathway of the individuation process is the *Shadow*. The Shadow is represented as an essentially negative figure, the bearer of our limits, but to encounter, or rather, acknowledge this figure implies acceptance of the same, thus shedding light on the positive aspects of its essence. It should not be overlooked that, in Jung's views, all symbols convey a dual meaning; every negative has a positive counterpart and vice versa, in a continuous dialectic relationship. To quote Jung's description of this archetype:

> Though the shadow is a motif as well known to mythology as anima and animus, it represents first and foremost the personal unconscious, and its content can therefore be made conscious without too much difficulty. In this it differs from anima and animus, for whereas the shadow can be seen through and recognised fairly easily, the anima and animus are much further away from consciousness and in normal circumstances are seldom if ever realised. With a little self-criticism, one can see through the shadow – so far as its nature is personal. But when it appears as an archetype, one encounters the same difficulties as with anima and animus. In other words, it is quite within the bounds of possibility for a man to recognise the relative evil of nature, but it is a rare and shattering experience for him to gaze into the face of absolute evil.[215]

The Shadow represents the unknown aspects of an individual's personality, and can thus be interpreted as an essentially unpleasant and negative side of the psyche, corresponding to largely instinctual impulses, which the individual tends to repress. The Shadow thus personifies everything the individual denies about himself but which, at the same time, influences and affects his behaviour by expressing itself through unpleasant traits of the character or tendencies that are incompatible with his conscious personality. In a certain sense, it represents our dark side, that which, for moral, ethical or rational reasons, we deny, due to its guise of social unacceptability.

However, it is only through an encounter with one's own Shadow, through acknowledgment of its existence and its essence, and acceptance of the same as essential part of one's personality, that the individual can attempt to build his total identity, clearly and necessarily including the darker side.

The second stage of the process, the second archetype, relates to the pair of masculine/feminine opposites, with the former being referred to as *Animus*, and the feminine side represented by the *Anima*. Jung maintained that each individual bears within himself the corresponding unconscious archetype of the other gender, which, as in the case of the Shadow, must be acknowledged and accepted as an integral part of the individual in order to complete the pathway of Self-achievement.

In his definition of these archetypes, Jung once again underlines the fundamental difference between an archetype, which by nature cannot be accessed directly, and its contents, the forms or images through which it manifests itself:

> Though the contents of anima and animus can be integrated they themselves cannot, since they are archetypes. As such they are the foundation stones of the psychic structure, which in its totality exceeds the limits of consciousness and therefore can never become the object of direct cognition. Though the effects of anima and animus can be made conscious, they themselves are factors transcending consciousness and beyond the reach of perception and volition. Hence they remain autonomous despite the integration of their contents, and for this reason they should be borne constantly in mind.[216]

These two parts of the pair, Animus and Anima, are openly manifested as symbolic, yet unconscious contents; indeed, in our dreams and in the emotions we feel, each individual perceives emotions routinely attributed to the opposite sex, which are therefore archived and rejected, due to their being incongruous within the individual *Persona*.

It should be pointed out that the latter term had maintained, according to Jung, its original meaning, the meaning attributed by the Greek, i.e., the mask that conceals the actor, the sum of the roles we assign ourselves and that others assign to us. On the contrary, the term 'Individual' refers to all that is behind the Persona, the true essence comprising the archetypal, unconscious contents that clash with the role we assume; an integral part of Self, which should be encountered, acknowledged and accepted to enhance individuation. The Persona (from the Latin word that designated the theatre mask) may thus be viewed as the public face of an individual, the way he appears in society, in line with the accepted rules and conventions. It reveals what each of us is willing to put on display, but does not necessarily coincide with one's true inner being:

> It is only because the persona represents a more or less arbitrary and fortuitous segment of the collective psyche that we can make the mistake of regarding it in toto as something individual. It is, as its name implies, only a mask of the

> collective psyche, a mask that feigns individuality, making others and oneself believe that one is individual, whereas one is simply acting a role through which the collective psyche speaks...Fundamentally the persona in nothing real: it is a compromise between individual and society as to what a man should appear to be. He takes a name, earns a title, exercises a function, he is this or that. In a certain sense all this is real, yet in relation to the essential individuality of the person concerned it is only a secondary reality, a compromise formation, in making which others often have a greater share than he.[217]

The image of the Anima or Animus thus *balances* the Persona, it represents the unconscious side of the latter and affords creative opportunities in the individuation process.

In the context of the individuation process, the Anima represents the exquisitely psychic and mental aspects capable of transforming the Anima into the first initiatic contact the individual experiences with his own psychology. It is represented as a woman, a feminine figure, one of the most communicative archetypes as it inundates the individual with images from the unconscious, it creates illusions and complications, as well as crises:

> No man is so entirely masculine that he has nothing feminine in him. The fact is, rather, that very masculine men have – carefully guarded and hidden – a very soft emotional life, often incorrectly described as 'feminine'. A man counts it a virtue to repress his feminine traits as much as possible, just as a woman, at least until recently, considered it unbecoming to be 'mannish'. The repression of feminine traits and inclinations naturally causes these contrasexual demands to accumulate in the unconscious. No less naturally, the imago of woman (the soul-image) becomes a receptacle for these demands, which is why a man, in his love-choice, is strongly tempted to win the woman who best corresponds to his own unconscious femininity – a woman, in short, who can unhesitatingly receive the projection of this soul...The first bearer of the soul-image is always the mother; later it is borne by those women who arouse the man's feelings, whether in a positive or in a negative sense.[218]

The Animus, on the other hand, represents the ensemble of typically masculine, practical and concrete, rational, and real aspects, i.e. the contact with the sphere of the direct and the tangible, the 'here and now'. This is the most combative and pragmatic archetype, seen as dangerous in view of its instrumental ability to overwhelm the individual; its portrayal in dreams thus corresponds to the war, the blacksmith and similar symbols. Jung synthetically described the characteristics of the two archetypes as follows:

> We must therefore expect the unconscious of woman to show aspects essentially different from those found in man. If I were to attempt to put in a nutshell the difference between man and woman in this respect, i.e., what it is that characterises the animus as opposed to the anima, I could only say this: as the anima produces moods, so the animus produces opinions; and as the moods of a man issue from a shadowy background, so the opinions of a woman rest on equally unconscious prior assumptions. Animus opinions very often have the character of solid convictions that are not lightly shaken, or of principles whose validity is seemingly unassailable.[219]

In the same way as men with the Anima, women also need to enter into a strictly dialectic relationship with the Animus:

> The technique of coming to terms with the animus is the same in principle as in the case of the anima; only here the woman must learn to criticise and hold her *opinions* at a distance; not in order to repress them but, by investigating their origins, to penetrate more deeply into the background, where she will then discover the primordial images, just as the man does in his dealings with the anima. The animus is the deposit, as it were, of all woman's ancestral experiences of man – and not only that, he is also a creative and procreative being, not in the sense of masculine creativity, but in the sense that he brings forward something we might call the *lògos spermatikòs*, the spermatic word.[220]

An understanding of one's own Anima, or Animus, thus represents a fundamental element in the journey towards the approach of Self. If this fails to take place the achievement of a total personality will be impossible:

> The immediate goal of the analysis of the unconscious is to reach a state where the unconscious contents no longer remain unconscious and no longer express themselves indirectly as animus and anima phenomena; that is to say a state in which animus and anima become functions of relationship to the unconscious. So long as they are not this, they are autonomous complexes, disturbing factors that break through the conscious control.[221]

A non-understanding of these archetypes will, as a consequence, inevitably lead to a block, a standstill, a neurosis, as both are in possession of a creative and a destructive potential; in his work *Aion* Jung summarised these first two stages:

> The first of these is the shadow, that hidden, repressed, for the most part inferior and guilt-laden personality whose ultimate ramifications reach back into the realm of our animal ancestors and so comprise the whole historical aspect of the unconscious. Through analysis of the shadow and of the processes

contained in it we uncover the anima/animus syzygy. Looked at superficially, the shadow is cast by the conscious mind and is as much a privation of light as the physical shadow that follows the body. For this superficial view, therefore, the psychological shadow with its moral inferiority might also be regarded as a privation of good. On closer inspection, however, it proves to be a darkness that hides influential and autonomous factors, which can be distinguished in their own right, namely anima and animus. When we observe them in full operation – as the devastating, blindly obstinate demon of opionionatedness in a woman, and the glamours, possessive, moody, and sentimental seductress in a man – we begin to doubt whether the unconscious can be merely the insubstantial comet's tail of consciousness and nothing but a privation of light and good. If it has been believed hitherto that the human shadow was the source of all evil, it can now be ascertained on closer investigation that the unconscious man, that is, his shadow, does not consist only of morally reprehensible tendencies, but also displays a number of good qualities, such as normal instincts, appropriate reactions, realistic insights, creative impulses, etc. On this level of understanding, evil appears more as a distortion, a deformation, a misinterpretation and misapplication of facts that in themselves are natural. These falsifications and caricatures now appear as the specific effects of anima and animus, and the latter as the real authors of evil. But we cannot stop even at this realisation, for it turns out that all archetypes spontaneously develop favourable and unfavourable, light and dark, good and bad effects. In the end we have to acknowledge that the self is a *complexio oppositorum* precisely because there can be no reality without polarity.[222]

The Wise Old Man or the archetype of the Initiate and Self

The third stage is represented by an encounter with the *Wise Old Man*. This archetype is conveyed as the masculine, paternal, specular counterpart of the *Great Mother*. The Wise Old Man embodies the archetype in which the entirety of the individual's potentials, i.e. his predictions, reasoning ability and experience, are locked. As the Great Mother represents the ultimate goal for the feminine psychology, the Wise Old Man symbolises everything the individual will become on completing the previous stages, a man, a *Wiseman* who knows, has encountered the past, the present and the future, a counsellor, a philosopher. Based on these potentials, the Wise Old Man represents what the individual strives to become; he symbolises consideration, wisdom and intuition on the one hand, and moral qualities on the other. Failure to recognise the Wise Old Man will therefore immobilise the individual, and will hamper his achievement of a spiritual evolution.

It is not by chance that the Wise Old Man was defined by Jung as the archetype of the *Spirit* in human form, or rather, the personification of the spiritual principle, represented as a judicious, authoritative, perceptive, sensitive and decisive figure capable of leading those seeking enlightenment; he potentially symbolises the Master. A disciple of the Initiatic Schools feels the necessity to encounter this archetype, which 'preserves the hidden secret of experience'; only after meeting the same will he be able to venture beyond the search for Self, having acquired the power to see things no longer in a horizontal-material manner, but rather from a *vertical-spiritual* viewpoint.

Between 1934 and 1939, Jung held a number of seminars on the interpretation of Nietzsche's best-known book, *Thus Spoke Zarathustra*; this in-depth study provided the Swiss psychoanalyst the opportunity to further develop the archetype of the Wise Old Man. During the seminars, Jung highlighted how Nietzsche himself maintained that Zarathustra personified an ancient experience, the primordial experience of the Wise Old Man, a figure that embodies the centennial wisdom we 'inherited', the bearer 'of the truth that has become instinctive through experience, one could say, having been lived millions of times, a sort of wisdom of nature that is born in us and to which we owe the coordination of our whole biological as well as psychological system – that old experience which is still visible in our drams and in our instincts'.[223] It was Jung's belief that Tradition thus originated within man himself, and represented the result of his deepest *experiences* aimed at the discovery of the Divine, which also lies within us:

> Now, there are numbers of archetypal situations and the whole of them make up the world of mythology. Mythology is the textbook of archetypes, of course not rationally elucidated and explained, but simply represented like a picture or a storybook. But all archetypes were originally real situations.[224]

Jung also highlighted how the archetype of the Wise Old Man could sometimes be represented by a distinctly historical figure, which was later transformed into an archetype, a figure:

> Which brings with it the flavour of past centuries, a feeling of the actual presence of remote times, as if time were at a complete standstill...I am quite certain, from what Nietzsche says about Zarathustra, that he experienced him as an identity within himself that had existed many thousands of years before him, that always had been.[225]

In the context of the Masonic initiatic experience, the presence of the archetype of the Wise Old Man is manifested in the figure of King Solomon, the wisdom of whom is proverbial. Freemasons are called upon to represent King Solomon, and thus discover this archetype, only at the apex of their initiatic experience; indeed, at this point they will have assumed the role of the Lodge's initiatic guide, the Venerable Master, who, in turn, initiates others:

> The sun within, an illuminating factor, the sun of understanding, the light of the Gnosis...in the Gnostic texts you always find that light symbolism associated with the wise old man who is the initiator, the bringer of light.[226]

To this regard, Jung warned against a full identification, as to do so would signify a return to use of the mask, that of the Persona: 'The old wise man is surely the figure of the great teacher, the initiator, the psychopompos'; it should however be borne in mind, that to encounter the Wise Old Man does not signify to identify with him, as this would determine an inflation in which individuality is once again lost, 'for one cannot possibly live as the wise old man day and night; one would be something between a corpse and a fool'.[227]

As mentioned previously, the Sapiential Schools, the environment in which the disciple meets the archetype of the Wise Old Man, were created in times of crisis in which the individual risked losing his own Centre; in fact, Jung remarked with regard to this archetype:

> Whenever he appears, he also refers to a certain situation: there is some disorientation, a certain unconsciousness, people are in a sort of confusion and don't know what to do. Therefore these Saoshyants, these wise men or prophets, appear in times of trouble, when mankind is in a state of confusion, when an old orientation has been lost and a new one is needed.[228]

To return to our reference ideal, the Initiate, in the light of what has been discussed so far, we are now in a position to further define this figure. The initiate is an individual who, having embarked on a journey aimed at achieving the evolution of his consciousness, is about to encounter the archetype of the Wise Old Man, indeed, he feels a need to do so on having completed the first stages of the process; he has, indeed, already met his Shadow, his Anima, and is now ready for the final stage of the initiatic, conscientious and psychic journey. Through the experience of an authentic Initiatic School, this individual, our ideal type, an Initiate from the point of view of his qualification and his essence, also becomes an Initiate from a ritual perspective; in other words, he becomes part of a Tradition, and can thus aspire to know Tradition. He is keen to undertake the hardest part of his journey of conscientious evolution in the environment he deems the most fitting for achievement of his chosen goal. As discussed previously, he has already met the previous archetypes and now, aiming to extend further his consciousness, adopts the instruments of intellectual intuition (or *Active Imagination*) to conclude his process of Self-discovery.

The fourth and last stage of this path is characterised by the encounter with the archetype of Self. By drawing a parallelism with alchemical dynamics, an encounter with the Shadow represents the alchemical process of *Nigredo*, followed by the further elaboration of the contents of the unconscious and the appearance of the following archetypes, the Anima or Animus and the Wise Old Man, symbolising the *Albedo*. The conclusion of the pathway, the discovery and achievement of one's deepest Self, is viewed as the alchemical representation of the third and final stage, *Rubedo*.

The Self symbolises the peak of the pathway of realisation of one's personality, in which the totality of the conscious and unconscious aspects of a subject are ultimately united.

When the individual encounters the archetype of Self, this implies that the latter is aligned with the Ego; until this takes place, the 'pathway' is not deemed to be complete:

> Intellectually the self is no more than a psychological concept, a construct that serves to express an unknowable essence which we cannot grab as such, since by definition it transcends our powers of comprehension. It might equally be called 'the God within us'...Nor does it imply a deification of man or a dethronement of God. What is beyond our understanding is in any case beyond its reach. When, therefore, we make use of a concept of God, we are simply formulating a definite psychological fact, namely the independence and sovereignty of certain psychological contents that express themselves by their power to thwart our will, to obsess our consciousness, and to influence our moods and actions...Therefore, by affixing the attribute 'divine' to the workings of autonomous contents, we are admitting their relatively superior force. And it is this superior force that has at all times constrained humans to ponder the inconceivable and even to impose the greatest sufferings upon themselves in order to give these workings their due. It is a force as real as hunger and the fear of death.[229]

Accordingly, this archetype represents the sum of the individuation process, the *goal* and objective of our ideal type, or reference figure, the Initiate. The archetype of Self is represented by Jung, varying according to the work in which it is mentioned, as a light, a mandala, a quaternary, as a Centre and as God, it symbolises the central *point* of the personality; it is, indeed, around Self that all other systems are grouped, it ensures cohesion and provides the personality with balance, stability and, above all, *unity*.

In line with the Jungian theory, the Ego represents the conscious side of our psyche, whereas the archetypes represent its unconscious element; consequently, just as the Ego is placed at the core of consciousness, so Jung places Self at the core of personality. Reaching one's Self, therefore, signifies reaching the *wholeness*, that is, the union of the conscious with the unconscious, as clarified by Jung:

> Psychologically the self is a union of conscious (masculine) and unconscious (feminine). It stands for the psychic totality. So formulated, it is a

> psychological concept. Empirically, however, the self appears spontaneously in the shape of specific symbols, and its totality is discernible above all in the mandala and its countless variants.[230]

According to Jung, Self also generates an authentic ethical reaction in the individual, at variance with the ethics imposed by the collectivity in which we live, as described by Von Franz:

> A subdued inner voice, the *vox Dei* or voice of the Self. In other words, what Jung calls the ethical reaction of the human psyche is not identical with the Freudian superego. On the contrary, the two concepts can even clash and be opposed. Jung expresses his view that we are under the pressure of two factors: that of the collective ethical code, which differs from nation to nation and generally dictates our ethical behaviour, and that of a personal moral urge, which is individual and often does not coincide with the collective code.[231]

At times, the two morals fail to coincide and the individual finds himself faced with a critical choice between his intimate moral vision and that of the social context, which surrounds him:

> Then you are in the soup, and then you realise that really there are two things which dictate human behaviour: the collective ethical code, which we can also call the Freudian superego, and the personal moral individual reaction. The latter is generally referred to as the voice of God, even when it sometimes coincides with the collective moral code. The Romans would call it genius, Socrates would say 'my daimonion', and the Naskapi Indians of the Labrador Peninsula would call it Mistap'eo, the 'great man who lives in everybody's heart. In other words, it is a figure which we would call an archetype of the self, the divine centre of the psyche which naturally, in different cultures, has different names and connotations.[232]

The fundamental function of Self-achievement is to restore order to the psychic chaos of the individual; the Self, which lies latent within us from the outset, thus develops a tendency to solve our decompensations and applies its energy to encourage us to seek psychic wholeness. The process was clearly described by Jeffrey Raff:

> Balancing this disorder, however, is the self, the principle of order and harmony… From the perspective of personified images, the self as a totality includes the whole array of images and voices that arise from the unconscious. In addition, the self is the centre of the psyche, around which all the other parts orient themselves. The self brings order to the psyche, and harmonises all aspects of the psyche to create an orchestrated composition. Seen in this way,

> the self is the centre of the soul around which the archetypes are grouped in their respective order. The mandala is the symbol for the self when it functions in this manner. To distinguish between the self before and after individuation, I speak of the 'latent' and the 'manifest' self. The latent self is a weak centre, possessing only limited power to organise psychic life. Within the latent self, the complexes and archetypes vie for control of the…The power and energy of the self, manifests as an almost irresistible urge to be oneself. The self, pushes one to the experience and expression of one's own uniqueness; to this end it must order the archetypal world. The archetypes are collective forces, and the images that they produce are universal. An individual might simply follow these images, and, thereby, have numinous experiences… As the self brings the archetypes into harmony, it affects the patterned order of the mandala structure with each archetype in a complementary relationship to the whole. In this process, the archetypes lose their universal and collective qualities, and actually contribute to the uniqueness that is the self.[233]

The Self therefore, could be described as the archetype of *wholeness*; it leads towards the realisation of a more complete personality by integrating the unconscious into the consciousness. To this regard, we can ascertain how the rituals and doctrines of the Sapiential Schools comprise these very dynamics, highlighted by the goal that both the Initiate and the individual set themselves: the search for wholeness.

In the Eleusinian rituals, Gnostic and Hermetic essays (particularly the *Ogdoad* and the *Ennead*), alchemical papers and in the Masonic rituals, the archetype of Self becomes conscious, by satisfying the need of the Initiate for Transcendence as a conscious self-realisation of his own wholeness. The disciple of the Sapiential Schools, by means of an initiatic pathway of self-improvement, seeks from within the requests of the archetype with the aim of integrating these into his consciousness and providing them with an individual solution. Within this vision, the Self represents the divine component of the personality, that which in Gnosticism and the Kabbalah was represented by a spark of light seeking conscious realisation.

Whereas in normal conditions archetypal images are projected outside the Myth and into religion, in the presence of collective crises they return to the unconscious from which they originated, giving rise to chaotic situations and spiritual confusion. In the event of a spiritual crisis, when the external values of the revealed credo collapse, this archetype returns to the psyche from which it originated, and man needs to *restore* his sense of the sacred within himself through a more emphasised individuation.

For this reason, the main objective of the Initiatic Schools was unfailingly to provide, in times of crises of conscience, the opportunity, an alternative to the official religions and cults, to carry out a project of improvement of the individual, which would allow him to find his Centre, his own Self. This process was rendered possible thanks to a *transcendent* action, i.e. displacement of the psychic centre from the Ego, the centre of consciousness, to the Self, the centre of conscious and unconscious personality. The *condicio sine qua non* for this operation would have been the subordination of the Ego to the Self in a metaphysical project, the 'death' of the Ego, better known as *initiatic death*, as we are reminded by René Alleau:

> We often forget that the primary sense of the expression 'to initiate' literally signifies 'to let die'. An 'initiate' is no less separated from the profane world than a dead person is. Despite the illusions with which the unhappy appease themselves, neither the dead nor the initiates speak directly with beings who are placed on a different level to theirs. It is up to us to raise to them, rather than demanding that they descend to us.'[234]

The great Ibn 'Arabi maintained that it is necessary to 'die before you die', to overcome the *illusion* of separation.

The initiatic death is present in all sapiential doctrines, from Osiris, to Orpheus, to Demophon in the Eleusinian Mysteries, to Hiram Habif in the Masonic rituals; it symbolises the mystic drama of God, his passion, death and resurrection, which, in the alchemical work, the Black Work, the *nigredo*, is projected onto the matter in order to cause its transmutation. To this regard, alchemist Basil Valentine wrote that:

> Neither human nor animal bodies can be multiplied or propagated without decomposition; the grain and all vegetable seed must decay before it can spring up again...But you who should know more than the vulgar herd, must search into the causes of things, and endeavor to understand how the process of generation and resuscitation is accomplished by means of decomposition.[235]

As Eliade recalls, the alchemist deals with *Matter* in the same way as divinity is handled in the Mysteries: the mineral substances 'suffer', 'die', 'are reborn' to another way of being, they have been, in other words, transmuted. Alchemists project onto Matter the initiatic function of suffering and it is precisely thanks to the 'tortures', the 'death' inflicted by the alchemist to Matter that the substance is transmuted and the *miste* resurrects, and becomes, allegorically, Gold. Gold, as Eliade recalls, represents the symbol of immortality; the ancient Egyptians believed that the flesh of the gods was made of gold and that the pharaoh, by becoming a god, would also acquire a flesh of gold. The alchemical transmutation thus corresponded to the perfection of matter, or if interpreted in Christian terms, to its redemption. The latter represented, according to Eliade, the substantial novelty of the alchemical concept: the life of Matter is no longer designated in terms of *vital* hierophanies, as it was in the outlook of primitive man, but it has acquired a spiritual dimension; in other words, by taking on the initiatory significance of drama and suffering, matter also takes on the destiny of the Spirit. The initiation tests which, on the spiritual plance, culminate in freedom, illumination and immortality, culminate on the material plane, in transmutation, in the Philosopher's Stone.[236]

The initiatic death is thus the key to a full comprehension of the individuation process; death is necessary for the deeper Self to be generated by the Ego: 'By means of putrefaction, fermentation, and trituration – all of which take place in darkness - the materia is divested of its initial form'.[237] And indeed as Masonic initiates we are compelled to *leave all Metals behind*, a purification that is strictly necessary for the initiatic path to start:

> A creature of heaven...dies and rots. Then the stars, by means of the elements, will give life again to this putrid corpse, so that from it may rise a new celestial body...Once this is done, thou shalt see the terrestrial completely consumed by the celestial and the earthly body forever in a heavenly crown of honor and glory.[238]

French Alchemist and writer Eugène Canseliet, the only disciple of the great Fulcanelli, perfectly defined in one of his writings the putrefaction process with regard to initiatic death:

> Amongst the writings united in the golden Ars, at times reduced to the size of a pamphlet, there is not one that speaks of the indispensable and fecund putrefaction, in which black is the perfect sign, and the first of all philosophical operations destined to succeed. Sublime blackness, divine alpha, unyieldingly denied to the unworthy, to those who, masked spectators of occultism in the most pejorative sense of the term, slaves to falsehood in search of miserable sordid gains, throng before the still valid remains of some old man sacrificed by the abominable negotiations:
> *Ah, black hirsute corset of splendid flies*
> *Buzzing betwixt cruel miasmas*
> *Gulfs of shadow*
> We do not fear to insist; in the case of future births, putrefaction will not take place in the absence of a simultaneous dissolution, and both together will accompany the darkness the thickness of which was indicated by the ancients, hyperbolically pronouncing that it is 'blacker than the blackest of blacks' (nigrum nigrius nigro). However, the certain sign of death does not lie merely in the funereal hue, and is frequently accompanied by the observance of infectious issuances, commonly reported by the authors, among which the 'ancient philosopher Artephius' commented 'And in this putrefaction and resolution of the body three signs will be manifested, being a black colour, discontinuity and separation of the parts, and a fetid odour resembling that perceived in the sepulchres.[239]

The Gnostic journeys of the Sapiential Schools (Mystery, Hermetic, Rosicrucian, Alchemical, Masonic) reveal the presence of a dynamic which recalls, in its practice and goal, albeit with the due differences, the 'individuation process', the conscious realisation of our yearning for wholeness, of our peculiarity and diversity. The activation of Self, achieved by means of the above journey generates an experience that can be defined as *religious* (or sacred), and it is precisely this synergy of conscious and unconscious aspects that determines an *expansion* of the personality.

For the purpose of the present book, Jung's influence is mainly relevant with regard to the equivalence between the conscious Self-realisation of one's own personality and religiosity (or search for sacrality). The road that leads to the realisation of one's own peculiarity would thus be comprised within a greater transcendent project.

Active Imagination as a gnostic and initiatic pathway.

I shall now progress to the concept of Active Imagination. The latter is essentially a method aimed at the development of a patient's imagination during psychotherapy, to expedite the process of formation of individual or collective symbols and images. More precisely, this method is employed to artificially extract the diverse unconscious contents, to enhance the setting up by the Ego, once the latter becomes visible, of a *confrontation*; we are therefore dealing with an introspective method by means of which an intentional, direct and alert relationship may be established with the unconscious psyche.

Active Imagination can thus be interpreted as an instrument the individual applies to awaken the archetypal contents of the psyche, a practice aimed at facilitating the individuation process and, as a consequence, Self-realisation.

Active Imagination facilitates ease of access, through exploiting our potential, to the Tradition we possess and that lies within us, and can thus be viewed as a powerful and efficient method contributing to the recovery of an integrated intuitive-sensorial-imaginal-emotional-cognitive-spiritual knowledge corresponding to a largely forgotten ancient wisdom.[240]

The method, even when explained in the simplest way possible, is highly complex and Jung himself considered it accessible only to a restricted number of individuals; it took a long process for it to form itself within the Jungian theory, as testified by the recurring presence of the issue in Jung's writings, starting from *The Transcendent Function* (1916) to the last references that can be found in the essay 'Mysterium Coniunctionis' (1958).

In *The Transcendent Function* Jung did not employ the term Active Imagination but defined the latter 'spontaneous fantasy', to be preferred even to dreams thanks to its potentiality to conjure images:

> Since the energy-tension in sleep is usually very low, dreams, compared with conscious material, are inferior expressions of unconscious contents and are

> very difficult to understand from a constructive point of view, but are usually easier to understand reductively. In general, dreams are unsuitable or difficult to make use of in developing the transcendent function, because they make too great demands on the subject.[241]

For this reason, to activate the transcendent function Jung considered the possibility of using 'other sources', the most efficient of which was, indeed, represented by Active Imagination:

> Another source is spontaneous fantasies. They usually have a more composed and coherent character and often contain much that is obviously significant. Some patients are able to produce fantasies at any time, allowing them to rise up freely simply by eliminating critical attention. Such fantasies can be used, though this particular talent is none too common. The capacity to produce free fantasies can, however, be developed with practice. The training consists first of all in systematic exercises for eliminating critical attention, thus producing a vacuum in conscience. This encourages the emergence of any fantasies that are lying in readiness. A prerequisite, of course, is that fantasies with a high libido-charge are actually lying ready. This is naturally not always the case.[242]

Having been preferred over dreams, which represent a pure product of the unconscious, the method of Active Imagination conferred to the *inner* factor an expression that Jung referred to as 'transcendent function', i.e. the function that triggers a *synthesis* of the conscious and unconscious personality.[243]

Jung described Active Imagination as a form of dialectical psychological confrontation, the most specific procedure of integration between the conscious and the unconscious, through which the Ego and the psychic processes confront each other within the field of fantasy by creating common expressions in terms of meaning and value:

> The method is based on evaluating the symbol (i.e., dream-image or fantasy) not semiotically, as a sign for elementary instinctual processes, but symbolically in the true sense, the word 'symbol' being taken to mean the best possible expression for a complex fact not yet clearly apprehended by consciousness. Through reductive analysis of this expression nothing is gained but a clearer view of the elements originally composing it.[244]

Certain scholars, likewise interpreted active Imagination, as a form of *meditation*, based essentially on an inner confrontation between the personifications of the unconscious, whose goal, as we have seen, is the conjunction of the opposites that have been observed during the analysis of the unconscious.

Active Imagination mainly represents an imaginal dialogue between the Ego and the figures of the unconscious, which triggers the 'transcendent function', a substantial alteration of consciousness, obtained, indeed, through the conjunction, *coniunctio*, between the conscious and the unconscious minds. To this regard, Prof Antonella Adorisio, member of the Italian Centre for Analytical Psychology, wrote:

> A powerful and efficient method to turn our attention to the invisible world of our interiority; it is a central and self-reflective psychological attitude which promotes the occurrence of the symbolic function in the inner encounter with the Other. By giving space and form to the tension that is implicit in the contrast between diverging positions, active imagination sets out to create unifying symbols which, in their containing of and transcending both positions, can identify new possibilities and facilitate the individuation process.[245]

As discussed previously, the goal of Active Imagination is to stimulate the 'transcendent function', the psychic mechanism which transcends the pair of opposites constituted by incompatible conscious and unconscious tendencies, and which symbolises our *inner* mode of psychological and spiritual growth, enabling the passage from one behaviour to another and thus allowing us to overcome the opposition without necessarily rejecting it, but rather assembling it in an original synthesis.

The structure of the method is undoubtedly linked to the work Jung performed on himself, particularly the experiences which characterised the period 1912-1917, as elegantly testified by the images and explications produced in the *Red Book*. Despite Jung listing a number of methods to *activate* Active Imagination (painting, sculpting, dancing), he believed that the most efficient consisted in allowing a vision to spontaneously present itself. As far as the other methods are concerned, as correctly observed by Jungian analyst and psychiatrist Michael Fordham, it is imperative to understand the clear distinction between *imaginative activity* and Active Imagination, in order to avoid the risk of considering all paintings, sculptures or other as indistinct expressions of the latter:

> Painting pictures, fantasying, etc., may just as well be imaginative activity as active imagination, the distinction depending upon the activity of the go. In favourable circumstances imaginative activity leads to growth of the ego, active imagination to consciousness of the self.[246]

Indeed, through Active Imagination one is not abandoned to free association, which merely allows complexes to prevail, but rather grabs an element of fantasy and *consciously* adheres to it. Practice determines an ability in following the evolution of the material and in carrying out an actual 'dialogue' with the latter, as described by Jung:

> The point is that you start with any image...Contemplate it and carefully observe how the picture begins to unfold or to change. Don't try to make it into something, just do nothing but observe what its spontaneous changes are. Any mental picture you contemplate in this way will sooner or later change through a spontaneous association that causes a slight alteration of the picture. You must carefully avoid impatient jumping from one subject to another. Hold fast to the one image you have chosen and wait until it changes by itself. Note all these changes and eventually step into the picture yourself, and if it is a speaking figure at all then say what you have to say to that figure and listen to what he or she has to say.[247]

The first phase of the method, the 'letting things happen', requires the creation of a true psychic void, to enable us to reach a state of total relaxation bringing the conscious and the unconscious closer together, a state of tranquillity in which the subject remains conscious and aware. Thereafter, we should concentrate on the image that will be produced with an open and welcoming attitude; the term used by Jung to this regard, *betrachten*, designates a sort of observation able to make the image 'pregnant'.

If the image is pregnant, it implies that a birth and, subsequently, further creation of new images is to be expected, all of which confirms the *transforming potential* of the relationship between the observer and the observed.

The image produced should then be represented objectively by means of an *expression outlet*, to include a series of different forms of expression, such as writing, painting, dance, poetry, music. Finally, an 'ethical confrontation' between the Ego and the unconscious should be stimulated, by interpreting the images and messages from the unconscious as real and, thus, maintaining the same ethical behaviour we would adopt in a real situation. It can thus be gathered that the term 'active' specifically refers to the *active* role of the Ego towards the personifications of the unconscious, allowing for a differentiation of the latter from complexual possessions.[248] The importance of assuming ethical responsibility with regard to the images that are conjured plays a central role in the Jungian method, as emphasised by Federico de Luca Comandini:

> The psychic event within the procedure culminates when it urges the parties involved to actively intervene in the imaginal context that has been created. Assuming a conscious position is essential for the establishment of a fruitful relationship with the unconscious. Should the Ego not assume its share of responsibility with regard to the stream of images, the latter would disappear leaving no traces like prints in the desert.[249]

By practicing the method of Active Imagination therefore, the initial state of psychotic void, a void that is nevertheless full of potential, is gradually filled with personifications originating from the unconscious, which, subsequently, in view of the attention bestowed on the same by conscious behaviour, become saturated and undergo a transformation through the observation of the generator. These images reconnect us to symbols that, in turn, bear a forgotten knowledge and *primordial wisdom* that continues to lie within our unconscious, awaiting a return to the light, a Tradition.

As mentioned previously, caution should be applied to not confuse Active Imagination with passive fantasy, as the Ego plays no part in the latter and images emerge in consciousness without the evocation or participation of the receiver.

On the contrary, in Active Imagination the Ego establishes a *voluntary* relationship with the images, which, through its intervention, are brought to light; the acting subject thus does not limit himself to allowing the image to emerge from the unconscious, but assumes an *active* position towards it and seemingly seeks an ethical confrontation. To quote Federico de Luca Comandini on the matter:

> To promote an ethical confrontation between the Ego and the unconscious is ultimately the crucial question for Jung, in favour of a symbolic behaviour of the mind able to transcend the acute antinomy scattered between the psychic opposites (rational/irrational, conscious/unconscious, etc.) in the current vision of the world. In the psychological approach to imagination, therefore, it is essential for the Jungian perspective not to limit oneself to a contemplative and/or interpretative (in the ordinary sense of the word) fruition of what emerges from the unconscious, but for there to be an active participation of the Ego in the development of the event.[250]

Once the method of Active Imagination is in a position to enhance a vital tension between opposites, a state of expanded consciousness is generated, an operation resembling the results achieved by a Gnostic or Mystic experience, as explained by Antonella Adorisio:

> The dialogue with the unconscious cannot but be a secret experience with the mystery within which the symbolic function can develop; in this sense, it can also be defined as a mystic (linked to mystery) experience which leaves us transformed, in a similar manner to what happened during the ancient Mystery cults...Active imagination, as a form of self-treatment, can also represent an *actual initiatic journey* that requires departure to take place with empty hands, by leaving everything that one owns behind, in order to access the void 'full' of potential that allows for deep and radical transformations. A journey that expects to have to face everything that stands in the way of change, which should thus be accomplished by carrying the torch of one's own awareness.[251]

To this regard, I should like to quote an excerpt from the Red Book by Jung, which offers an explanation of the meaning and essence of the method of *Active Imagination*:

> I earnestly confronted my devil and behaved with him as with a real person. This I learned in the Mysterium: to take seriously every unknown wanderer who personally inhabits the inner world, since they are real because they are effectual. It does not help that we say in the spirit of this time: there is no devil. There was one with me. This took place in me. I did with him what I could. I could speak with him…I must have it out with him, as I cannot expect that he as an independent personality would accept my standpoint without further ado. I would be fleeing if I did not try to come to an understanding with him. If ever you have the rare opportunity to speak with the devil, then do not forget to confront him in all seriousness. He is your devil after all. The devil as the adversary is your own other standpoint; he tempts you and sets a stone in your path where you least want it. Taking the devil seriously does not mean going over to his side, or else one becomes the devil. Rather it means coming to an understanding. Thereby you accept your other standpoint.[252]

Of course, in this instance the devil is identified as the allegory of any other personification of the unconscious expressing a different point of view from that conveyed consciously.

Jung's words convey how Active Imagination is capable of producing, for the selected few that succeed in activating the same, a true *development of consciousness*, with his method revealing the dynamics and objectives of a true gnostic journey, a gnosis represented by a confrontation between the conscious and the unconscious (both personal and collective) sides of the individual. The completion of the journey will allow the individual to achieve a realisation of his personality, a process referred to by Jung as 'individuation'. Over the course of this journey the individual will encounter and collide with archetypal (unconscious) organisations of his personality and, only by facing them, will he be able to further *expand* his consciousness, by means of a method which represents the royal road through which the Ego establishes a vital relationship with the archetypal images known as Tradition.

Active Imagination and the Alchemical 'Opus'

Before delving deeper into Jung's studies on alchemy, it seems appropriate to remember that the first scholar to carry out a psychoanalytical interpretation of alchemical writings was not Jung but Viennese psychoanalyst Herbert Silberer, who discussed alchemy in his essay 'Probleme der Mystik und ihrer Symbolik' (1914). Silberer, as James Webb reminds us, had specialised in the application of Freudian interpretations to legends, Occultism and Religion, but, strangely, Webb neglected to mention Silberer's strong interest in Freemasonry, which was thoroughly analysed in connection with alchemy and Rosicrucianism in the essay 'Problems of Mysticism and its Symbolism'.

In the above essay, Silberer declared to have discovered the religious significance of Alchemy thanks to Ethan Allen Hitchcock's works, which encouraged him to examine the Vedanta and several authors involved with Occultism, such as Papus and Elifas Levi. Silberer's study on Alchemy offered three interpretations: the psychoanalytical (Freudian-sexual), the chemical, and the one he referred to as anagogical, which made use of a Hermetic exegesis, thus representing a true 'esoteric' interpretation of alchemy.

According to Silberer, man's unconscious remained approximately the same throughout great periods, meaning that the unconscious of a man of today would be in its fundamentals not significantly different from that of alchemist Zosimus; Silberer believed, in fact, that the aspect that an individual reveals of himself is essentially 'the soul of the race', his humanity. Starting from this assumption, he defined alchemy as a true 'way of thinking', a sort of vision of the world common to all those who, throughout the different historical periods, were involved with the *Ars Regia*.

Silberer's text provides an analysis of the various element of the Alchemical Opus and, particularly, the concept of Prima Materia, and underlines how Alchemists attributed numerous, over a hundred, definitions to this expression, some of which continue to represent a true enigma today. Indeed, alchemists provided clues for interpretation, which were soon however revealed to be far from exhaustive, as only the predestined individual, he who was 'destined' to comprehension, was capable of finding the keys for the entire Work.

Silbered listed some of the definitions used to refer to the Prima Materia, interpreted both as 'original material' and as 'first condition': *Lapis philosphicus* (philosopher's stone), *aqua vitae* (water of life), *venenum* (poison), *spiritus* (spirit), *medicina* (medicine), *Coelum* (Sky), *nubes* (clouds), *Ros* (dew), *Umbra* (shadow), *stella signata* (marked star), *Lucifero, Luna* (moon), *aqua ardens* (fiery water), *sponsa* (betrothed), *coniux* (wife), *mater*, *madre* (Eve), *lac vorginis* (virgin's milk), *mestruum, materia hermaphrodita catholica Solis et Lunae* (Catholic hermaphrodite matter of sun and moon), *espettorato Lunae* (moon spittle), *uruna fimus* (children's urine), *affronta dissolutae* (loose stool), *fimus* (muck), *materia omnium formarum* (material of all forms), Venus.

Having highlighted how the original material in the above definitions was often identified with secretions and excretions, saliva, milk, dung, menstrual fluid, urine, Silberer underlined the correspondences with childhood's theories of procreation, which, in his opinion, related to the fantasies that refer to symbols originating from man's primitive activities.

In the paper Silberer also outlined the differences between high alchemy (commonly known as speculative alchemy) and practical alchemy (the so-called 'metal blowers'), proposing an interesting analogy with operative and speculative Freemasonry. Silberer particularly highlighted the contamination between high alchemy and speculative Freemasonry, which he believed to have taken place through the Rosicrucian thought. Indeed, despite the fact that the origins of the Masonic and Rosicrucian thoughts are believed not to coincide, the German scholar considered speculative Freemasonry to have derived specifically from the Rosicrucian Alchemical thought, and argued his theory by highlighting the parts of the Masonic doctrine in which he believed the Rosicrucian Alchemical symbolisms and dynamics to be evident. In order to support his thesis, Silberer quoted the theories of German philologist and Freemason Ludwig Keller who, with regard to alchemical, Rosicrucian and Masonic symbols, declared that 'we meet a language that has found acceptance among all occidental peoples in analogous form, not indie a letter or word language, but a language nevertheless, a token or a symbol language of developed form, which is evident even in the rock temples of the so-called catacombs, once called latomies and loggie. The single images and symbols have something to say only to the person who understands this language. To the man who does not understand it, they say nothing and are not expected to say anything.'

As discussed previously, there is no proof of a direct filiation between the Rosicrucian movement and thought and Freemasonry, but, as in the case of Neoplatonism, Hermetism and alchemy, there undoubtedly exists a contamination between the above doctrines and the Masonic thought.

Moving on to the Jungian studies on alchemy and their position within the wider category of the 'identification process', I should start by saying that, despite Jung's involvement and extensive examination of gnostic symbols (particularly in the essay *Aion*), the Swiss scholar identified a close analogy with the method of Active Imagination particularly in alchemical meditations. According to Jung, the alchemists were those who allowed their unconscious to manifest itself freely in their laboratories by projecting its contents onto Matter, a prominent object in their researches. In the words of Jung:

> Since the practical, chemical work was never quite free from the unconscious contents of the operator which found expression in it, it was at the same time a psychic activity which can best be compared with what we call active imagination.[253]

Accordingly, for Jung the archetypes represented a sort of 'primordial image', similar to the a priori forms advocated by Kant, to be held responsible for the formation of symbols. These unchanging 'primordial images' may at times be returned to the light through a transcendent function, an individuation process and, particularly, by means of Active Imagination, by projecting the individual beyond his physical confines, on the plane of collective unconscious thought.

The idea that Jung attempted to highlight in his studies on alchemy was how, in certain cases and particularly through the method of Active Imagination, the unconscious pursues processes manifested by means of alchemical symbolisms, processes which tend to produce psychic results comparable to the results obtained in Hermetic operations. Despite attracting the criticism of numerous thinkers who shared the alchemical thought, Jung maintained that alchemists performed Active Imagination in complete unawareness; during their complicated 'operations' they unconsciously projected their inner images onto materials, with the unconscious being projected onto matter:

> While working on his chemical experiments the operator had certain psychic experiences which appeared to him as the particular behaviour of the chemical process…He experiences his projection as a property of matter.[254]

In the *Opus*, alchemists replaced the Ego and the unconscious, which in the individuation process led to Self, with the king and queen, who produced the alchemical gold. Jung maintained that whereas the alchemist starts from the raw material, i.e. lead or other non-noble metals, which he later elaborately transforms into alchemical Gold, the initial raw material is nothing other than a non-individuated Ego, tormented by his neurosis, anxiety and depression, the Ego which: 'Like the prima materia, it goes through a dissolution, what the alchemists call the nigredo; for Jung this is the confrontation with the "shadow", one's "dark side".'[255]

By Active Imagination, therefore, Jung conducts an in-depth psychological assessment aimed at assuming the *legacy* of the task carried out by alchemists, reactivation of the spiritual function with the unconscious foundation of human nature;[256] the individuation process is thus represented as a true 'gnostic' journey that leads man towards his own 'Centre' (the *Self*) and is undertaken by the unconscious without the authorisation of the conscious, invariably against the will of the latter. This journey towards discovery is therefore a mere version of the *opus alchymicum* or, more precisely, an 'unconscious imitation', to be freely used, of an extremely difficult initiatic procedure reserved for a limited spiritual élite. To quote Raff:

> Alchemy provides a model and a map for defining inner experiences, as well as a symbolic system for their expression. There were a number of factors that influenced Jung's conclusion that the stone was symbol for the self. He conceived of the self as the union of opposites and the centre of the psyche. The stone was the union of opposites, and often portrayed as centre. The self could be personified as an inner figure, as could the stone. The self was the repository of wisdom and so, too, was the stone. The self was the goal of all psychic life, and the end state to which the individuation process led, while the stone was the goal of the all alchemical endeavours. Moreover, Jung thought that the self-created symbols in order to make its attributes known and the stone was one such image. Jung always operated under the assumption that what was said of the stone was true of the self, for in the stone the self had found a way to symbolically express itself…But what is the self?

> Experientially, the self is an inner and subjective figure or centre that feels powerful, numinous, and complete in itself. As a theoretical construct, the self has a number of attributes. It is the centre of the whole personality and is thus related to what Jung calls the ego, the centre of consciousness.[257]

It is mainly in his work *Psychology and Alchemy* that Jung organically developed the historical parallelism between his psychology and the alchemical Opus, proposing an analogy between his method of *Active Imagination* and the alchemical concept of *imaginatio*. The volume comprises two studies presented during the 'Eranos' sessions in Ascona, and published, respectively, in 1936 (*Dream Symbols of the Individuation Process*) and 1937 (*Ideas of Redemption in Alchemy*).

Psychology and Alchemy highlights Jung's belief that the latter represented far more than a *pseudo-science*, as it was often identified, as testified by his depiction of alchemy almost as a sort of religion, whose 'disciples' possessed an inner and innate impulse to transform the 'prima materia' of experience in order to redeem the human soul and entire humanity from the darkness of ignorance. In the Jungian interpretation, the alchemist often symbolises the *atanòr* through which the alchemical Opus is carried out, as the figure who will undergo the changes and transformations to provide, in the modified Materia, confirmation that the task has been carried out correctly. Luigi Auriemma, editor of the Italian version of *Psychology and Alchemy*, wrote an exquisite introduction to the Italian version of Jung's above-mentioned work:

> The aim of Jung's essay is clear: to prove, through an exacting and comprehensive analysis of the historical materials that were diffused in extremely wide areas, that his hypothesis of the existence of a psychic collective foundation was not an arbitrary and anti-historical individual fantasy, but the discovery of a common root in which universal behaviours and ample materials materialise themselves, and are then clad by history with specific characters that are typical of singular and unrepeatable conditions...it is precisely this solitude that reveals to Jung the original meaning of Alchemy, which cannot in any way be reduced to a prescientific stutter but rather compared to a marginal form of religiosity: by accepting, or rather, seeking solitude, the Alchemist seems to have acknowledged the unrepeatable, completely personal aspect of the process, in which he can actually live himself, as the material executor, the crucible, the 'vase' transformed by his implication in the operations performed, by the emotion, the hope and the wait in connection with the awaited result: gold, the redeemer of the matter itself in which it lies hidden and buried.[258]

It is clear that the point of contact between Jung and the Alchemists is mainly constituted by the *transformative power* identified both in Active Imagination, in its confrontation between the Ego and the unconscious, and the alchemical *imaginatio*, in which the Alchemists' inner representations were connected to transformation of the Materia, which constituted for Jung the grounds for projections of one's own unconscious.

For these reasons, to Jung, the analysis of alchemical *imagination* represented a fundamental aspect in achieving a comprehension of alchemical studies. Through an analysis of a series of alchemical texts, Jung reached the conclusion that in the alchemical imagination, just as in Active Imagination, the essential part of the process was represented by the initial phase, in which the Alchemist attempted to achieve a state of deep meditation, from which the Work would stem.

The description of the different stages of the alchemical Opus revealed Jung's extensive knowledge, gained as the result of many years of study and examination of alchemical symbolism and allegories in numerous, frequently rare, texts:

> Alchemy, as is well known, described a process of chemical transformation and gives numberless directions for its accomplishment. Although hardly two authors are of the same opinion regarding the exact course of the process and the sequence of its stages, the majority are agreed on the principal points at issue, and have been so from the earliest times, i.e., since the beginning of the Christian era. Four stages are distinguished, characterised by the original colours mentioned in Heraclitus: *melanosis* (blackening), *leukosis* (whitening), *xanthosis* (yellowing), and *iosis* (reddening). This division of the process into four was called the quartering of the philosophy. Later, about the fifteenth or sixteenth century, the colours were reduced to three, and the xanthosis, otherwise called the *citrinitas*, gradually fell into disuse or was but seldom mentioned. The *nigredo* or blackness is the initial state, either present from the beginning as a quality of the *prima materia*, the chaos or *massa confusa*, or else produced by the separation (*solutio*, *separatio*, *divisio*, *putrefactio*) of the elements. If the separated condition is assumed at the start, as sometimes happens, then a union of opposites is performed under the likeness of a union of male and female (called the *coniugium*, *matrimonium*, *coniunctio*, *coitus*), followed by the death of the product of the union (*mortificatio*, *calcinatio, putrefactio*) and a corresponding nigredo. From this the washing (*ablutio*, *baptisma*) either leads direct to the whitening (albedo), or else the soul (anima) released at the 'death' is reunited with the dead body and brings about its resurrection, or again the 'many colours' (*omnes colores*) lead to the one white colour that contains all colours. At this point the first main goal of the process is reached, namely the albedo, *tinctura alba*, *terra alba foliata*, *lapis albus* etc., highly prized by many alchemists as if it were the ultimate goal. It is the *silves* or moon condition, which still has to be raised to the sun condition. The albedo is, so to speak, the daybreak, but not until the rubedo is it sunrise. The transition to the rubedo is formed by the citrinitas, though this, as we have

> said, was omitted later. The rubedo then follows direct from the albedo as the result of raising the heat of the fire to its highest intensity. The red and the white are King and Queen, who may also celebrate their 'chemical wedding' at this stage.[259]

It is, however, the unconscious that the Alchemist projects onto the Materia, or rather, the unconscious is the *true* raw material; during the processes of the Task the disciple is subjected to something on a *psychic* level, assimilated to the original reaction of the substances on which he worked, implying that the Alchemist was performing the true *Opus* on himself through *imaginatio*:

> The real nature of matter was unknown to the alchemist: he knew it only in hints. In seeking to explore it he projected the unconscious into the darkness of matter in order to illuminate it. In order to explain the mystery of matter he projected yet another mystery – his own unknown psychic background – into what was to the explained: 'Obscurum per obscurius, ignotum per ignotius'! This procedure was not, of course, intentional; it was an involuntary occurrence...While working on his chemical experiments the operator had certain psychic experiences, which appeared to him as the particular behaviour of the chemical process. Since it was a question of projection, he was naturally unconscious of the fact that the experience had nothing to do with matter itself (that is, with matter as we know it today). He experienced his projection as a property of matter; but what he was in reality experiencing was his own unconscious. In this way he recapitulated the whole history of man's knowledge of nature.[260]

According to Jung, in the course of their experiments, alchemists were frequently gripped by hallucinations or actual visions, events which could not be explained if not by their presence as projections of unconscious contents, visions produced unconsciously by the essential instrument that was *imaginatio*:

> The imaginatio, or the act of imagining, was thus a physical activity that could be fitted into the cycle of material changes, that brought these about and was brought about by them in turn. In this way the alchemist related himself not only to the unconscious but directly to the very substance which he hoped to transform through the power of imagination...Imagination is therefore a concentrated extract of the life forces, both physical and psychic.[261]

Jung concluded the essay with a consideration on the singularity of the historical contexts in which the various alchemical texts were produced, underlining the presence in said contexts of a certain fractiousness, or rather, a 'necessity for redemption' from a condition of darkness and dissatisfaction in which the individual felt overwhelmed, a situation that was also typical of other contexts which eventually determined the creation of other Sapiential Schools:

> The alchemy of the classical epoch (from antiquity to about the middle of the seventeenth century) was, in essence, chemical research work into which there entered, by way of projection, an admixture of unconscious psychic material. For this reason the psychological conditions necessary for the work are frequently stressed in the texts. The contents under consideration were those that lent themselves to projection upon the unknown chemical substance. Owing to the impersonal, purely objective nature of matter, it was the impersonal, collective archetypes that were projected first and foremost, as a parallel to the collective spiritual life of the times, the image of the spirit imprisoned in the darkness of the world. In other words, the state of relative unconsciousness in which man found himself, and which he felt to be painful and in need of redemption, was reflected in matter and accordingly dealt with in matter. Since the psychological condition of any unconscious content is one of potential reality, characterised by the polar opposites 'being' and 'not-being', it follows that the union of opposites must play a decisive role in the alchemical process.[262]

In conclusion, the method of Active Imagination afforded an opportunity for the symbols previously discovered by alchemy to be returned to the light; indeed, the process activated by the method of Active Imagination placed the operator in a truly alchemical situation, aimed at determining an improvement, which, on a psychic level, corresponded to the result yielded by alchemical operations.

As mentioned previously, Jung interpreted alchemy, with its symbolisms and operations, as a projection onto the Materia of the archetypes and processes of the collective unconscious, the 'soul of the world', the *anima mundi*, identified by alchemists as the *spiritus mercurius*; the latter was, indeed, imprisoned in the 'matter', which led alchemists to believe in the truth of Materia, as Materia symbolised their psychic life. The aim of the *Opus* was to free this Materia, to 'redeem it', in other words, to obtain the *Philosopher's Stone*, to which Jung attributed the meaning of 'wholeness' and 'order', that is, a personality modified by the integration of the unconscious.

Whereas alchemical thought was based on the belief in the existence of a sole substance from which all others originated, that the union of contrasting forces gave rise to mutations, that the final elements of matter were characterised by a specific structure, and, above all, that the Materia was brought to life by a reciprocal compenetration of body and soul, Jung similarly considered Self-achievement as a unitary process, and believed that mind mutations took place by means of a conflict of opposites, that archetypes provided the psyche with a basic structure, and, above all, that the psyche of every individual influenced that of everybody else, a dynamics which will later be observed also in biologist Rupert Sheldrake's theory of *Morphic Fields*.

The Process of Identification in the Initiatic Schools

Based on what has emerged so far from our attempt to define and identify the ideal type which represents the cornerstone of this study, the human figure or type who averts the need to understand or be a part of a Sapiential School is represented by individuals situated *a priori* in an advanced state of the Self-awareness process and who, through the initiatic experience, progress towards the completion of their pathway towards wholeness, i.e. towards integral personalities.

Although Active Imagination is the specific method that Jung identified in alchemical practices, which recalled the 'individuation process', the doctrines and rituals of other Initiatic Schools likewise revealed the presence of specific experiences which, as mentioned previously, were largely manifested in times of social and moral crisis when the individual, in a state of *disorientation*, perceived a need to regain an inner balance in order to achieve the *reintegration* of his no longer integrated personality, to *reacquire* his Centre, as illustrated by Jung:

> Under certain conditions the unconscious spontaneously brings forth an archetypal symbol of wholeness. From this we must conclude that that some such archetype occurs universally and is endowed with a certain numinosity.[263]

In several of his studies, Jung developed an interest in the dynamics pertaining to the Sapiential Schools (Mysteric or Gnostic) and analysed these dynamics from both a biological and genetic viewpoint, as well as in terms of the cerebral structure, representing them in a metaphysical or mystic sense as something which followed the experiences of the old Eleusinian Mysteries; to this regard one of the greatest experts in Jungian theories, Prof Sonu Shamdasani, wrote that:

> A distinctive feature of Jung's work was its attempt to provide psychological understanding of the processes of personality transformation which he claimed underlay religious, hermetic, gnostic and alchemical practices.[264]

The Eleusinian Mystai

Mystery cults have always been particularly thriving in times of crisis and social uprising, when individuals started to develop a certain dissatisfaction with traditional forms of life and thought, and started asking themselves new existential questions to which they could not find an answer within the traditional institutions. Mystery Societies clearly distinguished themselves from official Religions and Cults; at a time in which the official cult, the gods who made up the Olympus of Greek mythology, did not fully satisfy the religious needs of men of the time, a new system was therefore created in which the dynamics for the approach of the sacred presented a different emotional and spiritual involvement. The relationship of a Mystery Initiate with its relative deity is of a different nature to that of a man of the ancient world with the god of an official cult, a relationship of a deeper nature, almost metaphysical as initiates are left the freedom to experiment with the sacred, an element which is non-existent in the official cult.[265] To this regard, in her *Mystery Religions in the Ancient World*, Marion Giebel stresses that:

> At the time of initiation, mystery disciples are delivered a secret knowledge that allows them to deepen their understanding of the divine and human thus reaching a special relationship with their mystery deity, which promises them support and protection. Although showing similar characteristics, the development of mysteries cannot be attributed to a direct descent from tribal initiation or fertility rites. The Eleusinian Mysteries, for instance, present similarities and differences, but a certain aspect never varies: initiation always grants access to a more noble existence, extending beyond human life and portraying man as the link on a chain connecting divine to human life.[266]

The Myth narrated in the *Hymn to Demeter* represented the foundation on which the ritual was structured, in which two classes of participants to the ceremony were present, the initiands, called *mystai*, and those who had already undergone initiation, the *epòptai*. The mystagogue was the person that guided the initiate to the sanctuary in Eleusis and assisted him during the ceremony, much of which saw the mystai blindfolded.

The Eleusinian Mysteries were divided into 'Lesser' and 'Greater' Mysteries: the former were celebrated once a year in Kheria, a suburb of Athens, during the month of Anthesterion in the Spring. The ceremonies comprised a series of rituals, fastings, purifications and sacrifices, all regulated by a mystagogue. The Greater Mysteries were also celebrated once yearly, from the 7th to the 13th of the month of Boedromion (September-October); the ceremony lasted for eight days, the first seven of which were taken up by preparations for the ceremony.

We do not know many of the rituals, which took place during the Greater Mysteries, and we may therefore only *deduce* what happened inside the sanctuary; we may hypothesise that the initiates, *remodernising* the legend of Demeter, were placed mystically in the condition to receive the revelation that was transmitted by the *dromena*, the *legomena* and the *deinkymena*.

The dromena, in substance, were the dramas, with the hall in which the Initiation took place being arranged as an actual theatre, a square atrium with steps at each side.

The dromena were accompanied by a verbal revelation, the legomena. These consisted probably in *secret formulas* (aporrheta) for recognition, actual *laisser-passer* (symbola). The legomena however had a rather limited importance, indeed, in the words of Aristotle, 'initiates do not need to understand anything; rather they undergo an experience and a disposition – become, that is, deserving.'

Indeed, all ancient authors agree in stating that the essential moment of the revelation consisted in a vision or illumination.

The apex of the epòpteia, the deinkymena, is reached when the mystai, on having their blindfolds removed and under a blinding light, were 'shown' the 'secret' object, purportedly a cut *ear of wheat* representing the complete life cycle. The epòpteia, which could be translated by the term 'contemplation', and consequently denote the epòpts as 'contemplators', corresponds therefore to the *revealing* of the secret concealed in the ritual.

The dynamics applied in the Eleusinian rite underline therefore how the purpose of the Initiation to the Mysteries did not have a soteriological aim; on the contrary, the ceremony resulted in an actual ontological change, a mutation of 'state', a *psychological* change elicited by an active-realizatory metaphysical dynamic rather than a quiescent and quietist one, an actual 'transformation of personality' which closely resembled Jung's individuation process.

Many scholars of the Eleusinian Mysteries are still astounded by how the secrets of Eleusis, with the exception of the few references made by Clement of Alexandria and Hippolytus of Rome, have been so well preserved throughout the centuries, a fact which is easily and logically explained by the possibility that there may have never been a secret to be revealed, and that, as explained by Sabbatucci:

> The true secret was represented by a subjective mystic experience that would not have been deemed credible, nor even communicable by others. This experience maintained its validity, as a secret to be guarded, as long as one believed in it.[267]

The same dynamics can be observed in Masonic rituals and fit perfectly with the *personal* experience of a Freemason, whose wholly inner secret, and for this reason incommunicable, may be discovered solely by means of a spiritual realisation and a subsequent transformation of his personality.

Thus, the 'secret' referred to in the Eleusinian Mysteries are comprised in a *personal* and *spiritual* dynamics which is prevalently, as already stated, *incommunicable*; it can thus be concluded that the vision evoked in the epopt, which caused his frame of mind to be modified by the initiatic experience, consequently brought him closer to a state of awareness of the existence of a deep, purely rational Self, differing from the conscious Ego, with which he undertook his initiatic journey.

In conclusion, by observing the ritual dynamics of the Mysteries, and other later Initiatic Schools, it can be deduced that those who prepared themselves for the complex ritual underwent an actual 'individuation process', an experience which, as we will see again centuries later with the Masonic rituals, aspired to a 'Brotherhood' beyond which, by giving up one's own individuality, or rather one's own Ego, we could identify a search for wholeness, for psychic totality:

> We are therefore in the midst of a mystic phenomenology: in Eleusis there was no catechisation and neither was the initiate exalted in the name of an ideal human brotherhood, but this brotherhood was achieved involuntarily when he accepted to undergo a rite in which he would be asked to give up his individuality.[268]

The Hermetic path

Hermetism was a philosophical-religious current conceived between the second and third centuries A.D. in the pagan environment of original Christianity, with Oriental influences deriving from the gnostic representation of the Greek Platonic, Neoplatonic and Stoic philosophies. Its fascinating doctrine constitutes the first historically documented example of interaction between the Greek rationalist tradition and Oriental wisdom as a form of revealed knowledge.

Hermetic gnosis can be interpreted, both as a religious practice and a cognitive aspiration, aimed at removal of the veil of ignorance which prevents us from reconnecting with our Divine side. Its objectives are represented by a search for unity and the foundation of all things, a search for unity, which, in the Jungian vision, was accomplished especially at a psychic level through the union of the conscious with the unconscious, and the integration of the Ego with one's deeper Self.

The goal of Hermetic communities was the search for a Divine *intuition* without the intervention of a religion characterised by a personal God, thus making use only of a totalising *comprehension* of the Universe. Among the Hermetic Treatises, the *Ogdoad* is deemed a paradigmatic example of that which the renowned scholar Garth Fowden defined an actual 'Hermetic text of initiation',[269] a pedagogic and philosophical initiatic pathway which, in the latter stages of the process leads to awareness in the initiate of his true nature and his union with the Divine.

The *Ogdoad* and the *Ennead* indeed represent the final part, the eighth and the ninth, of a spiritual development preceded naturally, by another seven stages. The Treatise does not describe all the stages, although it is implied that in order to attain the final two stages the candidate should have lived a pure life and, above all, removed ignorance and replaced it with the knowledge imparted in the specific texts.

The entrance of the initiate into the Ennead represents a ritual in itself, which concludes with the pronunciation of the mysterious name of God in the form of invocations, which are supervised by Hermes, acting a 'mystagogue', and symbolised, from a Jungian perspective, the archetype of the Old Wise Man.

The Treatise opens with the disciple reminding Hermes of his promise to raise him to the Ogdoad and Ennead, and being given a positive reply by Hermes who deems the disciple as being 'intellectually' ready, underlining moreover how the inner growth of the initiate is produced by the teachings imparted from the books. Following the prayers conducted under the exhortation of Hermes to perform these with 'the mind, heart and soul', a verbal sequence commences followed by a request to see the image of truth. On having reached a state of *ecstasy* Hermes is begged by the disciple to assist him in achieving this visible ecstasy, with Hermes then requesting that to achieve this aim he utters a silent prayer; finally the disciple achieves ecstasy, the vision of the Ogdoad, the Ennead and, lastly, of God himself, or if we wish, of our deep Self.

In the above-described visible ecstasy, preceded by a profound meditation, we cannot help but identify the two crucial phases of Jung's method of Active Imagination, as previously discussed. In the act referred to as 'ecstasy', he who produces the same, Hermes, remains conscious and aware to the extent that he can enable the disciple to achieve, in turn, the same 'vision', the 'same image', the achievement of the Ogdoad and the Ennead, the 'vision' of God, or, from a Jungian perspective, of his own Self. This represents the conclusion of the individuation process, the achievement of the disciple's psychic wholeness.

Synchronicity

To conclude, I wish to analyse briefly Jung's studies on the phenomenon of *Synchronicity*, intended as an experience of *access* to the archetypes. Jung's theories on Synchronicity are likely those which, beyond all others, were the object both of curiosity and evident criticism. Jung himself was increasingly aware of the difficulties he would encounter in gaining the comprehension of his theory, which indeed was frequently misinterpreted compared to what Jung had intended:

> I would like to call attention to a possible misunderstanding, which may be occasioned by the term 'synchronicity'. I chose this term because the simultaneous occurrence of two meaningfully but not casually connected events seemed to me an essential criterion. I am therefore using the general concept of synchronicity in the special sense of a coincidence in time of two or more casually unrelated events which have the same or a similar meaning, in contrast to 'synchronism', which simply means the simultaneous occurrence of two events...The main characteristic of these events is the absolute relativity of the concepts of space and time, as in synchronicity: An unexpected content which is directly or indirectly connected with some objective external event coincides with the ordinary psychic state: this is what I call synchronicity, and I maintain that we are dealing with exactly the same category of events whether their objectivity appears separated from my consciousness in space or in time...But since experience has shown that under certain conditions space and time can be reduced almost to zero, causality disappears along with them, because causality is bound up with the existence of space and time and physical changes, and consists essentially in the succession of cause and effect. For this reason synchronistic phenomena cannot in principle be associated with any conceptions of causality.[270]

In Jung's vision, therefore, synchronicity essentially consisted in two linked factors: a) an unconscious image accesses consciousness in a direct or indirect manner in the form of a symbol, a dream, an idea or a premonition b) an objective situation – which actually takes place in everyday reality – coincides with the above content. In order to understand Jung's vision, it is essential to underline how the two events do not necessarily need to be *casually* connected, but should simply present a common meaning: Synchronicity takes the coincidence of events in space and time as meaning something more than mere chance, namely, a particular interdependence of objective events among themselves as well as with the subjective states of the observer.

Thanks to his personal experiences on the matter, Jung maintained that in order for synchronicity to take place, a lowering of the *mental* functions of the conscious sphere would need to occur. In these circumstances, according to Jung, the tone of the unconscious is *amplified*, allowing it to emerge to the surface of the conscious. It is only then that the conscious encounters the primordial images representing the archetypes. Physicist Wolfgang Pauli realised that all synchronicities took place in nature, as, be they human synchronicities or synchronicities that took place in the quantic domain, they were obliged to share a common matrix, which should have been able to unite synchronically the world of the psyche with the world of the matter.

Jung opined that alchemy itself gave rise to frequent phenomena of synchronicity, i.e. processes synchronically impinging upon both Matter and psyche. Upon completion of the alchemical process, the Work, indeed, the chemical and spiritual substance together were transformed into a *single* everything. However, as observed previously, Jung maintained that medieval Alchemists were not fully aware of the process of 'psychological transformation' that took place in their unconscious whilst carrying out their experiments. They certainly knew that the above was a process that originated from the soul and projected it onto the external world; however, they only made use of it in an empirical and perhaps instinctive manner.

Thanks to his discovery of synchronicity, Jung demonstrated that what we believed to be our psyche was not our psyche at all, but rather our ability to connect to a great *universal matrix* that unites us all. The Ego, the separation, the distinction between objects and particles are the different parts of a single, endless dance, and if taken separately, as distinct elements, they would be nothing but an illusion.

Physicist Massimo Teodorani defined all of the above as an actual 'cosmic web', a complex of truths and information which is only accessible to individuals possessing specific abilities:

> In other words all of this reminds us of the mythical kingdom of Akasha, which Oriental civilisations have been talking about for thousands of years. Some scientists started from the void and found themselves in the concept of synchronous interconnection and unity of all. Other scientists, such as quantum physicist David Bohm, have landed in the so-called 'implicate order'; in order to describe the abstract realm that represents the foundation of all known

> matter and constitutes its consciousness, physicist Marco Tedeschini, by reviving and re-elaborating an old Cartesian conception of the Universe, defined this realm as 'ether' whereas quantum physicist Wolfgang Pauli and depth psychologist Jung laid the foundations of the so-called 'collective unconscious'. There is good reason to believe that collective unconscious, ether, void, implicate order and Akasha are different ways of representing the same concept, that is the matrix of Universal unity and synchronicity.[271]

This *cosmic web*, this sort of universal library containing the universal knowledge, could symbolise a further representation of the concept of Tradition.

Synchronicity is thus a peculiar phenomenon that can only be explained by definitively abolishing the distinction between psyche and matter, as it can only occur, according to Marie-Louise Von Franz:

> When an archetype is activated in the observer's unconscious, producing a state of high emotional tension. In such moments psyche and matter seem no longer to be separate entities but arrange themselves into an identical, meaningful symbolic situation. It looks at such times as if physical and psychic worlds are two facets of the same reality. This unitary reality Jung called the unus mundus (the one world). Synchronistic events are, according to Jung, sporadically and irregularly occurring parapsychological phenomena. But they seem to be only special incidences of a more general principle which Jung termed acausal orderedness. The latter means that certain factors in nature are ordered without its being possible to find a cause for such an order...What is different in the 'one world' from Jung's unus mundus is that the latter also includes psychic reality, or rather that it transcends both psyche and matter. The ultimate reality of both, the unus mundus itself, is transcendental; it cannot be grasped by our consciousness. Synchronistic events are 'singularities' in which the oneness of psyche and matter, the unus mundus, becomes sporadically manifest.[272]

5
Tradition and Science – Sheldrake's 'Morphogenetic Fields'

Tradition and Science

Whereas with Jung we stepped away from the pure metaphysics of the Perennialist current, the theories of English biologist Rupert Sheldrake, which, as we will see, present significant analogies with certain elements of the Jungian thought, can be placed entirely within the scientific field.

Before analysing Sheldrake's theory, it should be highlighted how another scientist, Basarab Nicolescu, the founder of an International Association devoted to *transdisciplinarity*, also proposed his own personal and original interpretation of the meaning of Tradition.

Nicolescu's theory was also based on the certainty of the existence of a collective unconscious interpreted as the storehouse of all human 'experiences', a psychic deposit resulting from man's evolutionary development, which has hoarded itself in memory generation after generation.

His idea of Tradition was thoroughly discussed in his essay 'Nous la particule et le monde' (1985), in which Nicolescu presented an interesting comparison between Jacob Bohme's Christian Theosophy and contemporary sciences, particularly physics. His representation of the word Tradition from an interdisciplinary perspective is specifically analysed in the chapter 'Contemporary Physics and Western Tradition', in which Nicolescu refers to it as a concept that incorporates all the different Traditions, maintaining that it concerns 'the transmission of an ensemble of knowledge of the spiritual evolution of the human being, of our position in the various worlds, and of our relationship with various cosmoses. This body of knowledge is thus inevitably invariant, stable, and permanent, despite the many forms assumed in its transmission and despite the distortions introduced by time and history.' [273]

The Romanian scientist, although appreciative of Fritjof Capra's innovative studies on the convergence between certain scientific themes and Tradition, highlighted the excessive alignment of the latter with Oriental thought, and proposed an alternative personal approach based on the identification of a link between contemporary science, in its Western form, and Western Tradition; according to Nicolescu, indeed:

> Tradition also exists in space and time. Although its content is unique, its form of expression and the language used to express it are of great diversity, under the inevitable influence of history and of the cultural environment. One of the fundamental ideas of Tradition – that of unity in diversity and of diversity through unity – applies to Tradition itself. The ensemble of a tree's branches does not preclude the existence of a unique trunk. And a tree without branches would be a dead tree. It would be enough to let ourselves be imbued with the impressions of a Zen monastery in Kyoto and of a baroque church in Bavaria in order to understand the considerable differences in a nevertheless unique search. For a Western scholar, most of the traditional extreme Eastern and African forms of art and spirituality are as far away as Sirius. For a traditional education to have the chance of being truly understood by the modern man or woman, it must necessarily respect language, mentality, cultural, and personal history.[274]

It is interesting to underline how, despite approaching Tradition from a typically scientific viewpoint, Nicolescu regarded the origin of the latter as being of an exclusively metaphysical nature:

> Traditional knowledge proceeds from immemorial times, but it would be futile to search for an origin of Tradition. In its deep roots, Tradition may be conceived outside geographical space and outside historial time. It is eternally present, here and now, in every man and woman, in a continuous emergence. The origin of Tradition can only be metaphysical.[275]

How can science and Tradition, in Nicolescu's opinion, therefore be brought closer together? It is common knowledge that the scientific language evidently differs from the traditional language; indeed, whereas 'experience' is considered as the supreme judge of science, Tradition, on the contrary, lays claim to the 'right to inefficiency' on the plane of spatio-temporal materialism, which can be observed directly. Concepts such as 'God', 'transcendence', 'light' or 'darkness' repel the man of contemporary science, as their adoption would question the very foundations of scientific knowledge. So, Nicolescu wondered, how can a connection be found between science and Tradition? Nicolescu replied that contemporary physics is the one to provide us with the answer to this question, as the latest physical discoveries show us how science and Tradition address the same and invisible reality:

> In light of the essential differences between science and Tradition, the general opinion is that no rigorous relationship can be established. This conclusion is entirely logical and honourable, and the discussion could stop there. Nevertheless, the conclusion has the disadvantage of being too simplistic and even in contradiction with some fundamental conclusions of modern physics. There is no question of recommending a Hegelian synthesis between science and Tradition, because this could only lead to a hybrid design, which would be fatal for both science and Tradition. The attempt to deal with Tradition by employing the means of science or to deal with science by employing the means of Tradition inexorably leads to destruction and disappointment. There is another way, which consists in recognizing science and Tradition as two poles of a contradiction and accepting this contradiction, with all its consequences, as a sign of a unique and invisible reality.
>
> A possible point of contact between science and Tradition is to be found within the limits of the mind itself, limits that can be found in turn by the mind and by science. The characteristic movement of science reaches its own limits, and from there, if these limit areas, border areas, are common to science and Tradition, there could be a lea pinto another kind of understanding. In other words, contact points can be found in the fundamental axioms of science or in the most general results obtained by science.[276]

To this regard, I would like to present a brief, and clearly incomplete, overview of some of the innovative discoveries of the current scientific research.

It is undeniable that we are currently going through a phase of scientific exploration leading to a radical reconsideration of man's place in the universal scheme and, as a consequence, to the establishment of a different relationship between *Science* and the *Divine*. Well-known academic scholars of esotericism have often considered as 'New Age scientific theories' those which, on the contrary, are state-of-the-art scientific discoveries and researches, whose results have also been accepted by the most sceptical detractors.[277] Unfortunately, the attribution of the New Age epithet, often in a denigrating manner, to these innovative researches contributed to lessening the credibility of a number of important discoveries which, albeit summarily, will be brought to your attention in this book.

I have already extensively analysed some of these themes in my book *Introduction to Freemasonry*, including Danish physicist Nils Bohr's 'Principle of Complementarity', according to which the elementary particles of matter, the *Quanta*, can be seen both as particles and waves, depending on the way in which the phenomenon is observed, a theory which recalls alchemy, in which the mercurial feminine principle explained the protomorphism of natural phenomena, their fluid variability.

In this interpretation, the Universe might not be the Newtonian materialistic one made of determined, visible objects moving along defined trajectories, a substantially static Universe, but a *dynamic* one, constituted by *waves of possibility* or mere potentialities which eventually become actuality and thus matter, a manifest world, thanks to the 'observer', who is represented by the scientist when inside a laboratory, and by us in everyday life.

In this vision, which opens itself to science, man is the Centre and the sense of the Universe, exactly as theorised by Pico della Mirandola in his *Oration on the Dignity of Man*.

Another interesting theory is represented by the 'Principle of Non-Locality' by Austrian physicist and Nobel-prize winner Wolfang Pauli, who revealed how the elementary particles within an atom are in continuous and immediate communication between themselves in order for each one of them to know its position with regard to the others and the global situation, without the need to exchange signals. According to scientists, this would prove that every particle is *connected* to the entire system and that all parts of the Universe are therefore *interconnected* by electromagnetic fields as if they were linked by a single intelligent energy.

For the first time, science has found itself forced to theorise on the existence of a dimension that *transcends* the one in which we live, meaning that it nowadays needs to turn to the *transcendent* to explain the phenomena it observes, as this *transcendent* dimension, which had until recently been excluded from scientific investigations, appears to influence the behaviour of nature. [278]

'Morphogenesis' and the 'Morphic Fields'

Moving on to Sheldrake's theories, it should be underlined how the latter are based on a specific process that the English biologist defined 'morphogenesis'. The concept of morphogenesis is closely linked to the one of 'formative causation', that is, the mechanism thanks to which things acquire their form or their organisation. This dynamics concerns a wide range of phenomena: the formation of galaxies, atoms, crystals, molecules, plants, animals, cells, societies, practically all phenomena characterised by forms, structures or self-organisational properties. Sheldrake himself described his theory as follows:

> The hypothesis of formative causation starts from the assumption that morphogenetic fields are physically real, in the sense that gravitational, electromagnetic and quantum fields are real. Each type of cell, tissue, organ and organism has its own specific field. These fields shape and organise developing plant and animal microorganisms, and stabilise the forms of adult organisms. They do this on the basis of their own space-time organisation.[279]

According to Sheldrake's theory, the form of societies, ideas, crystals and molecules would essentially depend on the *manner* in which the previous phenomena of the same kind were organised. This would be made possible thanks to a sort of *innate memory* present in *the* morphic fields of every type of phenomenon, a discovery which would lead us to the conclusion that the regularities of nature more closely resemble *habits* rather than phenomena that are ruled by unmodifiable, eternal and unchangeable mathematical laws which also exist outside of nature:

> My hypothesis is that the formation of habits depends on a process called morphic resonance. Similar patterns of activity resonate across space and time with subsequent patterns. This hypothesis applies to all self-organising systems, including atoms, molecules, crystals, cells, plants and animal societies. All draw upon a collective memory and in turn contribute to it.[280]

Morphic resonance would thus refer to the ability to share the habits that organisms acquire during their evolutionary process: these habits appear to resonate within the species by creating the opportunity for new acquisitions, ranging from the ability to resist a virus to new collective learnings, taking place in subjects who might be situated at great distances from one another.

Sheldrake often made use of his writings to remind us how, to modern science, all natural things are vibration, form and activity, which is why his theory of a memory of nature, which he defined 'morphogenetic resonance', was based on similar forms of vibrations that influenced each other. By referring to the example of mandala obtained through the vibration of sand, Sheldrake highlighted how his theory had elements in common with several mystic and religious traditions, which told us of primordial vibrations, the original sound, and informed us that at the beginning of creation there existed vibrations which later gave form to all other things.

Sheldrake's approach placed itself within a new vision of science that was radically opposed to the mechanistic interpretation underlying many of the canonical paradigms of scientific research. In his first text on the topic, *A New Science of Life,* from 1981, Sheldrake defined this new approach as follows:

> However, the organismic or holistic philosophy of nature provides a context for a more radical revision of the mechanistic theory. This philosophy denies that everything in the universe can be explained from the bottom up, as it were, in terms of the properties of subatomic particles, or atoms, or even molecole. Rather, it recognises the existence of hierarchically organised systems which, at each level of complexity, possess properties that cannot be fully understood in terms of the properties exhibited by their parts in isolation from each other; at each level the whole is more than the sum of its parts. These wholes can be thought of as organisms, using this term in a deliberately wide sense to include not only animals and plants, organs, tissues and cells, but also crystals, molecole, atoms and sub-atomic particles. In effect this philosophy proposes a change from the paradigm of the machine to the paradigm of the organism in the biological and in the physical sciences.'[281]

But what kind of matter makes up the morphic fields? Morphic fields, according to Sheldrake, are 'physical' but differ from the other fields of contemporary physics; in substance, the morphic fields, albeit an integral part of nature, are not made up of matter. Indeed, they are not of an electromagnetic nature, nor are they fields of quantum possibilities, and they do not concern the creation of particles or similar; they are something more complex, 'fields of information' underlying the development or growth of all things, fields which subtend the reason behind the form and disposition of things, behind the repetition in nature of similar, yet never identical, forms, such as in the case of crystals or plants:

> Fields are nonmaterial regions of influence. The Earth's gravitational field, for example, is all around us. We cannot see it – it is not a material object – but it is nevertheless real. It gives things weight and makes things fall. It is holding us down to Earth at this moment; without it we would be floating. The moon moves around the Earth because of the curvature of the Earth's gravitational field...The gravitational field pervades the entire universe, curving around all matter within it. According to Einstein, it is not in space and time: it is space-time. Space-time is not a bland background abstraction; it has a structure, which actively shapes and includes everything that exists or happens within the physical universe...Electromagnetic fields are of a significantly different nature to gravitational fields and have several functions. They integrate all material systems, from atoms to galaxies. They underlie the functioning of our brains and bodies. They are essential for all our electric devices...Objects affect each other through fields even when they are not in material contact...

> In addition to these familiar kinds of fields, according to quantum field theory there are various kinds of matter fields – electron fields, neutron fields, and so on – microscopic fields within which all the particles of matter exist as quanta of vibratory energy. None of these fields is reducible to the others. Physicists have hoped for a long time to understand them all as aspects of a single unified field. Contemporary theoretical fields attempts to derive them from the hypothetical original unified field of the cosmos, which then differentiated within itself into the known fields of physics by curling up in various was as the universe grew and evolved.[282]

In conclusion, according to the English biologist:

> The nature of fields is inevitably mysterious. According to modern physics, they are entities of an even more fundamental nature than matter. Fields cannot be explained in terms of matter; rather, matter is explained in terms of energy within fields…What exactly are morphogenetic fields? How do they work? Despite the widespread use of this concept within biology, there are no clear answers to these questions. Indeed, the nature of these fields has remained as mysterious as morphogenesis itself.[283]

We could attempt to provide an explanation for *morphogenesis* through a number of examples. When a new chemical compound is created for the first time in a laboratory it is usually extremely hard to crystallise, but the more it is synthesised, the easier it becomes for its crystals to be formed in laboratories throughout the world. This theory, applied to the animal world, is based on the idea that every species, and every member of the same, draws from a *collective memory* of the same species, by tuning in with past members and, in turn, contributing to its further development, by means of a resonance between individuals and groups within the species (subgroups, races, ethnic groups, tribes, families, in the human case). These morphic fields would be essentially responsible for the form and specific organisation of systems at all levels of complexity, not only in biology but also in chemistry, physics and social systems.

When the member of a species learns a new behaviour or a new way of thinking, the morphogenetic field of that species, changes, transforms itself, albeit slightly, within the context in which it is placed, and if the behaviour and the new thought structure is repeated long enough, its morphic resonance will hoard itself and start to *influence* the entire species. The more individuals of the same species learn to execute a new task or think in a different way, the more powerful the reference morphogenetic field will become and the easier other individuals will find it to execute that task.

The process through which the morphic fields of every system exercise their influence on the subsequent systems is called morphic resonance. This process, as specified by Sheldrake, does not only take place within a defined system, such as a plant or the body of an animal; morphic fields, in fact, are interconnected in a time that goes beyond linear time, a time of present memory which carries with it information that is necessary for the creative design of things.

Every smallest and insignificant thing, be it mineral, vegetable or animal, possesses a corresponding field which relates to the rest of the Universe; in order not to give rise to any easy misunderstandings, however, Sheldrake himself underlined that:

> My idea of morphic fields is that, even though they are extended and non-local in their effects, they are still part of our individual and collective mind, but not to be equated with some ultimate Universal Mind. The morphic fields are not God...

Morphic Resonance

As we have seen, morphic resonance represents the ability to share behavioural changes, also including the way of thinking, which organisms acquire during their evolutionary process, behaviours that are transmitted within the same groups thus allowing a development and an evolution of the same, even though the members of said species occupy distant positions from one another. According to Sheldrake, there thus appear to exist connections within the fields that link members of social groups to one another, connections that act as channels for the transfer of information between separate members of the group. An analogy to this process can be observed in the field of quantum physics: if two particles have belonged to the same quantum system and are separated in space, they nevertheless maintain a mysterious connection, meaning that a change in a separate part of a system can have an immediate impact on the other; this phenomenon is known as *non-locality* or *quantum non-separability*.

As we have observed, Sheldrake's theory hypothesises that the learning process is also carried out by the *species* and not only by the single members, so if a certain number of individuals develop specific behavioural, psychological or organic properties, the latter are automatically *acquired* by the other members of the same species. In the case of man, we would thus achieve, according to the English biologist, a synchronistic transmission of *spiritual awareness* to members of our same species even at superior levels.

As a consequence, if a fair share of humanity were to be able to achieve a certain level of *spiritual awareness*, this same awareness could be extended, by means of morphic resonance, to other groups, thus involving the entire system (the number of people or individuals belonging to every other species in which a similar phenomenon takes place is called 'critical mass') and upgrading the level of *planetary awareness*. Every individual transformation would therefore determine a transformation of the entire system and influence all individuals situated within the same.

If we approach this theory from an initiatic perspective, we will see that the disciples of a Sapiential School (Freemasons in our case) do not represent solitary spiritual researchers, isolated members of the species, essentially an entity cut off from the system, but, on the contrary, they are *connected* to all present, past and future creatures, by virtue of a powerful, albeit thin and mysterious, physical connection. More importantly, the entire humanity will benefit from their initiatic work, bearer of a superior *conscientious development*.

Which conclusion can therefore be reached? Certainly, that, in the light of what has been discussed above, political or social activism does not necessarily represent the only viable way to carry out concrete changes to a system which desires to improve itself. On the contrary, it runs the risk of resulting in nothing if an external change is sought by means of a mere material action carried out without first changing the interior. Real *action*, indeed, originates from the achievement of a new *vision*, of a new awareness developed within ourselves, which will indelibly *imprint* itself in the external field thus determining its evolution, an evolution that can by all means be sudden and unexpected.

According to Sheldrake, systems are organised in the manner in which they manifest themselves to us because *analogous* systems in the past used to be organised in the same way. More specifically, the forms and behaviours typical of all currently existing chemical, physical and biological, but above all social, systems are guided and shaped by *fields of organisation*, which, like an invisible hand, supposedly act through space and time. The entire social group would thus be organised by a field, a structure that has been appointed not only to organise the present but that also contains the *memory* of the past of that social group, a memory of similar social groups which existed in the past.

The concept of morphic resonance, as explained by Sheldrake, implies that every complex and organised ensemble of activity of an individual (superior animal or man), which also includes dreams, mystic experiences, altered states of consciousness, possesses its own structure: these mental states and activities can be transferred from one individual to another, specifically thanks to the mechanism of morphic resonance.

A transposition of this concept into the dynamics of Initiatic Schools revealed how the vehicle of Initiation, in particular, represented the instrument which allowed the Disciple to be *transported* into the group's collective memory, thus enabling him to *connect* with Tradition, and enter into a sort of 'communion' with all those who have already belonged to the group, placed in what Freemasons refer to as the 'Eternal Orient'. As a consequence, if within the Initiatic Schools 'qualified' individuals work towards superior states of consciousness, it can be concluded that the higher the number of individuals who manage to elevate their spiritual awareness, the easier it will be for other individuals, both within and outside of the same group, to proceed in that direction. Similarly, Freemasonry, if interpreted as an Initiatic Order rather than as a profane service club, an opinion group, a political party or a merely charitable association, will be able to act not only upon the Society in which it is spatially located, but also on the entirety of Humanity, thus facilitating its evolution.

The Brain and the Mind

In his essay 'The Presence of the Past', Sheldrake hypothesised that our memories are not stored in our brain, but that there exists a field of information which can be accessed *through* the brain. This would lead to the conclusion that human consciousness, personal memories and our sense of the Ego can outlive biological death. According to the English biologist, our mind, albeit centred in our body, and specifically in our brain, is not 'limited' to the latter, and would indeed extend *beyond* it through the fields of the mind, or mental fields, which exist both within and beyond the brain itself. Our minds would thus not be imprisoned within the limited radius of our skull, separated from each other, but, on the contrary, they would be *interconnected* with one another, just as individuals are interconnected among them. All of the above would provide an explanation to phenomena such as telepathy and similar phenomena, which so far have never been clarified scientifically.

For centuries, we have adopted, in Sheldrake's opinion, two different positions, a materialistic one, in which the mind coincided with the brain and the one of Cartesian dualism, in which the mind was regarded as a non-physical, non-local entity, which mysteriously interacted with the body. In rejecting these theories, Sheldrake proposed an alternative in which the mind is composed of fields, which penetrate the brain and extend *beyond* it, exactly as it happens with magnets or on Earth. Sheldrake's theory, therefore, is based on the belief that the mind is not localised in space or time, and that it cannot be limited to the current moment but on the contrary, that it possesses an immortal, non-energetic quality, which is not, above all, influenced by spatial separation. The mind is therefore not restricted to the brain but neither is it *produced* by it, although it can act through it.

Sheldrake's theory thus gave rise to the idea of a *collective consciousness* with extremely similar characteristics to the Jungian concept of Collective Unconscious, a collective consciousness which could essentially be represented as a single, unique mind. Sheldrake himself confirmed the similarities between the representation of the collective unconscious offered by Jung and his idea of a *connection* between the individuals due to a sort of 'collective memory' deriving from morphic resonance; to this regard, Sheldrake wrote:

> The collective unconscious of the psychologist Carl Jung has much in common with the concept of the group mind, and what Jung called the archetypes resemble what Durkheim called 'collective representations'...Jung's idea of the collective unconscious did not make sense in the context of the mechanistic theory of life; consequently, it was not taken seriously within orthodox science. But it makes good sense in the light of formative causation. By morphic resonance, structures of thought and experience that were common to many people in the past contribute to morphic fields. These fields contain the average forms of previous experience defined in terms of probability. This idea corresponds to Jung's conception of archetypes as 'innate psychic structures'.[284]

According to Jung, the origin of archetypes cannot be explained but by assuming that they are the sediments of experiences which have been *repeated* by humanity; as a consequence the collective unconscious can be identified with the part of the psyche that can be distinguished negatively from the personal unconscious due to the fact that its existence does not derive from personal experience.

Whereas the personal unconscious is essentially made up of contents that used to be conscious but were subsequently forgotten or removed, the contents of the collective unconscious were never a part of consciousness and were not therefore acquired individually, their existence deriving exclusively from *legacy*. Additionally, whereas the personal unconscious mainly consists of complexes, the contents of the collective unconscious, on the contrary, are constituted essentially by archetypes.[285] It can lastly be highlighted how certain elements of Jung's thought in a certain way forewarned Sheldrake's theories:

> The concept of collective unconscious is neither speculative nor philosophical but an empirical matter. The question is simply this: are there or are there not unconscious, universal forms of this kind? If they exist, then there is a region of the psyche which one can call the collective unconscious.[286]

This 'region of the psyche' will be represented several decades later by the concepts of morphic fields and 'extended mind' of the English biologist.

Both in Sheldrake's and Jung's theories psyche and matter are connected; it is a well-known fact that Jung accompanied his experiments with the *I Ching*, observations on his patients' dreams that often contained images which singularly corresponded to external events, and which seemed to possess the same sense of oneiric images.

This happens when an archetype is activated in the unconscious of the subject who experiences it, and a state of strong emotional tension is thus produced. In said moments, psyche and matter appear no longer as separate realities but rather as entities coordinated with a single symbolic situation filled with sense. It is as if the psychic and the physical worlds were facets of an identical reality; Jung called this 'unitary reality' *unus mundus*. The Swiss scholar regarded synchronistic events as sporadic parapsychological phenomena that emerge irregularly and appear to illustrate only special cases within a general principle, which he referred to as a causal coordination, meaning that certain natural facts seem to possess an order, without anyone being able to identify a cause for this. As underlined by the Jungian scholar Marie-Louise Von Franz:

> What is different in the 'one world' from Jung's unus mundus is that the latter also includes psychic reality, or rather that it transcends both psyche and matter. The ultimate reality of both, the unus mundus itself, is transcendental; it cannot be grasped by our consciousness. Synchronistic events are 'singularities' in

> which the oneness of psyche and matter, the unus mundus, becomes sporadically manifest.[287]

The theories of the 'new' Science redirect us to the Neoplatonic and Alchemical concept of 'Soul of the World', whereby everything is connected to everything as everything is only a part of a large organism, the Universe, and, above all, every single man is strictly linked with the totality of the Cosmos. Italian astrophysicist Massimo Teodorani, who carried out interesting studies on David Bohm's theories and the phenomenon of 'Synchronicity', starting from the combined studies of physicist Pauli and Jung, stated the following:

> What we believe to be our psyche is not our psyche but our ability to connect to a large universal matrix which unites all of us. The Ego, the separation, the distinction between objects and particles are many parts of a single, endless dance, but if considered separately as distinct entities they are nothing but an illusion. Our own Ego is an illusion. Certain psychic issues, indeed, similar to the ones experienced by Pauli, are a way to warn us that we are detached from our real 'Self'. The key to happiness, peacefulness and life itself is to gain awareness of our being part of an infinite universe...The only way to access the latter is to connect with the realm of archetypes, which is nothing other than a huge library containing in symbolic form all the knowledge of the universe. After all, this realm situated beyond space and time and the mysterious and mythical 'Akasha', which has been handed down in Oriental traditions, are exactly the same thing. In order to access the laws of the universe in its proper light, it is essential for the psyche to connect with this 'cosmic web'.[288]

Sheldrake's theory of the morphogenetic fields is not, therefore, based on isolated theories, but rather boasts scientific correspondences with other interesting theories such as Jung's *collective unconscious*, David Bohm's *implicate order*, Penrose's and Laszlo's *sub-quantum field*, Pribram's *holographic mechanism*, Radin's and Nelson's *global consciousness*.

To return to the doctrines of the Sapiential Schools, the solicitation present in the Second Degree of the Masonic ritual to 'extend one's researches into the hidden mysteries of Nature and Science' symbolises the directions to a path to be followed, filled with exciting and sometimes incredible discoveries which surprisingly seem to correspond to an ancient knowledge that we refer to as Tradition, which was kept alive and transmitted thanks to the contribution of the Initiatic Schools. During the 'Passage' Ceremony, we are asked to *make the liberal Arts and Sciences our future study* and, above all, as mentioned previously, *to extend our researches into the hidden mysteries of Nature and Science*. We should now ask ourselves, what do the 'hidden mysteries of Nature and Science' consist of? If one of the duties of a Freemason is the study of Science, we cannot help but notice how the latter has been transforming its foundations over the last few decades, moving incredibly closer to certain theories that until recently only belonged to the 'esoteric-alchemical' world.

Should we wish to define this scientific approach, we would need to compare it to the Neoplatonic and Spinozian vision of the man-nature relationship, the search for a *unified* knowledge, and the result of a *holistic vision* of reality. According to this vision man and Nature are seen as part of the same harmonious, living and sentient organism, an expression of the Spirit, rather than separate and independent parts of the same.

The traditional science of Cartesian and Illuministic derivation, the limits of which are increasingly evident, is becoming widely criticised. The undeniable merit of Illuminism was to free the researcher from the chains of theology and religious dogma dominant at the time, although throughout the centuries it has degraded into a dry materialism, insufficient in both methodology and results to explain many aspects of our existence. Today there is a new frontier of science represented by scientists and scholars from all over the world, at times collocated beyond the confines of the orthodox scientific community (the same community that condemned Galileo and Copernicus) which supports a new, no longer fragmented but unified knowledge. A knowledge frequently substantiated by scientific discoveries that challenge the certainties of orthodox scholars.[289]

We have seen how every new knowledge and discovery, every spiritual conquest, every new individual awareness, does not concern the single Initiate but the entire collectivity; it is for this reason that a Freemason, even from within his Temple, will always be able to deeply impact on the surrounding reality, by carrying out the only real action towards a progress of the entire Humanity: he performs an actual 'Cosmic Action'.

CHAPTER THREE
'WORKING THE ROUGH STONE' AND ATTAINMENT OF SELF

This multitude of beings come forth again and again
and, once emerged, is dissolved at the coming of night ...
and comes forth again at the coming of day.
Bhagavagita

1
The Rituality of Freemasonry.

From the 'Rough Ashlar' to the 'Perfect Ashlar'

In my opinion, the doctrines and rituality of the Initiatic Schools feature elements that resemble the dynamics of the Jungian 'process of individuation', or rather, an attempt to *transform* one's personality, an essentially psychological and consciential transformation yielded by the innate tendency of man to seek an integral personality, to conquer, or to attain knowledge of Self.

Regrettably, an exclusively moralistic interpretation of the Masonic symbology has frequently represented the aims and doctrines of the latter in a dismally banal and dismissive manner. This is particularly true with regard to the symbology of the *Raw Stone*, the key symbol in the Masonic initiatic pathway. Indeed, the Raw Stone is generally represented, from a typically moralistic point of view, as a symbol of an individual overcome by his imperfections, be they material physical, bodily, emotional, behavioural or cultural, with the Frenchman Jean-Marie Ragon maintaining that:

> The object of Masonic research is focussed on attaining knowledge of the art of perfecting the imperfections left in mankind by nature, and on discovering the treasure of the true moral...... An artist should work on a body created by nature, to which sulphur and mercury had been added and that subsequently would need to be removed and, at a later stage, purified, in order to reunite the two. This body is known as the raw stone. This raw stone is the very same smoothed by Freemasons with the aim of removing superfluities, and is known in the Masonic ethics as the *obliteration of defects*.[290]

Casting morals aside and seeking to gaze into the depths of our very being, we may be able to see how, in the Masonic symbols and ritual dynamics, the ritualist, likely *unknowingly* in the same way as the alchemist, created within the ritual the premises for an overt 'identification process', achieving the recognition by his conscience (I), the *Ego*, depicted by the *Rough Ashlar*, of the central nucleus of his psyche (Self), or rather the *Perfect Ashlar*. I have adopted the term 'unknowingly' as the Masonic rituals, particularly at the outset, were rarely proposed, either by their compilers or subsequent users, under any other than the 'moral' form (naturally with the rare exceptions commented on in this book), although they clearly contained elements that went far beyond an essentially ethical scope. Indeed, the symbology of these rituals possessed, and still possess today, a content that, if 'revealed' through a detailed exegesis, would contribute towards *evoking* the specific archetypes that were merely waiting to be returned to the light; in his inner self, the Initiate to the Mysteries of Freemasonry is aware that the desired hewing of the *Ashlar* represents so much more, being the symbol of an entity that may only be restored in the depths of the human psyche.

Freeing oneself of conditionings

In the Masonic ritual, prior to undertaking the Initiation ceremony, we are asked to 'leave the Metals outside' the Temple into which we are to be subsequently introduced; the 'Metals' to be relinquished represent our 'conditionings', acquired throughout experiences lived in our profane life, as highlighted by Titus Burckhardt:

> The chaotic and 'opaque' bodily consciousness, encumbered with passions and habits, is 'base' metal. In it soul and spirit seem suffocated, darkened, mixed with earth. On the other hand, 'illumined' bodily consciousness ('noble' metal), is itself a spiritual mode of existence. The soul must first be extracted from base metal, the alchemists say. The remaining body is to be purified and burnt until it is no more than ashes. Then the soul is to be reunited with it. When the body is thus 'dissolved' in the soul, so that both constitute a pure materia, the Spirit acts on the soul and confers on it an incorruptible form. That is to say, it transmutes individual bodily consciousness back into its own purely spiritual possibility, where, in all its fullness and according to its own essence, it remains motionless and indivisible.[291]

Although, even before this, during the ceremony for the consecration of a Lodge, the place in which the Opus of the Initiate will subsequently take place, the first fundamental action is to scatter grains of wheat on the floor of the Lodge, thus symbolically representing the building as the 'field' from which 'regenerated men' will subsequently germinate:

> The Field, as Earth, generally stands for the group of conditions and possibilities contained within corporeality that it understood in an all-embracing sense. The Seed is, first of all, vulgar Gold, which 'separated from the Mine (Universal Life) is as dead': but when thrust into the Earth, or the Field, and after putrefying, it is reborn and brings to full flower the principle whose potentiality it held: whence is drawn a further symbolism taken from the vegetable kingdom, which is born in and rises up out of the 'depths' of the Earth: trees, flowers, gardens, etcetera.[292]

Subsequently, as the ceremony progresses, the numerous circumambulations will contribute further towards transforming the sire into a *Témenos*, a sacred place, or, alchemically speaking, into an *alchemical vase*, i.e. the transformative recipient inside which the *Endeavour* will be accomplished. The circumambulation therefore will result in the construction of an 'enclosure' (Témenos) constituting not only a place in which to carry out the sacred function, delimiting and, at the same time, creating the sacred space, but also a 'container' in which the initially chaotic and opposed energies will be freed and reunited, in the same way as the alchemical dynamics of *solve et coagula*. Accordingly, the symbol of the Témenos does not merely represent a form of expression, but also explicates the action of drawing a *sulcus primigenius*, a magical groove surrounding the centre of the innermost personality aimed at preventing dispersion of the same, or shielding it from distractions originating from the outside world.[293]

Identical meanings can be observed in the circumambulatory rites practiced in ancient Rome, rites which were also present in other Indo-European populations (Greeks, Celts, Indians, etc); these rites, performed on the earth's surface (epictones) appeared to originate from the circular, or rather elliptical, movement of the stars, as commented on by the traditionalist scholar Marco Baistrocchi:

> The rotatory movement, coadjuvated by the element concerned, was thus intended to purge, remove, separate, wash the impurity, and therefore atone for the error made, paying the penalty: only once the impurity had been 'dissolved' and the mud liquefied (lues), could one be considered free from impurity, from the task undertaken, and thus restore the equilibrium with the deities.[294]

These circumambulatory rites were essentially of two types, both featuring substantially diverse meanings and values. The right-handed circumambulatory rite was undertaken clockwise from the left towards the right, thereby following the movement of the sun, it was seen as being happy and propitious, expressing the development of life, thus being performed in a joyful and harmonious environment. The left-handed circumambulatory rite was undertaken anti-clockwise from the left to the right, therefore in the opposite direction to the apparent diurnal movement of the sun; contrary to the previous rite, this was deemed inauspicious and deadly, and was therefore performed in a sad and gloomy environment.[295]

In the light of the above, one of the most widely renowned Landmarks of Freemasonry, i.e. 'prohibition to discuss politics and religion within the Lodge', largely interpreted as a need to avoid unpleasant 'discussions' between the Brothers over divergent political or religious views. However, if viewed from a strictly initiatic viewpoint, as it should be, we are beseeched to enter the Masonic Temple whilst leaving behind all external ideological and religious conditionings, thus fully freeing oneself of experiences acquired throughout one's profane collective experience, which would inevitably compromise the journey towards consciential development aimed at gaining knowledge of the 'Ultimate Principles' of existence.

2
The Circle as a symbol of Self

A 'Point within a Circle'

The Masonic rituals display elements that resemble the dynamics of the 'individuation process', particularly in the phase of the ritual in which the candidate is told he will be able to find the Mysteries (Self) lost following the premature death of the architect Hiram Abif (the Ego) through the *Centre*, a point within a Circle, or rather, a 'Circumference'. We know that Jung, taking the cue from alchemical symbols, identified the Circle in the 'Quaternity', i.e. the archetype of totality or Self (the Circle due to its perfect shape, and the Quaternity due to the fact that four is the smallest number of parts a Circle can naturally be divided into): 'Quaternity and Circle, the former motif emphasises the Ego's containment in the greater dimension of the Self, the latter emphasises the rotation, which also appears as a ritual circumambulation. Psychologically, it denotes concentration on and preoccupation a centre, conceived as the centre of a circle and thus formulated as a point.'[296]

The symbol of the Circle is constantly present throughout the texts of alchemistry, with Evola highlighting in his *The Hermetic Tradition*:

> The alchemical ideogram of the 'One the All' is the circle: a line or movement that encloses within itself and contains in itself both its and beginning. In hermetism this symbol expresses the universe and, at the same time, the Great Work...This 'all' has also been called chaos ('our' chaos), and egg, because it contains the undifferentiated potentiality of every development or generation: it sleeps in the depths of each being as a 'sensed myth' – to use Olimpiodorus' expression –and it extends to the chaotic multiplicity of scattered things and forms in space and time here below. The closed line, the circle of Ouroboros, also has another meaning: it alludes to the principle of 'exclusion' or 'hermetic sealing' that metaphysically expresses the idea of a unilaterally conceived transcendence being extraneous to this tradition.[297]

Indeed, in Freemasonry this symbol is again manifested, with the Masonic rituals recapturing the dynamics of the alchemical opus, replacing the 'impure' Metals from which the Gold will subsequently be extracted, the symbology of the Unhewn Stone destined, after considerable efforts, to be transformed into a perfectly Smooth Stone.

As mentioned previously, the symbol of the Circle is generally associated with its Centre. In the field of analytical psychology the word 'Centre' is used to convey an image of completeness, totality and globality; intended as the product of a psychological process driven by a sense of incompleteness and inadequacy of the conscience. The Centre is substantially a spaceless and timeless image which, rather than emerging, so to speak, through a leap of the individual, by starting from the current condition of the latter, i.e. through his awareness of being confined to a limited space and time, thus explaining why the transcendent function has been activated in his psyche.[298] In the Masonic ritual, the revelation of the sacred symbol (God) tells us that this is situated at the Centre (Self) of the building, in Solomon's Temple (our conscience). From a mystical point of view, the ritual may be likewise interpreted: discovery of our inner Self signifies that we find ourselves in front of the Deity, of God.

The *process of identification of the centre*, a term frequently used with regard to the dynamics of initiation, also refers to the 'psychic transformations' undergone in the renewal and completion of one's personality. The Initiate, in identifying his psyche as a 'centred' system compared to Self, and a 'scattered' system with regard to the Ego, by embarking on the initiatic journey, seeks gnosis, an integration between the conscious and the unconscious, an integration between the inner Ego and Self.

Attainment or return to Self

According to the Art historian Luc Benoist, the purpose of Initiation is the active achievement of a higher state, defined by the author as a 'communion with Self', access to a state of deep harmony, of complete balance all individual elements. Based on these premises, which I strongly support, the Three Degrees of Freemasonry should thus be viewed as *Consciential States* rather than *Intellectual States*. An intuitive knowledge is seen as an organ of immediate knowledge, of pure intelligence, that reaches beyond reason *tout court*. The backwards journey undertaken by the Initiate, in this instance under the semblance or form of the Freemason, thus represents an inner awareness or return of the finite Self, projecting towards the divine Principle, or rather an integration of the individual Self with the Divine Self.

The tools of Freemasonry, i.e. its symbols, should be seen as an archetype. As an example, the Hammer, symbol of the conscience and tool used by the Worshipful Master to open the initiatic undertakings of the Lodge, is present in various forms throughout the history of mankind, as illustrated by:

> The tools of the smith also share this sacred quality. The hammer, the bellows and the anvil are revealed to be animate miraculous objects. They were

> regarded as capable of operating by their own magico-religious force, unassisted by the smith. The smith in Togo, speaking of his tools, describes them as 'the hammer and its family'. In Angola the hammer is venerated because it forges the instruments necessary to agriculture; it is treated like a prince and pampered like a child...All these beliefs do not stop at the sacred power of the metals, but extend to the magic of the instruments. The art of creating utensils is essentially superhuman – either divine or demoniac (for the smith also forges murderous weapons). Remnants of ancient myths belonging to the Stone Age have probably been added to, or woven into, the mythology of metals. The stone tool or the hand-axe were charged with a mysterious power; they struck, inflicted injury, caused explosions, produced sparks, as did the thunderbolt...The hammer, successor to the axe of the Stone Age becomes the emblem of powerful gods, the gods of the storm...The storm gods strike the earth with 'thunderstones'; their emblem is the double axe and the hammer; the storm is the signal for the heaven-earth hierogamy. When striking their anvils, smiths imitate the primordial gesture of the strong god; they are in effect his accessories.[299]

When the Worshipful Master strikes the hammer to open the function, he is imitating the gesture of God the Creator, the Lodge, *atanòr* in which the *alchemical opus* will take place, is ready for the initiatic process.

Hiram Habif and the 'initiatic death'

It is in the Third Degree of Freemasonry, in the legend containing the allegory of the death of Hiram, that we find the most important analogy between the Masonic rituals and those of the ancient Initiatic Societies, i.e. the initiatic death. The discovery of the body of God and the sacred Archetype, known as *euresis* in the Mysteries, and its recovery from the ground to be worshipped in a sacred place, played a fundamental part in the rituals of the Mystery Societies, as well as in the rituals used today in Freemasonry.

The aim of the initiatic death is to *die to yourself*, i.e. the death of our collective Persona, to reveal the Divine that is within each of us, our inner Self, as Guido De Giorgio writes:

> The presence of tradition implies that on finding himself, Man will find the former, he will find God, but however, on finding himself, man must necessarily die, as he is required to retrace the pathway to the abyss generated by the fall, he is required to kill ignorance, to abolish it, to elicit a return to wisdom, to ensure that his death becomes his true life, and the his knowledge of his inner self becomes the knowledge of God.[300]

In the same way as the Eleusinian *mystai*, likewise Freemasonry in actualising the

Myth of Hiram Abif, endures some aspects of an Initiation, the Initiate is subjected to the same fate as the archetype, as the *first initiate*. The sufference is thus likened to an aspect of Initiation, and the overcoming of the *fear* of death can therefore be lived and interpreted as an anticipation, but above all, *overcoming* of death itself. The aim of the Third Degree of the Masonic ritual is, we are told, to 'teach us how to die'.

The initiatic death, the acme of all Initiation rituals, thus produces a restorative effect on the Candidate, culminating in the generation of an overt ontological change. In his renowned study *The Mystic Birth*, Mircea Eliade describes the dynamics of the latter:

> The majority of initiatory ordeals more or less clearly imply a ritual death followed by resurrection or a new birth. The central moment of every initiation is represented by the ceremony symbolising death of the novice and his return to the fellowship of the living. But he returns to life a new man, assuming another mode of being. Initiatory death signifies at once the end of childhood, of ignorance, and of the profane condition…All the rites of rebirth and resurrection, and the symbols that they imply indicate that the novice has attained to another mode of existence, inaccessible to those who have not undergone the initiatory ordeals, who have not tasted death.[301]

In light of the above, we may thus conclude that Initiation, although featuring a preliminary phase in the First Degree, is only completed, from an esoteric point of view, in the Third Degree with the initiatic death which, through the ages, has concluded initiations to all Mysteries, as underlined by René Alleau:

> It is too often overlooked that the verb 'to initiate' literally means, in the main sense of the word, 'to make die'. An 'initiate' is no less separated from the profane world than a dead man. In spite of the illusions in which the unhappy take pride, neither the dead nor initiates communicate directly with the beings situated on a different plane. It is we who should be elevated to their plane, not they who should be expected to descend to ours.[302]

To conclude, the renowned Arab mystic Ibn 'Arabi teaches us that we need to 'die before we die', meaning that the Candidate should overstep the illusion of separateness, and only then will he become an Initiate.

To Alphabetise, Solve et Coagula

To alphabetise means to pronounce slowly and clearly, enunciating the letters and syllables of each word, an expression that reminds us of children when they are learning to read; 'all those children alphabetising in a chant', wrote D'Annunzio in the *Novelle di Pescara*. Today, with our routine use of foreign words, the term 'spelling' is frequently used, although 'to spell' has a slightly different meaning, referring to a solemn pronunciation, particularly used in magic formulas. On the contrary, to alphabetise implies, above all, uncertainty, the careful taking of one step at a time.

The Masonic ritual should indeed be interpreted in this sense, when the Initiate, asked to pronounce the Sacred Word replies: 'I can neither read nor write, I can only alphabetise'[303], and in taking his first steps on the initiatic journey, is identified as a 'child passing from the mother's womb to the world.[304]

However, particularly the act of alphabetising should be seen as one of the ritual allegories most clearly displaying a likeness with the dynamics of the alchemical Opus, as it recalls the fundamental process of 'solve et coagula'. In the ritual (Emulation), we observe how the Word, initially *decomposed*, or rather alphabetised, will subsequently be pronounced as a *whole*. Naturally, from an initiatic viewpoint, the term 'Word' should not be intended merely as a series of sounds or graphic signs, and from an esoteric point of view a sequence of sounds or signs makes up a word only if it is capable of meeting a purpose, of evoking a meaning in the mind of he who hears or reads the same, and thus become a symbol. On an initiatic plane therefore, the reiteration of the Word, pronouncing it in full after having previously alphabetised it one letter at a time, reuniting what was previously divided, allegorically signifies the discovery of the signs of the Principle (this is the meaning) throughout the various stages of the manifestation.

In the context of the dynamics of the ritual, the Word is thus interpreted as a symbol, a term deriving from the Greek (*sun-bolon*) that indicates 'the reunion of two parts of a divided object, each of which is capable of recalling the original object'. Here then the concept of Word reminds us of the concepts of *purpose* and *order*, where order is construed as the conformity of parts (in this case letters) that make up a specific group (the Word) and result in the purpose of the group (the evoking of a meaning). The alphabetising of a Word may thus symbolise the passage from One (the Word) to a series of differentiated forms within the physical world (letters), from the supreme order of the unmanifested Principle to the relative order of the universal manifestation.

Therefore, one cannot fail to grasp the relationship between the symbolism of alphabetising (and subsequent enunciation as a whole) and the alchemical process of *solve et coagula*, both intended as a representation of the non-equivalent complementarity of two inverse phases; it will indeed be precisely this enunciation subsequent to the alphabetising to achieve 'order, or rather to correspond to the purpose of the Word.

The symbolism of alphabetising and the alchemical principle of solve et coagula, by evoking the hierarchised complementarity of the two ascending and descending inverse phases of the cosmic manifestation, may both be traced to a sole universal symbolic model. It is this model, the primordial archetype, that we can detect expressed in numerous forms of the Kabbalah (fragmentation and reintegration of the *Adam Qadmon*), in Hinduism (disintegration and reconstruction of the *Purusha*), in the ancient Egyptian rites (break up and reconstitution of *Osiris*), as well as in the Jungian process of individuation, in which dissolution of the initial Persona subsequently, and by degrees, leads to the knowledge of one's innermost Self (God). If, through use of the term *Solve* or *Solutio*, the elements are broken down, the subsequent expression *Coagula* will refer to their being reunited; in the same way, for he who seeks the Spirit, if *solve* implies the dissolution of the forced positions, of the negative states of the mind and body, the need to dissolve and remove negative energies, *coagula* refers to the coagulation of the elements dispersed within an integrated environment, representing a new synthesis.

The Chequered Pavement, reconciling the conscious with the unconscious

As a general rule, the symbology of the *Chequered Pavement* is interpreted, quite simplistically, and from a typically moralistic point of view, as the contrast between good and evil.

However, let us overlook morals for a moment, and approach the symbol from a more profound point of view. On referring to the Chinese text of *I Ching* and its primary symbols *yin* and *yang* (a circle divided into two black and white halves), by likening the Ego to a Circle, and a Circle with a Point in its midst, the Self, we might likewise interpret the Chequered Pavement as the symbol of the mind, divided between the conscious (white) and the unconscious (black).

If an integration between the conscious and the unconscious represents the aim of the process of individuation, the search for the integral personality, the Self, the walking on a Chequered Pavement will symbolically represent the union between our conscious and unconscious parts, an integration of opposites, the *coniunctio*. If, alchemically speaking, the idea of coniunctio was capable of illuminating the obscure mystery of chemical compositions, from the mythologem viewpoint; it expresses the archetype of a unification of opposite, thus assuming the semblance of the *unio mystica*.

3
The Royal Arch

The Quaternity - symbol of an Integral Personality

We have previously seen how the esotericism of the symbolic Three Degrees is fully representative of the Masonic initiatic journey, not requiring any further superfetations or additions. The only specification to be made refers to the fact that this esotericism is naturally accomplished by means of the Royal Arch ritual, generally not viewed as an additional Degree, but rather as a sort of further advancement of the Third Degree.

If the prevailing theme of Freemasonry is constituted by the Three Degrees, and the construction of King Solomon's Temple, in the Royal Arch reference is made to the symbolic reconstruction of the Temple following the demise of Babylon.

Substantial differences can be observed between the structure of a chapter of the Royal Arch and a Craft Lodge. The Three Degrees Freemasonry comprises Lodges made up of Brethren, whilst in the Royal Arch the Chapters are made up of Companions. The Chapters are presided over by three Principles representing Zerubbabel, the Prince of Jerusalem, Haggai the Prophet, and Joshua the High Priest, assisted by two Scribes, Ezra (Chapter Secretary) and Nehemiah, a Principal and two Assistant Sojourners, a Treasurer and a Guardian, the latter of which encharged with defending the Chapter.

Before embarking on an analysis of the symbology of the Quaternary present within the context of the Royal Arch ritual, a few brief notes on this Ritual should first be provided, due to its lesser degree of familiarity compared to the so-called Blue Lodge Freemasonry (the *first Three Degrees*).

In the introduction to his fundamental *Freemasons Book of the Royal Arch*, the British historian Bernard Jones writes:

> There has been long argument on how Royal Arch masonry came into existence. Was it present in some slight form in the earliest fabric of speculative masonry or was it, frankly, just an innovation in the first half of the eighteenth century? Those accepting the first possibility believe that long before the earliest recorded dates of Craft masonry - the Acception in the London Company of Freemasons in 1621 and the 'making' of Elias Ashmole in 1646 - there was a legend or a series of legends from which was developed (a) the Hiramic Degree (Third Degree) which was working in a few lodges certainly as early as the 1720's; (b) the Royal Arch Degree known to be working by the 1740's and 1750's; and (c) some additional degrees. All three were thought to have come from one common source and, although developed on very different lines, to have running through them a recognizable thread.[305]

From a strictly documental point of view, there is currently no proof that the Three Degrees Freemasonry and Royal Arch Freemasonry hailed from a common root or origin. Likewise, there is no reliable demonstration attesting that the rituals of the Royal Arch were created from a 'mutilation' of the Degree of Master. This said, it cannot however be ruled out, indeed, there are signs of 'contaminations' at the very least between the rituals of the symbolic first Three Degrees and the rituals of the Royal Arch. To this regard, Jones points out: 'we know that mention of any stone-turning in the Craft ritual of the 1730s known to John Coustos did not remain in the Craft working, but that the *motif*, amplified and drastically developed, does find a place in the Royal Arch ritual,[306] consequently, Jones concludes:

> We do not believe that the Royal Arch developed from the same source as the Hiramic Degree, and we have found no trace of any connexion with operative masonry. But neither do we believe that the Royal Arch Degree was an

> out-and-out fabrication. We feel that some masons and some lodges were early acquainted with elements now associated with the Royal Arch ceremonial, in which respect we have been greatly influenced by the reference to stone-turning and the finding of the Sacred Name made by John Coustos in his evidence when in the hands of the Inquisition. And we cannot disregard Gould's suggestion that the much-talked-of and little-known Scots degrees, worked in the early eighteenth century, were cryptic in character and might well have provided ideas that developed on the Royal Arch pattern...In the main the theme of the Royal Arch story is provided by versions of an ancient crypt legend with which many learned men would have been quite familiar. The arranger might first have gone to one or more of these versions (as in our opinion he undoubtedly did) and then incorporated an idea or ideas present in the Craft ceremonials in use by some few lodges. The arranger - with the material of the old crypt legends, the references in the Craft ritual, and the Old Testament story of the Jewish exile - was able to erect what was actually a new degree or rite containing the features of the vault, the discoveries and the reiterated belief in the Word.[307]

The majority of scholars, in the uncertainty as to whether or not the Legend of Hiram and the Royal Arch share a common origin, maintain that the Royal Arch should be viewed as a clear accomplishment of the Third Degree. It was undeniably the view of the Antients (the 'secessionist' Obedience that, in 1751, contrasted the original Grand Lodge, defining it contemptuously as the Moderns) that the Royal Arch ritual contained some elements that had been lost in the Third Degree; for this reason, the ceremony of the Third Degree concluded by *preparing* the candidate for an additional step to be undertaken in a subsequent, and conclusive, ritual.

The first Masonic documents, the *Old Charges*, contain a potential terminological reference to the Royal Arch in the *Dumfries Manuscript* of 1710 which wrote: 'No lodge or group of masons shall thoughtlessly convey to others the Royal secret, but shall only do so following extensive deliberation', an expression that is present in an amended version, although implying a similar significance, in the Aldersgate ritual currently in use in the British Chapters.

The theory of the introduction of the Royal Arch to England by the Scottish Knight Andrew Michael Ramsay, based on a hypothetical speech he delivered on occasion of a meeting of the Grand Lodge of France in Paris on 21 March 1737, is a matter of legend.

Documents referring to John Coustos, previously mentioned by Jones, are more reliable; Coustos was a Swiss-born protestant residing in Britain, and member of a Lodge in Lisbon made up largely of French Catholics, who was betrayed and jailed during the Inquisition in 1742, in compliance with the Papal Bull on Excommunication dated 1738. Coustos was likely initiated in a London Lodge in 1730, subsequently moving to Paris and then Lisbon, where he worked as a diamond cutter. He was freed from the Inquisition thanks to the involvement of the British Representative in Lisbon in October 1744, subsequently returning to England. The original documents of the Inquisition highlight how in March 1743 Coustos was coerced into giving a confession that contained interesting elements relating to both the Three Degrees of Freemasonry, as well as to symbolic elements present in the rituals of the Royal Arch, as follows:

> The reason and foundation that the Masters of this Fraternity have for causing those who newly join to take the Oath upon a Bible, or a Book of the Gospels, at the place of that of St. John is the following, - that when the destruction took place of the famous Temple of Solomon there was found below the First Stone a tablet of bronze upon which was engraved the following words – JEHOVAH – which means 'God', living thereby to understand that that Fabric and temple was instituted and erected in the name of the said God to whom it was dedicated, the same Lord the beginning and the end of such a magnificent work, and as in the Gospel of St. John there are found the same words and doctrine they, for this reason, cause the Oath to be taken at the place, thus to show that the whole institution of this Fraternity is founded on the same doctrine which Solomon observed in his sumptuous work, and the reason he has for saving this is for having heard it so declared by some of the French and English Masters, though he does not know from whence they obtained this doctrine for its propounding.[308]

In addition to the clear reference to the rituals of the Royal Arch, the document relating to the interrogation of Coustos is of particular interest as it provides an important key to the comprehension of the true attitude of the Catholic Church towards Freemasonry at the time. This occurred within a few years of publication of the Bull *In Eminenti Apostulatus Specula* by Pope Clement XII, a document in which Freemasonry was outlawed and its members excommunicated; historians have taken great enjoyment in assigning a series of interpretations to the Papal Bull, among which that of a political 'opportunity' of condemnation by the Roman Church has curried the greatest favour. On the contrary, in my opinion, one should merely attain, without any extravagant dietrologies, to the justification provided in the document itself, i.e. to the crime committed by the Freemasons, namely heresy. Likewise, the documentation relating to the trial of Coustos, as confirmation of the consistency of his accusers, and above and beyond the reason for the sentence, that I shall not comment on for the sake of brevity, highlights how each time the Inquisitors refer to Freemasonry, they use the term 'Religion', once again confirming how the Catholic Church and its theologians were indeed apt to view the latter as an antagonistic Religion, or rather a degeneration of the orthodox Christian religion (the Masonic rituals of the period contained clear references to the Trinity and to Saint John, that were subsequently lost, and to the use of the Bible), and therefore as heresy.

To return to our topic, Coustos' words reveal that at the time of his visits to the London Lodges, the latter featured ritual elements from the Three Degrees, which subsequently disappeared from the actual Craft ritual, but instead appeared in the Royal Arch.The origins of the Royal Arch are as uncertain as those of the Craft in terms of documented evidence. The historian John Hamill, one of the greatest experts in the history of English Freemasonry, wrote that:

> It is now generally accepted that Royal Arch originated in the 1730s, but whether in England, Ireland or, possibly, France is still highly arguable...The search for origins has not been helped by the marked lack of early evidence.[309]

Historians Douglas Knopp and G. P. Jones found references to the Royal Arch from as early as 1723 but concluded that no real evidence could be gathered of the fact that actual ceremonies were held in the same period:

> Casual references to an Arch can be traced in masonic literature from 1723 onwards. Thus at the end of the historical section of the Constitution of 1723, Anderson refers to the Royal Art being duly cultivated and the cement of brotherhood preserved, 'so that the whole Body resembles a well-built Arch.' Two of the early printed masonic catechism have the question 'Whence is an Arch derived', to which one replied 'From Architecture' and the other 'From the rainbow'. In this connection it may be noted that arms of the Grand Chapter of All England at York contained a rainbow, but the arms were not added until the second half of the eighteenth century.[310]

According to the historians, the first reliable document referring to a Royal Arch ceremony is represented by a letter dated 1 February 1734 written by Mick Broughton to the Duke of Richmond (Grand Master from 1724 to 1725, in which Broughton made a joking reference to a 'super excellent' and 'refers to three masons being 'made chapters' in a lodge in the library at Ditton, when Dr Desaguliers (Grand Master, 1719–20) was visiting the Duke of Montagu'.[311]

The document in which the term Royal Arch was first used in England dates back to 4 March 1752 and is represented by minutes of the Antients, whereas the first known minutes documenting an 'Elevation' ceremony belong to a Moderns Lodge and date back to 1758.

The birth and subsequent development of the Royal Arch in English Freemasonry were undoubtedly influenced by the severe hostilities between the two Obediences, which competed against each other in England from the mid-1700s to the early 1800s.[312] After the establishment of the Grand Lodge in 1717, another Grand Lodge was founded in 1751; the historians' opinions on the reasons for this occurrence diverge significantly. Some interpreted the latter as an actual schism, whereas others identified its cause in the preponderant presence of Scots and Irishmen who joined other Englishmen in their displeasure at a series of important decisions taken by the original Grand Lodge with regard to the publication of Samuel Prichard's pamphlet entitled 'Masonry Dissected', in which the Sacred Words of the ritual were revealed. As a consequence to Prichard's pamphlet, the Grand Lodge introduced a number of variations to the ritual (such as the inversion of the words), a decision which caused intense disagreements (as these were seen as an evident violation of the Landmarks) and further encouraged a schism that had perhaps already begun. The future schismatics had long been accusing the Grand Lodge of several interventions which had been jeopardising the Masonic orthodoxy, the most serious being omitting prayers, de-Christianizing the ritual, ignoring saints' days, failing to prepare Candidates in the traditional manner, abbreviating or abandoning the lectures (catechisms), abandoning the Ancient Charges, causing the ceremonies, particularly Initiation, to be more austere, and, finally, allowing the Installation of the Venerable Master.[313]

Following the establishment of another Grand Lodge in 1751, which, as we have seen, was attributed to the Antients, as opposed to the original one, which was paradoxically attributed to the Moderns, the Royal Arch, too, developed in two different manners. The documents currently available seem to reveal that the ritual of the Royal Arch was received positively within the Antients Grand Lodge whereas it was never completely integrated in the Moderns. The 1764 edition of the Antients Grand Lodge *Constitution*, which was named *Ahiman Rezon* by the compiler Laurence Dermott (the first edition was published in 1756), stresses the concept that the Royal Arch represented 'the root, the heart and the essence of Freemasonry', with the document's frontispiece displaying two series of heraldic coats of arms, one of which portrayed a Lion, an Ox, a Man and an Eagle (symbols pertaining to the ritual of the Royal Arch) with an arch on top, supported by cherubs. There is thus no doubt that the Antients were more open towards and felt fully involved in the ritual of the Royal Arch, although the documents currently available reveal they might not have been the first ones to perform it. Indeed, despite the lack of chemistry, the first Grand Chapter to be founded in England, and in the world, was precisely that of the Moderns, in 1766, thanks to the Grand Master of the Grand Lodge who then became its First Principal. The new organism was named Grand Royal Chapter, which was changed to Grand Lodge of Royal Arch Masons in 1795 and again in 1801 to Supreme Grand Chapter. The birth of the Grand Chapter, brought to light thanks to the initiative of the Grand Master, Lord Blayney, was not well-accepted by the Grand Lodge; for this reason someone subsequently modified the foundation document by postponing the date and inserting a 'P' (which stood for Past) in front of Blayney's rank, effectively trying to place Blayney's intervention after his official appointment as Grand Master. To this regard Hamill wrote that:

> Evidently the involvement of their Grand master in the formation of a Masonic body which they did not officially recognise upset the premier Grand Lodge,

> for the Charter of Compact shows evidence of having been tampered with. The date was altered to 1767, a 'P' was inserted between 'Blayney', and 'Grand Master' implying that the event took place after Blayney had finished his term as Grand Master.[314]

The Antients founded their Grand Chapter five years later, in 1771, with a substantial difference; in fact, whereas the Moderns' Grand Chapter initially established itself as a sort of body *separate* from the Grand Lodge, the Antients was somehow contained within the structure of the Grand Lodge and was never organised independently, thus creating a sort of single institution between the Grand Lodge and the Grand Chapter.

In 1817, the current Supreme Grand Chapter of Royal Arch Masons of England was established, born from the union of the Modern' and Antients Grand Chapters (the previous meeting of the two Grand Lodges had taken place in 1813).[315]

What is the current situation? The *Book of Constitutions* of the United Grand Lodge of England declares that 'By the solemn Act of Union between the two Grand Lodge of Free-Masons of England in December 1813, it was declared and pronounced that pure Antient Masonry consist of three degrees and no more, viz., those of the Entered apprentice, the Fellow Craft and the master Mason, including the Supreme Order of the Holy Royal Arch' and, above all, the 'exalted' Royal Arch candidate is informed that what he received is not a Fourth Degree but a *completion* of the Third.

The introduction of the above formula gave rise to a new and endless controversy on what should be considered as *Pure Antient Masonry*. Without becoming involved in the debate, it would appear that Douglas Knopp, with the usual sobriety that characterised his studies on Freemasonry, provided the most plausible interpretation, explaining that, without needing to take the declaration to the letter, the Pure Antient Masonry could be identified not only with the Three Degrees but rather with the esoteric knowledge associated with it, independently of the expression of said knowledge in one, two or three portions.

The claim of the Royal Arch to be part of Pure Antient Masonry can be judged by considering whether the principal esoteric knowledge associated with the Royal Arch can be shown to have existed when the Premier Grand Lodge was founded.[316]

With regard to the question of whether the Royal Arch should be considered the Fourth Degree of Freemasonry or simply the completion of the Third, we know that before the Unification of 1817, the Grand Chapter of the Antients believed that the Royal Arch should undoubtedly be considered as a Fourth Degree, but after the unification matters changed, as reported by Harry Mendoza:

> The premier Grand Lodge did not recognise the Royal Arch as part of Craft masonry; they had no objection to it so long as it was considered as a separate and distinct Society. The Grand Lodge of the Antients however held the opposite view; they claimed it as a fourth degree. These views had to be

> resolved if the two Grand Lodges were to be united. This was done in a superficial manner by the wording in the Articles of Union, now incorporated as the Preliminary Declaration to the Book of Constitutions...The Royal Arch is now an integral part of Freemasonry, directly connected with the Craft. Designated officers in the Craft hold comparable offices in the Royal Arch; a Chapter has to be attached to a Lodge and bear its number...The Royal Arch is not a separate degree; it is an Order which has grown out of, and dependent upon, the Craft.[317]

According to the English historian Neville Barker Cryer, when the definition of 'completion' of the Third Degree was chosen in 1817, this never intended for the ritual of the Royal Arch to be interpreted as a sort of 'second part' of the Hiramic Degree:

> Though the Union of 1813 statement declared that the Royal Arch was included with the three degrees of the Antient Craft this was never intended to mean that now, or even in living memory then, the Royal Arch was simply the second part of the 3° as we know it.[318]

Indeed, Cryer argued that, at that time, Exaltation required the candidate to possess the degree of Past Master, to have been an Installed Master, and, more importantly, the ritual contained a particular ceremony, named 'Passing of the Veils', which later disappeared (except from the Bristol Chapter), all of which, according to Cryer, could not possibly contribute to the portrayal of the Royal Arch as the 'simple completion', or, even worse, the 'second part' of the Third Degree. Moreover, Cryer wondered, if the Royal Arch were the 'completion', a part of the Third Degree, why is the candidate not admitted to the Temple with the canonical three knocks? Why are different regalia worn? Why are members of a Chapter called Companions? Why are there Three Principals and not one Venerable Master and his Guards? Why do Sojourners exist? These and other anomalies represent for Barker Cryer the evidence that the Royal Arch cannot reductively be considered as the simple completion of the Third Degree but certainly something rather more complex.

After this brief historical excursus on the foundation of the Royal Arch in England – due to space restrictions the interesting realities of Scotland, Ireland and America will have to be overlooked – let's move on to analysing the ritual contents of the ceremony. The latter is based essentially on the 'Legend of the Crypt', the discovery of an underground room underneath the Temple of Jerusalem. The oldest document available regarding the legend dates back to the fourth century A.D. and is attributed to a Church historian, Philostorgius, who however placed the events at the time of Emperor Julian, known as the Apostate (331-363), successor of Constantius. The legend presented in the ritual, albeit featuring the same dynamics narrated by Philostorgius, temporally places itself many centuries before, more precisely to coincide with the return from the Babylonian captivity (circa 536 BC) after Nebuchadnezzar's destruction of the first Temple in 586 BC.

Approximately seventy years later, Cyrus, King of Persia, after also conquering Babylon, allowed the Jewish exiles back into Palestine and authorised the rebuilding of the old Temple. The story narrated in the ritual informs us that Governor Zerubabbel, assisted by Joshua the High Priest and Haggai the Prophet, spared no expenses for the reconstruction, during which the crypt, the centre of the esoteric message of the ritual, was discovered.

The first anachronism[319] we come across is the 'vaulted arch' that is referred to in the ritual, which is a typically medieval element, as nothing similar existed at the time of the story narrated; what is interesting from an initiatic perspective, however, is the allegory represented by the moment in which the Sojourners, after removing some stones from the vault, are able to enter the crypt. It was precisely within the crypt that the Sojourner found a roll, the lost Volume of the Sacred Law, and a pedestal engraved with the initials of the Three Grand Masters who contributed to the construction of the first Temple, King Solomon, Hiram King of Tyre and Hiram Habif (the Temple architect who was subsequently killed), and 'some characters and mysterious words', which, if interpreted in connection with what was *lost* in the Third Degree and *found again* in the Royal Arch, could be believed to refer to God's name. The latter is, however, subject to widely diverging opinions.

The historian Harry Mendoza does not agree with the explanation that the lost Word is God's name, supporting his theory with the fact that according to many theologists and experts in Biblical exegesis God's name was never lost, even in the darkest moments of the Jewish diaspora. How should the lost and newly found Word thus be interpreted? Mendoza suggested that the problem be approached from a 'metaphysical' point of view: lost in the sense of 'failing to keep something in mind' and found as 'discovering something for the first time'.[320] In our opinion, Mendoza's interpretation cannot be considered metaphysical, let alone esoteric or initiatic. Indeed, if we wanted to confer a *metaphysical*, or *mythical*, meaning to the symbols we are presented with, we would have to presume that the Disciple was trying to recover a lost *awareness*, that of his divine nature, supported by the revelation, at the culmination of the ritual, of God's name.

The English historian Harry Carr, believed that the Word on which the Exaltation ceremony was based was not the same Word which was referred to in the Third Degree and now rediscovered, but rather represented a completely new Word. The ritual itself, however, invalidates Carr's theory, as it specifies that: 'the degree is conferred with the communication of the Ineffable Word which was lost at the traditional time in which the Third degree was originally enacted, and subsequently rediscovered, again according to masonic tradition, at the time when the Royal Arch ceremony first took place'. Without delving deeper into the matter, I believe that neither Mendoza nor Carr grasped the essential meaning of what the ritualist hoped to communicate. We shall thus look for a different interpretation.

It is undeniable that certain lost Mysteries were found again, and the fact that these Mysteries concern the event in question is once again confirmed by the ritual itself, in which references are made to Mysteries recovered 'in a dramatic and providential manner'. It is also specified that the lost Mysteries refer to the Word, as the ritual reads: 'Freemasonry is full of allegories, but the most important one is the *research* of the Word', but, subsequently, it adds that the Word 'is not the Holy name, but it is hidden in it and leads us in the same direction'. So we ask ourselves, what is the Word?

In my opinion, in order to comprehend the real meaning of lost and found Mysteries, that which should be emphasised is the meaning of 'research', a research that *leads* to God. The *actual* research should thus be emphasised, what we need to find is a path, as over time we have lost awareness of our divine nature, and the ritual can help us remember, retrace our origins, recognise the divine particle that resides within us.

There also exist other open questions regarding the terminology of the Royal Arch, such as the reason for which the latter is referred to as 'Holy'(Holy Royal Arch) in the English tradition. Given that in the Scottish ritual the word 'Holy' is not used, a reliable explanation is provided by Barker Cryer, who sees the word 'Holy' as the right attribute for an Order which constantly refers to the Holy Scriptures in its ritual:

> Why Holy? First and most obviously this is because of the great reliance placed in this ceremony on the words and teaching of Holy Scripture. Whilst it is true that there are odd references in the three Craft degrees to various Bible events – the pillars at the porchway or entrance of King Solomon's temple, the story of Jacob lying down with his head on a stone and in a dream seeing a ladder raising towards heaven, Jephthah and the Ephraimites, the trade of Tubalcain – there is nothing like the passage of Scripture which are actually read in the course of the ceremony here. As our ritual says, man 'would have remained in a state of darkness had it not pleased the Almighty to call him to light and immortality by the revelation of His Holy Will and Word'. This is underlined as the candidate is exalted and reads from the Book of genesis, to which the M.E.Z. responds with 'Such are the first words of the Sacred Volume which contains the records of founded and rooted in the Holy Words'.[321]

This markedly spiritual interpretation is not shared by other scholars, such as Richard Sandbach, who, in an essay on the history and symbolic content of the Royal Arch specifies that the undeniable references to the 'holy' in the ritual do not mean that the latter should be considered as something different from an essentially 'moral' code: '

> This does not imply that Royal Arch is itself more than a code of morality. Freemasonry is in no sense a religion and thus the Order may and should lead us to think about religion it does not try to provide a substitute.[322]

According to Sandbach, the possibility of living truly spiritual experiences can present itself only within the religious experience, and because Freemasonry is not a religion, despite the evident presence within its rituals of elements displaying an undeniable link to the holy, it will never be able to represent, according to Sandbach, anything other than a 'code of moral behaviour'. The question, however, arises as to why to go out of one's way to conceive complex allegories and elaborate symbols to represent a simple ethical code. And moreover, if we were to accept this pithy representation of the symbolic Three Degrees, it is the ritual itself that reminds us that once the Three Degrees have ended, there is still a journey to be undertaken: 'The degrees that you received in the Order have taught you that Freemasonry is a system of morality…The Exaltation ceremony suggests that we still have much to learn and encourages us to lift our gaze…'

Of course, as already demonstrated in a previous paragraph with Wilmshurst's writings, there also exist those who see Masonic symbols as the expression of an actual spiritual journey, such as the American George H. Steinmetz, who, with regard to the symbology of the Royal Arch, wrote that, after the acquisition of the Third Degree, the candidate is expected to:

> Continue on the plane of the spiritual, continuing to acquire knowledge through personal experience. This expectation is realised and he finds he is 'again caused' to 'represent' another and in that representation he actually experiences for himself that which Masonic tradition credits those whom he represent with having experienced.[323]

Moving on to the study of the symbology of the Royal Arch and its possible alchemical roots, we wish to highlight how, even the Anglosaxon Masonic historiography, generally reluctant to accept esoteric interpretations, reached the conclusion, with regard to the Royal Arch, that 'we must accept the likelihood that Royal Arch masonry borrowed directly from the alchemical store of symbolism'.[324]

The historian Bernard Jones asked himself, after having rightfully identified a lack of esoteric elements in the founding documents of Freemasonry, the *Old Charges*, when the esoteric connotation was introduced, and by whom. The answer Jones gave himself is that:

> Much of the more important symbolism was provided by high-principled, classically educated men who discovered in the course of a life-absorbing study of alchemy the rich store of symbolism that had been gathered together by their learned predecessors.[325]

Jones subsequently recommended a number of texts for an in-depth analysis of the alchemical doctrine, listing among them also *Psychology and Alchemy* by Jung, which, curiously, is only recommended for its 'provocative illustrations, not for the text'. It seems superfluous to recall the notable recognitions awarded to Jung's essay, mainly by influential religion historians, led by Mircea Eliade.

With regard to the alchemical connections, or rather 'contaminations', of Freemasonry, the American scholar Timothy Hogan was even more explicit, maintaining that:

> Alchemy first and foremost sought to join the physical with the spiritual. In alchemical symbolism, the physical world was represented by the square (like the four corners of the earth), and the spiritual world by a circle which had no beginning or end. The two tools used in making this symbolism are the square and compasses, and in the three degrees of symbolic blue lodge Masonry, the spiritual compasses gradually overcome the physical square as the candidate receives further light. In fact, early alchemical texts from the 1500s flatly state that in order to attain the famed Philosopher's Stone of alchemy, you needed to 'square di circle'.[326]

Quaternary in the Royal Arch

The symbol of Quaternary can already be observed in Craft rituals; the Fellow Craft, indeed, is put to the test by the *Squad*, a symbol of Quaternary by reason of the presence of a 90° angle, i.e. the fourth part of a circle. It was, however, mainly with the Royal Arch rituals that the symbols of Quaternary and totality started to acquire their essential nature. The symbol of the 'Four', indeed, is a recurring element in the symbology and rituality of the Royal Arch, appearing in the 'raps' or 'knocks' of the Three Principals, and the four Standards featuring the symbols of the Lion, the Man, the Eagle and the Ox. The quaternary is, more significantly, summarised in the Seal of Solomon, a symbol composed of two intersecting equilateral triangles, with the one with its vertex pointing upwards representing Fire, and the one with its vertex pointing downwards representing Water. The triangle of fire, with the horizontal side of the other triangle, represents Air, whereas the inverted sign represents Earth; in conclusion, it includes the representation of all elements and, subsequently, the union of 'opposites', as illustrated by Burckhardt:

> The signs of the four elements derived from the Soul of Solomon are particularly lucid when it comes to their application to the soul. From them can be seen that the plurality of the elements derives from the opposition of fire and water, that is, from the pair activity-passivity (which of course corresponds to the pair forma-materia). It is the same opposition we shall encounter in the form of sulphur and quicksilver. Through the union of opposites the soul becomes 'fluid fire' and 'fiery water', and at the same time

> also acquires the positive qualities of the other elements, so that its water becomes 'stable' and its fire 'non-burning'; for the 'fire' of the soul is that which confers stability on its 'water', while the 'water' of the soul confers on 'fire' the mildness and ubiquity of 'air'.[327]

The Seal of Solomon thus represents the symbol of wholeness, of totality, and it is not a coincidence for it to be encountered at an advanced stage of the initiatic journey, the one we identified as a further phase of improvement of the Master Degree. 'Morality' was definitively abandoned to move into the field of 'mystique' and 'transcendence', as reported by Wirth:

> The most brilliant gifts of Intelligence and willpower would never make anyone other than a fake magician into the disciple who has not nurtured the qualities of the heart. Those who are able to elevate themselves with sentiment as much as with science will be rewarded with the Seal of Solomon. These two intertwined triangles form the Star of the Microcosmos or the Great World. They symbolise the union of the Father and the Mother, of God and Nature, the singular Spirit and the universal Soul, the fire that procreates and the Water that generates. It is the pentacle par excellence, the symbol of a power that cannot be contrasted, which will be made available to us only after effectively attaining the degree of Master.[328]

A further reference to the Quaternary in the symbology of the Royal Arch is the *Tetragrammaton*, which is inscribed within a Triangle, and composed of four letters, which symbolise the emanation number, or representation of the Word. Whereas Ternary is understood as an actual emanation of Unity, the union of the Unity manifested with the Ternary originates the Quaternary, which is therefore represented by a Circle within a Triangle. The Quaternary identified possesses within it the numbers 1+2+3+4=10, thus creating the image of full Manifestation. The Quaternary is statically expressed by a square, but its dynamic projection consists in a cross which, by rotating around the intersection of its arms (the Centre), forms a Circle. A transition from Triangle to Square to Circle is therefore activated, involving symbolic elements that make up the Royal Arch *Plate of Gold*.

The triple Tau

Another key symbol in the Royal Arch ritual is the triple *Tau*, a letter of the Jewish alphabet which, as mentioned in the ritual itself, represented the seal that the angel who appeared to Zechariah made reference to, as confirmed in the Aldersgate ritual:

> This mark was set on those who had been acquitted by their judges, as a symbol of innocence. The military commanders placed it on soldiers who escaped unhurt from the field of battle, as a sign of their safety under the

> Divine Protection. For this reason it has ever been considered a mark or sign of life. The union of the Taus symbolises Divinity.

The triple Tau symbolises the completion of the spiritual journey of a Masonic disciple; the apron of the installed Venerable Master features three separate Taus: their union will take place in the Royal Arch, a journey which will lead the disciple to Divinity, the discovery of his own Self, the achievement of his full personality.

Similarly to the Tau, a further symbol of unity or totality is represented by the 'Throne of God', yet another symbol of union and power, which the Candidate will be faced with at the height of his initiatic journey. To this regard Elemire Zolla writes that:

> Unity manifests the power of everything, from zero to the undefined, of which it represents the intersection. Unity was an inexhaustible object of meditation...In ancient times a series of images were evoked to stimulate its conception, an experience for man, and was referred to as accomplishment and profound quiet, an unextended point of creativity, the hearth of everything, scale, cross, cosmic altar, Tau or first and last harmonic connection, Throne of God, star of the Everything, of the Pleroma.[329]

The Caternary Arch

The symbol of the Caternary Arch is particularly significant for the comprehension of the profound esoteric value of the ritual of the Royal Arch.

The Symbolical Lecture explains that once a Chapter of the Royal Arch is properly arranged, it takes the form of a Catenary Arch, to symbolise the vaulted sanctuary in which the Sacred Word was kept.

The 'Vault' which the candidates have to pass through is composed of two or more Catenary Arches that protect the room which, as they find out after their descent, houses the Altar on which the Sacred and Mystic Name is engraved; in order to do this, the 'vault key' placed on top of the Catenary Arch, a vault key which acts as seal to the room itself, will need to be uprooted (by physically reproducing the act).

From a strictly architectural point of view, we know that the structure of the Catenary Arch is able to support exceptional loads and stress, which exceed the sum of its single parts. The presence of the Catenary Arch can already be foreseen in the Craft ritual, as testified by the words *Boaz* (Strength) and *Jakin* (Solidity), which combined lead to 'Stability'; the union of the two columns, indeed, is necessarily achieved by means of a Catenary Arch which represents the highest structural stability.

The stability obtained, achieved and strengthened by the Disciple in the Master Degree, a stability which can be identified in a purely moral behaviour, however, is not sufficient to achieve a further spiritual progress; we should thus interrupt this state of (apparent) balance, and, by removing the vault key, push ourselves to the depths of our conscience, our soul, even at the, temporary, expense of our 'stability'. By descending into the darkness of our conscience we will find our Shadow.

Opening the vault and 'descending' into the darkness of one's soul

A number of scholars have provided a mystical interpretation to the ritual and symbol of the Royal Arch, such as C.R. Manasseh, who, in his essay 'The Mysticism of the Royal Arch', wrote that: 'There is, in my opinion, a very good reason for separating the three Craft or blue degrees from the Royal Arch ceremony; for the blue degrees take us through our experiences during our life on this earth and the Royal Arch then tries to initiate us into the Grand Mystery of the Life hereafter. And just as death on earth is not the final end of Man's saga, so the Third degree in the 'Blue' is not the end of our Masonic teaching. In fact, this is implied when the candidate is 'raised from a figurative death' but is left wondering in the Limbo of Unknowing, when he is told that 'the genuine secrets of a master mason were lost by the untimely death of our Master Hiram Habif'. To tide him over, however, the candidate is given certain 'substituted secrets', a sort of Ariadne's thread or guide through the maze which mystically points out the timeless transition between life on earth and hereafter.'

According to Manasseh, therefore, the main goal of the ritual of the Royal Arch is to 'reintegrate us with the True and Living God Most High, in the same way as the Craft rituals try to integrate us with the spiritual Birth, Life and Death respectively. This re-integration with the Supreme Source and Essence can only be achieved by a mystical union'.

Again, according to Manasseh, in the ritual of the Royal Arch, and particularly in the so-called Lectures, seven Schools of Mystical revelations can be identified: the prehistoric cave mysticism (Cromagnon and others) and the Eleusinian Mysticism of Germination (i.e. the mysteries of Nature, as hinted by the Vault and its sacred contents; Kabbalitic mysticism, as evident in the arrangements of the lights, and the Seal of Solomon in the Jewel worn by the Companions; Phytagorean and Neo-Platonic mysticism, both in the brief reference to the five platonic bodies and in the more detailed explanation of the triangulation of the lights and the geometry of the Triple Tau and the Jewel; finally, the two famous mysticisms which in fact probably belong to one and the same School, because they are so strikingly similar that they have the appearance of being identical, i.e. the Hebraic mysticism of the Merkabah vision of Ezekiel (Ezekiel, chapter 1), and the Christian mysticism of the Apocalyptic vision of St John (Revelation, chapter 4). Both have the same mystical vision of the Shekinah Glory or 'Divine Immanence' riding in an incandescent chariot of flames, drawn by the same four Angelic Beasts: the Man, the Lion, the Ox and the Eagle, the emblems of the Patriarchal Blessing, which were later borne on the standards of the four leading tribes who ruled respectively over the South, East, West and North columns in marching, camping or fighting order, during the Exodus (Numbers, chapter 2).

In light of the above, Manasseh maintains that, the ceremony of the Royal Arch should by all means considered as the 'Mystical' phase of Freemasonry: 'glimpsed in most religions and seen in all the mysteries enacted throughout the ages; as in most religions and mystery plays, it refers to the Resurrection, or Rebirth or Regeneration on a higher spiritual plane after death in our present material plane, depicted in the Third Degree of the Craft, which followed the working life of man, represented in the Second Degree, the whole preceded by birth on this same material plane, illustrated most forcefully by our Initiation ceremony'. Offering partial support to Manasseh's interpretation, the ritual itself reiterates that those which will be performed should be considered essentially as 'Mystical Rites'.

With regard to the symbology and goals of the ritual of the Royal Arch, and to the symbology of the Three symbolic Degrees, we could conclude that the two symbologies and the two different rituals present certain similarities with the Lesser (Three Degrees) and Greater (Royal Arch) Mysteries of ancient Greece. Only the Greater Mysteries, indeed, allowed the Disciple to reach that 'metaphysical' dimension that brought him closer to the Divine.

After this mystical interpretation of the symbology and ritual of the Royal Arch, I would now like to propose a personal 'psychological interpretation', which will highlight how the goal of the ritual journey is essentially the transformation of the Disciple's *personality*, that is, the integration of the conscious part with the unconscious part of his personality, the Ego and the deep Self.

As mentioned previously, the Disciple will metaphorically descend into the 'crypt', where he will meet his Shadow. Only by meeting his Shadow, indeed, will he be able to achieve his full personality, the height of his initiatic, or psychological, journey, and discover his own Self, which, in the Jungian doctrine, represents the Divinity, God. This is the reason why the Disciple, only *after* falling into the Crypt, will register the presence of God's Name, thus fulfilling the goal of his initatic and spiritual journey.

The journey in the underground world accessed through the initiatic death in the Third Degree continues in a more explicit manner with the allegorical representation of the crypt as the deep 'centre' of our being, our psyche, within which we can finally find God's name, i.e. our Self. If we operated from an initiatic perspective, we will have reached our full personality.

The rope with which the Sojourners climb down into the crypt, to show the legend to the Disciple, and which they again use to clamber up, symbolically represents the *link* (such as Jacob's Ladder in the First Degree) between our conscious side and the unconscious side, which we climb down to meet. The Oracle of Delphi invited the Disciple to 'Know Thyself', to proceed in the initiatic journey to achieve the 'Construction of one's own Temple' and discover one's own Self, and thus obtain a transformation of one's own personality and the achievement of psychic totality.

In conclusion, I would like to point out how, regrettably, a review of the ritual between 1834 and 1835, aimed at the creation of a homogeneous ritual due to the high number of existing different rituals, removed a part of particular esoteric importance, the Ceremony of the passing of the veils, most likely of Christian origin, which is nowadays preserved in the Bristol Chapters, in a ritual which still bears the same name.[330]

CHAPTER FOUR
LOSS OF THE 'CENTRE'

Descates, Locke and Newton took away the world and gave us its excrements instead.
William Butler Yeats
Exploration

1
The Symbology of the 'Centre'

The Centre

What do we mean when we speak, in reference to the crisis of contemporary man, of a 'Loss of centre'? As mentioned in previous chapters, in the Masonic ritual the symbolism of the Centre plays an important role; it is indeed through the Centre that the Freemason finds the lost 'Mysteries', symbolically it is represented in the form of a *Point* within a circumference, symbols that, as we shall see, once more take us back to the alchemical theme of *Gold*.

Before moving on to our 'sociological' investigation relating to the loss of the Centre in modern and contemporary man, we should attempt to observe what is hidden and 'veiled' behind the symbolism of *the Centre*. The *symbolism of the Centre* is an ancient symbology, an 'archetype'. From a Jungian perspective, unfailingly present throughout all civilisations; it is brought to light and refreshed, or, as Jung would say, it emerges from the collective unconscious, depending on the circumstances (or, from a Traditional viewpoint, following the cosmic rhythms). To this regard, Mircea Eliade writes:

> The validity of the symbol considered as a form of knowledge does not depend upon any individual's degree of understanding. Texts and figured monuments provide us with abundant proof that for some, at least, of the individuals of an archaic society the symbolism of the 'Centre' was transparent in its totality; the rest of the society remaining content to 'participate' in the symbolism. Moreover, it is not easy to draw the limits of such a participation, for it varies in function with an indefinite number of factors. All we can say is that the actualisation of a symbol is not automatic; it occurs in relation to the tensions and the vicissitudes of the social life, and, finally, with the cosmic rhythms.[331]

As reiterated punctually by Marcello De Martino, Eliade provided an exhaustive expression of all the material in his work *Symbolism of the Centre* (in *Images and Symbols*), although this topic had previously been addressed by Eliade himself in a chapter of *The Quest - History and meaning in Religion* (1969) entitled *Meaning and function of a cosmogonic myth*. For Eliade, De Martino explains, the Centre is the definitive *Axis Mundi*, the pivot on which the Universe turns, the Tree, the Mountain or the Pillar situated at the Centre of the world:

> This is a powerful symbol aimed at carrying out a regulatory function in the context of the cosmonological myths of a series of ancient cultures, including the Sumerians, Assyrian-Babylonians, Hebrews, Indian. According to Eliade the peak of the Cosmic Mountain is the highest point on the earth, and at the same time the umbilicus of the same, from which the creation of the world commenced. The Centre contains the Cosmic Tree that provides a connection between Heaven and Earth: although the Centre is also a conceptual reality that can be constructed, a sacred space symbolically representing the imago mundi, the mandala, or rather a 'circle' that is likewise a 'centre''.[332]

This explains the need, in Freemasonry as in all other Initiatic Schools, for the consecration of the place in which the ritual, the initiatic work, the creation of a sacred space within which to conceive a Centre, will subsequently be performed; the subsequent 'deambulations' in a circular form will be aimed at regenerating, renewing and updating the same.

A first reference to the symbolism of the Centre or 'Point' can be observed in the most important book of the Kabbalist tradition, the *Zohar*, or the *Book of Splendour*. In this fundamental text, the maximum expression of Hebrew esotericism, we find references to the symbolism of the Centre that will later be assumed by all other esoteric Traditions, I report below the wonderful initial paragraph highlighting the correspondences between the *Micro* and *Macro* cosmos:

> With the beginning of the manifestation of the King's will, a hard spark made an engraving upon the supernal light. This hard spark, which emanated from the most concealed of all concealed things from the secret of the En Sof, the Endlessness, Light took a shapeless form. The spark was then inserted into the centre of a circle that was neither white nor black nor red nor green, nor any color at all. When it began its measurements, it created colors that shone into the empty space and the engraving. From within the spark - this hard spark - a fountain spouted, from which the shades down below received their colors. From the most concealed of all concealed things, from the secret of the Endlessness Light, a concealed supernal point shone (this primordial point is identified by the Zohar as the Wisdom of God, Hochmah, the ideal thought of creation). Beyond this point, nothing is knowable and, because of this, it is

> called by the name Re'sit, 'beginning', being the first of the sayings (the ten by means of which the world was created).
>
> When King Solomon penetrated into the depths of the nut garden (Song of Solomon 6.11), he took up a nut shell and studying it, he saw an analogy in its layers with the spirits which motivate the sensual desires of humans....and, as stated, the impulses of man are male and female spirits (Eccl., 2.8). God saw that it was necessary to put into the world so as to make sure of permanence all things having, so to speak, a brain surrounded by numerous membranes. The whole world, upper and lower, is organised on this principle, from the primary mystic centre to the very outermost of all the layers. All are coverings, the one to the other, brain within brain, spirit inside of spirit, shell within shell. The primal centre is the innermost light, of a translucence, subtlety, and purity beyond comprehension. That inner point extends to become a 'palace' which acts as an enclosure for the centre, and is also of a radiance translucent beyond the power to know it. The 'palace' vestment for the incognizable inner point, while it is an unknowable radiance in itself, is nevertheless of a lesser subtlety and translucency than the primal point. The palace extends into a vestment for itself, the primal light. From then outward, there is extension upon extension, each constituting a vesture to the one before, as a membrane to the brain. Though membrane first, each extension becomes brain to the next extension. Likewise does the process go on below; and after this design, man in the world combines brain and membrane, 'nut and shell', spirit and body, all to the more perfect ordering of the world.[333]

Subsequently, particularly in alchemy the symbolism of the Centre, represented by a Point within a Circle, will be applied, and Freemasonry will draw inspiration from the same, representing it using the same image within its rituals.

As we shall see in the following paragraphs, in the alchemical doctrine the *Point* is above all the symbol of a creative and mysterious centre of Nature. In his treaty *Novum lumen* (1664) the German alchemist Johann Rudolph Glauber wrote:

> But you, dear reader, will have above all to consider the Point, in nature..., and you will need nothing else, but take care unless you seek that Point in the vulgar metals, where it is not. For these metals, the common gold more especially, are dead. But our 'metals' are alive, they have a spirit, and they are the ones you must take. For know that fire is the life of the metals.[334]

Another well-known German alchemist, philosopher and mathematician, Athanasius Kircher, in his famous work *Oedipus Aegyptiacus*, a treaty of Egyptology printed in Rome in 1652, in the same way as the previous authors identified in the symbolism of the *Centre* an unequivocal representation of the Divine, of God, who 'permits the existence of everything' and who 'governs and conserves everything':

> Everything shines wondrously in the infinite circle: as such a circle is an extreme circle, its radius will also be extreme, and likewise its diameter; and given that there cannot be a plurality of extremes, this circle is therefore unique, as its diameter is equal to its circumference; now, the infinite diameter has a Midpoint, or Centre, which is also infinite, and thus the infinite diameter has a midpoint, or centre, which is likewise infinite, and therefore diameter, circumference and centre are as one. The Hermetic Circle we have often referred to in the course of this work is thus, a circle the Centre of which is everywhere, and the circumference nowhere. And in the same way as the Supreme is therefore perfect, simple and inseparable within all things, as its centre is infinite and all-embracing, thus surrounding everything, as its circumference is infinite; likewise, it penetrates everything, as its diameter is infinite; it is therefore the beginning of everything and the centre, the end of everything and the circumference, and the midpoint and the diameter. As a Centre it is an efficient cause, as a diameter a formal cause, and as a circumference a final cause. As a Centre it permits the existence of everything, as a diameter it governs everything, and as a circumference it conserves all. See how the Supreme is not equal to any thing, nor is he indifferent to them; and how all things are contained within, by him and for him, as he is centre, diameter and circumference. It is moreover clear how all attributes of God are identified in Him in perfect unison, and how in Him all contradictions are solved …On the basis of the above, in the same way as in the infinite sphere the Centre, the circumference and the volume are a sole being, likewise, the Supreme is the centre, or beginning, the midpoint and the end, and all things are merely as one.[335]

Once again in the seventeenth century, another renowned alchemist, Francesco Maria Santinelli, known as Crassellame, who frequented the Academy of Christine of Sweden in Palazzo Riario, essentially adhering to the view expressed by Kircher, wrote:

> The point of the centre, no less inseparable than invisible, can only be understood through the circumference: the Word of the invisible God is intelligible only through his creatures. All lines radiate from the 'Centre of the Point ' and are reconducted to the 'Centre'; all things were born from the Word of God, and this circular revolution is accomplished, they will return from whence they came. The point of the centre is immobile, whilst spheres rotate; the Word of God is immutable, whilst all things perish. As from the Centre all things were issued to go forth and expand, so all things will return to the Centre for contraction: for the eternal goodness and for occult knowledge. Consequently, the ineffable Word of God is, as it were, the Centre of the World: from here this visible circumference was enacted which, in some way, contains the matter of its primary principle.[336]

From the above steps, it is clear that in the doctrines of alchemy, despite the differences and nuances with which habitually the different symbols were represented by the alchemists, the symbolism of the Centre remains unfailingly and unequivocally a symbolic representation of God and his 'Word'.

Carl Gustav Jung, Self as a 'Centre' and 'God'

The Swiss psychoanalyst Carl Gustav Jung likewise concurred that the origin of the symbology of the Centre in the alchemical tradition presented a *leit motiv* present throughout his studies relating to this topic:

> This strong emphasis on the midpoint is another fundamental idea of the alchemists. According to Michael Maier, the centre contains the punctum invisible, which is simplex, and therefore the same is no longer subject to decomposition, but lasts eternally. Its parallel on a physical plane is gold, the symbol of eternity. The centre is compared by Christianos to paradise with its four rivers; the latter symbolise the moods of the philosophers, who are likewise emanations of the centre...Dorneus reports how there is nothing more like the gods than the centre; indeed, it does not take up any space, and can be neither understood nor seen nor measured. The nature of God and the spirits is similar to this. The centre is therefore an 'abyss of boundless mysteries.[337]

Once again, Jung, in another of his works *Alchemistry and Mysterium Coniunctionis*, reiterated the significance of the symbology of the Centre, and in referring to a note published by the renowned British alchemist John Dee, stated:

> The point is identical with the prima materia of the metals, which is an 'aqua pinguis' (fatty water), the latter being a product of the moist and the hot. John Dee (1527-1607) speculates as follows: 'It is not unreasonable to suppose, that by the four straight lines which run in opposite directions from a single, individual point, the mystery of the four elements is indicated.' According to him, the quaternity consists of four straight lines meeting in a right angle. 'Things and beings have their first origin in the point and the monad'. The centre of nature is 'the punctum divinitus ortum', (the point originated by God) the punctum Solis in the egg.[338]

It should be underlined that Jung addressed the symbolism of the Centre prior to his studies on alchemy, indeed, the symbolism of the Centre was in fact already widely used to represent the basic concept of his studies, the 'process of individuation':

> The basic motif is the premonition of a centre of personality, a kind of central point within the psyche, to which everything is related, by which everything is arranged, and which is itself a source of energy....This centre is not felt or

> thought of as the ego, but if one may so express it, as the self. Although the centre is represented as the innermost point, it is surrounded by a periphery containing everything that belongs to the Self...This totality comprises consciousness first of all, then the personal unconscious, and finally an indefinitely large segment of the collective unconscious whose archetypes are common to all mankind.[339]

Starting from the symbolism of the Centre, Jung delved further into the complex symbolism of alchemy in the context of which a series of concomitant factors led him to the conclusion that the Philosopher's Stone of the alchemists was the symbol of Self, a Self representing the union of opposites, i.e. the Centre of the psyche. According to his theory of archetypes, the Self, in the same way as Stone, could thus be personified and become an inner figure, and, similar to Stone, the Self was custodian of wisdom, representing the ultimate goal of all alchemical processes. The Self acted as a repository for all psychic life, and, above all, represented the culmination of the process of individuation.

Jung moreover believed that it was indeed Self that was responsible for creating the symbols in order to make its attributes known, with Stone being one of these images; the Self was 'expressed' symbolically through the figure of the Stone. In conclusion, the Jungian scholar Jeffery Raff asks himself, what then is Self? From the point of view of experience, he responds, the Self is an inner subjective figure that can also be defined as a Centre, perceiving itself as powerful, divine and complete. As a theoretical construct the Self possesses a number of attributes, being the Centre of the personality, and thus related to what Jung referred as the 'Ego', the Centre of consciousness.[340]

The Self therefore represents the Centre of the personality even before it embarks on the process of individuation, although in principle its striving towards integrity is merely symbolic, since the true union requires a considerable effort; it is for this reason that Jung refers to the Self prior to this union as the 'latent' Self. As the process unfolds, the Self moves rapidly towards its manifestations and, once concluded, will ultimately reach what is termed by Jung as the 'manifest' Self.

It is however essentially the alchemical symbol of Gold which the Point within a Circle leads us to continuously; indeed, Jung referred that:

> Hence the gold, as Maier says, obtains a simplicitas approaching that of the circle (symbol of eternity) and the indivisible point. The gold has a 'circular form.' 'This is the line which runs back upon itself, like the snake that with its head bites its own tail, wherein that supreme and eternal painter and potter, God, may rightly be discerned.' The gold is a circulus bis sectus,' i.e., one divided into four quadrants and therefore a quaternity, a division made by nature 'that contraries may be bound together by contraries...The point as the centre of the quaternio of the elements is the place where Mercurius 'digests and perfects'.[341]

In more modern times, the traditionalist thinker Julius Evola addressed the issue of the symbology of the Centre in his fundamental work *The Hermetic Tradition*:

> The alchemical ideogram of 'One the All' is the circle: a line or movement that encloses within itself and contains in itself both its end and beginning. In hermetism this symbol expresses the universe and, at the same time, at the same time, the Great Work...This 'all' has also been called chaos ('our' chaos), and egg, because it contains the undifferentiated potentiality of every development or generation: it sleeps in the depths of each being as a 'sensed myth' - to use Olympiodorus' expression, it extends to the chaotic multiplicity of scattered things and forms in space and time here below. Moreover, The closed line, the circle of Ouroboros, also has another meaning: it alludes to the principle of exclusion or 'hermetic' sealing that metaphysically expresses the idea of a unilaterally conceived transcendence being extraneous to this tradition.[342]

...and to conclude: The 'One' is determined in the sense of a centre manifested in the midst of the chaos (the 'all') and which affirms itself there as a principle of incorruptible fixity, of stability, of transcendence.'[343]

Therefore, according to the Roman traditionalist, one progresses from the 'raw material', the Circle, to the Circle with a Point within, i.e. to the archaic hieroglyph of the Sun, a transformation that involves the transition from 'chaos' to 'order':

> And that which in the originating matter was undetermined possibility, a passive potentiality for any quality, change, or chaotic transformation, is turned into a quite different principle, which in hermetism corresponds to the feminine symbol of the Moon. This is the fundamental hermetic duality ...Transposed to hermetic metallurgical symbols, the principle of the Sun corresponds to Gold, that substance that no acid can alter – and the principle Moon corresponds fluid Silver or Silver-Water (the ancient name for Mercury)... Gold or the Sun, in one of its main practical senses, expresses what we can call the Ego principle; whether it manifests itself in 'earthy,' 'vulgar' form, (where it is only a mirror of the true Sun projected by the fortuitous Waters of the 'Current'), or whether it unites only to itself, or is pure, in the form of noble living metal and then acquires effectively the value of centre as in the primordial state.[344]

To conclude, we should not overlook Rene Guenon who, in agreement with Evola, defined the symbolism of the Centre as the quintessential image of the primordial, unalterable 'unit' from which everything would subsequently derive. Guenon writes:

> The Centre is before all else the origin, the point of departure of all things; it is the principal point, without form, without dimensions, therefore indivisible, and consequently the only image that can be given to primordial Unity. From it, by its radiation, all things are produced, just as unity produces all numbers without its essence being modified or affected in any way.[345]

In the light of these premises, we might thus define the 'process of centring' as the true and main purpose of the initiatic opus, not merely a search for Truth (God), but to be construed primarily as the *formation of a new centre of personality*, a regenerated, transmuted, or, as Jung would say, *integral* personality that on shedding the profanities (conditioning) is directed towards a metaphysical dimension aimed at reuniting us with the divinity already present within. We might thus conclude that rather than a search for God, this is an overt 'deification', as exceptionally described by one of the leading representatives of traditional thought, the Swiss Titus Burckhardt:

> Man, on the other hand, is created for the purpose of actively participating in the Divine Intellect, of which he is the central reflection. Only when he does so is he truly the centre of the earthly state, and even, in proportion to his identification with the Intellect, of the whole of formal manifestation or of the whole cosmos. The realisation of the centre of the earthly state is the real goal of alchemy, and also the deepest meaning of gold. Gold is a 'body' like other metals, but the mass, density and divisibility of bodies have in it been transmuted into pure, symbolical quality. It is incarnated light. The alchemists themselves often describe the goal of their work as a 'volatilization of the solid and a solidification of the volatile', or as a 'spiritualization of the body and an embodiment of the spirit'. Gold is nothing else than this. Only in the sign for gold is the midpoint of the circle represented, which indicates that in gold alone does the essential unity of the prototype with its material reflection find expression. Likewise, it is only in perfect man that the similarity of the creature with God becomes spiritually effective.[346]

This 'differentiated' man is he who advocates a transmutation of his own conscience, his own soul, an acceleration of his evolutionary path, thanks to his singular predisposition, namely a totally unconditioned thought, and freedom from all kinds of ideological, religious or social superstructures.

Search for the 'Centre' as an operative-realisationally metaphysical pathway

Freemasonry today is the last representative of a long chain of Wisdom Schools that have alternated throughout the history of mankind. If interpreted in the authentically traditional manner, it is capable of providing the cognitive and methodological tools required to address a path of personal and spiritual refinement and improvement.

The method used by the Freemasons is a method enhancing the achievement of an active process of inner and outer transformation, establishing a full-blown 'mutation of status' enabling us to perceive the essence of things, the metaphysical or 'noumenical' reality that goes beyond the real and visible through the intervention of a faculty known in traditional doctrines as 'intellectual intuition' or 'intuitive knowledge'. The purpose of the Masonic method, in the same way as all Wisdom Schools that have preceded it, is the reuniting with our Divine principle (*being* God), being freed of material constraints (leaving behind the 'metals'), or, from a Jungian viewpoint, the achievement of the 'integral personality', i.e. a psychological transformation, a transformation of personality.

This metaphysical and psychic realisation represents the supreme achievement, being the highest that can be conceived and accomplished; to succeed in achieving the latter, the Initiate is required to resort to a sort of consciential synthesis, the opposite of a mere rational discursiveness of an empirical and analytical mind which remains within the restricted confines of the manifest and the relative.[347]

The purpose and aim of the Freemason is focused on his *individual* development, an upwards climb of the Ego, in which he strives to realise himself using resources specific to his own particular nature. It is indeed precisely at the point of his evolution that a being actually becomes aware of the purpose of his journey and the true Initiation commences; once he has become aware of himself, he will be led along a personal pathway, to achieving a full realisation, accompanied by the onset of maturity, harmony and a hierarchy of all the possibilities virtually involved in the essence of the being. In this regard, man and his Creator are as one.

Once again we return to the ideal type of Initiate, which in turn is presented in the figures or forms which cyclically, and in particular historical contexts (crisis), are reiterated. Ernst Junger in his representation of the modern archetype of the Initiate proposed, amongst other things (Father Lampros, Antonio Peri, Nigromontanus), a last, suggestive figure, that of the *Anarch*, characterised by these features:

> The best definition is still in terms of the anarch's relationship to the anarchist. The anarchist, contrary to the terrorist, generally has goals. The anarch has no such intentions. His inner strength is far greater. In fact, the anarch's state is the state that each man carries within himself. He embodies the viewpoint of Stirner that the anarch is Unique. Stirner says: 'Nothing gets the better of me." The anarchist really is the natural man. He is corrected only by the resistance he comes up against when he wishes to extend his will further than is permitted by the prevailing circumstances. In his ambition to realise himself, he inevitably encounters certain limits; but if they didn't exist, his expansion would be indefinite. That was the fate of, say, the Caesars. So barriers have to be imposed. The anarch can don any disguise. He remains wherever he feels comfortable; but once a place no longer suits him, he moves on. He can, for instance, work tranquilly behind a counter or in an office. But upon leaving it

> at night, he plays an entirely different role. Convinced of his own inner independence, he can even show a certain benevolence to the powers that be. He's like Stirner, he's a man who, if necessary, can join a group, form a bond with something concrete, but seldom with ideas. The anarchist is often an idealist; but the anarch, on the contrary, is a pragmatist. He sees what can serve him and the common good, but he is closed to ideological excesses. It is in this sense that I define the anarch's position as a completely natural attitude. First of all, there is the man, and then comes his environment. That is the position that I favour at present.[348]

The figure of the Anarch appears in the novel *Eumeswil*, Martin Venator, the Anarch, despite being a historian prefers the activity of barman, and historical events hold no appeal; he prefers to remain a mere spectator.

To conclude, the symbolism and doctrines of both alchemy and Freemasonry clearly highlight how the Initiate (the alchemist or Freemason is prompted to engage in an actual *process of identification*, bringing its conscience (I), depicted by the *Unhewn Stone* (or 'vile Metals') into contact with the central core of his psyche (Self), namely the *Smooth Stone* (the alchemical Gold).

Beyond the exquisitely moralistic interpretations of the Masonic rituals, the Initiate to the mysteries of Freemasonry warns that the sought after 'hewing' of the Stone is no more than a symbol of the essence, the Self, which can only be achieved through descending into the depths of one's psyche, thus transforming his personality. For this reason the 'Initiate' may be defined as a 'self-centred' individual.

2
Dissociation from Nature

The 'Romantic' vision and respect for Nature

We shall now attempt to ascertain the causes that led to the loss of the *Centre* in modern and contemporary man by broadly analysing the origin of this process.

Over the last two centuries a series of fundamental changes in the fields of science, social dynamics, economy and even art, have overwhelmingly modified the *psycho-social balance* of the individual, forcing him into a sudden and continuous adaptation to new realities. The latter has resulted in the creation of confusion, despair and neurosis. At the beginning of this century Rudolf Steiner reminded the West that every step forward in scientific knowledge should necessarily be of a constructive nature - two steps ahead in the development of human moral conscience. A huge conscious effort to march towards technical progress has been undertaken over the last century, and not, I may add, devoid of consequences.

Among the scholars who have addressed the problem, the art historian Hans Sedlmayr, in his well-known essay *Loss of the centre*, indicated a series of issues that, from the end of the eighteenth century produced in Europe a radical change in the artistic and social perception of mankind, these included: the romantic English garden, the figurative architectural monument, the museum, the exhibition and the factory.

With regard to the creation of the English garden, the author highlights how in its conception and in the intentions of its creator man would be required to place himself in total *empathy* with Nature, an approach that Sedlmayr defines as 'passive' but in the positive sense of 'respect' of *Nature*:

> The 'English' landscape garden had its origin in England about 1720 as a conscious protest against the architectural gardens of France. The French product's use of geometric forms in its layout was now rejected as something unnatural. From 1760 onwards the 'English' garden swept the continent ... The landscape garden was something much more than a new kind of garden. It implied a revolt against the hegemony of architecture, a wholly new relationship between man and nature, and a new conception of art in general. One condition was essential if the landscape garden was to come into being; the active relation of man to nature had necessarily to become a passive one. This new passive subordination to nature answers an ethical and religious need: indeed, the word 'nature' itself now gained a religious colouring, the concept being interpreted in a pantheistic sense. Nature is raised to the rank of an all-pervading spiritual power. She no longer stands confronting man as an alien thing, man is 'sympathetically' woven into her being. In both man and nature is revealed the same animating entity, 'an ineffable being, a being friendly towards us all that works its will in things'...These gardens then are the cult centres of a nature cult, in which all is calculated to fix the feeling and imagination onto an omnipotent directing being. The aim was that in a multiplicity of ways this being should be felt to be speaking to anyone who wandered through these great expanses of space. Men no longer approach these cult centres as a community or congregation. The ideal is that they should come there as solitary individuals, though they may in certain circumstances appear in the company of their beloved, or of a friend, or at best in very small groups, groups united in a common devotion by the bond of friendship.[349]

In the same period, More and Cudworth, two of the most important representatives of the philosophical system of the Cambridge Neoplatonists, believed that the macrocosm necessarily reflected the microcosm, and elaborated accordingly a cosmological theory that took into account the primacy of man over the world due to his possession of freedom.

In *The true intellectual spirit of the Universe* by Cudworth, we detect the fundamental concept of 'the freedom of man', that Pico della Mirandola first exposed in his *Oration on the Dignity of Man*. Man is not the victim of a strange mechanism far removed from himself, but is *master* of his own affairs and responsible for the same. The world is thus seen as the mirror of man, i.e. the reflection of a higher spiritual reality, and not, as Hobbes opined, a blind mechanism.

An exhaustive fresco of English civilisation and the cultural climate of the time is provided by one of the best known English historians, George Macaulay Trevelyan, in his *English Social History*:

> If the England of the Eighteenth Century, under aristocratic leadership, was a land of art and elegance, its social and economic structure was assistant thereto. As yet there was no great development of factories, producing goods wholesale, ruining craftsmanship and taste, and rigidly dividing employers from employed...Architecture was safe in the plain English style now known as 'Georgian.' In those days all buildings erected in town or country, from town halls and rural mansions to farms, cottages and garden tool-houses, were a pleasure to the eye, because the rules of proportion, in setting doors and windows in relation to the whole, were understood by common builders: those simple folk, by observing the rules of proportion laid down for their guidance in Gibbs' handbooks, kept hold of a secret afterwards lost by the pretentious architects of the Victorian era, who deserted the plain English Georgian style to follow a hundred exotic fancies, Greek, mediaeval or what not and were book-wise in everything concerning their work, except the essential.
>
> In the Eighteenth century art was a part of ordinary life and trade. The pictures of Hogarth, Gainsborough, Reynolds, Romney and Zoffany; the school of miniature portraits that culminated in Cosway, the engravings of Vertue and Woollett, the busts and statues of Roubillac, the furniture and decorations of the Adams brothers - these were not outbreaks of genius in protest against its surroundings, but the natural outcome of the ethos of the age, parts of a process of supply and demand. And the same may be said of the literary world of Gray, Goldsmith, Cowper, Johnson, Boswell and Burke. In its quiet, settled unity of aim and thought it was a classical age, unlike the vexed Victorian, when most of the great men—Carlyle, Ruskin, Matthew Arnold, the Preraphaelites, William Morris, Whistler, Browning and Meredith—were in a state of revolt against the debased ideals of their time, or were fighting baresark each to impose his own strange genius upon the public. Yet the Eighteenth Century, it is true, produced the greatest rebel of all: William Blake was born in 1757...But wealth and security cannot alone account for a great age of taste and art. The Victorian age was even more wealthy and even more secure; yet the houses it built and the things it put into them (except the books) were of no high order. In the Eighteenth Century, taste had not yet been vitiated by too much machine production. Both the maker and the purchaser of goods still thought in terms of handicraft. The artist and the manufacturer were not yet divided poles asunder. They were both men of a trade supplying a limited public, whose taste was still unspoiled because it

> had not yet seen much that was really bad. Life and art were still human not mechanical, and quality still counted far more than quantity.[350]

As this chapter progresses, we may observe how, in contemporary times, following the birth and development of a 'mass society', these dynamics are altered drastically and dramatically, leading, in an unstoppable progression, to the current consumer society that can be ineluctably defined as an 'ugly' society, the society of 'mass production', of the lapse of good taste.

'Listening to the voice of Nature...'

The socio-cultural picture traced by Sedlmayr and Trevelyan is interesting in that it shows the period in which the speculative Freemasonry, similar to that practiced today, slowly took shape in England, and is indicative of the cultural stratum in which a more complex and organic, undeniably esoteric, Masonic ritual started to develop. A ritual in which the Initiate is reminded of how the fundamental and indispensable purpose of his journey of initiation includes 'Listening to the voice of Nature', i.e. to retrieve an intimate relationship with Nature, with the elementary.

The Masonic ritual teaches how in the Second Degree of Fellow Craft, the occult mysteries of Nature and Science are revealed. Subsequently, in the Third Degree, the Worshipful Master beseeches the Candidate to 'listen to the voice of Nature, which bears witness that even in this perishable frame resides a vital and immortal principle'.[351] It is clear from these words how the ritual relationship with Nature is conceived as an intimate relationship, a relationship with the elementary in which the subject interacts with the object, or rather, subject and object *mingle* holistically. Through the contemplation of Nature and the divine principle that is revealed within, having acquired the *Moral Truth and Virtue* (as imparted in the First Degree) and the *Intellectual Knowledge* through the study of Liberal Arts (in the Second Degree) , the Freemason is ready for his Initiatic Death. The intellect is conceived as a tool for the acquisition of prodromal knowledge alone, and therefore of an inferior grade compared to the true knowledge, which is reached only by intuition. The 'occult mysteries' referred to by the ritual reveal to the Freemason the existence of something that goes far beyond the sensitive field, the subject of scientific investigation.

By analysing the rituals of the speculative English Freemasonry, it can be observed how the Stability[352] ritual was developed, in the same way as the subsequent Emulation, through the work of the Lodge of Reconciliation, an interesting reference is made to the path of Nature and science, whilst in the corresponding step of the Emulation ritual the word 'Nature' is replaced by 'Virtue', a first clear move of the ritual content towards an increasingly moralistic connotation. The change manifested at the point at which the candidate is asked what goals he aims to achieve is of even greater interest, and we can revel in a wonderful and metaphysical statement - 'to be restored', which could be translated as a reinstatement (with one's Divine nature), assumes the semblance of a more generic and obvious 'light'.

If the Masonic pathway represents introspection, a reunification of the finished Self with its Divine Principle, or on seeking a reintegration of the individual Self with the Divine Self, the Masonic method is the instrument to be adopted on this pathway. But this method however, and here I refer in particular to the ritual through which it is expressed, will continue to remain on the outside and to be transmitted by means of forms, and thus will invariably continue to represent the mere 'preparation' of the Freemason to receive the true teachings of initiation, achieved as a result of his personal endeavours.

The etymology of the term 'Initiation' is presented as the transition from a 'profane' state of lethargy to a state of *awakeness* from which the Initiate' gains access to an awakening of consciousness, an enlightenment, a state that corresponds in a certain sense to a rebirth, an overt *ontological* change. The Initiation might thus be defined as a kind of awakening of man to the *awareness* of his identity and the place he occupies in the cosmos, the possibility of rediscovering the spark of the Divine that is within us. For these reasons, I believe the phrase 'to be restored', present in the Stability ritual, constitutes an excellent metaphor to indicate a similar reunion.

Intuitive Knowledge and *Vis Immaginativa*

One of the aims of the man-Nature holistic vision is to impart the means of knowing intuitively. This ability is critical in research, or better still, in the discovery of the Centre.

To explain the meaning of Intuitive Knowledge is an arduous task, as to *explain* in words what can only be *sensed* is an apparent contradiction of terms. However, I can attempt to do so by stating that the *condicio sine qua non* for an approach to Intuitive Knowledge is the ability of an individual to learn to *think* esoterically.

The intent is to perceive the *essence of things*, the metaphysical or *noumenal* reality that goes beyond the real and visible. In Intuitive Knowledge, or Intellectual Intuition, the intervention of reason or of discursive thought should not be evident, but rather 'the organ of immediate knowledge, namely the 'pure intelligence', which goes beyond the simple reason, a 'metaphysical' knowledge, supra-individual and supra-rational, in practice an operation of the mind through which the results of intelligence are obtained without the use of intelligence'.[353]

By Intuitive Knowledge therefore, we may define the type of gnoseological, cognitive experience based on a *super-sensitive* and *super-rational* perception of the Being in the *pure* state, i.e. of reality as it is, even before the individual senses and reason make it seem as divided into a series of *things* and manifestations (for mankind alone) of particular significance.[354]

The purpose of intuitive knowledge is to oblige us to *transcend* the mind to unite with the Absolute, to leave behind the relative and the manifold to tend to the One. The Indian school of thought teaches us that the conditions of human suffering are caused by an erroneous perception of reality, indeed, by entering the world of the phenomena (Samsara), which we perceive as real, man forgets and thus is removed from his universal identity. The classic example of the jug is useful to help us understand the concept: if we take a jug and break it, the air inside is indissolubly reunited with the air outside, inevitably returning to its *primordial state of inseparable unity*, the air in the jug does not become 'part' of the outside but at one with its totality, by all accounts is becomes the air *itself*. Thus, when an initiatic pathway, of whatever nature, be it hermetic, alchemical, or Masonic, reaches its conclusion, the 'liberation' has taken place, the notion of being identified souls makes way for the expanded consciousness of being present in nothing and in being in no way from God.

He who uses intuitive knowledge is the Initiate, an individual in perfect *communion* with *Nature*, who reclaims his direct relationship with the world, the elementary core that constitutes the ultimate essence of things. The social spheres do not concern him, the 'Initiate' moves at ease particularly in the elementary areas of Nature. Intuitive Knowledge allows him to explore new horizons; whereas rational knowledge has alienated man from Nature and its original language, by contrast, in knowledge by intuition the observer, the Initiate, is tuned to the same line as the observed, it grants him access to the indistinct, the undivided or rather the atemporal. Faced with disenchantment he advocates a new esoteric and mythical enchantment. The Initiate, now a Freemason, has created his own 'bubble in space and time', the Lodge, which allows him to operate in the absence of time, because only by stopping time can he aspire to achieve the elementary.

The Initiate is a man with a predisposition for asceticism, for self-realisation, rendering him potentially suitable for inclusion in a spiritual elite, an ecclesia, an Order emerging from the organisation or hierarchisation of those who with a similar *predisposition* of mind.

Through Intuitive Knowledge the Masonic Method teaches us to be free of *constraints* and to avoid using solely our rational mind to pursue a random knowledge of things. It is an acknowledged fact that if our mind is conditioned towards the search for Truth, if it is not completely free, it can only *augment* information pertaining to one's status in a process of mere accumulation of data aimed ultimately at strengthening our own conditionings and prejudices. Thus, only a totally free mind will have the potential to undertake a genuine initiatic pathway.

But I would like to examine in depth when and in what form Intuitive Knowledge is first manifested in our ritual, within the context of the progressive initiatic teachings it stems from. In this brief *excursus* I shall attempt to highlight how the focus will gradually shift from the *external* physical feature to the immortal, *interior* Self, situated, so to speak, behind the mind. We should bear in mind that the Masonic Ritual is 'esoterically' conceived, and for this very reason is *veiled* by symbols and allegories, *images*, due to their innate holism, representing the immediacy of perceptual knowledge meeting the requirements of pure, naked thought which has not been shattered by words.

In the First Degree we are told (in the *Exhortation* following Initiation) how the foundation of Freemasonry implies adhering to a series of moral and social Virtues.

Indeed, the Degree of Apprentice, characterised by the *Principles of Moral Truth*, could be defined as the Degree of Ethics. The Volume of the Sacred Law is the infallible guide to truth and justice and governor of our actions. We are encouraged to behave in an exemplary way in fulfilling our civic duties. Prudence, Temperance, Fortitude and Justice are advocated as a guide in our actions (Cardinal Virtues). We are moreover invited to practice Discretion, Loyalty and Obedience (to abstain from discussions relating to politics and religion).

In the Tracing Board related to the Degree concerned, we are symbolically reminded that Jacob's Ladder is made up of steps or rungs that indicate an identical number of moral virtues, particularly the three major virtues: Faith, Hope and Charity. 'Intuitive Knowledge' is not present in this Degree, and indeed is not yet required, as the intent is to form a good individual on both a personal and moral level, as well as in all areas of social interaction.

In the Second Degree the search is extended to the Occult Mysteries of Nature and Science. Order, we are informed, is based on the principles of Brotherly Love, Comfort and Truth. The Degree of Fellow Craft is therefore characterised by the 'Divine Science' and by the relationship between man and his notion of the Divine. A Freemason is led in this Degree to 'admire the intellectual faculties and trace their development through the pathways of celestial science, until the Throne of God himself'. We could define the latter as the Degree of Metaphysics, intellectually speaking. The Worshipful Master reminds us indeed how the candidate is expected to make the study of Liberal Arts and Sciences his future concern. Intuitive Knowledge is still not referred to, the intellect with all its faculties, although oriented towards a metaphysical sense, is however present and hence must be fortified through investigation and study.

The Third Degree, through contemplation, prepares us for the last hour of our existence; and when, thanks to this contemplation, it has led us through the intricate paths of our mortal life, instructs us, finally, how to 'die'. It is clear how the Degree of Master is unfailingly characterised by the exclusive man-God relationship, but which can no longer be placed in a historical and social context, nor interpreted using the instrument of human reasoning, but is seen rather as a 'mysterious veil which the eye of reason cannot penetrate'. To continue on our journey, we are required to possess a new faculty, contemplation, from which Intuitive Knowledge will stem.

Therefore, in the Degree of Master, once can no longer rely solely on the intellectual and moral faculties, as the ineffable is based on intuition rather than reason, on the perception of a *Whole* rather than its single parts.

This leads us into the delicate terrain of *mysticism*, introduced in the second degree by the symbolism of the Throne of God (symbolism found in the Book of Ezekiel, in the Jewish mysticism of *Merkavah*, in the apocryphal Book of Enoch) and the concept of *death* construed not as a physical death, but rather as a 'mystical' death, namely the dissolution of the *thinking Ego*.

Based on these premises, it is clear how the basis behind our reasoning is that 'thought', i.e. a logic-rational approach, will never permit us to view things as a whole, to see their *true* and *final* nature, and should, for a specific part of the journey, be *abandoned* in favor of contemplation, which opens the doors of Intuition and true knowledge.

The Indian philosopher Jiddu Krishnamurti masterfully addresses the issue of knowledge unassociated to the logical-rational form, explaining how it is possible 'to know intuitively'. He focuses his process on sheer 'observation', stressing the importance in the observer of an *awareness* that our habitual form of thought unfailingly and inevitably superimposes the observation itself, thus modifying the result obtained:

> Observation is the instrument of thought. You may observe, then conclude, conceive, create through that observation. The creation, the activity through that observation is the movement of thought. Can one observe without any of the movement of thought? Does that require a kind of discipline? Discipline, the root of it, is to learn, not to conform, not to imitate. Now can one learn to observe without the thought creating an image? Can one merely observe?[355]

Thus, may we merely 'observe', meaning that we may know the object of the observation and *sense* the nature, its *true* nature, without the overlay of thought? And what is the purpose of this pure observation, unaffected by the conditioning and logical-rational accretions and, above all, time?

The ultimate goal is the search for the *Absolute*, the *Essential*, the absolutely *Incorruptible*, for the alchemists the *Philosopher's Stone*, for Freemasons the *Cubic Stone*, for all of us *Truth,* an experience that ultimately leads to an enlightenment, a *transformation*. This human search for things that reason cannot understand, points precisely to the value of intuition as the highest form of knowledge. It is undeniable that you cannot look for what you do not know, indeed, within us, beyond the mind, there must be a space in which the Absolute and the Eternal resonates, and somehow, intuitively, we perceive the latter, and otherwise would not be pushed relentlessly towards them, despite reasoning persuading us that these are dimensions foreign to our human and earthly existence.

However, as mentioned previously, to be able to carry out this work, alchemically speaking the *opus*, we must first be freed from all illusions and conditionings that we bear ('metals' in the symbolism of Freemasonry), to prevent the mind from deceiving itself. We should thus observe, without any kind of illusion, the illusions that thought has created previously. In this way, by freeing the mind from its own creations, we will render it lighter, integral and honest; we may then start to investigate, asking ourselves whether there is a timeless, a timeless truth.

It is moreover of the highest importance that on carrying out the act of pure observation, at the moment we seek to Know Intuitively, the agent, or observer, is pervaded by a total 'freedom':

> From childhood we are trained, educated to control, to suppress. The controller is unnecessary, only observation is necessary. When you observe, there is no controller or the controlled, just observing. Observing your envy, without naming it, without denying it or accepting it, the sensation, this reaction, which arises, which has been called envy, look at it without the word (because this represents the past) and you will be able to live without a sense of control. So there is a possibility of living without any sense of control, of conflict, of division, only when there is *pure observation*.[356]

The method proposed by Krishnamurti is presented as a full-blown mystical approach that tends towards a 'union or reunion' between the *observer* and the *observed*:

> First you must look at things for what they are. What relations are there between us and mankind? And when you observe the tree what is going on in that observation? There is that thing, and you call it a tree. You call it a tree because the memory has come into operation, and it is generally recognised, that thing is a tree. You give it a name, from recognition. Now can you observe the tree without naming it? Just look at the tree, sir. Just look at it and see, if you can look at it without the operation of a single word or memory, then the word 'tree' is not a real fact, the Word is not the Thing. So a description of a tree is not the described ... If the Observer and the Observed are no different, then there is only Observation.[357]

I am therefore referring to an *expansion* of the Personality, in which the distance between the subject and the object seems to be removed, and all dimensions annulled, in which the subject of the experience seems to merge with the object experienced. Following this experience, a cosmic consciousness penetrates the individual consciousness, and the exterior and interior become as one.

It is common experience that where there is *division* a conflict will arise, the division obliges us to perceive separate entities, on one side me and *my* religion, *my* ideals, *my* language, *my* nation, and so on. If we perceive reality and ourselves as separate entities, fragmented and isolated, in addition to conflict there cannot fail to be a sensation of helplessness, frustration and fear, all characteristics of a human existence.

The problem therefore rises from the thought that generates division:

> All thinking is limited, fragmentary, thought can conceive the whole, but the conception is still thought...What happens if we know intuitively? Scientists have today have provided scientific proof (although the alchemists and esotericists had sensed the same many centuries earlier) that when you watch something without a theory, without memories, through a microscope, the very thing we are watching undergoes a change, the thing we watch is moving,

> changing, is never the same; when we watch our 'greed', our 'hatred', our 'jealousy' in this way, the thing that is being observed changes. To observe myself, my whole structure and nature of myself, a watching without a past association, that very watching brings about a change in what is happening.[358]

On our initiatic journey therefore we will refer to 'Intuitive Knowledge' as a form of knowledge devoid of definitions, concepts, notions and mental processes, being rather a 'state of consciousness'. Besides, the same symbols and metaphors we use are directed precisely at stimulating this form of platonic knowledge or 'reminiscence'.

The first step consists in changing our means of purveying the world and indeed ourselves, directing our gaze in the right direction: from a tendency to become alienated in multiplicity, to concentrating on one's inner senses, veering towards increasingly sophisticated stages of perception, reaching ultimately a state of contemplation, the highest form of knowledge and 'Union'.

To persevere in the profane interpretation of an initiatic pathway is misleading, as we know that the 'perfection', 'transformation' and 'fulfilment' of which we speak, which we strive towards, is an inner, spiritual, *esoteric* achievement, and should not therefore be sought except within our very selves.

The essence of a truly accomplished life resides in the awareness of the identity of one's soul with the *Universal Soul*. The essence of life is pure consciousness.

In one of the magnificent illustrations of the *Atalanta fugiens,* Michael Maier accompanies the Forty-second Emblem with the sentence: *For those who apply themselves to chemical things, may nature, reasoning, experience and reading be the guide, the stick, the glasses and the lamp*, signifying that the implementation of a process of transformation and integral realisation of the individual is not a simple matter, and to succeed in this intent Nature will need to act as a guide, as a book of observation, reasoning is merely a stick to lean on, and glasses will help to discern the true from the false on the basis of experience; the lamp of knowledge will shine constant light on the entire journey.

Without the 'lamp' of Intuitive Knowledge we should wander in a world of shadows where all intellectual efforts to understand the meaning of things would be futile.

3
The Consumer Culture

To return to the initial theme, the loss of the *empathetic* relationship between man and Nature, accentuated by the dynamics of industrialisation and technological development, would result in the final degeneration gradually made evident by the needs of an increasingly frantic production. Here I refer to the phenomenon of 'consumerism'. Man has moved inexorably away and has become estranged from Nature, seeing it increasingly as a resource to be exploited, he has thus gradually lost the perception of balance and correspondence between macro and microcosm and their place within Creation. Mankind has therefore inevitably started to lose its centre. The German historian Friedrich Georg Junger clearly emphasises this dynamic in his essay *The Failure of Technology*:

> Underlying strict rationality of technical working methods, we find a way of thinking which cares nothing for the preservation and the saving of the substance. What is euphemistically called production is really consumption. The gigantic technical apparatus, that masterpiece of human ingenuity, could not reach perfection if technological thought were to be contained within an economic scheme, if the destructive power of technical progress were to be arrested. But this progress becomes all the more impetuous, the larger the resources at its disposal, and the more energetically it devours them...Where wastage begins, there begins desolation, and scenes of such desolation can be found even in the early days of our technology, in the era of the steam engine. These scenes are startling by the extraordinary ugliness and the Cyclopean power, which are characteristic of them. The machine invades the landscape with destruction and transformation; it grows factories and whole manufacturing cities overnight, cities grotesquely hideous where human misery is glaringly revealed.[359]

During the nineteenth century therefore, man's approach to Nature will be subject to change, or rather a 'degeneration'. Sedlmayr outlines this process of progressive loss of empathy between man and Nature by taking as a paradigm the transformation of the idea of a 'garden' in which the plants have likewise become 'objects' exposed to the general public; indeed, subsequent to the English garden:

> The decline begins around 1830. The park acquires the character of a museum, a kind of nature museum. Exotic plants are planted in it as in a botanical garden. The original genuine spiritual impulse behind the thing, the sense of an all-pervading presence, in a word, the religious elements, begins to disappear. This fading out of the original content can be traced in certain utterances of the aging Goethe. By the middle of the century the park's successors have acquired certain unmistakable characteristics of an exhibition.[360]

Sedlmayr, continuing his analysis, detected this distancing and alienation from *Nature*, and by Nature likewise the human body is implied, particularly in the world of art, with sculpture providing a clear example, as it:

> It extrudes from itself all that pertains to the pictorial element and timidly withdraws into its own boundaries. It addresses itself through the eye exclusively to the sense of touch. It becomes fundamentally monochrome, whereas in the baroque and the Rococo monochrome sculpture was a marginal phenomenon. Coloured sculpture was the rule. There arises a form of sculpture white and chaste, a sculpture of pure lines and disciplined forms, a sculpture that sets its face against the pictorial and luxuriant, but it is a sculpture from which all creative abandon had disappeared, a sculpture that knows too much, that is governed by the prescriptions of archaeology and keeps on saying with wearisome clarity how exquisitely pure a thing it has become. Yet the real plastic and creative power behind it has in fact disappeared. Regarded as an art that calls dead matter into life, that of a Canova or a Thorwaldsen stands far below that of a despised Bernini. It lives by its very hostility to the pictorial, it lives by negation, it lives by its very distaste for colour, for fullness, gaiety and movement. For sculpture too, the material with which it works is dead. As dead as plaster.[361]

It is particularly in the mutation of the subjects painted that the relationship between man and Nature highlights its most substantial change, Nature has now become almost 'hostile', removed from man, threatening, a Nature that is no longer understood by humans and has consequently abandoned mankind. This topic is highlighted particularly in the powerful paintings of Caspar David Friedrich, they portray how man is left at the mercy of Nature, now hostile, menacing; the image of the ship trapped by giant blocks of ice is a markedly emblematic representation. In this ghostly vision the solitude of man is fully pronounced.

At the end of his journey Sedlmayr leads us back once again to the initial theme, the 'Loss of the Centre', for Sedlmayr the move away from classical art implies a turning away from God, the inspiration of artists:

> If we group all these symptoms together and examine them carefully we arrive at a diagnosis which we might well characterise as loss of the Centre...Man seeks to get away from art which should be the mediating element between senses and spirit, and art itself struggles to escape from art in which it has as little satisfaction as man now finds in man. Art strives away from man and from all that pertains to man and measure.... From 1880 onwards a sense of man is diffused with an increasing sense of Nullity and, at the start of the twentieth century, a tendency is observed whereby artists are no longer either capable of or wish to depict a human figure unless deformed. Thus, if the diagnosis reached following a close examination of the symbols revealed by modern art allows us to establish that the world has lost its Centre, this implies a consequent hypertrophy of man in the lower compared to the higher spiritual forms. If we look at the matter thus, the disturbance which we called the 'loss

> of centre' is seen to have its origin in the forcible separation of the human and the divine, in the tearing apart of one from the other, and in the loss of the mediator between man and God, the God-man. The lost Centre of man is simply God, and the innermost core of his disease is the loss of his relationship with God.[362]

This is the point, to move away from the Centre means, ultimately, to forsake the Divine, although the Divine is within ourselves; man therefore, in the process of alienation from God ultimately departs increasingly from himself. To combat this trend, which recurs cyclically in humans, the Initiatic Schools were set up with the main aim of restoring man to his divine essence, of helping him to once again find his Centre.

As mentioned previously, the process of alienation of man from God commenced specifically with the removal of man from Nature. Whereas the doctrines of alchemy, to be viewed as much more than the mere expression of a rudimentary chemistry, as they often were, and with more than a hint of contempt, transmitted to the alchemists a faith in the transmutation of Nature and its ambition to dominate time, we are certain that the alchemical opus highlighted the 'sacred' respect of alchemists for Nature.

This respect towards Nature, emphasises the religious historian Mircea Eliade, began to decline in the same way as Alchemy:

> It is true that this heritage has been interpreted and realised by modern man in a totally different way from that of the alchemist. The alchemist was still continuing the behaviour of primitive man, for whom Nature was the source of sacred revelations and work a ritual. But modern science could only come into its own by divesting Nature of these sacred attributes. Scientific phenomena are only revealed at the cost of the disappearance of the hierophanies. Industrial societies have nothing to do with the liturgical activity identifiable with craft rites. That kind of work was useless in a factory, even if only for lack of any industrial initiation or 'tradition'...of course, man has from time immemorial been condemned to work, but there is a difference, and it is a fundamental one: to supply the necessary energy to the dreams and ambitions of the nineteenth century, work had to be secularised. For the first time in his history, man assumed this very harsh task of 'doing better and quicker than Nature' without now having at his disposal the liturgical dimension which in other societies made work bearable. And it is in work finally secularised, in work in its pure state, numbered in hours and units of energy consumed, that man feels the implacable nature of temporal duration, its full weight and slowness. All in all, one may say that man in modern society has taken on, in the literal sense of the word, the role of Time, exhausting himself by so doing and becoming a uniquely temporal being. And since the irreversibility and vacuity of Time has become a dogma for the modern world

> (or more exactly, for those who do not recognise themselves as being at one with the Judaeo-Christian ideology), the temporality assumed and experienced by man is translated, on the philosophical plane, into the tragic awareness of the vanity of all human existence.[363]

For Eliade, it was indeed particularly the 'secularisation' of work, first experienced in a liturgical, and subsequently sacred form, that produced the conditions that led to the inevitable expulsion of the individual by Nature; in this degeneration, it was the 'dictatorship' of time that rendered man more and more enslaved, and planted a pessimistic idea as to the significance of his existence. This is one of the most evident consequences of the 'loss of Centre'. Subsequently, I shall analyse further the topic of Time.

Underlying the development of modern science was the Baconian program of dominion over Nature, this need to dominate however has been emptied of its moral content, its prevailing assumption in the tradition of magic. This constitutes an instrumental and utilitarian approach to the environment. Man is no longer the administrator of Nature, but has become its master. The world no longer exists to arouse wonder and be explored, to be used but at the same time protected, but is now to be exploited in a way that has no moral dimension, because the world is an 'it'.[364]

The modern scientific paradigm, child of the Enlightenment, was developed using the *empirical- instrumental* method, in an intellectual speculation in which the totality of all that surrounds us becomes a mere projection of human intellect rather then a process in itself. The outside world, Nature in particular, is transformed on the ground on which all inventions of reason are carried out, thus losing its natural features and its role as a vehicle of knowledge given to man to aid a harmonious and empathic understanding of life.

There is nowadays an increasingly urgent need to overcome the rationalism and scientism of the Enlightenment generated from the Cartesian view that *Nature* is a lifeless, inert machine, developed largely beyond the confines of mankind, devoid of any divine or spiritual significance, vitality or intrinsic harmony.

From this *de-divinisation* of the world, from this opposition between spirit and matter, the modern cult of science would subsequently be born in the belief that technical progress invariably corresponds to an inner evolution of man. The German sociologist Max Weber showed admirably how scientific rationalisation had produced an irreversible disenchantment (Entzauberung), secularising the ancient visions of the world derived from a mythological-religious source and replacing them with an objective image.

On the expulsion of modern man, the absolute master of 'technique', by Nature, it is of interest to recall the analysis of the philosopher and German historian Oswald Spengler. In his renowned *The Decline of the West*, he highlights the 'betrayal' of Nature by Faustian man, cause, in the view of Spengler, to the *civilisation*, i.e. expulsion, although inevitable and 'organic', from *society*:

> The Civilisation is the inevitable destiny of the Culture, and in this principle we obtain the viewpoint from which the deepest and gravest problems of historical morphology become capable of solution. Civilisations are the most external and artificial states of which a species of developed humanity is capable.... Pure Civilisation, as a historical process, consists in a progressive exhaustion of forms that have become inorganic or dead. The transition from Culture to Civilisation was accomplished for the Classical world in the fourth, for the Western in the nineteenth century. The term civilisation therefore designates the stage in a civilisation in which tradition and personality have lost their immediate worth, and all ideas should first be translated in terms of gain if one wishes to see it realised. Initially one had goods in line with their power. Nowadays, one is powerful in line with the amount of money he possesses. Money alone can raise the spirit to a throne. Democracy signifies a perfect identity between money and political power'.[365]

Thus, according to Spengler, a civilisation inevitably linked to an organic relationship with money and all that this entails.

In this dynamic, Spengler opines, 'Faustian' man, who approached the world as an 'organism' rather than as a 'mechanism', who saw Nature as a living thing, not as a mere object of exploitation, who detected in his very existence an inescapable *symbolic* meaning, in an interaction between micro and macro cosmos (although his form- soul and world, life and reality, history and nature, law and sentiment, destiny, God, future and past, is the sole, extreme means of grasping this inaccessible essence, a kind of metaphysics, in which everything undefinedly assumes the significance of a symbol'), the man who fully represented the soul of the West with his desire for unlimited spaces, an impulse towards the profound, the awareness of an Ego that observes himself and realises that next to the light there is shadow, this man, to conclude, essentially *betrays* his duty. Faust loves the great distances, the dynamics of unlimited space, polarised rays, molecules of gas, magnetic fields, electric currents, the upward force of the Gothic cathedrals, the desire for the unknown of the great travels. The soul of Faust was born here, in the conjunction between the force of man and the cosmic powers of Nature and of God, but all this, as mentioned previously, is, in the view of the German historian, subsequently forsaken by Faustian man. Spengler is no enemy of progress or technique, far from it, but for the author technical thought is of a religious origin, it is capable of even sanctifying inventions and innovations created by man, thereby bringing the individual soul closer to immortality and therefore to God.[366]

The *betrayal* of the Faustian soul is for the German historian a clear sign of an ongoing secularisation, a forsaking of the 'sacred' vision that man has had since the start of life and the world. Indeed, Spengler states 'An irreligious era is an era of decadence'.

The West inevitably wanes because it separates its organic fraction, i.e. it divides the unity and integrity of its living soul, but, as mentioned before, in his assessment, Spengler does not criticise progress and technical developments, deemed essential and inherent to the essence of man, but rather highlights the loss of their *symbolic* meaning, evident in the dynamics that combine the idea of the immortality of the soul with the powers of the cosmos:

> Never before has a microcosm felt so superior to the macrocosm. Today we see small living things that through their spiritual strength have reduced non-winners to a state of dependency. Nothing seems to match such a triumph that has succeeded in one civilisation alone, and indeed perhaps only for the period of a few centuries. But for this reason, Faustian man has become a slave of his creation. Both his steps and his customs will be pushed by the machine in a direction leading to no rest, and to no chance of return. The farmer, the craftsman, even the merchant suddenly become insignificant faced with the three figures that the development of the machine has forged: an entrepreneur, an engineer and an industrial worker. In this civilisation, and this alone, from a small branch of craftsmanship, i.e. the economy of manufacturing, the mighty tree that obscures all other professions has developed: the economic world of the mechanical industry. And this world has forced both the employer and the worker to obey. Both are slaves, not the masters of the machine that is starting to manifest its occult demonic power.[367]

In modern and contemporary society the role of man changes, he is no longer Faust, the manipulator, but has become dramatically the spectator, instrument and object of his own creations, he has become the manipulated. The French sociologist Jean Baudrillard masterfully summarises this unstoppable degenerative process in his famous essay 'The system of objects':

> Technical power can no longer be mediated, for it has no common measure with the human being and the human body. Nor by extension can it any longer be symbolised: functional forms can do no more than connote it…It is here perhaps that we should seek the reason for the morose technical satisfaction to the initial euphoria over mechanical achievement has so quickly given way, for the peculiar anxiety that takes hold of all beneficiaries of the wonders of the object, of obligatory non-involvement, and of the passively observed spectacle of their own power. The uselessness of habitual gestures and the breakdown of everyday routines founded on movements of the body have a profound physiological impact. Indeed, a genuine revolution has taken place on the everyday plane: objects have now become more complex than human behaviour relative to them. Objects are more and more highly differentiated, our gestures less and less so. Objects are no longer surrounded by the theatre of gesture in which they used to be simply the various roles; instead their

> emphatic goal-directedness has very nearly turned them into the actors in a global process in which man is merely the spectator.[368]

Accordingly, the man of the 'Third Millennium' will be called upon to deal with this situation of deep distress, commenced many decades ago and now at its highest manifestation, a situation in which even culture does not escape unscathed by the decline.

The French scholar Alain Finkielkraut likewise agrees that the major cause of the problem is represented by the modern consumer society:

> Once needs and desires were rigorously controlled, now they receive solicitous attention. Vice becomes virtue. Advertising replaces asceticism, and the spirit of capitalism inspires the relentless pursuit of life's immediate delights from the moment of birth. Extraordinary as it may seem, this ideological revolution maintains deep ties to the Puritan tradition. By saying simultaneously 'Get Rich!' and 'Have Fun!', by making free time profitable in lieu of condemning it, present day hedonism turns bourgeois reason against the bourgeois: calculative thinking overcomes its previous tendency to be exclusive; it discovers the usefulness of the useless; it methodically invests in appetites and pleasures and, after having reduced culture to an unproductive waste of time, it awards all forms of distraction with the status of culture. No transcendent value should stand in the way or determine how people use leisure and develop a taste for consumption'.[369]

The loss of 'Tradition' with its function of Centre is a consequence, and the most severe harm produced by this process, and the French philosopher thus concludes: 'In the name of 'Democracy', all links with our 'Tradition', with the structures that have long 'centreed' the individual in his culture are abandoned'.[370]
With this indiscriminate, voracious consumption, the spirit of the times in which we live is manifest, the 'machine' that has replaced man and is largely responsible for its 'loss of Centre', dictates the timing and decides, in the absence of limitations, what to produce and what use to make of the production, in a whirl of publicity that *numbs* the consumer and delivers exactly where needed.

Among those who have clearly illustrated the phenomenon of consumerism and manipulation of 'conformism' in Western society, the sociologist David Riesman is certainly worthy of mention; in his well-known work *The Lonely Crowd*, to define the alienation of the individual and particularly its lack of autonomy in modern urban society, he introduces a term that has now entered into the current sociological lexicon - Western man is represented by Riesman as an *other-directed* individual.

Riesman in his study divides the history of humanity into three periods, each of which is characterised by a type of individual that represents the collective character: the first societies, in the pre-industrial period, are defined by Riesman as 'Traditional', being societies in which the past and tradition, governs individuals, a society modelled substantially on a cohesion of the patriarchal family group with a significant predisposition towards religion; the second, ranging from the Renaissance up to the mid-twentieth century, feature man who has undergone a transformation generated by major social changes, an individual who has acquired an awareness giving him an increased sense of judgment, the 'inner-directed' individual, who should be capable of adapting to new and ever-changing situations, is thus born. Finally, in the third and current era, a historical moment in which we move from *production* to *consumption*, an individual whose goals are set by the group, an 'other-directed' individual, is introduced - we are now in a mass society. Riesman writes to this regard:

> What is common to all the other-directed people is that their contemporaries are the source of direction for the individual – either those known to him or those with whom he is indirectly acquainted, through friends and through the mass media. This source is of course 'internalised' in the sense that dependence on it for guidance in life is implanted early. The goals toward which the other-directed person strives shift with that guidance: it is only the process of striving itself and the process of paying close attention to the signals from others that remain unaltered through life.[371]

Of particular interest in Riesman's analysis is the diversity between the second, clearly individualistic, phase and the third in which individualism is markedly attenuated. In the second period the author, in referring to the teachings of Weber, links individualism to proto-capitalism, or rather, to a competitive capitalism within a society economically based on free competition, which later, in the third, is illustrated as a development the previous capitalist monopoly, where a higher degree of bureaucratisation and depersonalization of relationships lead to an inevitable decline in the importance of the individual, who has become increasingly easy to replace.

In analysing modern Western society, it is interesting to observe how Riesman describes the evolution of the relationship between adults and young people, a report rendered increasingly difficult by the rapid socio-cultural changes, and to the emotional changes elicited by scientific discoveries that, as we shall see in the next section, continually modify the space-time dimension in which we live.

There seems to be an almost frantic chase, all forms of contact between the adults and youths seem to disappear, even conflict is lessened, ultimately leaving room merely for a laconic mutual indifference. Everything relentlessly undermines the foundations of self-confidence amongst the adults, paradoxically implying that they mutate from being 'guides' into 'gregarious' beings, leaving young people with no model to follow, other than that of the group, thus obliging them to inevitably conform to the latter:

> The typical other-directed child grows up in a small family, in close urban quarters, or in a suburb. Even more than in the earlier epoch the father leaves home to go to work, and he goes too far to return for lunch. As the size and living space of the family diminish and as the pattern of living with older relatives declines, the child must directly face the emotional tensions of his parents...The parents lack not only the self-assurance that successful inner-direction brings but also the strategy of withdrawal available to many unsuccessful inner-directed types. The loss of old certainties in the spheres of work and social relations is accompanied by doubt as to how to bring up children. Moreover, the parents no longer feel themselves superior to the children...In this change of parental attitude the mass media of communication play a dual role. From the mass media – radio, movies, comics – as well as from their own peers, children can easily learn what the norm of parental behaviour is, and hold it over their parents' heads...The parents also have their sources of direction in the mass media. For in their uneasiness as to how to bring up children they turn increasingly to books, magazines, government pamphlets, and radio programs. These tell the already anxious mother to accept her children...In contrast, what the other-directed child does 'learn' from his parents is anxiety – the emotional tuning appropriate to his other-directed adjustment.[372]

Today we live in an essentially 'bad' world, and the dramatic thing is that we are not even aware of this; in the past, the objects of our daily life were designed with aesthetic sense and love, art and work were conceived as a *unicum*. In modern day society this bond no longer exists, the objects of daily use are manufactured in 'series', work produces only atrocious tools that will need to be replaced after a pre-determined period of time, and even works of art become 'usable' items, being reproduced in countless copies, as the art historian Coomaraswamy writes:

> We have come to think of art and work as incompatible, or at least independent, categories and have for the first time in history created an industry without art...An industry without art provides a necessary apparatus of existence: houses, clothing, frying pans, and so forth, but an apparatus lacking the essential characteristics of things made by art, the characteristics, viz., of beauty and significance. Hence we say that the life that we call civilised is more nearly an animal and mechanical life than a human life.[373]

When work, productions, manage to progress in the absence of art, the field inevitably becomes more uncouth, returning to an unbridled, primitive state, the divine condition of which is definitively forgotten:

> To say that the artist works for art is an abuse of language. Art is that by which

> a man works, supposing that he is in possession of his art and has the habit of his art; just as prudence or conscience is that by which he acts well. Art is no more the end of his work than prudence the end of his conduct...On behalf of every man we deny that art is for art's sake. On the contrary, 'Industry without art is brutality'; and to become a brute is to die as a man. It is a matter of cannon fodder in either case; it makes but little difference whether one dies in the trenches suddenly or in a factory day by day.[374]

Where should we seek the main cause of all this? The prime suspect is undoubtedly the 'consumer'; indeed, over time the need to 'consume' has come to represent the unstoppable engine of the entire mechanism, its uncontrollable and indiscriminate growth has inevitably changed the relationship with the object, once expression an interiority conveyed in view of its function, the reflections of a 'view of the world', an *internal* expressions of the external nature – this ratio has now been radically altered.

Let me conclude by recalling one last, but not for this less important, cause that led to the progressive removal of the individual from his Centre, what might be referred to as a 'loss of Form'. The alchemists teach us that the initiatic work, the opus, is a means of intervening on the 'matter', in an attempt to achieve a perfect 'Shape', it is represented by the transformation of the Unhewn Stone in Freemasonry, an ontological undertaking that will result in the Initiate assuming the 'Form' capable assimilating him to the Divine that is already present within, a 'Form' however, that likewise comprises a behavior and an externality. Today, we are witnessing a continuous and relentless move away from 'Form', and terms such as 'informal', 'free', etc., have now become part of our everyday lexicon, the 'convenient' has indeed become 'sacred', but, as noted by the French philosopher Alain de Benoist:

> Shabbiness – either in dressing or intellectual, is indeed no more than one of the forms of regression. 'Letting go' under the pretext of being more 'unrestrained' or 'comfortable' implies a loss of form. The purpose of life is to give oneself a form - and subsequently to give one to the world. Likewise, the 'distinction' tends to assume a form. It is a catcgory of being even more than an appearance. Who could give us a form if we fail to give on to ourselves? ...The common illusion that modern societies secrete is that, as life becomes easier, less effort is required. Actually, the exact opposite is true. Effort merely changes its focus. There are more elements on which to direct our attention, more energy is required to forge a shape. Will rather than hope is a theological virtue. It is also a form of self-control, which in Italian is rendered using the term *maestrìa*.[375]

Without the opus, the work that leads to a restoring of one's dignity, of the lost cognition of human divinity, man is but a mortification of his potentials:

> To build oneself, to form oneself, may likewise imply to progress from the status of an individual to that of a person. We are all individuals, but are not all people; the Roman distinction between the animus and soul is well known: the person is an individual who has acquired a soul. It would certainly be unjust for all men to have a soul; it is right that some, at the end of his self-creation, may succeed in obtaining a soul. Only he who is master of himself, who reigns over his inner empire may aspire to achieving a soul. Honour is nothing more than loyalty to the rules established, to the image one has assumed...Hence the importance of 'style'. There is a clear relationship between 'style' and 'form'. To form the world, to assume a form, implies the simultaneous establishing of a style. For this reason, letters can never be divided from the spirit, from the underlying form, containing the content. 'Style is man': the means of doing things: questions of form are never superfluous.[376]

To give a form to the world, to adopt a certain type of form is the main task of the Initiate, together with the figures who have cyclically represented the same, figures that recur in history under different semblances, but whom all bear the same essence: a substantial and unlimited freedom of action and soul.

Ultimately, there is an impelling need to recover our Centre, to return to an 'organic', or rather 'holistic' relationship with nature, to restore a connection with the micro and macro cosmos. In order to achieve this, a rediscovery of Tradition, or better still, a recovery of its distinctive dynamics that have unfailingly accompanied the development of consciousness and human knowledge, is an unforegoable necessity. This will indeed be possible within an authentic Initiatic Order, in which, together with other Initiates, the individual will 'adopt a form' to be maintained throughout his entire life. It is indeed only in an Initiatic Order that the individual 'may experience an initiatic tradition, but accompanied by a forming of a virile character expressed through a specific lifestyle and by means of a more real contact with the world of action and history.[377]

4
The 'Dictatorship' of Time

'Public' time and 'private' time

An even more detailed analysis of the upheaval produced by scientific progress to the fragile equilibrium of the modern individual is that of the American historian Stephen Kern who, in his work *The Time and Space*, highlights how the great scientific discoveries have modified these concepts, developed in the individual the perception of living no longer in a unique time and space, but rather in a multiplicity and plurality of spaces.

As we know, space and time are the setting in which reality, and all concepts, theories and ideas are ascertained; indeed, these need to be situated in a specific space and a time. However, as underlined by Kern in his interesting essay, the relationship between 'time-space' and the 'sacred' produces a singular dynamic, a phenomenon already partially analysed previously by the American theologian Harvey Cox in his work *The Secular City*: 'In the same way that a new religious vision may change the sense of time and space, a new sense of time and space may change the view of religion'.[378]

Kern began his study by referring to the concept of time; between the late nineteenth and the early twentieth century, a clear conflict could be observed between the so-called *personal* and *public* time; the author cites examples in the field of literature including the famous novel by Oscar Wilde *The Picture of Dorian Gray* and, particularly, the masterpiece written by Marcel Proust *Search for Lost Time*. In this last novel, the plot is set in a *public* time with which we can easily identify. We are in the period of the Dreyfus Affair and the subsequent World War I; Proust highlights the personal time of the main character, Marcel, represented by the writer as non-linear and irregular, not in sync with the other characters. Marcel was convinced that his body its own time while he slept 'not on a dial superficially marked but by the steadily growing weight of all my replenished forces which, like a powerful clockwork, it had allowed, notch by notch, to descend from my brain into the rest of my body'. In seeking the lost time of his existence, the traditional measurement of time will prove to be of little use as Proust teaches us to listen with the aim of intercepting barely perceptible fluctuations of dormant memories etched in our bodies, which are however ready to spring to life once again according to an unpredictable dynamic.[379]

The Proustian image of Marcel leads us to think, by analogy, of the Freemason's relationship with time; on his journey towards initiation, in the same way as the character in the novel, he attempts to escape the 'dictatorship' of public time and seeks a *lost* time, that of 'Tradition', represented by his attempt to regain the *Lost Word*; in this context, the Freemason will be called upon to use his intuitive faculties and, like Marcel, try to capture the 'barely perceptible oscillations', as it is only by means of these intuitive abilities that he can aspire to gain access to the essence of things.

Breaking free from the slavery of time and once again finding one's 'personal' time thus assumes the connotations of an exercise of individuality and freedom, as affirmed by Bergson:

> Absolute consciousness acquired through intuition is not only a better means of knowing reality: it is essential in living in the context of a better life, and out ability to integrate the past into the present is a source of freedom.[380]

The public time, deemed superficial by Proust, terrifies Kafka and, particularly in the short story *The Metamorphosis* and his novel *The Trial* will become an element of additional anguish for his characters. Whilst for Joyce, the public time is totally inadequate for use in representing the human condition and its expressions, thus he squeezes the twenty years that *Odysseus* spent travelling into a mere sixteen hours in the life of Leopold Bloom spent wandering about the city of Dublin.

The intrusiveness of the public time in the life of the common individual is likewise evident in other novels, including the magnificent *Atlas Shrugged* by Russian writer Ayn Rand, in which Eddie Willers, one of the characters of the novel:

> He turned a corner. In the narrow space between the dark silhouettes of the two buildings, as in the crack of a door, he saw the page of a gigantic calendar suspended in the sky. It was the calendar that the mayor of New York had erected last year on the top of a building, so that citizens might tell the day of the month as they told the hours of the day, by glancing up at a public tower. A white rectangle hung over the city, imparting the date to the men in the streets below. In the rusty light of this evening's sunset, the rectangle said: September 2. Eddy Willers looked away. He had never liked the sight of that calendar. It disturbed him, in a manner he could not explain or define. The feeling seemed to blend with his sense of uneasiness; it had the same quality. He thought suddenly that there was some phrase, a kind of quotation that expressed what the calendar seemed to suggest. But he could not recall it. He walked, groping for a sentence that hung in his mind as an empty shape. He could neither fill it nor dismiss it. He glanced back. The white rectangle stood above the roofs, saying in immovable finality: September 2.[381]

In the field of painting, if the Impressionists tried to give a direct impression of the time, placing their works at specific times of the day and the seasons, it was in particular the *Cubists* who, with their multiple perspectives succeeded in progressing beyond the immediate moment. Already Sociologists such as Mauss and Herbert (*A brief study of the representation of time in religion and magic*, 1909), discern in the conception of public time, especially in phenomena linked to the 'sacred', an interpretation of *discontinuous* time, expandable (even reversible) and substantially heterogeneous. Indeed, although the commonly held notion maintained that time represented an *orderly* sequence of separate parts, a highly innovative cultural trend upheld that 'personal' time represented the only *true* time, featuring a fluid rather than a rigid structure. This, as seen previously, is clearly indicated in the manipulation of present time in the works of novelists, whilst psychiatrists and sociologists have contributed through their studies towards further changing the traditional idea whereby personal time flows passively parallel to public time.

The importance of the *past* time reaches its maximum expression with the historicisation of thought. It took off from Locke, according to whom all knowledge is derived from sensation; with the Enlightenment this idea developed further and ultimately rejected innate ideas and the possibility of human essence *a priori*, asserting that society and history are capable of 'constructing' man. The systems advocated by Comte, Hegel, Darwin, Marx and Spencer (living forms that develop into what they are as the result of progressive transformations over time) confirmed the ideas of those who favoured the decline of the religious conception of man, and the possibility of living in a Godless world. Accordingly, the process of 'secularisation' was finally commenced.

However, some people refused outright this idea of the past exalted by a historicist and genetic setting, among which the playwright Ibsen who, in his works *Ghosts* and *Hedda Gabler*, represented the negativity of a past that crushed his characters, and, particularly, Friedrich Nietzsche who introduced, in his book *Thus Spoke Zarathustra*, the notion of 'will to power', whereby the latter is constantly hampered, in the vast majority, by a burden of memories, regrets and guilt. In the fundamental chapter '*On redemption*' Nietzsche vehemently maintained that the sole true redemption was represented by the victory of will power over the time and obstacles that the past placed in its way:

> Impotent towards what hath been done, the Will is a malicious spectator of all that is past...To redeem what is past, and to transform every 'It was' into 'Thus would I have it' – that only do I call redemption! Thus the past becomes an appropriation of will, and acts as a seer, a purposer, a creator, a future itself, and a bridge to the future.

Disorientation and pessimism

To return to the main topic of this chapter, the 'Loss of Centre' in modern man, the *leit motiv* of the century is overwhelmingly the sensation of *inadequacy* and *disorientation* produced in man by the drastic changes currently taking place, as skilfully highlighted by the sensitivity of a series of writers.

One example is afforded by the apocalyptic novels of H.G. Wells, in one of which, *The Time Machine*, the protagonist of the novel, the Time Traveller, creates a machine capable of travelling into the future, choosing as his destination the year 802.701. At this time the traveller comes across a new population on the Earth, the Eloi, a peaceful race lacking any predisposition towards conflict. They are threatened only by the Morlock, a creature that lives hidden underground and attacks the Eloi at night to eat them. The story, states Kern:

> Is a compendium of nineteenth century theories projected into the future: Marx's vision of a growing stratification of the classes is amplified in the conflict between the Eloi and the Morlock; the eugenetics are represented by the education of the Eloi; the ideal of preventive medicine has been reached, and all illnesses have been eradicated; the erosion of the family, feared by the majority in Wells' time, is now complete and the genders have developed and become exceedingly similar.[382]

The pessimism of contemporary man is also represented in other novels, to the authors cited by Kern I would like to add the Hungarian writer Sandor Marai who, in one of his narrative works reaches the very brink of pessimism and indicates suicide as the sole means of finding God. The main character of the novel utters the following subsequent to the suicide of two lovers:

> There may be relationships between nature and man that we are not aware of. Because behind all things is God...Many ignore this, and many deny the existence of God. It has been so throughout the ages. Our era is unfortunate because it has lost touch with God...Religion still exists, it is true, but it is not like it used to be...And there are men who think they are religious because they have a fear of God, and pray for the intercession of saints. But this is certainly not an absolute and vital relationship with God, without which existence is no more than a series of terrible accidents. He who knows God is not necessarily religious. I, for example, am not at all religious. I go to church every now and then, but most of all to admire the works of art, or to enjoy the ancient music and watch the austere gestures of the rites. This is all very nice, but you cannot come close to God so easily. There must be sacrifice...Men desire sacrifice as only thus can they aspire to an encounter with God.[383]

The marked sense of inadequacy, fruit of the sudden changes taking place in the daily routine, would later be analysed on a medical level; from 1869 the North-American neurologist George M. Beard, started to study the phenomenon and introduced the diagnostic class of 'neurasthenia' (nervous breakdown) into the psychiatric nomenclature, resulting in the publication of the paper 'American Nervousness' in 1881. In his studies Beard upheld that an increase of working rhythms and interactions between individuals (which had increased thanks to the discovery of the telegraph and the construction of the railways) allowed businessmen to deal with a considerably higher number of transactions compared to the previous century. By multiplying in this way, the competition and the pace of work began to manifest a growing number of diseases, ranging from neurasthenia, neuralgia, and nervous dyspepsia to early tooth decay and premature baldness.

The Hungarian sociologist Max Nordau highlighted how in the same period a significant increase was observed in the manifestation of violence and criminal episodes, likewise caused, in his opinion, as a result of the new discoveries and inventions, which 'thus penetrated deeply, tyrannically, into the life of all individuals', producing a burden on the nervous system and an erosion of body tissues.

The 'Forms' of Time

That time is fundamentally subjective and that Western man, in his perception of the latter has a tendency to control and uniform it, is confirmed by one of the most interesting findings of the 'split brain physiology', according to which if the right part lacks all sense of time, the left, on the contrary, is obsessed with it. In his interesting work *The dance of life* the anthropologist Edward T. Hall describes the sense of time of Western man, in whom the left side is predominant, as 'monochromatic', to signify 'along a straight line'. The Arabs, the Turks, the Indian tribes of South America, in whom the right side is dominant, feature, on the contrary, a 'polychromatic' sense of time, i.e. time may be represented as a network capable of extending in numerous directions. Hall introduces his theory as follows:

> Some things are not easily bent to simple linear description. Time is one of them. There are serious misconceptions about time, the first of which is that time is singular. Time is not just an immutable constant, as Newton supposed, but a cluster of concepts, events, and rhythms covering an extremely wide range of phenomena. It is for this reason that classifying time, in the words of the English Africanist E. E. Evans-Pritchard, 'bristles with difficulties'. At the microlevel of analysis one might say that there are as many different kinds of time as human beings on this earth, but we in the Western world view time as a single entity. It is possible to philosophise endlessly on the 'nature' of time. While such an exercise can be engaging and even at times enlightening, I have found it more productive to use a different approach. In my approach, behaviour comes first and words follow. Looking at what people actually do (in contrast to what they write and say when theorizing) one quickly discovers a wide discrepancy between time as it is lived and time as it is considered. As people do quite different things (write books, play, schedule activities, travel, get hungry, sleep, dream, meditate, and perform ceremonies) they unconsciously and sometimes consciously express and participate in different categories of time.[384]

Subsequently, Hall lists a series of manifestations and relative descriptions of temporal 'forms' - Biological Time, Personal Time, Physical Time, Metaphysical Time, Sync Time, Sacred Time, Profane Time, Meta Time, going on to describe the substantial differences present between the East and the West in the means of conceiving time:

> Years of exposure to other cultures demonstrated that complex societies organise time in at least two different ways: events scheduled as separate items – one thing at a time – as in North Europe, or following the Mediterranean model of involvement in several things at once. Like oil and water, they don't mix.

Each has its strengths as well as its weaknesses. I have termed doing many things at once: Polychronic (P-time). The North European system – doing one thing at a time – is Monochronic (M-time). P-time stresses involvement of people and completion of transactions rather than adherence to preset schedules. Appointments are not taken as seriously and, as a consequence, are frequently broken. P-time is treated as less tangible than M-time. For polychronic people, time is seldom experienced as 'wasted', and is apt to be considered a point rather than a ribbon or a road, but that point is often sacred...There are imponderables in the chemistry human of human transactions. In Latin America and the Middle East, North Americans can frequently be psychologically stressed. Immersed in a polychronic environment in the markets, stores and souks of Mediterranean and Arab countries, one is surrounded by other customers all vying for the attention of a single clerk who is trying to wait on everyone at once. There is no recognised order as to who is to be served next, no queue or numbers to indicate who has been waiting the longest. To the North European or American, it appears that confusion and clamour abound...Particularly distressing to Americans is the way in which appointments are handled by polychronic people. Being on time simply doesn't mean the same thing as it does in the United States.[385]

5
The 'Inhomogeneity' of Space

The end of 'absolute' Space

Between the end of the nineteenth and the beginning of the twentieth century the concept of space underwent a radical change, and, in the same way as time, its homogeneity became the subject of debate. As anthropologists discussed the varying spatial perceptions of different cultures, painters radically altered the conception of perspective space established during the Renaissance.

The Spanish philosopher Ortega y Gasset developed the philosophy of *perspectivism*, which proposed the existence of a series of different spaces equal to the number of different points of view; whence the rationalist stance affirmed the homogeneity of space, Ortega contended, on the contrary, that there were in fact as many spaces as there were prospects. In a conference focussing on the meaning of Einstein's concept of 'relativity', Ortega linked perspectivism and the general theory of relativity, stating that the coincidence of their publication in 1916, was an unequivocal sign of time. Indeed, in Gasset's opinion, the two doctrines indicated a clear confirmation of the collapse of the old notion of the existence of a sole reality in a sole absolute space:

> There is no absolute space because there is no absolute perspective. To be absolute, space has to cease being real – a space full of phenomena – and become an abstraction. The theory of Einstein is a marvellous proof of the harmonious multiplicity of all possible points of view. If the idea is extended to morals and aesthetics, we shall come to experience history and life in a new way.[386]

The fundamental discovery of quantum physics led to a further change in outlook, with its perpetual oscillation between a sense of 'reality' and a sense of 'possibility' reiterating what was referred to by the German philosopher Hegel as the *amphibious nature* of man:

> Spiritual culture, the modern intellect, produces this opposition in man which makes him an amphibious animal, because he now has to live in two worlds which contradict one another. The result is that now consciousness wanders about in this contradiction, and, driven from one side to the other, cannot find satisfaction for itself in either of the one or the other.[387]

This amphibious nature faces man with the constant need to achieve and maintain an active and dynamic balance with the world in which he lives, avoiding a fall on one hand into a temptation to remain above reality, with utopia, and on the other to remain below, with resignation.

These considerations allow us to focus increasingly on the foundations, the indispensable condition of all identities, intended as an authentic and effective expression of the aptitude to plan and to design oneself: an ability to hear and see reality not merely as an 'already finished' and 'defined' entity, to be taken merely into account, but rather as an ongoing process which assumes a series of different forms compared to those currently displayed, thus to not only authorising, but rather demanding from the observer, an ability to perceive and think outside the box.[388]

In the field of Mathematics, the appearance of non-Euclidean geometries further revolutionised the traditional idea of space. Over a period of two thousand years, the two- and three-dimensional Euclidean geometry was deemed the sole form of geometry in a position to represent space; in the nineteenth century however the two mathematicians Lobachevsky and Riemann questioned the assumption that the above form of geometry might represent the only universally valid process. In particular the Euclidean *fifth postulate* represented a stronghold that as yet remain unchallenged by any mathematician, citing: 'Through a given point can be drawn only one parallel to a given line'. However, in 1830, the Russian Nikolay Lobacevskij criticised this postulate, announcing the discovery of a two-dimensional geometry in which through any parallel point an infinite number of lines could be traced on the same plane. Subsequently, in 1854, the German Bernhard Riemann proposed another form of 'elliptic' geometry (geometry relating to the surface of a sphere), according to which the sum of all angles in a triangle amount to more than 180 degrees. This radically changed the two-dimensional Euclidean concept of space that the world had adopted up to that time (the sum of the angles of a triangle was 180 degrees), Riedmann's space was *elliptic*, whilst Lobachevsky's was *hyperbolic*.

'Cubism', inadequacy and desperation

The revolution in geometry was consequently joined by a revolution in painting in which Cézanne and subsequently the Cubists had contributed towards annihilating the traditional *perspective* space. The two main exponents of Cubism, Picasso and Braque, united with the innovations of Cezanne and the Cinema, thus leaving behind the homogeneous space, the result of a linear perspective, and proposing the subjects of their paintings in a variety of spaces and perspectives, abandoning the search for three-dimensionality and representing the surface on which they painted exactly for what it was, a *flat* surface.

The themes of Cubism however also represented representation the inadequacy and despair of the individual in the world in which he lived, the separation from God and the lost hope of finding him, as highlighted, among others, by the Russian philosopher Sergej Bulgakov:

> Although it cannot be termed religious, it is undeniably the painting of the mystery and in some way resembles the icon, in spite of its diversity. Despite the rapid development and radical changes in artistic processes, the spiritual content of Picasso's art remains unfailingly uniform and consistent; from the beginning to the end it is permeated by a sense of growing sadness and horror of life...Picasso's work - particularly in the second period - is the result of a demonic possession. His painting reveals an intensity in the world as purveyed by the prince of evil, detesting and cursing the creation of God, and at the same time writhing in a hellish torment...This ice in the heart, this lack of love for God's creation, likewise, although it may seem strange, represents the pathos of his work: a painful atheism, which invariably oscillates between pride and vulgarity, and swings effortlessly from one to the other.[389]

These words are echoed by those of another Russian philosopher, Nicolaj Berdjaev who, particularly with the birth of *futurist* art, opined how this disintegration of perspective and a Centre of reference is presented in all its terrible negativity and with all its consequences:

> The boundaries of solidity of the being are violated, everything loses crystallinity, flakes, is pulverised. Man passes through the objects, and the objects through man, an object encroaches another, all surfaces are moved, all planes of being are conjoined. This is the new perception of universal life that the futuristic art attempts to convey. Cubism was but one expression of this cosmic vortex that changes the place of all things. Futurism in all its shades took a step further. It represents a total violation of the dwelling of a being, the disappearance of all images of the world of objects using well-defined contours. In ancient art, which had seemed eternal, the image of man and the human body featured clearly marked boundaries, was distinct from the images of the other objects of the world, from minerals, plants and animals, from rooms, from houses, roads and cities, from machines and the infinite spaces

> of the world...The image of man disappears in this process of cosmic pulverisation and decay.[390]

With regard to the concepts of time and space, I should like to conclude with the typically Traditionalist vision of Julius Evola who, in his work entitled *Revolt against the modern world*, underlines the contrast between 'linear' time and the meta-historic view of traditional society, in which a homogenous and essentially passive space in the modern world is accompanied by a 'dynamic' space, a 'vital ether' of traditional civilisation:

> Time in traditional civilisations was not a linear, 'historical' time. Time and becoming are related to what is superior to time; in this way the perception of time undergoes a spiritual transformation…If traditional man had an experience of time essentially different from that of modern man, it follows that analogous considerations must be made concerning the experience of space. Space is considered today as the simple 'container' of bodies and of motions, totally indifferent to both. It is homogeneous…In the experience of traditional man, on the contrary, and even in its residues (at times present among some savage populations), space is alive and saturated with all kinds of qualities and intensity. The traditional idea of space is often confused with the same idea of 'vital ether' – the akasa, or mana – which is a mystical, all-pervasive substance-energy, more material than immaterial, more psychic than physical, often conceived as 'light'.[391]

6
Secularisation and Nihilism

'Secularisation' as a distancing from the 'Sacred'

As observed from the examples proposed in this foray into the realms of science and the arts, a change in the representation of time and space constituted an important 'litmus test' for the current identity crisis pervading modern man.

The Belgian thinker Hendrik de Man in his *Massification and the decline of culture* demonstrated how the elimination of spatial and temporal distances has contributed to the loss of the historically natural and biologically conditioned measures and perspectives, leading man into a full-blown *disorientation*. Likewise, the Italian sociologist Sabino Acquaviva, in his work *The eclipse of the sacred in industrial society,* represents these dynamics, emphasizing how the modification of the concepts of time and space reveal the changes and evolutions of society registered from the pre - modern (pre-technical) era to the present, the first being related to ad the second unrelated to the natural rhythms, thus eliciting a dangerous hiatus between mind and body:

> The evolution in representation, in the same way as in the perception of space and time, is therefore an essential component of the global evolution of human experience. We progress from an almost biological representation of the primitives and their cultures to modern scientific theories...The pace of pretechnical society is natural: in its intensity work is constantly linked to the rhythms of nature, the seasons, the rain, the sun, day, night, to the rhythm of life of animals, the natural rhythm of the human body and so on. But, as noted by Mauss, man is a unitary fact, and therefore there must be a close connection between the rate of physical activity and the rate of intellectual activity, although the channels of this connection are scarcely known. Even in previous historical eras the mind and the body of man were dominated by these rhythms, to varying degrees, in both a rural and an urban environment.[392]

Throughout the historical period prior to that in which we currently live, the idea of 'slowness' beat the rhythms of the daily routine, for this reason, as seen previously, the absence of 'speed' rendered the concepts of time and space totally different to those featured in modern day society. In modifying the concepts of time and space and, particularly, the consequent chronic lack of time to devote to the relationship with the 'sacred', the Italian sociologist sees an inevitable development of the process of 'secularisation':

> The gradual elimination of prelogical thoughts (prelogical, of course, from the point of view of modern logic), such as magical phenomena, superstitious beliefs, and so on, take place over the last two hundred years: by purifying itself in this way, our logic is simultaneously permeated by concepts derived from the most recent scientific and technical evolution. At this point, when the parameters of judgment of the majority of men have changed substantially, is it not perhaps easier to provide a negative interpretation of religious phenomena? ...Is it not true that the vast majority are left devoid of parameters of judgement in the matter of religious phenomena, once these parameters have been swept away by modern logic?'[393]

The progressive secularisation of the sacred, according to Acquaviva, would lead to the loss of traditional points of reference, a removal from the 'institutionalised' religions which, according to the author, are currently experiencing a clear period of crisis.

Essentially, the analysis carried out by Acquaviva, together with those of Kern and Sedlmayr mentioned previously, discern a clear manifestation of the secularisation of the prospects of man, his life and his thought, in the modification of the concepts of time and space.

Secularisation is one of the most widely used terms, at times inappropriately, to represent the cause of the condition of discomfort and disorientation experienced by modern man, aimed at representing the sense of *loss*, or rather, a departure from God and from the various forms of Religion it which he is represented, a process, in the view of several historians and sociologists that has been underway for several decades.

It is not my intention to enter into a discussion of the meanings of the controversial concept of 'secularisation' which, according to the authors and the eras in which it was approached has led to a wide series of frequently contradictory definitions. I shall therefore merely express my personal disagreement with those who see secularisation as a 'desecration' *tout court* of society, in the belief that the perverse degenerative process of modernity has led not so much to a *departure* from the sacred, but rather to the birth of a new means of *nihilistically* interpreting the sacred, what we might call a 'sick' sacredness.

Secularisation as a metamorphosis of the 'Sacred'.
Whilst accepting the above view of 'disenchantment' (caused by the ongoing process of rationalization of the modern world), the interpretation of the French sociologist Emile Durkheim, who sees in secularisation not a departure from God and the Religions, but a *metamorphosis* of the same and of the relationship with the sacred, in the light of this study, would appear, in my opinion, to be more readily acceptable.

This metamorphosis of the sacred in *degenerate* forms of religiousness had, as seen previously, been highlighted by Guenon and Evola with regard to Theosophy, and by the German philosopher Oswald Spengler who, in the margin of a dissolving civilisation in the twilight of its existence, at the end of the cycle of the current civilisation, revealed the presence of a 'second religiousness', a corrupt manifestation of authentic religiousness. However, although degenerated, nonetheless manifestations of a *need* of the sacred which, as observed by Jung, is naturally and unfailingly present in mankind, a sacred present within his unconscious, unveiled through the revelation of particular archetypes.

The emergence of phenomena such as Theosophy and Anthroposophy at the onset of the twentieth century, of the new religious movements and fundamentalisms which had been established by the mid-twentieth century, thus confirms the thesis put forward by Durkheim and Jung whereby the traditional religious institutions are challenged and new realities are born (Moon, Krishna, Scientology, the Christian fundamentalism in the US and others). These new *representations* of the sacred however, although, as mentioned, the result of an essential requirement inherent to mankind, bear the signs of the degeneration and loss of values known today as *nihilism*.

Nihilism in Contemporary Society
As stated previously, secularisation is only one of the many aspects in which the nihilism of modern society is present. The real issue should thus be sought at the source, in the origins of nihilism, in an attempt to ascertain how it can be fought and overcome.

The analysis of nihilism clearly underlines how the most harmful product generated relates largely to the *fragmentation* of the unity of being, accompanied by a systematic destruction of Nature and an uncontrollable gigantism of technology. The forms in which nihilism is presented, the demystification, secularisation, apostasy and, above all, rationalisation, have erased all symbols from the world together with the wisdom which resided within.

The solution afforded by Nietzsche is the super-man 'that lightning capable of overturning the dormant condition in which the world lies, thus bestowing on man an ability to transmute'. Once God has died, confirms Nietzsche, he reappears in he who killed him, man thus appropriates the creative power of God, he grasps the opportunity to be transformed into a super-man, a man beyond the common man, capable of facing the darkness of his own nature.

In particular, we can identify a 'condition' within nihilism, the modern condition. For Heidegger the fate of Western nihilism is contained in the genetic code, on an unavoidable journey that leads from Plato to Nietzsche. But the classical interpretation of nihilism as a philosophy of anomalies, of anarchy and iconoclasm, is likewise opposed by authors such as Ernst Junger who, at least initially, yielded an image of nihilism that lives and thrives on order. An order seen as a technocratic domination in which men work without seeking either purpose or meaning.

Can we therefore progress beyond nihilism? Although aware of the tragic fate of mankind, Nietzsche and Dostoevsky were able to catch a glimpse of its defeat: Nietzsche advocated, subsequent to a transvaluation of values, a trust in the *Beyond-Man* as he who would inherit the teleological by becoming the personification, joyously, the sense of the earth. Dostoevsky however continued to believe in a possibility of recovery from nihilism through suffering, his redemption from nihilism through pain still is still today entertained on the Christian horizon.

On the contrary, Junger and Heiddegger ('thinking in values is the greatest blasphemy imaginable against Being') maintained that no recovery from nihilism was possible, and that the only thing that remained was to speed up the dynamics in the hope achievement of the same would result in its depletion, its exhaustion. Heidegger in particular advocated a radicalisation of nihilism, a congregating in its essence with the aim of revealing the non-nihilist essence of nihilism. But what can on lean on whilst digging along the line of nihilism? As mentioned, initially Junger viewed the development of technique with benevolence, deeming its hegemony to be the ultimate expression of nihilism: 'The steel snake of science has added rings to the rings, scales to scales ...It now extends, an impressive dragon, over the earth and the seas, almost allowing its reins to be held a child, whilst elsewhere it reduces entire cities to ash with its incandescent breath' [394], idealising a figure capable of dominating it and use it for its own purposes, the figure of a 'Worker', the ' Lord of Technique', the individual who will elicit the development of Will to Power by means of the same technique, building a new civilisation on the ruins of the previous one, eliminating the 'ancient cults' and replacing them with a new reality that claims for itself veneration and faith [395]. Junger would subsequently amend his opinions, whilst in the Thirties he continued to view progress and its highest expression, technique, in a positive light, seeing in the 'song of the machines' an opportunity to claim the *elementary* and the possibility of a renewal of the bourgeois world that he so detested, he later began to have doubts as to the consequences of this limitless development, particularly on the *total mobilisation* required by a similar development, shifting the focus increasingly towards individualism. The vision of the world of this individual is represented by the two emblematic figures proposed by Junger, the Rebel and the Anarch, both well defined by Luciano Pirrotta:

> The 'rebel' is the integral man who has found - to use an expression of Eckhardt - the 'primordial bottom', the last (Urgrund) in which the 'spark of the soul ' lies, and with it the certainty of divine ascent, but it is concomitantly a subject capable of moving on the current plane, at ease in the same reality that hates and fights, perfectly camouflaged amongst ordinary people...The 'rebel', the other side of which is the 'Anarch', will experience the increase of disorder in the institutions, heightened social conflict, the chaos that mounts and the 'desert' that 'grows', in a position of instrumental symbiosis, exploiting each pre-set opportunity, the more outwardly 'integrated' he appears, the more he will be inwardly indifferent and detached. He will not be foolish enough to fall into the role, particularly useful to the 'Leviathan', of the warrior or protester, nor will he act as spokesman for the ephemeral ecologist or pseudophilanthropic protests, equally tolerated by the bourgeois state as entirely.[396]

For Junger it is indeed the Anarch in particular who is destined to overcome nihilism, he is 'beyond the line' of nihilism itself, has crossed it, relying solely on his ability, his own master, he is capable of reaching the deepest layer of his personality, or, as Jung would say, his deepest Self. The Anarch, who does not live isolated in the forest but continues to be part of society in a mode, defined by Giulio M. Chiodi as 'distant but physically present', interacting with the course of events only outwardly:

> He is a non-participating conformist, or a misfit who conforms, seeking the best suited angles, he is a stranger who complies to complete his journey, without conflict and with total indifference and neutrality. He is both present and regally detached, as he can adapt to all conditions although he will not identify with any of them.[397]

The Jungerian Anarch partly resembles Evola's Differentiated Man, a man 'characterised by an existential dimension not present in the predominant human type of recent times – that is, the dimension of transcendence,'[398] after the death of God, indeed all reference to *transcendence* is removed from human life, morality is now independent of theology and metaphysics, being based solely on the authority of reason, but as Evola recalls:

> Once morality has lost its root, which is the original and effective relationship of man with a higher world, it ceases to have any invulnerable foundation… In 'autonomous' morality, which is secular and rational, the only resistance to any natural impulse is an empty and rigid command.[399]

Nihilism, according to Evola, is a product of history that, in the same way as others, was directed against Tradition, a counter-traditional movement that only the Man of Tradition can face and overcome, the Man of Tradition who does not represent a *new* type of man, but the same ideal type who had long been the bearer of traditional principles and *weltshauung*.

As stated, the ideal type depicted by Evola is similar to that proposed by Junger, an ideal type who, in the same way as the Anarch 'cannot or do not wish to abandon the contemporary world, but are ready to face it and to experience it even in its most feverish aspects, all the while preserving a differentiated personality'[400]. The Differentiated Man, similar to the Anarch, is thus referred to a man 'who finds himself involved in today's world, even at its most problematic and paroxysmal points; yet he does not belong inwardly to such a world, nor will he give in to it. He feels himself, in essence, as belonging to a different race from that of the overwhelming majority of his contemporaries…Thus the principle to follow could be that of letting the forces and processes of this epoch take their own course, while keeping oneself firm and ready to intervene when 'the tiger, which cannot leap on the person riding it, is tired of running'.[401] In the Differentiated Man, his definition confirms that 'his differentiated character consists in facing the problems of modern man without being a 'modern man' himself; he belongs to a different world and preserves within himself a different existential dimension'.[402]

In the same way as Evola, likewise the German philosopher Karl Jaspers saw as the fundamental problem of modern man the abandonment of Transcendence. Jaspers provided an interpretation of Transcendence that complies with the doctrine of 'philosophical faith', a Transcendence that can only be approached by 'approximation', impossible to harness by dogmas or rigid hierarchical organisations of the 'sacred':

> Demonology, deification of man and nihilism, commit, albeit in a different way, the same mistake – they attempt to grasp the truth with a rapid coup. In the presence of the affirmation: God exists, all these falsehoods dissolve like mist in the sun. But the mists envelop us once again, because, in an attempt to reach out to God, we encounter the tangibility of truly present and visible things in the world, whilst the truth, unattainable in the invisibility in which it hides, appears to lead nowhere. To reach the latter we have no choice but to

> take the indirect route that bypasses the world, but in doing so we fall back on those falsehoods that must be overcome if we seek awareness of the profundity of being authentic, of divinity. God is the most distant being, the Transcendence before which all other realities, erect and absolute, is found to be lacking, and, in any case, gives the impression of being reached by means of an exceedingly rapid coup. We could argue endlessly over the nature of God and Transcendence, we could attempt to approach it by means of negatives, but we can never truly comprehend.[403]

Jaspers maintained that in nihilism man lost further the dimension of *Transcendence*. Particularly in his work *The spiritual situation of our time* the German philosopher emphasises how contemporary man lives in a world from which Transcendence has disappeared, as everything has resulted in an objectification of the institution by means of scientific rationalisation, a rationalisation that nihilistically sees nothing beyond itself, denying the profound nature of existence the possibility of de-situating, of progressing beyond the facticity of the evidence. The abuse by man of scientific rationality has thus inevitably led to an objectification of the totality of the institution and a consideration of each *transcendent* dimension equivalent to nothing.

Jaspers views the true essence of nihilism in the ignorance of being, the consequence of which will result in the deification of man as a general consciousness, i.e. an inter-subjective consciousness on which scientific attitude is based, by means of which the individual is persuaded of his ability to control the totality of everything through its objectification:

> A nihilist is he who believes in nothing beyond that which can be perceived in reality, he who sees as an illusion all that cannot be seen or touched, he who denies freedom and sees himself as a mere act of conclusion in his factuality.[404]

Although Jaspers recognises that Nietzsche identified the nihilism as the problem of contemporary man, i.e. his ability to *de-situate*, he also argues however that this possibility becomes impossible to put into practice following the abolition of *Transcendence*, which occurs in the Nietzschean philosophy at the moment of the 'death of God':

> Open unbelief is known as nihilism. The nihilist ventures to appear without disguise. For him all contents of faith are untenable, he has unmasked all interpretations of the world and of being as delusions: for him everything is conditional and relative; there is no fundament, no absolute, no being as such. Everything is questionable. Nothing is true. Everything is permitted.[405]

The ability of man to ex-ist, or rather to stay beyond the confines, to de-situate, and subsequently to progress beyond their situation through freedom, may thus be manifested, in the view of Jaspers, only by means of a reference to God as the *symbol* (or figure) of all possible transcendence. However, as pointed out by Katja Galimberti, it should be emphasised that the route advocated by Jaspers has no mystical intent, as the aim of the German philosopher is not to reach the absolute afterlife, but 'that immanent transcendence announced in its historic manifestations, which is not however depleted in the historicity of events'.[406] Indeed, Jaspers contrary to another renowned interpreter of European nihilism, Martin Heidegger, did not view Nietzschean nihilism as an unavoidable achievement of western metaphysics:

> If the regnant directive in Nietzsche's thought is the attainment in actuality of the highest and best that is possible for man without God, nevertheless, Nietzsche, in spite of himself and without being aware of it, shows decisively that the limited existence of man cannot fulfil itself without transcendence. The negation of transcendence brings about its own reappearance. It appears to thought in falsifying constructions of substitutes and to the authentic self in a still uncomprehended shattering confrontation of true transcendence in opposition to false...Because everything remains open to him, because he cannot pass on anything as a permanent possession but can only assist with preliminaries, Nietzsche presents to each individual the task of winning his ground through relation to transcendence in existential historicity. Nietzche's convulsive thinking, proceeding always from the transcendence that he denies, prepares us for the transcendence that he does not reveal and for the historicity of Existenz to which he never directly refers.[407]

For Jaspers therefore an escape from nihilism will only be made possible through a return to Transcendence, the only place in which man can once again find himself, his Centre; man is only truly a man when he lives in relation with Transcendence. Transcendence is the form of appearance of being, and only through the latter may can gain knowledge of the content of being and of himself. He cannot transcend this requirement; if he fails to recognise the same, then the place of the unrecognised entity will be taken by something different.[408]

In conclusion, the road towards the overcoming of nihilism and return to the Centre is constituted by a return to Transcendence, a return achieved by the rediscovery of the principles of Tradition, with the Wisdom Schools representing the place in which man can accomplish this task, uniting with other 'dispersed' seekers to await until the end of the dark period, 'riding the tiger'. In the doctrines of the Initiatic Schools this wait for the Eternal Return teaches us that the inevitable end of the Kaly Yuga will lead to the overcoming of nihilism itself 'converting it positively con the voluntary acceptance of returning to being. The Will to Power of that which seeks to return to possess eternally'.[409] We should therefore concentrate on surviving this era unscathed, using our highest faculties and skills, meeting our archetypes, understanding them, interpreting the same, to then know ourselves:

> Whoever speaks in primordial images speaks with a thousand voices; he enthrals and overpowers, while at the same time he lifts the idea he is seeking to express out of the occasional and the transitory into the realm of the ever enduring. He transmutes our personal destiny into the destiny of mankind, and evokes in us all those beneficent forces that ever and anon have enabled humanity to find a refuge from every peril and to outlive the longest night.[410]

To return to Transcendence and succeed in maintaining the Centre whilst awaiting the end of the Age of the Wolf ('Times of the axe and the sword, times of the wind, times of the Wolf, before the world collapses') represents the main task of the Initiatic Orders, of Freemasonry.

FOOTNOTES

INTRODUCTION *(pages 9-20)*

1 In my book *Introduction to Freemasonry*, I dedicated an entire chapter to the theory of the origins of Freemasonry. I believed this to be of use, due to the fact that the 'origins' of Freemasonry have long represented one of the most widely discussed and difficult arguments. The numerous theories put forward over the years have embraced a widely heterogeneous area, providing historic, sociological, economic, and religious interpretations, to name but a few. However, the most heated debate took place between historians or thinkers who, in the same way as Guénon, view modern-day 'speculative' Freemasonry as having descended *directly* from the medieval Guilds, and those who, on the contrary, see it as a purpose-created endeavour developed towards the mid-seventeenth century.

Among the historians, the main advocate of the 'direct' descent of modern Freemasonry, although devoid of any degree of continuity, from the medieval cathedral builders, is undoubtedly Henry Carr, one of the most widely renowned and established British historians in the field of Masonic studies. This 'Transitional Theory' was deemed by Carr to be demonstrable on the basis of a series of facts and documents (the oldest dating back to 1356) which, over a period of 600 years had provided proof of the descent of modern Freemasonry from the medieval Guilds. The first of these documents related to a dispute that took place in London in 1356, between the stonemason builders who carved the stone and the bricklayers and builders who erected the walls. The specific details of the debate are not known, but, as an outcome, 12 expert master builders, some of whom of high renown, stood before the Lord Mayor of London and his Councillors in the Guildhall where they were officially authorised to draw up an elementary *Code of Regulations for the Trade*. Over the next twenty years, the organisation evolved into the London Masons Company, the first Trade Guild of masons and, according to Carr, one of the direct progenitors of modern Freemasonry. In Carr's opinion, the 1356 document and other subsequent papers (the first testimony of an 'admission' ceremony is purported to date back to 1390), provide confirmation that the 'speculative' form of Freemasonry developed through a 'transition', lacking any form of continuity, from the ancient 'operative' Freemasonry, and first commenced in the London Masons Company: 'The transition from operative to speculative masonry was not the take-over of an old business under new management. It was the original business, which gradually changed its character according to the needs of its time, but with perfect continuity throughout'. (Henry Carr, *600 Years of Craft Ritual*, AQC Vol.81, 1978)

Carr's Transitional Theory has met with considerable criticism from historians who rejected the idea of a direct descent of modern-day Freemasonry from the medieval Guilds. One of the most strenuous opposers, was the historian Eric Ward, who emphasised how, in his opinion, the group established within the confines of the London Company of Masons. The so-called 'Accepted' Masons, was a completely *new* movement that emerged in England during the seventeenth century, being free and unassociated with commerce and, particularly, which bore no connection to the medieval stone masons. Ward referred how learned gentlemen from the Royal Society with an interest in scientific medicine, and the study and publication of ancient books and manuscripts, used the tools of the 'Operative' Masons as symbolic objects, and adopted the precepts of the Regius Poem written in 1390 (Eric Ward, *The Birth of Free-Masonry*, AQC Vol.91, 1978). In his theory, Ward gave due consideration to the initiatic aspect present, in his view, from the first forms of Freemasonry, presenting the latter, as mentioned previously, as an *ex novo* movement created towards the middle of the seventeenth century by borrowing both legendary material from the medieval stonemasons and, subsequently, the rituals employed by the Scottish Company of Masons. Ward moreover maintained that still today there is no tangible proof that Freemasonry may have originated from the medieval Corporations of Cathedral Builders, and consequently, 'accepted' Freemasonry was a movement first created in England in the seventeenth century, bearing no correlation to the corporation. This movement, affirmed Ward, comprised the ancient English 'operative' duties, which, by that time, had become almost obsolete, and, in the first stage of its development, borrowed several of the coeval traditions adopted by the Scottish Stonemasons. To conclude, Ward viewed the 'accepted' Freemasonry that had formed in England at the start of the seventeenth century as an initially limited society that gradually developed into something far more extensive over the following decades. The members of this society were apparently gentlemen of culture or successful squires who, in the opinion of the author, fitted better with the stereotype of men 'of the best rank' mentioned by Anderson in the eighteenth century. There are no written traces pointing towards an attempt to embrace the humble artisans, the salaried stonemasons, and the term 'Free-Mason' thus assumed the meaning of 'free from the corporation of masons'.

Largely in agreement with the above, John Hamill, British historian of international acclaim, previously Librarian and Curator of the United Grand Lodge of England, who, in line with the notions of Ward, adamantly ruled out the possibility of a 'transition' lacking any degree of continuity, from the medieval 'Operative' Stonemasons to the 'Speculative' Freemasons of the mid-seventeenth century. Indeed, Hamill underlined how, in an attempt to prove descent by transition from the 'operative' form to the 'speculative' form of Masonry, numerous historians assembled, frequently in a blatantly arbitrary fashion, fragments of information gathered from the four corners of the British Isles, although Hamill goes on to say how these theories contained nothing more than vague pretexts. For this reason, Hamill also suggested that Masonic studies should be differentiated into those he defined as being of the *Authentic or Scientific School*, based on irreproachable documents and consequential conclusions, and the *Non-Authentic School*. He moreover underlined how, on examining and evaluating the English documents pertaining to the origins of Freemasonry, he failed to detect any evidence of the existence of 'operative' Lodges. Hamill similarly refuted other aspects put forward in Carr's *Transitional Theory*, including the purported connection between the English and the Scottish operative movements of the period. Hamill forcefully denies any such connection, categorically excluding the presence of equal working conditions and activities carried out by the cathedral builders in England, Scotland and Ireland, particularly in view of the marked social, cultural political and religious differences present in each of these countries. Indeed, further corroboration was provided by the facts that, up until the passing of the *Act of Union* in 1707, England and Scotland, although linked by the Crown since 1603, were separate countries with a border in between.

Hamill goes on to recall how, during the Middle Ages, the 'operative' Lodges were no more than sites on which to store materials and where workers could rest; in addition to the fact that, as early as the 1600s, the Guilds system, with the exception of the London Livery Companies, was dying a fast death. Moreover, Hamill failed to recognise evidence of an 'English Mason Word' or of a particular sign of recognition among the English 'Operative' Masons. Indeed, evidence of 'non-Operative' or 'Accepted' Masons were all relegated to contexts unrelated to the trade, and the names listed in the documents available bore no connection to the building or architectural trades. As reported by Hamill therefore, the 'Accepted' Masons (there is some doubt as to whether they can be termed 'Speculative' in the seventeenth century), seem to have been first encountered in England as a *new* organisation which had no previous association with an 'operative' 'Craft', further emphasising how this new 'Free and Accepted' or 'Speculative' Freemasonry first originated in England, not in Scotland.

To conclude, what in Hamill's opinion were the dynamics that led to the birth of the modern form of Freemasonry? The author states that, although it is undeniable that the London Mason Company first originated from the operative Guilds of Masons governed by the London Trade, carrying out a purely operative role devoid of any speculative features, in the Seventeenth century the London Mason Company introduced a fundamental new phenomenon known as 'Acceptance'. All the documents held by the London Mason Company dating back to pre-1620 have been lost, although a document dated 1619, demonstrates the presence of paying members who were associated with the trade, and of others, on the contrary, who paid 'for making' and who were in no way linked to the trade. Thus, the latter gathered together to form an 'inner circle' within the Company, and were known under the term of 'Acceptance' from which modern-day Freemasonry subsequently originated (John Hamill, *The Craft*, Crucible, Great Britain, 1986, pg.32).

2 United Grand Lodge of England Pro Grand Master Address at European Grand Masters Meeting, London, 8 December 2007.

3 In his books Junger frequently refers to a particular 'figure', a magician, an alchemist, or, better still, an 'Initiate' among his protagonists. In the book *On the marble cliffs*, Father Lampros imparts secret metaphysical knowledge to the two brothers who live in the hermitage. He undertakes his botanical studies in the adjacent cloisters of Maria Lunaris. The mysterious Order of Mauretanians, which both brothers belong to,

constitutes an elitist gathering of magicians, scientists and warriors descending from the ancient Templars, entrusted with the task of keeping spirits burning, as the heritage of the few remaining aristocrats. Attempts have been made to liken the Mauretanians to Freemasonry, as in German the term for Masons or Builders is *Maurer*. The barbarians eventually destroy the Mauretania rock, and the knights retire to a distant castle belonging to their Order where they hold high the faith of the aristocratic soul awaiting the inevitable redress. Antonio Peri in *Heliopolis* is also clearly an 'Initiate':

'He did not travel to the islands on Sundays and holidays and did not frequent the taverns on Pagos beach. He locked himself up in his studio for trips into the dreamy regions. He said that all countries and unknown islands were woven into the tapestry. The drugs served him as keys to entry into the chambers and caves of this world...he also believed in the need for a classification of formulae. The highest of these formulae should have revealed, in the same way as the philosopher's stone, the secret of the universe'. Nigromontanus is another enigmatic figure emerging from Junger's fantasy, in The Adventurous Heart he writes: 'Nigromontanus narrated of solitary souls, who seemingly lived amongst us, but were nonetheless inaccessible. Accustomed to the pure heat of the fire on high, once the proximity of supreme danger makes the notions of leaving their solitude seem bearable, then they step forward.'

4 In this book I use the term *Schools of Wisdom* (Initiatic and Philosophical schools) when referring in particular to contexts indicated in a previous volume (*Introduction to Freemasonry*) as the bearers of doctrines and symbols that subsequently 'contaminated' Masonic thought and symbols throughout the eighteenth century. I shall refer therefore to Mystery Societies, Hermetic Communities, Neoplatonist circles and, in particular, the Cambridge Neoplatonists of the late Renaissance, to the representatives of Rosicrucianism and Alchemy.

5 With regard to Hermeticism, the discourse on the *Ogdoad and the Ennead* is considered a paradigmatic example of what Garth Fowden, the renowned scholar of hermeticism, termed an authentic 'hermetic text of initiation', an initiatic and pedagogic-philosophical journey, which during the latter stages of the process, develops an reveals to the initiate his true nature at the time of reunification with the Divine. The *Ogdoad and the Ennead* indeed represents the eighth and ninth parts, the final part, of a spiritual development preceded by seven other stages. The volume does not list all stages, although it is implicit that in order to reach the last two, an absolute purity of life must have been manifested, and, particularly, ignorance must have been expunged through the gaining of knowledge imparted by a series of specific writings.

6 *GRAND MASTER'S EDICT ANNOUNCED AT THE GRAND COMMUNICATION* - 13 JUNE, 2012:

On 12 May 2010, the Board of Management passed a resolution stating the principles governing esoteric research. These principles are central to the practice of Regular Freemasonry. In order that there be no doubt that they bind every brother and Lodge in this jurisdiction I have decided to make them the subject of a Grand Master's edict. At my request, the Board of Management has rescinded its resolution so that it may be substituted with the following edict that takes effect immediately.

1. Authorised, official Masonic Education and Instruction is only 'Regular' when applied to Free and Accepted or Speculative Masonry (Regular Freemasonry).
2. Because of the widely divergent interpretations, which can be placed upon it, I am

concerned about the unqualified use of the word 'esoteric', or any of its derivatives or extensions, within Regular Freemasonry. Such use needs to be avoided as it has been and can be misconstrued to the detriment of the Craft.

3. I encourage all Masons to make daily progress in the acquisition of Masonic knowledge. Speculation and discussion within the Landmarks of the Order are to be commended.
4. Within Regular Freemasonry, interpretive discussion and exposition concern only the progressive acquisition of Masonic knowledge towards an understanding of the secrets and mysteries of the Craft, promoting the brotherhood of man under the fatherhood of God. To avoid any misapprehension, such regular discussion and exposition shall be described as 'speculative' and the term 'esoteric' shall not be applied.
5. Regular Freemasonry does not permit within it any form of esotericism which encompasses or tends towards – occultism, sorcery, alchemy, astrology, profane mysticism, transcendentalism, supernaturalism, druidism, rosicrucianism, satanism or any concept or movement related to any of these. The presentation, endorsement and/or promotion of such subjects in any Lodge holding under the UGL of NSW and ACT whether the Lodge be open, adjourned, at refreshment or closed or at any connected or associated Lodge function should be deemed irregular and is strictly forbidden.
6. Any breach of this Edict constitutes serious un-Masonic conduct and shall be treated accordingly.
7. The Grand Master from time to time may grant dispensations to permit the presentation of papers on esotericism, which would otherwise constitute a breach of this edict. A dispensation may be granted on such terms and conditions as the Grand Master may impose. An application for a dispensation must be made to the Grand Master in writing through the Grand Secretary. Normally it will only be granted if the proposed paper is a genuine and proper piece of Masonic research.

CHAPTER ONE – Esotericism, interpretations and fabrications *(pages 21-60)*

7 In my essay *Julius Evola and Freemasonry, an inconvenient truth* (Settimo Sigillo, 2010), I highlighted how Evola, whilst focusing on modern-day degenerations, was less than critical when referring to the 'traditional' forms of Freemasonry.

8 Julius Evola, *The Mask and the Face of Contemporary Spiritualism*, Edizioni Mediterranee, Rome, 2008, p.41.

9 Julius Evola, *Il cammino del cinabro*, Scheiwiller, Milan, 1972, p.122.

10 Wouter Hanegraaff, *The birth of a discipline*, in *Western Esotericism and the Science of Religion*, Selected Papers presented at the 17th Congress of the International Association for the History of Religions, Mexico City 1995, p. XI.

11 Wouter Hanegraaff, Ibidem, p. XIV-XV.

12 Pierre Riffard, *L'Esoterismo*, Rizzoli, Milan, 1996, p. 325-342

13 W. Hanegraaff-A. Faivre, *Western Esotericism and the Science of Religion*, Peeters, Leuven, 1995, p. 1.

14 Antoine Faivre, *L'Esoterismo, storia e significati*, Sugarco, Carnago (Varese), 1992, p. 26-44.

15 Antoine Faivre, Ibidem, p. 40.

16 Although Riffard, at variance with Faivre, on referring to the esoteric phenomenon and to the esotericist, adopts a markedly more inspired approach than his colleague:

Esotericism is to push one's thoughts to extreme consequences and to once again find oneself in one's heart, and subsequently, from this intimate centre, throw oneself to the opposite extreme as the centre contains the completeness. The surface is travelled by starting from this point. This world and the other world coincide. This is esotericism: to ask oneself if the beings, individually, and in their completeness, possess the sense to grasp it, to grasp also the cowardice, the pointless cruelties of man, until they understand, they recognise themselves, they reveal in the limits of their evilness, in the brutality of the stupidities of possibilities, other potentialities...This is esotericism: to touch in this life the other side of things, to gain access here and now to the ultimate, primary reality, to become aware of the extreme in one's surroundings. 'If the other world exists, it is in this' stated the poet Eluard. Orpheus promises happiness here and now. Esotericism is the attempt, not merely the temptation, to achieve on high and all-embracingly that which is routinely carried out damply below. The artist does not walk, he dances, he does not speak, he sings; thus, the esotericist strives to see instead of looking. By taking in air, he is inspired...The esotericist rejects the possible, the initiate accomplishes what we all dream of. The Hindu yogi and the Buddhist wise man possess a divine gaze, knowledge of the thought of others, a memory of past existences...But the purpose of the esotericist is not to display his knowledge nor to acquire these powers. It is always the same question that is re-presented: is man capable of knowing fully, of being in full? Which methods of thought and which rules of life will grant access to the secret locked within ourselves? The esotericist is a person who has developed himself completely, like an eagle in the full of his flight. He opens, in the same way as folding a creased sheet of paper that contains the formula of the world. Microcosm-macrocosm... science can command. Religion must believe: in esotericism one either accomplishes or fails to accomplish. The alchemist does not verify whether the lead turns to gold (or rather, only in an accessorial manner), and does involve a question of faith: he transmutes, works, realises and is realised: we might say that he is aurified, he becomes gold, he is rendered valuable, simple, he wishes to shine. He who practices esotericism is an esotericist, he who studies esotericism is an esoterologist. On opting to speak of esotericism, one should first underline how esotericism refuses to be conveyed verbally, vulgarized, indeed it refuses to be the focus of attention, to be a topic of conversation. (Pierre Riffard, op. cit., p.11-14.

17 Wouter Hanegraaff, *Western Esotericism*, Bloomsbury, London, 2013, p.3.

18 Gilles Quispel, Interview with Cristopher Farmer, *Gnosis* (Fall/Winter) 1985): 28.

19 Ernst Junger, *L'Operaio, Dominio e forma*, Guanda, Parma, 1991, p. 295.

20 Pierre A. Riffard, op. cit., p. 26.

21 Pierre R. Riffard, op. cit., p. 54.

22 Nicholas Goodrick-Clarke, *The Western Esoteric Tradition*, Oxford University Press, New York, 2008, p.3.

23 Nicholas Goodrick-Clarke, ibidem, p.13.

24 Citation in John Holman, *Il ritorno della filosofia perenne*, Arethusa, Turin, 2011, p. 19.

25 Arthur Versluis, *Magic and Mysticism, An Introduction to Western Esotericism*, Rowman & Littlefield, USA, 2007, p.1.

26 Arthur Versluis, ibidem, p.5.

27 Arthur Versluis, *Religion of Light*, New Cultures Press, Minneapolis, 2013, p. 3-4.

28 John Holman, *Il ritorno della filosofia perenne*, Arethusa, Turin, 2011.

29 Frithjof Schuon, *L'Esoterismo come principio e come via*, Mediterranee, Rome, 1997, p. 8-20.

30 Guy G. Stroumsa, *La Sapienza nascosta, Tradizioni esoteriche e radici del misticismo cristiano*, Edizioni Arkeios, Rome, 2000, pag.137.

31 Curzio Nitoglia, *L'Esoterismo*, Centro Librario Solidatium, Verrua Savoia, 2002, p.12-14

32 Curzio Nitoglia, Ibidem, p. 32-33.

33 Curzio Nitoglia, Ibidem, p. 46.

34 Curzio Nitoglia, *L'Esoterismo*, Centro Librario Solidatium, Verrua Savoia, 2002, p.12-14.

35 Father Paolo M. Siano, *La Massoneria tra esoterismo, ritualità e simbolismo*, Casa Mariana Editrice, Frigento (AV), 2012, p.10-11.

36 Father Paolo M. Siano, Ibidem, p.11.

37 Father Paolo M. Siano, Ibidem, p. 202.

38 Father Paolo M. Siano, Ibidem, p. 210.

39 Pierre A. Riffard, op. cit., p.58.

40 Pierre Riffard, op. cit., p. 171-172.

41 Antoine Faivre, op. cit., p.123.

42 Antoine Faivre, op. cit., p.100.

43 Antoine Faivre *Esoterismo e Tradizione*, Elledici, Turin, 1999, p.72-73.

44 Jean-Paul Corsetti, *Storia dell'Esoterismo e delle Scienze Occulte*, Gremese Editore, Rome, 2003, p.276.

45 René Guénon, *Gli Alti Gradi Massonici,* in 'La Gnose', May 1910.

46 Oswald Wirth, *L'initiation Maconnique*, in 'L'Initiation', year 4°, n.4, January 1891.

47 Arturo Reghini, *Le Parole Sacre e di Passo*, Atanòr, Rome, 2008, p.92-94.

48 W.L. Wilmshurst, *The Meaning of Masonry*, Gramery Books, New York, 1980, p. 10-11.

49 W. L. Wilmshurst, Ibidem, p. 12.

50 W. L. Wilmshurst, Ibidem, p. 13.

51 W. L. Wilmshurst, Ibidem, p.14.

52 W. L. Wilmshurst, Ibidem, p.42.

53 W. L. Wilmshurst, Ibidem, p.106.

54 W. L. Wilmshurst, Ibidem, p. 46-47.

55 Wouter Hanegraaff, *Western Esotericism*, Bloomsbury, London, 2013, p. 117.

56 An interesting example is constituted by the works of the *Dormer Masonic Study Circle*, founded in 1938, membership of which is open to all Master Masons belonging to Lodges operating under the jurisdiction of the United Grand Lodge of England or of a recognised Grand Lodge. Its aims are to study the 'Hidden Mysteries' of Freemasonry, and in particular its esoteric elements; meetings are held informally once a month (in London). The titles of some of the books published by the Circle, highlight how the topics dealt with embrace the entire field of esoteric studies and its association with the Masonic symbology: The True Freemasonry: Exoteric & Esoteric, Seeking a Master (A. Cathcart Bruce), The Raising of the Dead – Freemasonry and the Pauline Doctrine of the 'Great Work', The Superphysical World, Freemasonry and the Reconstruction of the Spiritual Ideal, Masonic Anthropometric Cosmogenesis (J.R. Cleland), Freemasonry and

the Doctrine of Reincarnation, The Kabbalah and Freemasonry (J.R. Cleland), Freemasonry and the Message of Aquaria, Freemasonry and the Ancient Wisdom, The Mystical Quest in freemasonry, in Transaction (1 – 30). Concerning Belief (Freemasonry and Spiritual Disciplines (J. R. Cleland), Raising of Osiris, The Spiritual Significance of Some Symbols (F.V. Mataraly), Concerning God and Religion, The Illumination of the Craft (W.H. Topley) in Transaction (31 – 50). Freewill and Predestination (J. R. Cleland), The Ancient Mysteries and Modern Freemasonry (R.A.L. Harland), in Transaction (51 – 70).

57 Margaret C. Jacob, *Massoneria illuminata*, Einaudi, Turin, 1995, Pag.5. Original Title: *Living the Enlightenment*, Freemasonry and Politics in Eighteenth-Century Europe, Oxford University Press, 1991.

58 *Ibidem*, p.14.

59 *Ibidem*, p.26.

60 *Ibidem*, p.27.

61 *Ibidem*, p.32.

62 I devoted to this topic a recent book I wrote *The Influence of Neoplatonic Thought on Freemasonry* (Book Guild Publishing, Sussex, England, 2007), highlighting the fact that if we are to refer to philosophical influences on the origins of the Masonic doctrines, although I would particularly tend to term these 'contaminations', then they are undoubtedly to be found more in the Neoplatonic thought (I refer largely to the Cambridge Neoplatonists) than in the context of Illuminist ideals.

63 S. Bulgakov – N. Berdjaev, *Il cadavere della bellezza, La crisi dell'arte,* Medusa, Milan, 2012, p.43.

64 Julius Evola, *Cavalcare la tigre*, Edizioni Mediterranee, Rome, 1995, p.306.

65 Julius Evola, *L'Arco e la Clava*, Edizioni Mediterranee, Rome, 1995, p.97.

66 Julius Evola, ibidem, p.98-99.

67 Julius Evola, *Maschera e volto dello spiritualismo contemporaneo*, Mediterranee, Rome, 2008, p.87.

68 Julius Evola, Ibidem, p.88.

69 Julius Evola, Ibidem, p.45.

70 Julius Evola, Ibidem, p.45-46.

71 Julius Evola, *Idealismo, occultismo e il problema dello spiritismo contemporaneo*, in *Ultra*, year XVII, n. 6, December 1923.

72 Ibidem.

73 Giovanni Monastra, *Ananda K. Coomaraswamy: dall'idealismo alla tradizione*, Futuro e Presente, n.3, 1993.

74 A. More – R. Coomarswamy (edited by) *Selected letters of A.K. Coomaraswamy*, Oxford University Press, 1988, p.39.

CHAPTER TWO – Tradition *(pages 61-176)*

75 Antoine Faivre, *Esoterismo e tradizione*, Editrice Elledici, Turin, 1999, p.5.

76 Antoine Faivre, *L'Esoterismo*, Sugarco, Carnago (Varese), 1992, p.19.

77 Aldous Huxley, *La Filosofia Perenne*, Adelphi, Milan, 1995, p.11.

78 Aldous Huxley, Ibidem, p.13-14.

79 William W. Quinn Jr., *The Only Tradition*, State University of New York Press, 1997, p.67.

80 Wouter Hanegraaff, *On the Contruction of 'Esoteric Tradition'*, in *Western Esotericism and the Science of Religion*, Selected Papers presented at the 17th Congresso f the International Association for the History of Religions, Mexico City 1995, curated by Antoine Faivre e Wouter Hanegraaff, Peeters, Leuven, Belgium, 1998, p.26-27.
81 Frithjof Schuon, *L'esoterismo come principio e come via*, Edizioni Mediterranee, Rome, 1997, p.21-22.
82 René Guénon, *Le Sacré-Coeur et la Legénde du Saint Graal*, *Regnabit*, year 5, n.3-4, 1925, p.192.
83 Jean-Pierre Laurant, *René Guénon, Esoterismo e Tradizione*, Edizioni Mediterranee, Rome, 2008, p.11.
84 René Guénon, *Introduzione generale allo studio delle dottrine Indù*, Adelphi, Milan, 1989, p.31.
85 Antoine Faivre, *Esoterismo e tradizione*, Editrice Elledici, Turin, 1999, p.51-52.
86 René Guénon, op.cit., p.31.
87 René Guénon, *Vi sono ancora delle possibilità iniziatiche nelle forme tradizionali occidentali?*, in La *Tradizione e Le Tradizioni*, Edizioni Mediterranee, Rome, 2003, p.169-173.
88 R. Guénon, *Introduzione generale allo studio delle dottrine Indù*, Adelphi, Milan, 1989, p.78-79.
89 Renè Guénon, *Tradition et Inconscient*, Etudes Traditionelle, 1949.
90 René Guénon, *La crisi del mondo moderno*, Edizioni Mediterranee, Rome, 1991, p.44.
91 René Guénon, *ibidem.*, pag.119.
92 René Guénon, *La crisi del mondo moderno*, Edizioni Mediterranee, Rome, 1991, p.42-50.
93 René Guénon, *Ibidem*, p.153-154.
94 René Guénon, Ibidem,, p.207.
95 Giovanni Monastra, *Ananda K. Coomaraswamy: dall'dealismo alla tradizione*, Futuro e Presente, n.3, 1993.
96 Mircea Eliade, *Spezzare il tetto della casa*, Jaca Book, Milan, 1997, p.207.
97 A. More – R. Coomarswamy a cura di), *Selected Letters of A.K. Coomaraswamy*, Oxford University Press, 1988, p.26.
98 Wiliam W. Quinn Jr., *op. cit.,* p.5.
99 Marin Lings, *L'Undicesima Ora*, Settimo Sigillo, Rome, 2004, p.108.
100 Wiliam W. Quinn Jr. op. cit., p.21.
101 Ananda Coomaraswamy, *Selected Papers, Vol. I, : Traditional Art and Symbolism. Vol. II: Metaphysics. Vol.III: His Life and Work*, edited by Roger Lipsey, Bollingen Series, Princeton University Press, 1977.
102 Roger Lipsey in Ananda Coomaraswamy, op. cit., p. 277.
103 Ananda K. Coomaraswamy, *Sapienza Orientale e Cultura Occidentale*, Rusconi, Milan, 1998, p.91.
104 Ananda K. Coomaraswamy, *La Danza di Shiva*, Adelphi, Milan, 2011, p.22-23.
105 Ananda K. Coomaraswamy, ibidem, p.24.
106 Ananda K. Coomaraswamy, ibidem, p.27.
107 Ananda K. Coomaraswamy, ibidem, p.26-29.
108 Ananda K. Coomaraswamy, *Il Grande Brivido*, Adelphi, Milan, 2005, p.11.
109 Ananda K. Coomaraswamy, Ibidem, p.50.

110 Tommaso D'Aquino, *Summa Theologia*, I, 117, 1. Cfr. I, 45, 8 ad 4.
111 Ananda K. Coomaraswamy, *Il Grande Brivido*, Adelphi, Milan, 2005, p.54.
112 Ananda K. Coomaraswamy, Ibidem, p.57.
113 Ananda K. Coomaraswamy, *La Filosofia dell'Arte Cristiana e Orientale*, Abscondita, Milan, 2005, p.41.
114 Ananda K. Coomaraswamy, *La Trasfigurazione della Natura nell'Arte*, Abscondita, Milan, 2007, p.13 – 14.
115 Ananda K. Coomaraswamy, Ibidem, p.17.
116 Ananda K. Coomaraswamy, Ibidem, p.22.
117 Ananda K. Coomaraswamy, ibidem, p.31-32.
118 Ananda K. Coomaraswamy, ibidem, p.18-19.
119 The English *Emulation* Ritual reminds us that *Ornaments* make up the the interior of the Lodge. They constitute the *Mosaic Pavement*, the *Blazing Star* and the *Indented or Tesselated Border*, and recall a symbology of significant cosmological value.
120 Ananda K. Coomaraswamy, *Il Grande Brivido*, Adelphi, Milan, 2005, pag.197. Original title Selected Papers, Vol. 1, Princeton University Press, 1977.
121 Ananda K. Coomaraswamy, Ibidem, p.187-188.
122 Ananda K. Coomaraswamy, Ibidem, p.188-190.
123 Ananda K. Coomaraswamy, Ibidem, p.199.
124 Ananda K. Coomaraswamy, *Tempo ed eternità*, Luni Editrice, Milan, 1996, p.14-49.
125 Ananda K. Coomaraswamy, *Sapienza Orientale e Cultura Occidentale*, Rusconi, Milan, 1998, p.20.
126 Ananda K. Coomaraswamy, ibidem, p.58.
127 Ananda K. Coomaraswamy, *La Filosofia dell'Arte Cristiana e Orientale*, Abscondita, Milan, 2005, p.17.
128 Ananda K. Coomaraswamy, Ibidem, p.22.
129 Ananda K. Coomaraswamy, Ibidem, p.33.
130 Giovanni Monastra, *Ananda K. Coomaraswamy: dall'dealismo alla tradizione*, Futuro e presente, n.3, 1993.
131 Giovanni Monastra, op.cit.
132 Frithjof Schuon, *Sulle Tracce della Religione Perenne*, Edizioni Mediterranee, Rome, 1988, p. 9-10.
133 Frithjof Schuon, Ibidem, p.59.
134 Frithjof Schuon, *L'Uomo e la Certezza,* Borla, Turin, 1967, p.121-122.
135 Frithjof Schuon, ibidem, p.124-125.
136 Frithjof Schuon, ibidem, p.125.
137 Frithjof Schuon, *Caste e Razze*, Edizioni all'insegna del Veltro, Parma, 1979, g.24.
138 Frithjof Schuon, Ibidem, p.24-25.
139 Fritjof Schuon, *L'Unità trascendente delle Religioni*, Edizioni Mediterranee, Rome, 1997, p.9.
140 Frithjof Schuon, Ibidem, p.14.
141 Frithjof Schuon, Ibidem, p.23-35.
142 Frithjof Schuon, *L'esoterismo come principio e come via*, Edizioni Mediterranee, Rome, 1997, p.37-39.
143 Frithjof Schuon, *L'Uomo e la Certezza*, Borla, Turin, 1967, p.50.
144 Frithjof Schuon, Ibidem, p.195.

[145] Frithjof Schuon, Ibidem, p.61.
[146] Julius Evola, *Gli Uomini e le Rovine*, Edizioni Mediterranee, Rome, 2001, p.64.
[147] Julius Evola, *Imperialismo Pagano*, Edizioni Mediterranee, Rome, 2002, p.47.
[148] Franco Volpi, *Dizionario delle Opere Filosofiche*, Mondadori, Milano, 2000, pag.358.
[149] Julius Evola, *Rivolta contro il mondo moderno*, Edizioni Mediterranee, Rome, 1998, p.30-32.
[150] Julius Evola, Ibidem, p.47-48.
[151] Julius Evola, op. cit., p.73-74.
[152] Stefano Zecchi, Introduzione a *Cavalcare la Tigre*, Edizioni Mediterranee, Rome, 1995, p.13-18.
[153] Julius Evola, '*Sui limiti della 'regolarità' iniziatica*', Introduzione alla Magia Vol. II, Edizioni Mediterraneee, 1971, p.162.
[154] Julius Evola, Ibidem, p.165.
[155] Julius Evola, *La Dottrina del Risveglio*, Edizioni Mediterranee, Rome, 1995, p.37.
[156] Julius Evola, *La Destra,* n.3, Rome, March 1972, p.73-74.
[157] Julius Evola, op.cit., p.154.
[158] Julius Evola, op.cit., p.74-75
[159] Roberto Sestito, *Il Figlio del Sole*, Associazione Culturale IGNIS, Ancona, 2006, p.83-84.
[160] Julius Evola, *Introduction to 'I versi d'oro di Pitagora'*, Atanòr, Rome, 1959, p.16.
[161] Julius Evola, Introduction to René Guénon, *La crisi del mondo moderno*, Mediterranee, Rome, 1991, p.10-12.
[162] Karl Jaspers, *La filosofia dell'esistenza*, Laterza, Bari, 1995, p.82.
[163] Karl Jaspers, *Metafisica*, Mursia, Milan, 2003, p.278.
[164] Karl Jaspers, *La fede filosofica*, Raffaello Cortina Editore, Milan, 2005, p.191.
[165] Bruno Negroni, *Jaspes e la metafisica*, Marino Sofanelli Editore, Chieti, 1981, p.26
[166] Karl Jaspers, *La filosofia dell'esistenza*, Laterza, Bari, 1995, p.83.
[167] Umberto Galimberti, Introduction to Karl Jaspers, *La fede filosofica*, Raffaello Cortina Editore, Milan, 2005, p.11.
[168] Umberto Galimberti, ibidem, p.11.
[169] Karl Jaspers, *La fede filosofica*, Raffaello Cortina Editore, Milan, 2005, p.72.
[170] Karl Jaspers, ibidem, p.94.
[171] Umberto Galimberti, Introduzione a Karl Jaspers, *La fede filosofica*, Raffaello Cortina Editor, Milan, 2005, p.40-41.
[172] Karl Jaspers, *La fede filosofica*, Raffaello Cortina Editor, Milan, 2005, p.63.
[173] Karl Jaspers, ibidem, p.79-80.
[174] Karl Jaspers, ibidem, p.132-134.
[175] The *embracing* always merely announces itself – in present objects and within the horizons – but it never becomes an object. Never appearing to us itself, it is that wherein everything else appears. It is also that due to which all things not merely are what they immediately seem to be, but remain transparent. Jaspers, *La filosofia dell'esistenza*, p.18.
[176] Karl Jaspers, *La filosofia dell'esistenza*, Laterza, Bari, 1995, p.25.
[177] Julius Evola, *Cavalcare la tigre*, Edizioni Mediterranee, Rome, 1995, p.78.
[178] Julius Evola, Ibidem.
[179] Julius Evola, ibidem, p.86.

[180] Julius Evola, ibidem, p.89.
[181] Julius Evola, *Cavalcare la tigre*, Edizioni Mediterranee, Rome, 1995, p.80.
[182] Man is situated right in the middle of their complementarity, their reciprocal intimacy, or, in other words, Man fulfils God and his own personal being by letting himself be penetrated by this divine dynamism. From the perspective of Indian philosophy, it could be said that transcendence and immanence belong in an advaitic relationship, whereby one does not exist without the other and one cannot even be conceived without the other. The human mind distinguishes them but is mistaken in thinking that they are separate or that reality is divided. Whereas a separation would lead to a purely dualist illusion, reducing one to the other would similarly lead to an equally misleading monism. On the contrary, according to Panikkar, the fundamental structure of Reality is trinitarian, that is, cosmotheandric. No matter which element we start from, we will always reach the radical Trinity, Cosmotheandrism, interdependence. The world redirects to God and man. God redirects to man and cosmos. Man redirects to the world and God. The invisible harmony of Reality is based on the perichoresis of these three elements. Raimond Panikkar, Visione trinitaria e cosmoteandrica: Dio-Uomo-Cosmo, vol. VIII, Jaca Book, Milan, 2010, p. 87.
[183] Carl Gustav Jung, Sogni, Ricordi, Riflessioni, Rizzoli, Milan, 1978, p.352.
[184] Carl Gustav Jung, Il simbolo della trasformazione nella Messa, Opere Vol.XI, Bollati Boringhieri, Turin, 1979, p.251.
[185] Carl Gustav Jung, *Il problema spirituale dell'uomo moderno*, Bollati Boringhieri, Turin, 1985, p.120.
[186] Federico de Luca Comandini – Robert Mercurio, *L'Immaginazione Attiva*, Vivarium, Milan, 2002, p.176.
[187] Nicholas Goodrick-Clarke, *The Western Esoteric Tradition*, Oxford University Press, 2008. p. 246-247.
[188] Sonu Shamdasani, *Fatti e artefatti, Su C.G. Jung, sul Club Psicologico e su un culto che non è mai esistito*, Edizioni Magi, Rome, 2004, p.16.
[189] Sonu Shamdasani, *Fatti e artefatti, Su C.G. Jung, sul Club Psicologico e su un culto che non è mai esistito*, Edizioni Magi, Rome, 2004, p.43-44.
[190] Sonu Shamdasani, ibidem, p.103.
[191] Richard Noll, *Jung il profeta ariano*, Mondadori, Milan, 1999, p.105.
[192] Richard Noll, ibidem, p.117.
[193] Richard Noll, ibidem, p.113-114.
[194] Richard Noll, ibidem, p.120.
[195] Richard Noll, ibidem, p.129.
[196] Marta Tibaldi, *Pratica dell'Immaginazione Attiva*, La Lepre Edizioni, Rome, 2011, p.83.
[197] Carl Gustav Jung, *Il Concetto d'Inconscio Collettivo*, in Gli Archetipi dell'Inconscio Collettivo, Bollati Boringhieri, Turin, 1995, p.69.
[198] Carl Gustav Jung, *Ibidem*, p.70-72.
[199] Marie-Louise Von Franz, *Psiche e materia*, Bollati Boringhieri, Turin, 1992, p.7-12.
[200] Carl Gustav Jung, *Il Concetto d'Inconscio Collettivo*, in *Gli Archetipi dell'Inconscio Collettivo*, Bollati Boringhieri, Turin, 1995, p.78-79.
[201] Carl Gustav Jung, *Psicologia dell'Inconscio*, Bollati Boringhieri, Turin, 1998, p.120.
[202] Mircea Eliade, *Trattato di Storia delle Religioni*, Bollati Boringhieri, Turin, 1986, p. 446
[203] Mircea Eliade, *Mito e Realta*, Borla, Rome, 1988, p. 179-180

[204] Marie-Louise Von Franz, *Psiche e Materia*, Bollati Boringhieri, Turin, 1992, p.22.
[205] Massimo Teodorani, *Sincronicità*. Macro Edizioni, Cesena (FC), 2006, p.69.
[206] Colin Wilson, *Il Signore del Profondo*, Atanòr, Rome, 1986, p.61.
[207] Jeffrey Raff, *Jung e l'immaginario alchemico*, Edizioni Mediterranee, Rome, 2008, p.28.
[208] Carl Gustav Jung, *Aion*, Bollati Boringhieri, Turin, 1997, p.22.
[209] Carl Gustav Jung, ibidem, p.183.
[210] Carl Gustav Jung, Ibidem, p.187.
[211] Carl Gustav Jung, *Psicologia e Alchimia*, Bollati Boringhieri, Turin, 2006, p.18-19. 2006,.
[212] Mircea Eliade, *Il Mito dell'Eterno Ritorno*, Edizioni Borla, Rome, 1968.
[213] Mario Trevi, Introduzione a C.G. Jung, *L'Io e l'inconscio*, Bollati Boringhieri, Turin, 2008, p.18-23.
[214] Carl Gustav Jung, *L'Io e l'inconscio*, Bollati Boringhieri, Turin, 2008, p.85.
[215] Carl Gustav Jung, *Aion*, Bollati Boringhieri, Turin, 1997, p.10.
[216] Carl Gustav Jung, Ibidem, p.20.
[217] Carl Gustav Jung, *L'Io e l'inconscio*, Bollati Boringhieri, Turin, 2008, p.65.
[218] Carl Gustav Jung, ibidem, p.103-113.
[219] Carl Gustav Jung, ibidem, p.124.
[220] Carl Gustav Jung, ibidem, p.126-127
[221] Carl Gustav Jung, ibidem, p.153.
[222] Carl Gustav Jung, *Aion*, Bollati Boringhieri, Turin, 1997, p.251-252.
[223] Carl Gustav Jung, *Lo Zarathustra di Nietzsche*, Bollati Boringhieri, Turin, 2011, p.12.
[224] Carl Gustav Jung, ibidem, p.27.
[225] Carl Gustav Jung, ibidem, p.16.
[226] Carl Gustav Jung, ibidem, p.177.
[227] Carl Gustav Jung, ibidem, p.164.
[228] Carl Gustav Jung, ibidem, p.27.
[229] Carl Gustav Jung, *L'Io e l'inconscio*, Bollati Boringhieri, Turin, 2008, p.160-162.
[230] Carl Gustav Jung, *Aion*, Bollati Boringhieri, Turin, p.253.
[231] Marie-Louise von Franz, *L'Ombra e il male nella fiaba*, Bollati Boringhieri, Turin, 1995, p.110.
[232] Marie-Louise von Franz, ibidem, p.111.
[233] Jeffrey Raff, *Jung e l'immaginario alchemico*, Edizioni Mediterranee, Rome, 2008, p.28-37.
[234] René Alleau, *Aspetti dell'Alchimia Tradizionale*, Atànor, Rome, 1989, p. XXII.
[235] Basilio Valentino, *Le Dodici Chiavi della Filosofia*, VIII° Chiave.
[236] Mircea Eliade, *Arte del Metallo e Alchimia*, Bollati Boringhieri, Turin, 1987, p.133.
[237] Titus Burckhardt, *Alchimia*, Arché, Milan, 2005, p.170.
[238] Basilio Valentino, *Le Dodici Chiavi dell'alchimia*, p.55.
[239] Eugène Canseliet, *L'Alchimia, Simbolismo ermetico e pratica filosofale*, Edizioni Mediterranee, Rome, 1996, p.24-25.
[240] Antonella Adorisio, *Immaginazione attiva ed esperienza simbolica*, Quaderni di cultura junghiana, Year 2, number 2, 2013, p.70.
[241] Carl Gustav Jung, *La dinamica dell'inconscio,* Bollati Boringhieri, Turin, 1994, .92.
[242] Carl Gustav Jung, ibidem, p.93.
[243] Marie Louise Von Franz, *L'immaginazione attiva secondo C.G. Jung*, in Federico de

Luca Comandini – Robert Mercurio, *L'Immaginazione Attiva*, Vivarium, Milan, 2002, p.257-258.

[244] Carl Gustav Jung, *La dinamica dell'inconscio,* Bollati Boringhieri, Turin, 1994, p.89.

[245] Antonella Adorisio, op. cit., p.60.

[246] Michael Fordham, *Active Imagination,* Journal of Analytical Psychology, January 1967, p.208.

[247] Carl Gustav Jung, *Letters*, curated by Gerhard Adler, Routledge and Kegan Paul, London, 1973, Vol I, 1906, p.460. Cited in Gary Lachman, *Jung il Mistico*, Edizioni Mediterranee, Rome, 2012.

[248] Antonella Adorisio, op. cit., p.63.

[249] Federico de Luca Comandini – Robert Mercurio, *L'Immaginazione Attiva*, Vivarium, Milan, 2002, p.48.

[250] Federico de Luca Comandini, *L'immaginazione attiva di C.G. Jung*, Proceedings of the Conference 'Figure archetipali – Tracce sui sentieri dell'uomo', Bracciano 3-4 October 2009.

[251] Antonella Adorisio, op.cit., p.70.

[252] Carl Gustav Jung, *Il Libro Rosso*, Bollati Boringhieri, Turin, 2010, p.260-261.

[253] James Webb, *Il Sistema Occulto*, Sugarco, Milan, 1989, p. 273.

[254] Herbert Silberer, *Hidden Symbolism of Alchemy and the Occult*, Desmond Gahan, 2012, p.119.

[255] Herbert Silberer, ibidem, p.122-123.

[256] Herbert Silberer, ibidem, p.179.

[257] Carl Gustav Jung, *Psicologia e Alchimia*, Bollati Boringhieri, Turin, 2006, p.380.

[258] Carl Gustav Jung, ibidem, p.243.

[259] Gary Lachman, *Jung il mistico*, Edizioni Mediterranee, Rome, 2012, p.124.

[260] Federico de Luca Comandini, op.cit..

[261] Jeffrey Raff, op. cit., p.28-31.

[262] Luigi Aurigemma, Introduzione a Carl Gustav Jung, *Psicologia e Alchimia*, Bollati Boringhieri, Turin, 2006, p.XI-XII.

[263] Carl Gustav Jung, op. cit., 227-228.

[264] Carl Gustav Jung, Ibidem, p.242.

[265] Carl Gustav Jung, Ibidem, p.271.

[266] Carl Gustav Jung, Ibidem, p.454.

[267] Carl Gustav Jung, *Aion*, Bollati Boringhieri, Turin, 1997, p.66.

[268] Sonu Shamdasani, *Cult Fictions*, Routledge, London, 1998, p.120.

[269] Fabio Venzi, *Introduzione alla Massoneria*, Atanòr, Rome, 2012, p.110.

[270] Marion Giebel, *I Culti Misterici nel mondo antico*, ECIG, 1993, Genoa, p.10-12.

[271] Dario Sabbatucci, *Saggio sul Misticismo Greco*, Edizioni dell'Ateneo, Rome, 1965, p.143.

[272] Dario Sabbatucci, ibidem, p.129.

[273] Garth Fowden, *The Aegyptian Hermes*, University Press, Cambridge, 1986, p.97-99.

[274] Carl Gustav Jung, *La dinamica dell'inconscio,* Bollati Boringhieri, Turin, 1994, p.475.

[275] Massimo Teodorani, *Sincronicità*, Macro Edizioni, Cesena (FC), 2006, p.105.

[276] Marie-Louise Von Franz, *Psiche e Materia*, Bollati Boringhieri, Turin, 1992, p.81-82.

[277] Basarab Nicolescu, *Nous la particule et le monde*, Editions Le Mail, France, 2002, p.158.

[278] Basarab Nicolescu, *ibidem*, p.159.

279 Basarab Nicolescu, *ibidem*, p.158.

280 Basarab Nicolescu, *ibidem*, p.163.

281 Wouter Hanegraaff, *New Age Religion and Western Culture, Esotericism in the Mirror of Secular Thought*, State University of New York press, Albany, 1998, pagg.62-63. In his description of the peculiarities of the 'New Age' phenomenon, Dutch scholar Wouter Hanegraaff portrayed innovative scientific researches as illustrated below, also providing a description of the new methodological approach displayed by the same: '*Traditional science – associated with the academic establishment – is thoroughly condemned as materialistic and conducive to human alienation, but the New Age has discovered the new science as a potential ally against it. Following Thomas Kuhn's Structure of Scientific Revolution, New Age believers claim that established science reflects an outdate reductionistic paradigm bound to be replaced by a new paradigm based on a holistic perspective. The suggestion that the evolutionary thrust of science now leads it to reject the very materialism it once helped to create is an inspiring to some people a sit is outrageous to other. That New Age Science diverges from mainstream science is recognized by critics and sympathizers alike, but both interpret this fact differently. Critical outsiders prefer to speak of 'fringe science', an appellation which reflects their conviction that these approaches are borderline cases of genuine scientific research, if not nonsensical pseudo-science pure and simple. Defenders, on the other hand, turn the fact of their marginal position into an advantage by re-labelling their perspective as 'leading edge science'. They see themselves as the avant-garde of scientific progress: pioneers of a radical new worldview...Rather, New Age Science is typically concerned with developing unified worldview.*'

282 Fabio Venzi, *op. cit.*, p.274.

283 Rupert Sheldrake, *La Presenza del Passato, La risonanza morfica e le abitudini della natura,* Edizioni Crisalide, Spigno Saturnia (LT), 2011, p.124.

284 Rupert Sheldrake, *Le illusioni della scienza*, Urra, Milan, 2013, p.72.

285 Rupert Sheldrake, *A New Science of Life*, Icon Books, London, 2009, (first edition 1981), p.26.

286 Rupert Sheldrake, *La Presenza del Passato, La risonanza morfica e le abitudini della natura*, Edizioni Crisalide, Spigno Saturnia (LT), 2011, p. 113-114.

287 Rupert Sheldrake, *Ibidem*, pagg.115-118.

288 Rupert Sheldrake, *La Presenza del Passato, La risonanza morfica e le abitudini della natura*, Edizioni Crisalide, Spigno Saturnia (LT), 2011, pagg. 309-310.

289 Carl Gustav Jung, , Conferenza 1936, in *Gli Archetipi dell'Inconscio Collettivo*, Bollati Boringhieri, Torino, 1995, pag.69.

CHAPTER THREE – 'Working the Rough Stone' and attainment of Self

(pages 177-202)

290 Carl Gustav Jung, *Ibidem*, pag.72.

291 Marie-Louise Von Franz, *Psiche e materia*, Bollati Boringhieri, Torino, 1992, pag.83.

292 Massimo Teodorani, *Sincronicità, Il legame tra Fisica e Psiche da Pauli e Jung a Chopra*, Macro Edizioni, Cesena, 2006, pagg.64-69.

293 Fabio Venzi, *Introduzione alla Massoneria*, Atanòr, Roma, 2012, pagg.271-272.

294 Jean Marie Ragon, *Massoneria Occulta e Iniziazione*, Atanòr, Rome, 2011, p.9-10.

295 Titus Burckhardt, *Alchimia*, Arché, Milan, 2005, p.75.

296 Julius Evola, *La Tradizione Ermetica*, Edizioni Mediterranee, Rome, 2006, p.96.
297 Carl Gustav Jung, *Commento al Segreto del Fiore d'oro*, 1929, p.35.
298 Marco Baistrocchi, *Il Cerchio Magico, Riti Circumambulatori in Roma antica*, Libri del Graal, Rome, 2010, p.6.
299 Marco Baistrocchi, ibidem, p.123.
300 Carl Gustav Jung, *Aion*, Bollati Boringhieri, Turin, 1997, p.213.
301 Julius Evola, *La Tradizione Ermetica*, Edizioni Mediterranee, Rome, 2006, p.48-49.
302 Paolo Francesco Pieri, *Dizionario Junghiano*, Bollati Boringhieri, Turin, 2005, p.73.
303 Mircea Eliade, *Arti del Metallo e Alchimia*, Bollati Boringhieri, Turin, 1987, p.24-26.
304 Guido De Giorgio, *La Tradizione Romana*, Edizioni Mediterranee, Rome, 1989, p.95.
305 Mircea Eliade, *La Nascita Mistica*, Riti e simboli d'Iniziazione, Morcelliana, Brescia, 1974, p.12-13.
306 René Alleau, *Aspetti dell'Alchimia Tradizionale*, Atànor, Rome, 1989, p.XXII.
307 Rituale del 1° Grado del Rito Scozzese Antico ed Accettato.
308 Johannes Fabricius, *Alchimia*, Edizioni Mediterranee, Rome, 1997, p.67.
309 Bernard E. Jones, *Il Libro dei Liberi Muratori del Sacro Arco Reale*, Atanòr, Rome, 1988, p.9.
310 Bernard E. Jones, Ibidem, p.13.
311 Bernard E. Jones, Ibidem, p. 16-17.
312 A.Q.C., Vol.LXVI (1954), p.117.
313 John Hamill, *The Craft,* Crucible, London, 1986, p.100.
314 D. Knoop – G.P. Jones, *A Short History of Freemasonry to 1730*, Manchester United Press, Manchester, 1940, p.125-126.
315 D. Knoop – G.P. Jones, *The Genesis of Freemasonry*, Manchester University Press, Manchester, 1949, p.291-292.
316 The English historian Yasha Beresiner provided a clear and detailed representation of the dynamics that led to the birth of the Royal Arch in England in his *Royal Arch Freemasonry in England 1813-2013* (Lewis Masonic, London, 2013): '*By the 1740s, things were not going particularly well for the premier Grand Lodge. The anti-Masonic exposures mentioned, Masonry Dissected (London: J. Wilford, 1730) and other similar articles, led to the clandestine making of masons who were thus enable to apply for Masonic charity. This caused mayhem in the corridors of Grand Lodge. The long standing Grand Secretary (1734-56) of the premier Grand Lodge, John Revis, later to become Deputy Grand Master (1757-63), proved to be ineffectual in his duties, albeit a staunch and loyal Freemason. Not surprisingly, the Grand Masters appointed from the aristocracy, acting effectively as figureheads during the first half of the eighteenth century, were unable or, more likely, unwilling to attend meetings of Grand Lodge which, in any case, was not meeting regularly. The twenty-five year old William, 5th Lord Byron (1722-98), appointed Grand Master in 1747 for a five year span, is often cited. In the hole time of his tenure he didn't attend a single meeting, nor did he take any action whatever with regard to new appointments in the Grand Lodge. Meanwhile, there was an element of resentment in Masonic circles on the part of Irish brethren who had migrated to England following the Irish famine of 1740-41. They found it difficult, to put it mildly, to be welcomed or accepted as joining members of English lodges. Freemasonry in England was at its lowest ebb and the eventual emergence of a new and competing Grand Lodge was not surprising.*

It was in this ambiance of general anxiety in English Masonic circles that the Royal Arch first surfaced in the 1740s as a separate degree of Freemasonry. There is as little information on the origins of the Royal Arch as there is of the Craft. Theories abound. Bernard Jones (Freemasons' Book of the Royal Arch London, George Harrap, 1957) divides researches into two fields: those who believe the Royal Arch to have some origin in the fabric of freemasonry, and those who believe the Royal Arch to be a mid-eighteenth century innovation.

One clear mistake of many students of the Royal Arch is to fail to differentiate between 'origins of' and 'source to'. The former denotes a continuous lineal descent. Not so with sources, which are isolated islands of recorded information, often in the distant past such as the Bible, the single source for much of Masonic ritual and practices. We can hardly claim however, that any biblical legends are the origins of Freemasonry. With this distinction in mind, an excellent and acceptable possibility of a source behind the Royal Arch legend of the crypt is expounded by Ian Thorpe in his article 'The Origins of the Royal Arch Degree: a personal view' (The Square, December, 2012, p19). In a clearly written and convincing article, Thorpe traces the source of the Royal Arch legend, as used in today's chapters, to a ninth-century manuscript volume in the Bodleian Library, Oxford. This is an excellently researched article and appears to establish an undisputed source for the Royal Arch, previously mentioned in the preface to Bernard Jones' book cited above. It is not, however, in any way to be seen as the origins of Freemasonry, which would imply a direct link and continued pedigree from the ninth century to the ritual of the present day.

Though only speculations, among the most popular and credible explanations of the origins of the Royal Arch is the possibility that the third degree was fragmented after the introduction of the Hiramic legend (familiar to all Master Masons) in the late 1720s. Chronology favors the association of the Hiramic legend to the first Temple in 957 BC, which is then followed by the content of the Royal Arch ritual and its relevance to the Second Temple of 516 BC. The suggestion that the Royal Arch may have been instigated by masons belonging to the Modern Grand Lodge has not been substantiated. In practice, there is no link between the third degree and the Royal Arch. Harry Carr, in his paper entitled 'The relationship between the Craft and the Royal Arch' (AQC, 86, 1974, pp. 35-86), shows that the oft-quoted concept that the substituted word in the third degree, therefore, is not lost and the ritual does not state or even suggest that it is lost. Thus, the word that is found in the exaltation ceremony of the Royal Arch and referring to an event taking place four centuries later, is not the same word purportedly lost and now rediscovered. It is a totally new and un-associated word'. p.14-15.

317 Bernard E. Jones, op. cit., p.52.

318 John Hamill, op. cit. p.102.

319 Many historians maintain, rightfully so in my opinion, that the meeting of the Supreme Grand Chapters took place in a different manner to that of the Grand Lodges and, from a Constitutional perspective, cannot even be referred to as a 'Meeting'. As reported by A.R. Hewitt in issue LXXVIII of A.Q.C, *The Supreme Grand Chapter of England. A brief history from Blayney to Sussex*, (1965, pagg.111-129), whereas in the case of the Grand Lodges representatives from the two realities had met and negotiated the terms of the union, as far as the Grand Chapter is concerned, only Sussex, the *Moderns* Grand Chapter, was appointed to negotiate. The terms of the negotiation are not known and,

above all, no formal document was signed for ratification. A compromise was undoubtedly reached which conciliated the two opposite interpretations, that of the Antients who demanded that the Royal Arch be considered part of the pure and ancient Freemasonry, and that of the Moderns who demanded that the works of the Royal Arch not take place in the Lodges but rather in specific Chapters, separate but at the same time included in the Craft.

320 Quoted in Bernard E. Jones, *Il Libro dei Liberi Muratori del Sacro Arco Reale*, Atanòr, Rome, 1988, p.120-121.

321 Harry Mendoza, *Fifty Royal Arch Questions Answered*, September 1994, p.8.

322 Neville Barker Cryer, *What Do You Know About The Royal Arch?*, Lewis Masonic, Hersham, Surrey, 2002, p.25.

323 Further anachronisms concern the simultaneous presence of Zerubabbel, Joshua and Haggai during Cyrus' Kingdom; indeed, the three men did not find each other again until Darius' Empire, as only Zerubabbel had initially left for Palestine. Esdras' and Nehemiah's presence is also temporally incorrect, as Esdras arrived in Palestine seventy years after Zerubabbel, and Nehemiah thirteen years after Esdras, to take care of the rebuilding of the city walls and not of the Temple.

324 Harry Mendoza, *Fifty Royal Arch Questions Answered*, September 1994, p.12.

325 Neville Barker Cryer, *What Do You Know About The Royal Arch?*, Lewis Masonic, Hersham, Surrey, 2002, p.10.

326 Richard Sandbach, *Understanding the Royal Arch*, Lewis Masonic, Hersham, Surrey, 1992, p.12.

327 George H. Steinmetz, *The Royal Arch, Its Hidden Meaning*, Macoy Publishing and Masonic Supply Company, Richmond, Virginia, 1979, p.67.

328 Bernard E. Jones, op. cit., p. 10.

329 Bernard E. Jones, ibidem, p. 220.

330 Timothy Hogan, *The Alchemical Keys to Masonic Ritual*.

CHAPTER FOUR – Loss of the Centre *(pages 203-250)*

331 Titus Burckhardt, *Alchimia*, Arché, Milan, 2005, p. 57-63.

332 Oswald Wirth, *Il Simbolismo Ermetico*, Edizioni Mediterranee, Rome, 1997, p.101.

333 Elémire Zolla, *Le meraviglie della natura, Introduzione all'alchimia*, Marsilio, Venice, 1991, p.22.

334 Bernard Jones scrive che '*The passing of the veils symbolises the enlightenment that comes with the Masonic progression, but originally it might well be, the veils were the emblem of the mysterious veil that was rent in twain when the crucified Saviour passed through it. In an old Lancashire Craft lecture of the possible date of about 1800 the Veil of the Temple 'signified the Son of God, Jesus Christ, hanging upon the Altar of the Cross, as the true veil between God and us, shadowing with His wounds and precious blood, the multitude of our offences, that so we might be made acceptable to the Father*'. Op. Cit., p.201.

335 Mircea Eliade, *Immagini e Simboli*, Jaca Book, Milan, 1991, p.26.

336 Marcello De Martino, *Mircea Eliade Esoterico*, Edizioni Settimo Sigillo, Rome, 2008, p.391.

337 *Zohar, Il Libro dello Splendore*, curated by Gershom Scholem, Einaudi, Turin, 1998, p.6-7.

[338] Johann Rudolph Glauber, *Novum lumen*, 1664.
[339] Athanasius Kircher, *Oedipus Aegyptiacus*, Rome, 1652-54, vol.III, p.95.
[340] Crassellame, *Lux obnubilata suate natura refulgens*, Edizioni Mediterranee, Rome, 1981, p.44.
[341] Carl Gustav Jung, *Paracelso come fenomeno spirituale*, in *Studi sull'Alchimia*, Bollati Boringhieri, Turin, 1988, p.187-188.
[342] Carl Gustav Jung, *Mysterium Coniunctionis*, Bollati Boringhieri, Turin, 1998, p.48.
[343] Carl Gustav Jung, *Gli Archetipi dell'Inconscio Collettivo*, Opere, Vol.9, Bollati Boringhieri, 1977, p.427.
[344] Jeffrey Raff, *Jung e l'immaginario alchemico*, Edizioni Mediterranee, Rome, 2008, p.28-31.
[345] C.G. Jung, *Mysterium coniunctionis*, Opere XIV, Bollati Boringhieri, Turin, 1989, p.50.
[346] Julius Evola, *La Tradizione Ermetica*, Edizioni Mediterranee, Rome, 2006, p.48-49.
[347] Julius Evola, Ibidem, p.58.
[348] Julius Evola, *La Tradizione Ermetica*, Edizioni Mediterranee, Rome, 2006, p.58-61.
[349] René Guénon, *Simboli della scienza sacra*, Adelphi, Milan, 1990, p. 63.
[350] Titus Burckhardt, *Alchimia*, Arché, Milan, 2005, p.71.
[351] Fabio Venzi, *Introduzione alla Massoneria*, Atanòr, Rome, 2012, p.95-98.
[352] Julien Hervier, *Conversazioni con Ernst Junger*, Guanda, Parma, 1987, p.72.
[353] Hans Sedlmayr, *Perdita del centro*, Edizioni Borla, Rome, 2011, p.27-31.
[354] G.M. Trevelyan, *Storia della società inglese*, Einaudi, Turin, 1948, p.496-499.
[355] Emulation Ritual, p.183.
[356] The *Stability Lodge of Instruction* is the most ancient of the Lodges still in existence. Following the act of reunion between the two Grand Lodges in 1813 (Ancients and Moderns), the Lodge of reconciliation started to compile a common ritual, a work that lasted lapproximately two and a half years, until May 1816. The following year, 1817, the Stability Lodge of Instruction was founded under the aegis of the Lodge of Stability n°381 (currently n°217).
[357] Fernando Pessoa, *Pagine Esoteriche*, Adelphi, Milan, 1997, p.53.
[358] Massimo Scaligero, *Dioniso*, in *Testimonianze su Evola*, Edizioni Mediterranee, Rome, 1973.
[359] Jiddu Krishnamurti, *In total silence the mind comes upon the eternal*. Speech delivered in Sanaan, 1979.
[360] Jiddu Krishnamurti, ibidem.
[361] Jiddu Krishnamurti, *Are we aware of this division?* Speech delivered in Madras, 1979.
[362] Jiddu Krishnamurti, ibidem.
[363] Friedrich Georg Junger, *La Perfezione della tecnica*, Settimo Sigillo, Rome, 2000, p.38.
[364] Hans Sedlmayr, *op. cit.*,p.32.
[365] Hans Sedlmayr, *op. cit.*, p.109-110.
[366] Hans Sedlmayr, *op. cit.*, p.195-203.
[367] Mircea Eliade, *Arti del Metallo e Alchimia*, Bollati Boringhieri, Turin, 1987, p.161-163.
[368] Brian J. Gibbon, *Spiritualità e Occulto*, Edizioni Arkeios, Rome, 2004, p.95.
[369] Oswald Spengler, *Il tramonto dell'Occidente*, Guanda, Parma, 1995, p.1368.
[370] Stefano Zecchi, Introduzione a Oswald Spengler, *Il tramonto dell'Occidente*, Guanda, Parma, 1995.
[371] Oswald Spengler, *op. cit.*, p.1393.

[372] Jean Baudrillard, *Il sistema degli oggetti*, Bompiani, Milan, 2009, p.70-71.
[373] Alain Finkielkraut, *La sconfitta del pensiero*, Nuove Idee, Rome, 2007, p.118,
[374] Alain Finkielkraut, ibidem, p.120.
[375] David Riesman, *La folla solitaria*, Il Mulino, Bologna, 1999, p.81.
[376] David Riesman, *op. cit.*, p.111-114.
[377] Ananda K. Coomaraswamy, *La Filosofia dell'Arte Cristiana e Orientale*, Absondita, Milan, 2005, p.67.
[378] Ananda K. Coomaraswamy, ibidem, p.99-102.
[379] Alain de Benoist, *Le idee a posto*, Akropolis, Naples, 1983, p.32.
[380] Alain de Benoist, *Ibidem*, p.50-51.
[381] Julius Evola, Introduction to René Guénon, *La crisi del mondo moderno*, Edizioni Mediterranee, Rome, 1991.
[382] Harvey Cox, *The Secular City: Secularization and Urbanization in Theological Pespective*, SCM Press, London, 1966.
[383] Stephen Kern, *Il tempo e lo spazio, La percezione del mondo tra Otto e Novecento*, Il Mulino, Bologna, 2007, p.23-24.
[384] Henri Bergson, *Saggio sui dati immediati della coscienza*, Florence, 1958.
[385] Ayn Rand, L*a Rivolta di Atlante. Prima Parte: Il Tema,* Corbaccio, Milan, 2007, p.8.
[386] Stephen Kern, *op. cit.*, p.124.
[387] Sàndor Màrai, *La Sorella*, Adelphi, Milan, 2006, p.46-49.
[388] Edward T. Hall, *The Dance of Life, The Other Dimension of Time*, Anchor Books Editions, New York, 1984, p.13.
[389] Edward T. Hall, *op. cit.*, p.45-48.
[390] José Ortega y Gasset, *Il tema del nostro tempo*, Sugarco, Milan, 1985.
[391] G.W.F. Hegel, *Estetica*, Einaudi, Turin,1972, p.65.
[392] S. Tagliagambe – A. Malinconico*, Pauli e Jung*, Raffaello Cortina Editore, Milan, 2011, p.302-303.
[393] S. Bulgakov – N. Berdjaev, *Il cadavere della bellezza*, Edizioni Medusa, Milan, 2012, p.10-20.
[394] S. Bulgakov – N. Berdjaev , Ibidem, p.43.
[395] Julius Evola, *Rivolta contro il mondo moderno*, Edizioni Mediterranee, Rome, 1998, p.187.
[396] Sabino Acquaviva, *L'eclissi del sacro nella società industriale*, Mondadori, Milan, 1992, p.184.
[397] Sabino Acquaviva, Ibidem, p.187.
[398] Ernst Junger, *Il cuore avventuroso*, Guanda, Parma, 1986, p.72.
[399] Luisa Bonesio, *Fisiognomica del nichilismo*, in 'Ernst Junger e il pensiero del nichilismo, Herrenhaus, Seregno, 2002, p.199-200.
[400] Luciano Pirrotta, *La conoscenza ribelle*, Atanòr, Rome, 1994, p.24.
[401] Giulio M. Chiodi, *Forza elementare e forma in Ernst Junger*, in 'Junger e il pensiero del nichilismo', Herrenhaus, Seregno, p.55-56.
[402] Julius Evola, *Cavalcare la tigre*, Edizioni Mediterranee, Rome, 1995, p.52.
[403] Julius Evola, *Cavalcare la tigre*, Edizioni Mediterranee, Rome, 1995, p.30.
[404] Julius Evola, *Il cammino del cinabro*, Schweiller, Milano, 1972, pag. 198.
[405] Julius Evola, *Cavalcare la tigre*, Mediterranee, Rome, 1995, p.19-25.
[406] Julius Evola, ibidem, p.43.

407 Karl Jaspers, *La fede filosofica*, Raffaello Cortina Editore, Milan, 2005, p.194.
408 Karl Jaspers, *Cifre della trascendenza*, Marietti, Turin, 1990, p.29.
409 Karl Jaspers, *La fede filosofica*, Raffaello Cortina Editore, Milan, 2005, p.186.
410 Katja Galimberti, Galimberti Katja, *Nietzsche*, Feltrinelli, Milan, 2000, p.168.
411 Karl Jaspers, *Nietzsche*, Mursia, Milan, 1974, p.386.
412 Karl Jaspers, ibidem, p.387.
413 Miguel Serrano, *Nietzsche e la danza di Shiva*, Settimo Sigillo, Rome, 2013, p.31.
414 Carl Gustav Jung, *Psicologia e Arte poetica*, in Opere, Vol.X, Bollati Boringhieri, Turin, p.353.

INDEX